THE STUDENT
BIBLE COMMENTARY

G000153516

CANDLE
BOOKS

Designed by Peter Wyart, Three's Company

Published in the UK by Candle Books
ISBN 1 8598 5185 1
Distributed by STL, PO Box 300, Carlisle, Cumbria
CA3 0QS

Worldwide coedition organized and produced by
Angus Hudson Ltd,
Concorde House, Grenville Place,
Mill Hill, London NW7 3SA, England
Tel: +44 181 959 3668
Fax: +44 181 959 3678

Printed in Singapore

Picture acknowledgments
Illustrations
Frank Baber: p. 309
Peter Dennis: pp. 16, 192, 196
Alan Harris: p. 167
James Macdonald: pp. 20, 35, 96, 105, 106, 149,
159, 162, 174, 178, 181, 279
Richard Scott: pp. 126, 228

Photographs
Ancient Art & Architecture: p. 339
Bible Scene: pp. 263, 277, 284, 297
British Museum: pp. 27, 30, 100, 139, 158
Tim Dowley: pp. 22, 25, 26, 55, 57, 60, 66, 80, 95,
108, 110, 113, 120, 122, 125, 152, 168, 170, 171,
172, 180, 182, 188, 194, 198, 201, 203, 205, 208,
210, 213, 214, 218, 220, 225, 228, 232, 245, 246,
248, 260, 267, 269, 271, 285, 292, 301, 303, 307,
316, 325, 327, 329, 333, 334, 335
Jamie Simson: pp. 74, 142, 177, 179, 242, 254, 274,
281, 283, 286, 300
Peter Wyart: 3, 28, 36, 42, 53, 59, 61, 63, 67, 73, 79
82, 84, 91, 92, 119, 123, 124, 135, 137, 140, 150,
151, 163, 183, 186, 187, 189, 193, 199, 211, 226,
229, 234, 235, 238, 244, 259, 273, 288, 295, 296,
313, 315, 320, 321, 328, 336, 347,

THE
STUDENT
BIBLE
COMMENTARY

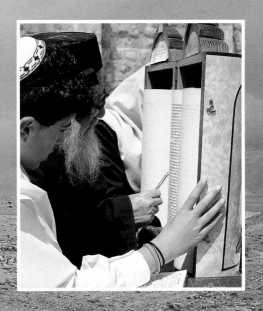

Contents

Old Testament

Introduction   8

Historical

Genesis   14
Exodus   28
Leviticus   36
Numbers   42
Deuteronomy   49
Joshua   55
Judges   60
Ruth   66
1 Samuel   68
2 Samuel   74
1 Kings   80
2 Kings   85
1 Chronicles   92
2 Chronicles   96
Ezra   100
Nehemiah   102
Esther   105

Poetical

Job   108
Psalms   111
Proverbs   120
Ecclesiastes   123
Song of Songs   125

Prophetic

Isaiah   128
Jeremiah   142
Lamentations   150
Ezekiel   152
Daniel   159
Hosea   163
Joel   166
Amos   168
Obadiah   171
Jonah   172
Micah   174
Nahum   176
Habakkuk   178
Zephaniah   180
Haggai   181
Zechariah   183
Malachi   188

Between the Testaments   191

New Testament

The Four Gospels

The Four Gospels 196
Matthew 198
Mark 208
Luke 216
John 226

The Letters of Paul

Acts 235
Romans 248
1 Corinthians 254
2 Corinthians 260
Galatians 265
Ephesians 269
Philippians 274
Colossians 277
1 Thessalonians 281
2 Thessalonians 285
1 Timothy 288
2 Timothy 292
Titus 297
Philemon 301

The Jewish Christian Letters

Hebrews 303
James 316
1 Peter 321
2 Peter 325
1 John 329
2 John 334
3 John 335
Jude 336
Revelation 338

Special Features

Creation Tablets	16
Tower of Babel	20
Land of the Patriarchs	25
Egypt	26
Assyria	91
The Chaldean Empire	98
The Minor Prophets	173
The Star of Bethlehem	199
Capernaum	210
Caesarea Philippi	211
Demonism	211
Miracles	212
Jericho	213
The Sea of Galilee	214
Time of the Second Coming	215
Bethlehem	218
Nazareth	220
The Dead Sea Scrolls	228
The synagogue	234
Caesarea	238
Corinth in Paul's day	242
The city of Ephesus	244
Rome of Paul's day	245

Charts

The 66 Books of the Bible	10
Chronology of the Dual Kingdoms	85
1 and 2 Kings in Contrast	87
Chronology of the Return	100
The Prophets and Their Message	127
Kings of Judah in the time of Jeremiah	143
Bible Weights and Measures	190
Events of the Intertestamental Period	193
Political background in New Testament times	195
Matthew and Mark Compared	207
Order of the events of the Crucifixion	215
Characteristic Features of Luke's gospel	216
Chronology of this period	217
Jesus' prayers in Luke	219
The resurrection authenticated	232
Chronological chart of Acts	237
Paul's life	246
Sanctification	251
Contrasts in Galatians	265
Great prophetic themes	339
The seven sevens of the Apocalypse	341

Maps

Ancient Near East	25
Route of the Exodus	27
Canaan divided between the Twelve Tribes	62
David's United Kingdom	77
Assyria	91
The Divided Kingdom	93
The Chaldean Empire	98
Jerusalem under Nehemiah	104
The Persian Empire	107
The Baylonian Empire	148
The Assyrian Empire	176
Palestine during Jesus' Ministry	206
Jerusalem during the time of Herod the Great	231
Paul's First Journey	239
Paul's Second Journey	241
Paul's Third Journey	243
Paul's Fourth Journey	247
The New Testament World	299
The Seven Churches of Asia	343

Abbreviations

Books of the Bible

OT	Old Testament
Gen.	Genesis
Ex.	Exodus
Lev.	Leviticus
Num.	Numbers
Deut.	Deuteronomy
Josh.	Joshua
Judg.	Judges
Ruth	Ruth
1 Sam.	1 Samuel
2 Sam.	2 Samuel
1 Kings	1 Kings
2 Kings	2 Kings
1 Chron.	1 Chronicles
2 Chron.	2 Chronicles
Ezra	Ezra
Neh.	Nehemiah
Est.	Esther
Job	Job
Ps., Pss.	Psalms
Prov.	Proverbs
Eccl.	Ecclesiastes
Song	Song of Songs
Isa.	Isaiah
Jer.	Jeremiah
Lam.	Lamentations
Ezek.	Ezekiel
Dan.	Daniel
Hos.	Hosea
Joel	Joel
Amos	Amos
Obad.	Obadiah
Jonah	Jonah
Mic.	Micah
Nah.	Nahum
Hab.	Habakkuk
Zeph.	Zephaniah
Hag.	Haggai
Zech.	Zechariah
Mal.	Malachi
NT	New Testament
Matt.	Matthew
Mark	Mark
Luke	Luke
John	John
Acts	Acts
Rom.	Romans
1 Cor.	1 Corinthians
2 Cor.	2 Corinthians
Gal.	Galatians
Eph.	Ephesians
Phil.	Philippians
Col.	Colossians
1 Thess.	1 Thessalonians
2 Thess.	2 Thessalonians
1 Tim.	1 Timothy
2 Tim.	2 Timothy
Titus	Titus
Philem.	Philemon
Heb.	Hebrews
James	James
1 Peter	1 Peter
2 Peter	2 Peter
1 John	1 John
2 John	2 John
3 John	3 John
Jude	Jude
Rev.	Revelation

Others

A.D.	*anno domini* (in the year of our Lord)
ASV	American Standard Version
B.C.	before Christ
c.	*circa* (about)
cf.	*confer* (compare)
ch.	chapter
e.g.	*exempli gratia* (for example)
et al.	and others
f., ff.	following
i.e.	*id est* (that is)
Jos	Josephus's *Antiquities*
KJV	King James Version
LXX	Septuagint (Greek translation of Old Testament)
p., pp.	page, pages
q.v.	*quod vide* (which see)
RSV	Revised Standard Version
v., vv.	verse, verses

Introduction

What the Bible is

The word "Bible" designates the Scriptures of the Old and New Testaments recognized and used by the Christian churches. Judaism recognizes only the Scriptures of the OT.

There is only *one* Bible—incomparable, unique as far as all other "sacred" literature is concerned, because: (1) It is *the* revelation of God. (2) It is "God-breathed" (2 Tim. 3:16) and inspired in a different sense from all other literature. (3) It discloses God's plans and purposes for the ages of time and eternity. (4) It *centers in God incarnate in Jesus Christ,* the Savior of mankind (Heb. 1:1-2).

Meaning of the name "Bible"
The word "Bible" comes from the Greek word *biblia* ("books"), denoting the inner bark of the papyrus reed (ancient paper) from which ancient books (scrolls) were made. Daniel 9:2 refers to the OT prophetic writings as "the Scriptures" (*ta biblia* in the Greek).

Scriptural designations of the Bible
Our Lord customarily referred to the OT books as "the Scriptures" (Matt. 21:42; Mark 14:49; John 5:39). His followers did likewise (Luke 24:32; Acts 18:24; Rom. 15:4). Paul referred to them as "the sacred writings" (2 Tim. 3:15, RSV), "the Holy Scriptures" (Rom. 1:2), "the very words of God" (Rom. 3:2).

Jesus once referred to them as "the Law of Moses, the Prophets and the Psalms" (Luke 24:44), echoing the formal arrangement in the Hebrew. The OT is more briefly termed "the Law and the Prophets" (cf. Matt. 5:17; 11:13; Acts 13:15). Even more briefly the term "Law" comprehends the other divisions (John 10:34; 12:34; 15:25; 1 Cor. 14:21).

Peter refers to Paul's letters as "Scriptures" (2 Peter 3:16).

The terms "Old Testament" and "New Testament"
The formal collection of Christian writings made after the middle of the second century was called the New Testament. This collection was placed alongside the Hebrew canonical books as of equal inspiration and authority. The Hebrew Scriptures were then called the Old Testament. Tertullian, an early Latin father (c. 200), first employed the term *Novum Testamentum.* Thereafter it came into general use, and the concept of a Christian Bible was crystallized.

The languages of the Bible
The OT was written almost entirely in Hebrew, a Semitic dialect akin to Phoenician and Ugaritic. The only parts written in Aramaic, another Semitic language akin to Hebrew, were Ezra 4:8-6:18; 7:12-26; Daniel 2:4-7:28, and Jeremiah 10:11. The NT was written entirely in Greek. Archaeology has shown this to be the common everyday language (*Koine*) of the contemporary Graeco-Roman world.

Order of books in the Hebrew Old Testament
The canonical books in a present-day Hebrew Bible number 24 and are arranged in a threefold

division—the Law (*Torah*), the Prophets (*Nebiim*), and the Writings (*Ketubim*), also referred to as "the Psalms" (Luke 24:44).

The form as it has come down to us from the Masoretic period (c. 600-900 A.D.) is as follows:

1. The Law, five books: Genesis, Exodus, Leviticus, Numbers, Deuteronomy.

2. The Prophets, eight books. Former Prophets, four books: Joshua, Judges, Samuel, Kings; Latter Prophets, four books: Isaiah, Jeremiah, Ezekiel, the Twelve.

3. The Writings, eleven books. Poetical Books, three books: Psalms, Proverbs, Job; The Scrolls, five books: Song of Solomon (Song of Songs, NIV), Ruth, Lamentations, Ecclesiastes, Esther; Prophetic-Historical Books, three books: Daniel, Ezra-Nehemiah, Chronicles.

This adds up to 24 books. When the Twelve (the books of the "Minor Prophets") are counted as 12 and not one, the total increases to 35. When the books of Samuel, Kings, Chronicles and Ezra-Nehemiah are counted as two books each, the number of the OT books is increased to 39.

The inspiration and authority of the Bible

Inspiration refers to the influence God exerted over the human authors of Scripture so that the words and thoughts they recorded were without error (cf. 2 Tim. 3:16; John 10:35; 2 Peter 1:19-21). This inspiration covers the original writings only, although a high degree of accuracy in the transmitted text is not only what is to be expected if God directed the process, but a fact demonstrated by textual criticism. Ferreting out any scribal errors that may have crept into the transmitted text is an activity belonging to the domain of lower criticism and the legitimate labors of consecrated scholars.

Divine inspiration makes the Bible uniquely the Word of God and not merely a book containing the Word of God, and as such it is different from any other book sacred or secular. It is an inspired revelation of God's redemptive plan and purposes in Christ, and not a revelation of natural science or a book of secular history. Alleged scientific discrepancies are due either to faulty scientific theories or inadequate interpretations of Bible thought forms. Alleged historical blunders may be due to such factors as a faulty textual tradition or wrong interpretation of historical or archaeological evidence or of the biblical text itself.

Authority resides in God's inspired Word (the Bible) interpreted by God's Spirit operating through Spirit-taught human agents. Orthodox Protestantism claims no other authority than canonical Scripture as the voice of the Holy Spirit.

The 66 Books of the Bible

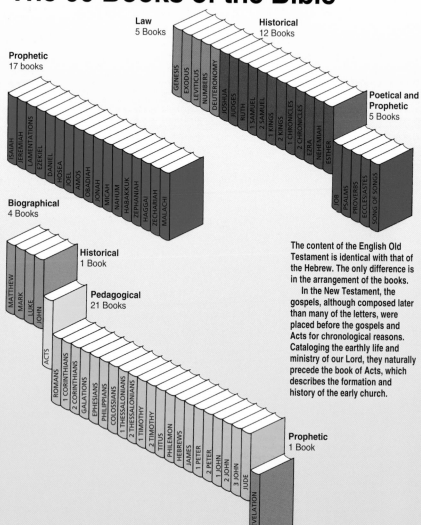

The content of the English Old Testament is identical with that of the Hebrew. The only difference is in the arrangement of the books.

In the New Testament, the gospels, although composed later than many of the letters, were placed before the gospels and Acts for chronological reasons. Cataloging the earthly life and ministry of our Lord, they naturally precede the book of Acts, which describes the formation and history of the early church.

Note on the 39 Books of the Old Testament.
The content of the English OT is identical with that of the Hebrew. The only difference is in the arrangement of the material. The English translators followed the order of the books in the Septuagint (Greek) translation made about 280-150 B.C. Roman Catholics followed the Septuagint tradition further by including 11 apocryphal books.

Note on the 27 Books of the New Testament.
In completed collections the Gospels, although composed later than many of the letters, were placed before Acts and the letters for chronological reasons. Cataloging the earthly life and ministry of our Lord, they naturally precede the book of Acts, which describes the formation and history of the early church.

The 21 letters consist of 13 by Paul, one (Hebrews) anonymous and addressed to Hebrew Christians, another (James) also addressed to the twelve tribes of the diaspora, two by Peter, three by John, and one by Jude.

Revelation, the capstone of biblical prophecy, completes the New Testament books.

Christ the unifying theme of the Bible
Although the Bible consists of 66 books, it is nevertheless *one* book. The unifying theme of Scripture is Christ. The OT prepares for Him and predicts Him in both type and prophecy. The gospels present Him redemptively in divine-human manifestation. Acts portrays Him preached and His gospel propagated in the world. The NT letters expound His redemptive work. The book of Revelation reveals Him as the consummation of all the purposes of God. From the offspring of the woman (Gen. 3:15) promised in paradise lost, to the "Alpha and Omega" (Rev. 22:13) realized in paradise regained, He is "the First and the Last" in God's revealed ways with mankind.

The purpose of the Bible
The Bible was given to bear witness to *one* God, Creator and Sustainer of the universe, through Christ, Redeemer of sinful man. It presents one continuous story—that of human redemption. This story is a progressive unfolding of the central truth of the Bible that God in His eternal counsels was to become incarnate in Jesus Christ for the redemption of fallen man. The unfolding of this central truth of redemption is set forth through history, prophecy, type, and symbol.

Typology of the Bible
Definition. A type (from the Greek *typos*, "a blow or mark left by a blow; a pattern or impress") is a double representation in action, the literal being intended and planned to represent the spiritual. A type is thus the divine impress of spiritual truth upon a literal event, person, or thing.

Extent. Scripture offers its own clues as to which passages permit typical interpretation. The book of Hebrews is a NT witness to the concentrated typical quality of the Pentateuch and Joshua. First Corinthians 10:11 offers a NT basis for the rich typology of the Pentateuch. Modern interpreters should exercise caution in going beyond Scripture's own program of typology.

Varieties of types. Types fall into several categories.

(1) Typical *persons* include Cain, a type of the natural person, destitute of any adequate sense of sin or atonement (Gen. 4:3; 2 Peter 2:1-22; Jude 11). Abel, by contrast, is a type of the spiritual person whose sacrifice of blood (Gen. 4:4; Heb. 9:22) evidenced his guilt of sin and reliance upon a substitute.

(2) Typical *events* include the Flood, the Exodus, the desert wanderings, the giving of manna, the bronze snake, and the conquest of Canaan.

(3) Typical *institutions* include the Levitical ritual where there is a concentration of typology. For example, the whole Levitical ritual in which lambs or other animals were slain to atone for sin (Lev. 17:11) prefigured the Lamb of God (John 1:29; Heb. 9:28; 1 Peter 1:19). The Passover (Lev. 23) portrayed Christ our Redeemer (1 Cor. 5:6-8).

(4) Typical *offices* include prophets, priests, and kings. For example, Moses as a prophet was typical of Christ (Deut. 18:15-18; John 6:14 7:40).

(5) Typical *actions* include Jonah's experience with the great fish, a prophetic type of our Lord's burial and resurrection (Matt. 12:39).

OLD TESTAMENT

Genesis
The book of creation

Nature of the book. Genesis, "the Book of Beginnings," is the indispensable introduction to the entire Bible, the foundation of all revealed truth. The book takes its name from the title given to it by the Septuagint (Greek) Version, derived from the heading of its ten parts *he biblos geneseos* ("This is the account of . . ."): 2:4; 5:1; 6:9; 10:1; 11:10; 11:27; 25:12; 25:19; 36:1; 37:2. The title of the book in the Hebrew Bible is *beeresit* ("In the beginning").

Outline

1-11	Primeval history of humanity
1-2	Creation
3	The Fall
4-5	From the Fall to the Flood
6-9	The Flood
10-11	From the Flood to Abraham
12-50	Patriarchal history of Israel
12-25	Abraham
25-28	Isaac
28-36	Jacob
37-50	Joseph

Genesis records nine beginnings:

1:1-2:3.	The beginning of the earth as man's habitation.
2:4-25.	The beginning of the human race.
3:1-7.	The beginning of human sin.
3:8-24.	The beginning of redemptive revelation.
4:1-15.	The beginning of the human family.
4:16-9:29.	The beginning of the godless civilization.
10:1-32.	The beginning of nations.
11:1-9.	The beginning of human languages.
11:10-50:26.	The beginning of the Hebrew race (covenant people).

Genesis records ten family histories:

1:1-4:26.	The generations of the heavenly posterity and the earthly seed.
5:1-6:8.	The generations of Adam.
6:9-9:29.	The generations of Noah.
10:1-11:9.	The generations of Noah's sons.
11:10-26.	The generations of Shem.
11:27-25:11.	The generations of Terah.
25:12-18.	The generations of Ishmael.
25:19-35:29.	The generations of Isaac.
36:1-37:1.	The generations of Esau.
37:2-50:26.	The generations of Jacob.

Genesis

1. The beginning of the earth as man's habitation

1. God. In the first phrase of revelation occurs the declaration of the existence of God, whose eternal being is assumed and asserted, and in no sense argued and defined. He is presented here as the infinite First Cause, the Originator and Creator of all things.

Creation and the six days of Genesis. The six days of creation in Genesis 1 can represent (1) literal 24-hour days of creation, (2) literal 24-hour days of divine *revelation* of creation, (3) extended geological ages or epochs preparatory for the eventual occupancy of mankind, or (4) a revelatory framework to summarize God's creative activity (Col. 1:16).

3-5. First day—light. God created *by his word* ("and God said"). The creation of light before the sun, moon, and stars (the agents of light) reminds us that light ultimately proceeds from God and only secondarily from His created "lamps."

6-8. Second day—waters separated from waters. The mixture of atmospheric waters was separated from the terrestrial waters.

9-13. Third day—land, sea, plants. The terrestrial waters were separated from the land to constitute the earth and to form the seas, making possible luxuriant plant and tree growth.

14-19. Fourth day—sun, moon, and stars. These heavenly bodies are now given responsibility as the source of light and heat on earth.

20-23. Fifth day—sea life and birds. God brings forth fish and birds.

24-31. Sixth day—land life and man created. Man was created (not evolved) as the crown and goal of God's creative activity. "Let us" (26) intimates the Triune God's counsel and activity in man's creation (cf. John 1:3; Col. 1:16). Man was given dominion over the earth.

2. Man in Eden

1-3. God's rest. This sabbath rest of God became the basis of the Mosaic Sabbath (Ex. 20:11).

4-6. Edenic climate. The creative work of God is summarized. This passage may suggest that before the Flood the earth was watered by vapor from subterranean water (cf. Gen. 7:11-12).

7. Man's creation. The creative act of 1:27 is described in detail. YHWH (Yahweh, traditionally vocalized Jehovah, printed LORD), the redemptive name of Deity, is introduced in vv. 4, 7, when man assumed control of the earth created for him.

8-14. The Garden of Eden. It was provided for unfallen man, 8-9. Its location, 10-14, was somewhere in the Tigris-Euphrates region.

15-17. Man's testing in Eden. Created innocent, placed in a perfect environment, man was put under a simple test of obedience, to abstain from eating the fruit of "the tree of the knowledge of good and evil." The penalty for disobedience was death—immediate spiritual death (Eph. 2:1-5), eventual physical death (Rom. 5:12).

18-22. Man provided with a companion.

Man's companion would be "a helper suitable for him," 18, on the same physical, mental, moral, and spiritual plane as he. The Lord God made woman from the man, and presented her to him.

23-25. Marriage instituted. The union of husband and wife prefigured the union of Christ and His church (Eph. 5:28-32).

3. The Fall of man

1. The Tempter. Satan used the serpent as his agent (2 Cor. 11:3, 14).

2-5. The woman tempted. Satan questioned God's word: "Did God really say . . . ?", 1, denied its teaching: "You will not surely die," 4, and, finally, substituted his own gospel, "You will be like God," 5.

6-7. The Fall. The woman fell through the lust of the flesh, the lust of the eyes, and the pride of life, 6 (cf. 1 John 2:16 KJV).

8-13. The Lord God seeks fallen man. God, 8, took the first steps in His new work of redemption to rescue fearful, ashamed, alienated, and confused fallen man.

14-15. The curse of sin in the serpent. Satan's tool, the serpent, was cursed, 14, but the first promise of a Redeemer was made, 15.

16. The curse and the woman. The status of the woman would be characterized by the headship of the man, and childbearing would bring pain and sorrow.

17-19. The curse and the man. Life was conditioned by inescapable sorrow, 17. Light occupation of Eden (2:15) was changed to heavy labor, 18-19. Physical death, 19, was pronounced.

20-21. Unity of the race. Adam named his wife Eve ("living"). The unity of the human race in Adam is here declared.

Creation Tablets

Creation tablets discovered. Between 1848 and 1876 the first tablets and fragments of tablets of the Babylonian creation epic called *Enuma elish* were found. Written in cuneiform characters, the seven cantos of the epic were inscribed on seven tablets and were recovered from the library of the Assyrian emperor Ashurbanipal (669-626 B.C.) at his capital Nineveh.

Similarities and differences with Genesis. Both accounts speak of the primeval ocean and both have a similar order of events—light, firmament, dry land, luminaries, man, and God or the gods of Babylon at rest. Both accounts have a predilection for the number seven, seven days, seven cantos. But the similarity is superficial, and the differences between the gross polytheistic Babylonian version and the Genesis account are vast. The Babylonian account is a corrupted version of an original tradition, the truth of which was granted to Moses by inspiration.

How cuneiform was inscribed on clay.

22-24. Expulsion from Eden. As a result of disobedience man lost his innocence and experienced knowledge of evil. Man was accordingly expelled from Eden lest by eating of the tree of life he should perpetuate his misery.

4. The first murder and civilization
1-5. Cain and Abel and their worship. Cain ("acquisition") was a type of a natural man of the earth. His religion was of works, destitute of saving faith and a sense of sin. The principal reason God rejected Cain's offering was that it was not offered in faith (Heb. 11:4).

6-15. The Lord's plea with Cain. God sought Cain, but he refused God's offer of reconciliation. In Cain, sin ran its full gamut, beginning with alienation from God, and proceeding to alienation from other men, nature, and even himself.

16-24. The first civilization. Cain "went out from the Lord's presence," 16, taking up residence in the land of Nod ("wandering"). Departure from God's presence always involves the absence of divine guidance. By this time Adam's progeny was numerous. Material growth and spiritual decline are portrayed.

25-26. Seth and the spiritual progeny. The Lord raised up Seth and Enosh to be those who passed on the messianic promise.

5. From Adam to Noah
1-32. The messianic line from Adam to Noah. The second division of the book of Genesis is introduced by the words: "This is the written account of Adam's line," 1. The next time the phrase appears is Matthew 1:1, where the lineage of the new Adam is set forth.

The great age of the pre-Flood patriarchs was

Archaeological light

The Babylonian flood story is preserved in the eleventh book of the famous Assyrian-Babylonian Epic of Gilgamesh, unearthed at Kuyunjik (Nineveh) in 1853. It describes a boat about five times larger than Noah's ark. In both the Babylonian and the biblical accounts, bitumen or pitch to close up the seams of the vessel appears prominently. Both accounts hold that the catastrophe was divinely planned. But in striking contrast to the monotheistic Hebrew account, the Babylonian account is polytheistic and has no adequate moral concept of the cause of the Flood. Both accounts assert that the hero of the deluge (Noah, Utnapishtim) was divinely instructed to build a huge boat to preserve life. Of all extra-biblical parallels that have come down to us from the vast cuneiform literature of the Tigris-Euphrates Valley of antiquity, the most striking remains the Babylonian account of the Flood.

due probably to greater physical vitality and a more heathful pre-Flood climate.

6-8. The Flood
6:1-7. The moral cause of the Flood. The view that this passage involved intermarriages of the "daughters of men," i.e., women in the flesh, with the "sons of God," 2, i.e., angels (cf. Job 1:6), is supported in 2 Peter 2:4 and Jude 6.

6:8-12. The Lord's grace toward Noah. Noah found grace because of his faith in the promised Redeemer and the need of vicarious atonement (Heb. 11:7). The ark was a type of Christ as the preserver of His people from judgment (Heb. 11:7).

6:13-22. Instructions for building the ark. The ark was 450 feet long, 75 feet wide, and 45 feet high with a displacement of 43,300 tons.

7:1-9. Instructions concerning the Flood.
Seven (or "seven pairs" RSV) of each of the
clean animals (i.e., acceptable for sacrifice—
Lev. 11:1-31; Deut. 14:3-20), are specified to be
taken, in addition to male and female of each
species for future increase (Gen. 6:19).

7:10-24. The earth is flooded. The causes of
the Noahic flood indicate a worldwide
catastrophe, not simply a local flood
(cf. 2 Peter 3:4-6).

8:1-6. The waters recede. A wind dried up the
water. The ark touched dry ground on one of the
mountains of Ararat, 4, that is, the general
mountainous territory of Armenia.

8:7-14. The sending out of the birds. A raven
was sent out first, 6-7; then a dove was released
on three occasions.

8:15-22. Noah leaves the ark and worships.
Noah offered burnt offerings on the altar that he
built, 20, gratefully worshipping the Beloved One
who had saved him and his family.

9. God's covenant with Noah

1-19. Elements of the covenant. (1) Promise
that every living thing should never again be
destroyed, 8:21. (2) Order of nature confirmed,
8:22. (3) Noah and his sons commanded to
increase and subdue the earth, 1, 7. (4) Meat
diet permitted but not with the blood, 3-4.
(5) Human government (capital punishment)
instituted, 5-6. (6) The rainbow appeared as the
sign of the covenant, 8-19.

20-29. Noah's prophecy. Noah dishonored
himself: salvation from the Flood did not change
mankind's sinful nature. Noah's son, Ham,
shamefully dishonored his father, 22-23. Noah
prophesied that a curse would fall on Ham's

Chronological light

It is highly improbable that the genealogical
framework of Genesis 5 was intended to be
used, or can be used, for calculating the
number of years (1656) between the creation
of man and the Flood, thus dating man's
creation 4004 B.C. (Ussher). The Hebrew
terms "begat," "son," "daughter" are used
with great latitude and may involve a distant
as well as an immediate descendant. The ten
generations from Adam to Noah and the ten
from Noah to Abraham evidently aim at
brevity and symmetry, rather than unbroken
father-to-son relation. Man is now
scientifically known to have existed long
before 4000 B.C., as both paleontology and
archaeology show.

"son" (descendant) Canaan, 25.

10. The Sons of Noah

W. F. Albright writes: "The table of Nations
stands absolutely alone in ancient literature and
remains an astonishingly accurate document" (in
Young's *Analytical Concordance to the Bible*,
22nd ed., p. 30).

1-5. The descendants of Japheth. These
formed the northern nations.

6-7. Descendants of Ham. These were
southern nations.

8-12. Hamitic imperial power. This appeared in
human history in Nimrod, founder of the
kingdom of Babylon.

Nineveh, 11 (modern Kuyunjik), about 60
miles north of Asshur, was the later capital of the
Assyrian Empire.

13-14. Other Hamitic nations— descendants of Egypt.

15-20. Other descendants of Canaan. *Sidon* (the oldest Phoenician city, 22 miles north of Tyre) represents the Phoenicians (Sidonians). The Hittites were an ancient imperial people of Asia Minor. The *Jebusites* settled in Jebus, the old name of Jerusalem (Josh. 15:63; Judg. 19:10-11) before David's conquest (2 Sam. 5:6-7).

Semites

21-31. Descendants of Shem. These made up the central nations. Shem is designated "the ancestor of all the sons of Eber," 21. *Eber* includes all the Arabian tribes, 25-30, as well as Israelites (11:16-26), Ishmaelites, Midianites (25:2), and Edomites.

Elam is Susiana, capital Susa (Neh. 1:1; Est. 2:8), with excavated levels going back to 4000 B.C. Asshur is Assyria, founded by Hamites (Gen. 10:11), but Semites overran the country.

11. From Babel to Abraham
The Tower of Babel

1-4. The building of the tower. Noah's descendants spoke *one* language, 1. They journeyed eastward from the mountains of Ararat to the fertile alluvial plain of Babylonia between the Tigris and the Euphrates. The human race had multiplied sufficiently and developed arts and crafts to build a city and "a tower that reaches to the heavens," 4. This is an expression of pride ("make a name for ourselves," 4) and rebellion against God and His command to "fill the earth."

5-9. The confusion of languages.

From the Flood to Abram

10-32. Genealogy from Shem to Abram. Ten names are recorded. These are apparently selective and the genealogy is symmetrically and telescopically abbreviated. The apparent intent of the narrative is to trace the messianic line with representative names.

12. The call of Abram

1. The divine call in Haran. God initially called Abram in Ur (Gen. 11:31; Acts 7:2-3) and renewed the call in Haran.

Haran, where Abram lived until the death of Terah, was a flourishing city in Abram's day and a center of the worship of the moon-god Sin (Sumerian, Nanna).

Through Abram and the creation of the nation Israel, God established for Himself a people through whom the Redeemer would come (Gen. 3:15; 12:3; 49:10; 2 Sam. 7:16).

2-4. The Abrahamic Covenant given. The covenant had seven parts: (1) Abraham to be a great nation. (2) Abraham to be personally blessed. (3) Abraham's name to become great. (4) Abraham to be a personal blessing. (5) Those who bless Abraham will be blessed. (6) Those who curse Abraham will be cursed. (7) All earth's families to be blessed in Abraham through his posterity, Christ (Gal. 3:16).

5-9. Abram in Canaan. Abram's wife Sarai, his nephew Lot, and the servants he acquired in Haran migrated to the land of Canaan with him.

10-20. Abram in Egypt. Abram, leaving Canaan because of famine, got into difficulty over Sarai's beauty. It was common in antiquity for men of power to confiscate beautiful women. Abram's subterfuge of calling Sarai his sister was partly true. She was his half sister (20:12). But the

Tower of Babel

The Tower of Babel is illuminated by the gigantic artificial mountains of sun-dried bricks in southern Babylonia called "pinnacle" or "mountain top." The oldest recovered ziggurat, one of more than two dozen known today, is at ancient Uruk (Erech, Gen. 10:10; modern Warka). It was a vast pile of clay buttressed on the exterior with brick and asphalt (bitumen), like similar ziggurats at Borsippa, Ur, and Babylon. Built in stages, three to seven stories high, ziggurats were varicolored. On the topmost stage, the shrine and image of the city's patron deity were housed. The tower of Genesis 11 may well be one of the first such towers attempted.

An artist's impression of a Babylonian ziggurat, which may be similar to the tower described in Genesis 11.

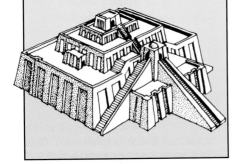

Archaeological light

In the Middle Bronze Age (2000-1500 B.C.) towns on the highland ridge were located only by springs. Archaeology has shown that Shechem, Bethel, Gerar, Dothan, Jerusalem (Salem), and Beersheba were in existence in Abraham's day.

seriousness of his lie must not be underestimated.

13. Abram separates from Lot
1-13. Abram and Lot return from Egypt and separate. Abraham made the choice of faith.
14-18. Abrahamic Covenant confirmed. The possession of Canaan and a natural posterity are stressed.

14. Abram the Hebrew warrior
1-12. Invasion of the Mesopotamian Kings. Four Mesopotamian kings fought against five kings of the Jordan Valley, 2, and were victorious, 3-12.
13-16. Victory of Abram the Hebrew. Abram is the first person in the Bible to be called the "Hebrew," 13.
17-24. Melchizedek and Abram. Melchizedek, "king of Salem" (Jerusalem) went out to meet Abraham. As a king-priest he prefigured Christ, who would arise as "a priest forever, in the order of Melchizedek" and thus fulfill the combined messianic offices of Prophet, Priest, and King (Ps. 110:4; Heb. 7).

15. The Abrahamic Covenant confirmed
1. The divine promise. The Lord gave

assurance of protection and reward for trusting Him.

2-3. The human predicament. Abram was childless. His steward Eliezer was his only heir. The adoption of a slave as an heir is attested to in records dating from 1950 B.C. and appears to have been common legal practice in Mesopotamia.

4-6. The promise of a son. Abram's faith grasped God's promise.

7-21. The covenant confirmed. The covenant announced (12:1-4) and confirmed (13:14-17; 15:1-7) was here ratified, 18-21.

16. Ishmael and Abram's faltering faith
1-6. Temptation to unbelief. The stalwart warrior of faith in Genesis 15 resorted to human means to help God in the fulfillment of the promise.

7-16. Results of unbelief. This son would father a prolific line, 10, and would be a wild, unruly, warlike man, 12. Future generations were bequeathed a division, full of animosity.

17. The covenant reconfirmed
1-2. Covenant sealed by revelation. God revealed Himself as El Shaddai (God Almighty), the All Powerful One.

3-8. Covenant sealed by change of name. The name Abram ("eminent father") was changed to Abraham ("father of a multitude"). Sarai's name was also changed to Sarah ("princess"), 15.

9-27. Covenant sealed by circumcision. Circumcision was a sign or token of the covenant, 9-10, a seal of the righteousness wrought by faith (Rom. 4:9-12).

Archaeological light
Now covered in water, in 2056 B.C. the Valley of Siddim, at the southern end of the Dead Sea, was fertile and populous. About 2056 B.C. the salt and free sulfur in this area were miraculously mingled, apparently by an earthquake common to this region. The violent explosion hurled the salt and sulfur into the air red-hot, so that it literally rained fire and brimstone (Gen. 19:24, 28).

18-19. Sodom and Gomorrah
18:1-16. The Lord's appearance at Mamre. The Lord in human form (theophany), apparently accompanied by two angels, appeared to the patriarch, "the friend of God" (Isa. 41:8, James 2:23) to assure the promise. Nothing is too difficult for Him, 14.

18:17-33. Abraham's intercession for Sodom. What boldness and humility combine in the patriarch's intercession, 22-33!

19. Sodom's sin and destruction, serving as a warning to God's chosen people (cf. Luke 17:32).

20. Abraham at Gerar
1-18. Abraham's lie. Abraham told Abimelech Sarah was his sister, repeating his earlier weakness.

21. Isaac's birth
1-8. Birth of Isaac. The name Isaac ("laughter") suggests the joy the child of promise was to bring not only to his aged parents but to all the redeemed through the greater Isaac, Christ.

9-21. Ishmael persecuted Isaac (Gal. 4:29), and Abraham under divine direction sent Hagar and

The Cave of Machpelah, Hebron, where tradition has it Abraham, Isaac, and Jacob were buried.

Ishmael away.

22-34. Covenant with Abimelech. This incident shows what an influential and powerful man Abraham was as a result of God's blessing.

22. The sacrifice of Isaac

1-14. The supreme test. The whole incident was filled with deep spiritual meaning. Abraham prefigures the Father who "did not spare his own Son, but gave him up for us all" (Rom. 8:32). Isaac pictures Christ "obedient to death" (Phil. 2:5-8). The ram sets forth substitutionary atonement through Christ offered as a burnt offering in our place (Heb. 10:5-10).

15-24. The covenant repeated, dramatically and solemnly, in response to the patriarch's faith and obedience.

23. The death of Sarah

1-20. Sarah's death and burial. Hittite documents illuminate the negotiations between Abraham and Ephron. Abraham demonstrated his faith by burying his wife in this land.

24. A bride for Isaac

1-67. The servant seeks and secures the bride. Obviously, Abraham's faith affected his household as his servant demonstrated great faith in his selection of Rebekah. Rebekah's willingness to follow the servant similarly reflects faith in the sovereign will of God.

25. Abraham's death

1-6. Abraham marries Keturah.

7-11. Abraham's death and burial. The record of Abraham's death, 8, provides a fitting epitaph for the man of faith.

12-18. Ishmael's generations. When Israel is restored, Ishmael will not be forgotten (cf. Isa. 60:7).

19-34. Birth of Esau and Jacob. With the announcement, "This is the account of Abraham's son Isaac," the eighth division of Genesis (25:19-35:29, Isaac's generations) begins, recording the perpetuation of the line through which the Promised One would come. Rebekah's sterility was cured by prayer, 21-22 (cf. Rom. 9:11-13). Esau's birthright involved paternal blessing and the place as head of the family, the honor of being in the promised line out of which the Messiah would come, and the exercise of the family priesthood.

26. Isaac in Gerar
The Abrahamic covenant is confirmed, 1-5, and the Lord appeared to Isaac at Beersheba, 23-24. Esau's carnality is further shown in his marriages, 34-35.

27-33 The story of Jacob
Main periods of Jacob's life. (1) In Canaan, the stolen blessing, ch. 27; the flight and Bethel vision, ch. 28; (2) servitude in Paddan Aram, ch. 29-31; (3) return to Canaan, ch. 32-33.

34. Dinah avenged by Simeon and Levi
1-31. Dinah's defilement. Jacob reaped what he had sown. The deceit of the father was to be reflected often in the deceit of his sons.

35. Renewal of the covenant at Bethel
1-15. Jacob restored to fellowship at Bethel. The divine command, 1, was obeyed by

destroying all idols that had contaminated them, 2-4. God protected on the journey, 5-6, and manifested Himself at Bethel, 7-15.

16-29. Rachel and Isaac die. Rachel died at the birth of Benjamin, 16-21.

36. Esau's line
1-19. Esau's country. Edom was the territory south of the Dead Sea reaching to the Gulf of Aqabah.

20-43. Horites. Hori or Horim were a tribe residing in Mt. Seir in Edom, 30.

37. Joseph introduced
1-11. The beloved son of Jacob. The vari-colored coat ("richly ornamented"), 3, his father gave Joseph was an indication of paternal favor.

12-27. The hatred of Joseph's brothers. They sold Joseph into slavery (cf. Judah's part, 26-27).

28-36. Joseph sold in Egypt.

38-41. Joseph's humiliation and exaltation in Egypt
Ch. 38. Judah's shame. God's Word deals realistically with sin even in preserved family registers in the line of messianic succession.

Ch 39. Joseph in prison. God's way up is often down, humiliation before exaltation.

Ch. 40-41. Joseph on the throne. He marries the daughter of the priest of On (Greek Heliopolis, "city of the sun"), a city of Lower Egypt. The On priesthood was powerful and closely identified with the throne.

42-45. Joseph revealed to his brothers
When Judah offered himself a hostage for Benjamin (44:18-34), Joseph could no longer

---

Archaeological light

Ample evidence of famines in Egypt exists. At least two Egyptian officials list among their good deeds the dispensing of food to the needy "in each year of want." One inscription (c. 100 B.C.) actually describes a seven-year famine in the days of Zoser of the Third Dynasty (c. 2700 B.C.). The story of Joseph swarms with correct local and antiquarian details.

---

refrain himself (45:1-15) and made himself known.

46. Jacob and his family migrate

1-4. The vision of God at Beersheba. In this last appearance to the patriarch, God assured him He would bring the Israelites again out of Egypt.

5-34. Arrival in Egypt. Jacob meets Joseph, 28-30.

47. Settlement in Goshen

1-10. Jacob before Pharaoh. The mighty monarch of the Nile graciously received the patriarch.

11-31. Israel's settlement in Goshen. Goshen, the northeast section of Egypt nearest Palestine, was called "the best part of the land" and "the district of Rameses." It was a valley some 35 miles long, excellent for grazing.

48. Jacob's adoption of Ephraim and Manasseh

1-14. Joseph's sons presented. Jacob adopted Joseph's two sons to secure for them the family blessing and to ensure that they would remain true to Israel's God.

15-22. Jacob's blessing and last words to Joseph.

49. Jacob's prophetic blessing of the twelve tribes

1-2. Jacob's call. He assembled his 12 sons to prophesy their tribal future.

3-27. The prophecy. This covers in a remarkable manner the entire sweep of Israelite history—past, present, and future.

28-33. Jacob dies.

50. Death of Jacob and Joseph

1-13. Jacob's death and burial. Joseph grieved, 1-3, and had his father embalmed, 2, this and v. 26 being the only direct Bible references to mummification by Hebrews. Burial was in the cave of Machpelah, 13.

14-21. The return to Egypt. Joseph's magnanimous treatment of his brothers is outlined.

22-26. Death of Joseph. Joseph's faith is shown by the oath he made his brothers take to transport his bones to Canaan (cf. Ex. 13:19).

Land of the patriarchs

Haran was an important junction on the rich caravan route between Nineveh, Carchemish, Mesopotamia, the Hittite Empire, and Egypt via Palestine.

Paddan Aram was the region in which Haran was located, and from which both Isaac and Jacob procured wives (Rebekah and Rachel) from among their relatives who had settled in Aram Naharaim.

Aram Naharaim, Genesis 24:10, is sometimes translated Mesopotamia. It denotes the territory east of the Middle Euphrates.

Village near Haran, southeast Turkey.

Ancient Near East in the Patriarchal Age

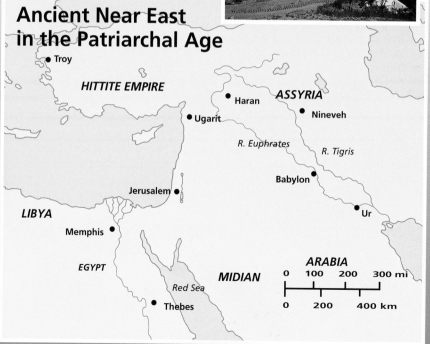

Egypt

Egypt. Egypt was a country two to thirty miles wide, situated along the course of the mighty Nile southwest of Palestine. The ribbon of fertile, alluvial land, watered by the annual flooding of the Nile, made Egypt the bread-basket of the ancient world. Brisk land and sea traffic with the other countries of the Fertile Crescent poured a steady stream of wealth into Egypt. But not until Egypt was several thousands of years old in the time of Abraham (c. 2050 B.C.) did its history touch the Bible narrative (Gen. 12 and onward).

Twelve of Egypt's thirty dynasties. In the third century B.C. an Egyptian priest named Manetho arranged Egyptian history into 30 dynasties from Menes, alleged to be the first king of united Egypt (c. 3100 B.C.), to the conquest of Alexander the Great, 332 B.C.

The Pyramids. Abraham may well have seen pyramids when he went into Egypt, for they were constructed in the Old Kingdom (third to sixth dynasties, about 2700-2200 B.C.).

The Great Pyramid of Khufu of the fourth dynasty is the largest, consisting of 2,300,000 blocks of limestone with a base occupying thirteen acres, originally towering 492 feet, and each block weighing about two and a half tons. Khafre, a successor of Khufu, constructed the Sphinx and at Giza a Second Pyramid, 447 feet high, which is almost as astonishing as the Great Pyramid.

History and early contact with Israel

Early and Predynastic Periods, c. 5000-3100 B.C. Neolithic and later cultures preceded the union of the kingdom by Menes.

Early Dynastic Period, c. 3100-2686 B.C. Menes reigned at This

Pyramid, Giza, Egypt.

The Sphinx at Giza.

below Thebes.

Old Kingdom, c. 2686-2181 B.C., dynasties three through six. Dynasties three and four were the age of the great pyramids and pyramid texts. Zoser (third dynasty) built the 190-foot high Step Pyramid at Saqqara.

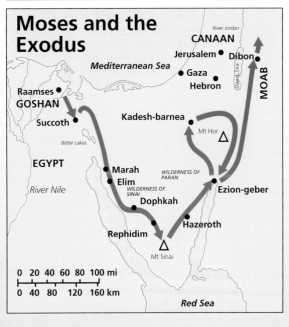

Moses and the Exodus

River Jordan

CANAAN

Jerusalem • **Dibon** •

Mediterranean Sea

Gaza •

MOAB

Raamses •
GOSHEN

Hebron •

Succoth •

Kadesh-barnea •

Mt Hor △

Bitter Lakes

EGYPT

Marah •

WILDERNESS OF PARAN

River Nile

Elim •
WILDERNESS OF SINAI

Dophkah •

Ezion-geber

Rephidim •

Hazeroth •

Mt Sinai △

0	20	40	60	80	100 mi

0	40	80	120	160 km

Red Sea

the heyday of pharaonic glory. Thutmose III (c. 1490-1436) was a great builder, conqueror, and enslaver of the Israelites. Amenhotep II (c. 1438-1425) was apparently the pharaoh of the Exodus, though many scholars place the Exodus and Conquest under dynasty 19; Ramses I (c. 1319), Seti I (1318-1304), Ramses II (c. 1304-1237), Memeptah (c. 1236-1222). Dynasty 20 was coeval with the period of the Judges.

First Intermediate Period, c. 2181-1991 B.C., dynasties seven to eleven, ruled at Memphis and Herakleopolis, 77 miles south of Cairo. This was a period of comparative weakness. Abraham's visit to Egypt was during this time.

Middle Kingdom, c. 1991-1786 B.C., dynasty 12, was ruled by native Thebans at Memphis and in the Fayum. It was coeval with the patriarchal period in Palestine. Probably during this period Joseph became prime minister.

Second Intermediate Period, c. 1786-1567, dynasties 13 to 17. The turmoil of dynasties thirteen 13 and 14 was followed by Hyksos, "rulers of the foreign lands" (dynasties 15 and 16) lasting 150 years. These foreign rulers governed from Avaris (Tanis) in the Delta. The horse and chariot were introduced. Some scholars place Joseph's rule in this period.

New Empire, c. 1567-1150 B.C., dynasties 18 to 20. This was the period when Egypt ruled the East,

Sculpture of Egyptian priest.

Exodus
The book of redemption

The book in general. Exodus means "departure," "a going," or "way out" (cf. Ex. 19:1; Heb. 11:22). The book focuses attention upon the great experience of redemption from Egypt as the type of all redemption, and upon the constitution at Mt. Sinai of the descendants of Jacob as a nation ruled by God. The Lord, heretofore connected with the Israelites only

Detail from an Egyptian wall-painting.

Outline

1-12	**Israel in Egypt**
1	Egyptian bondage
2-4	A deliverer
5-11	Struggle with Pharaoh
12	The Passover
13-18	**Israel in the wilderness**
13:1-15:21	The Exodus and pursuit
15:22-17:16	Journey to Sinai
18	Visit of Jethro
19-40	**Israel at Sinai**
19-20	Giving of the law
21-23	Social and ceremonial laws
24	Ratification of covenant
25-31	Tabernacle and priesthood instructions
32	Golden calf
33-34	Renewal of covenant
35-40	Erection of tabernacle and institution of priesthood

through His covenant with Abraham, Isaac, and Jacob, now brings them to Himself nationally through redemption and puts them under the Mosaic covenant signified by the tabernacle, the priesthood, and the Shekinah glory of His presence. The entire book is typical of the person and work of Christ, especially the tabernacle, priesthood, and sacrificial ritual, as 1 Corinthians 10 and the book of Hebrews show.

Exodus

1. Israel enslaved in Egypt

1-14. Israel's increase. Joseph died and several centuries elapsed. A "new king," 8, came to power. His oppression of the people is prefaced by an account of the expansion of the Israelites, 1-7.

15-22. Planned extinction. Pharaoh ordered every male Hebrew baby to be drowned in the Nile, 22.

2. Moses the deliverer raised up

1-10. Birth of the deliverer. To save her baby, Moses' mother, Jochebed (6:20), made an ark of woven papyrus plastered with tar and pitch. Pharaoh's daughter found him and named him Moses, 10.

11-23. Flight to Midian. At 40 (Acts 7:23), Moses cast his lot with his countrymen (Heb. 11:24). He killed an Egyptian taskmaster and so was forced to flee to Midian, 15-22, in northwest Arabia. Reuel, or Jethro (he had two names), was head priest and secular head of his clan.

24-25. God remembers the covenant. The foundation of God's redemptive work on behalf of Israel is His covenant with Abraham.

3-4. The call of Moses

3:1-3. The burning bush. The Angel of the Lord appeared to Moses in flames of fire from within a bush, 2.

3:4-12. The call and commission. It was no new god who spoke, 6, but the God of Abraham, Isaac, and Jacob.

3:13-14. The revelation of the name Yahweh. "I am who I am," 14, the One who is, who was, who is to come (Rev. 1:4), the eternal, unchanging living One, the name of our Lord who has redeemed us.

3:15-22. Directions for deliverance. Borrowing valuables from the Egyptians and despoiling them was not duplicity, but accorded with Oriental social custom and God's command.

4:1-17. Moses' objections. Moses had already pleaded *no ability,* 3:11, *no message,* 3:13; now he claimed *no authority,* 4:1, *no eloquence,* 4:10, *no inclination,* 4:13. God countered with the promise of *His presence,* 3:12, the manifestation of *His omnipotence,* 4:2-9, *His enablement,* 4:11-12, and *His direction* and *instruction,* 4:14-16.

4:18-31. Moses' return to Egypt. Moses' meeting with Aaron, 27-28, and their performance of signs signaled the progress of the redemptive plan.

5. Moses before Pharaoh

1-23. The results of the first encounter. The king cruelly imposed heavier burdens, requiring the same number of bricks, yet compelling the Israelites to gather their own straw, for which they blamed Moses, who in turn blamed God.

6. The Lord's reply to Moses' first prayer

1-13. The Lord's answer. The Lord reminded Moses of His covenant with the patriarchs under the name *El Shaddai* ("God Almighty," Gen.

Head of Pharaoh Rameses II of Egypt.

judgment upon the river deified on occasion as Hapi, "the giver of life," and at other times as Osiris, the god of fertility.

8. Second, third, and fourth plagues

1-15. The second plague: frogs. This was a miraculous intensification of a frequent natural phenomenon.

16-32. Third and fourth plagues: gnats and flies. The gnats were doubtless the stinging sand flies, notorious in Egypt.

9.Fifth, sixth, and seventh plagues

1-12. Fifth and sixth plagues: murrain and boils. "Nile scab" is a popular name of a skin disease prevalent at the rising and falling of the Nile.

13-35. The seventh plague: hail. This plague from the sky would impress the Egyptians that Jehovah is Lord of heaven as well as of earth.

10. Eighth and ninth plagues

1-20. The eighth plague: locusts. The locusts were brought by the east wind and carried away by the west wind.

21-29. The ninth plague: darkness. The chief god in the Egyptian pantheon was Re, the sun god. Here, Jehovah demonstrates that He has power over sunlight as well.

11. The tenth plague: death of the firstborn

1-10. The climaxing plague was announced, and its effectiveness predicted, but its execution is not recorded until 12:26-29.

12. The Passover and the Exodus

1-13. The Passover instituted. The Passover

17:1), but revealed the meaning of His personal redemptive name Yahweh (Jehovah), 2-3, now that He was about to deliver them from slavery.

14-27. The genealogy is obviously selective and abbreviated.

28-30. Renewed commission. Moses needs constant encouragement.

7. First of the ten plagues

1-9. Moses and Aaron assured. "God to Pharaoh," 1, means Moses' declarations were to have divine authority and Aaron was his appointed spokesman (cf. 4:16).

10-13. Sign of the rod. The miracles performed by the magicians were manifestations of evil supernaturalism.

14-25. First plague: Nile turned to blood, a

lamb slain spoke of Christ slain on Calvary. As the Israelites were shielded from the death angel, so the believer is shielded from the wrath of God (1 Cor. 5:7).

14-28. The Feast of Unleavened Bread. The lamb slain on the fourteenth day at sunset was followed immediately by the putting away of all yeast for seven days. Yeast in Scripture is an illustration of sin, "malice and wickedness" (1 Cor. 5:8).

29-51. Account of the tenth plague. The Exodus took place after a 430-year stay in Egypt, 40-42.

13. Consecration of the firstborn
1-16. The firstborn given to the Lord. Since the firstborn had been most miraculously delivered, the Lord commanded that they be given to Him, 1-2. Those whom the Lord redeems, He claims for Himself (1 Cor. 6:19-20).

Moses emphasized the importance of the Feast of Unleavened Bread (see 12:15-20) as a perpetual ordinance stressing holy separation of the redeemed, 1-10.

17-22. Traveling to the Red Sea. The pillar of cloud and pillar of fire were given, 21-22, symbolizing divine guidance and protection.

14. The crossing of the Red Sea
1-12. Israel's predicament. Shut in, perplexed, and confused by the wilderness, Israel was pursued by Pharaoh's light mobile chariotry.
13-31. Redemption by power. The Red Sea is really Reed Sea (Hebrew *yam suph*, the translation "Red Sea" coming from the Septuagint). It apparently refers to the region of the Bitter Lakes north of the Gulf of Suez.

15. The song of the redeemed
1-19. Israel celebrates deliverance. Filled with praise at the glorious rescue from the Egyptians, Israel sang ecstatically to the Lord.
20-21. The women's chorus, under Miriam, joined the praise.
22-27. Israel tested. The bitter trial at Marah was the brackish water.

16. Manna from heaven
1-13. The redeemed tested by hunger. In fertile Goshen, with two crops a year, there had never been any lack of food.
14-22. Manna from heaven. The manna (Hebrew *man-hu* "What is it?") foreshadows Christ, the food of God's people (cf. John 6:33-35).
23-30. Sabbath and manna. The Sabbath, a type of Israel's kingdom blessing (Heb. 4:8-9), was enjoined upon Israel in connection with the gathering of the manna.
31-36. Manna kept for a memorial, in the golden pot (Heb. 9:4), speaks of the true manna that we shall eat in God's own presence in glory.

17. Rephidim: water from the rock
1-4. The redeemed tested by thirst. At Rephidim, the Israelites were barred by the Amalekites from marching up the valley to natural springs.
5-7. Water from the rock. This beautifully symbolizes Christ, the giver of life (John 7:37-39).
8-16. Conflict with Amalek. This Bedouin tribe was a descendant of Esau (Gen. 36:12), and Israel's implacable foe.

Archaeological light

There is a structural similarity between the Sinai covenant and Hittite suzerainty treaties.

---

18. Moses and Jethro

1-12. Jethro's visit. Moses rehearsed for Jethro the way the Lord had judged Egypt for Israel's sake, and the Lord's deliverance, 8.

13-27. Government of the redeemed. Here God graciously supplied governmental administration.

19. Mt. Sinai and the covenant of the law

1-8. Israel at Sinai. The law was not *imposed* until it had been divinely proposed and accepted by Israel, 7-8.

9-25. The legal age introduced. This was done by the terrifying appearance of the Lord on Sinai, 9-11; by distance, 12-13; by smoke, fire, and threat of death. The law was designed to school the people in God's holiness. It was a "tutor to bring [them] unto Christ" (Gal. 3:24 ASV).

20. The Decalogue

1-17. The two tables. The first table, 1-11, lists duties to God, and the second table, 12-17, lists duties to people.

18-21. Israel asks for a mediator—Moses.

22-26. Additional regulations. Exodus 20:22-23:33, called the book of the covenant in 24:7, outlines in greater detail the stipulations of God's covenant with Israel.

St. Catherine's Monastery, near Mount Sinai.

21-24. The social ordinances

Ch. 21. Rights of persons. Laws were given about the regulations of slavery, 1-11; wrongs done to a fellowman, 12-27; injuries resulting from carelessness or neglect, 28-36.

22:1-15. Rights of property. Laws were given dealing with theft, 1-6, and dishonesty, 7-15.

22:16-23:19. Requirements of personal integrity.

23:20-33. Promise and prospect. Assurance of the divine presence with Israel, 20-23, was given and a blessed future predicted, if the people remained loyal to the Lord, 24-33.

24:1-17. Acceptance of the legal covenant

and worship. Again the voluntary acceptance of the law by Israel was stressed.

24:18. Moses on the top of the mountain. Moses spent 40 days and 40 nights on Mt. Sinai (cf. Matt. 4:1-2).

25. The tabernacle: ark, table, candlestick

1-9. The materials were supplied by the people's offerings. All was by divine direction, 9.

10-22. The ark. This box, 3 3/4 feet long, 2 1/4 feet wide and 2 1/4 feet high, was made of acacia wood overlaid with pure gold. It held a pot of manna, the Ten Commandments, and later Aaron's rod that budded. The mercy seat was the gold lid on top of the ark, illustrating how the divine throne is transformed from a throne of judgment to a throne of grace by atoning blood sprinkled upon it. The two cherubim represented guardianship of the holiness of God's throne, above which was enthroned the Shekinah glory presence of the Lord. The ark was the core of the tabernacle symbolism.

23-30. The table of bread. On it was placed the bread of the Presence made of fine wheat flour, baked in 12 loaves, renewed every sabbath and to be eaten by the priests only.

31-40. The golden candlestick. This was of pure gold, sevenbranched; a type of Christ our Light.

26. The tabernacle: its general construction

1-6. The ten linen curtains.

7-37. The tabernacle coverings, boards, veil, and outer screen. The veil of the tabernacle separated the holy place from the holy of holies, the inner sanctuary where the ark of the covenant was located. The OT high priest could only go behind the veil once a year.

27. The tabernacle: bronze altar, courtyard

1-8. The bronze altar. This was the great altar, 7 1/2 feet square and 4 1/2 feet high, for general sacrifice of animals.

9-19. The courtyard. The curtains of fine linen surrounding the courtyard suggest that righteousness is required for true worship since they shut out all who will not enter by the entrance, 16.

20-21. The oil for light. The fine olive oil is symbolic of the Holy Spirit (John 3:34; Heb. 1:9).

28. The tabernacle priesthood

1-5. Priesthood of Aaron and his sons. The holy garments for "dignity and honor," 2, represent the glory and beauty of Christ as our High Priest.

6-14. The ephod was an apron-like vestment worn under the high priest's breastplate.

15-29. The breastplate was richly embellished with twelve precious stones, each engraved with one of the names of Israel's tribes.

30. Urim and Thummim. They suggest the guiding ministry of the Holy Spirit.

31-35. Robe of the ephod. The gold bells on the hem of the robe spoke of God's acceptance of the priestly sacrifice. As long as the people heard the tinkling of the bells they knew that the high priest was still alive in the holy of holies and that God was satisfied with their atoning sacrifice, 35.

36-38. The gold headplate was inscribed with "Holy to the Lord," a reminder of the purity of the priestly ministry of Christ (Heb. 7:26).

39-43. Garments of the priests.

29. Consecration of the priesthood
1-4. The washing. This cleansing in water symbolizes new birth (John 3:5; Titus 3:5), in which Aaron participated, because he was a sinner and needed it.

5-25. The clothing and anointing. The consecration of the priests required various offerings in which the shedding of animal blood took place, 8-25.

26-46. Special food for priests. This was fitting for those, 26-37, who represented the people before God in sacrifice and worship, 38-46.

30. The altar of incense and the worshipers
1-10. The altar of incense was of acacia wood overlaid with gold, one and one-half feet square, three feet high. Equipped with inseparable horns and staves for transporting it, it was placed in the holy place in front of the veil. On it Aaron was to offer incense twice daily, 7-8. The incense fittingly symbolizes prayer, which like ascending sweet aromas rises acceptably to heaven (Rev. 5:8; 8:3).

11-16. The ransom money. Those who come as true worshipers must be redeemed.

17-21. The bronze basin. This washbasin placed between the altar and the door was used by priests to cleanse their hands and feet.

23-33. The anointing oil was a symbol of the Holy Spirit.

34-38. The incense. Genuine prayer, praise and thanksgiving, 34-38, is symbolized by the incense, which was to be uniquely made and reserved for God's adoration alone, 37.

31. The workmen and the Sabbath
1-11. The call of the workmen. Bezalel and Oholiab were filled with the Spirit of God, with ability and craftsmanship, 2-3, 6, to execute all the skilled labor necessary.

12-17. The Sabbath law restated. The Sabbath is a Jewish institution, connected with the legal or Mosaic covenant. Sunday is not a Sabbath, but the first day of the week, and belongs to the new age of grace.

18. Moses receives the tablets of stone.

32. The broken covenant
1-14. The golden calf. The legal covenant, so glibly accepted, was shamefully violated, showing the utter inability of the people to keep it in their own strength.

15-35. The broken tablets. Moses called for those who were on the Lord's side, and the Levites rallied to him, killing 3,000 of the worst offenders.

33-34. Restoration of the law
Ch. 33. Moses' new vision. Moses prayed for a new vision, 12-17, and was promised it for a new task, 18-23.

34:1-4. Second tablets of the law.

34:5-17. The new vision and commission. Moses saw the Lord pass by, 5-9, and his commission was renewed, 10-17.

34:18-35. The feasts and the Sabbath again commanded. Moses' face shone after he descended from the 40-day session with God, 28-35 (cf. 2 Cor. 3:6-18).

35-39. The tabernacle assembled
35:1-3. Sabbath regulations.

35:4-36:7. Gifts and workmen for the

The Tabernacle

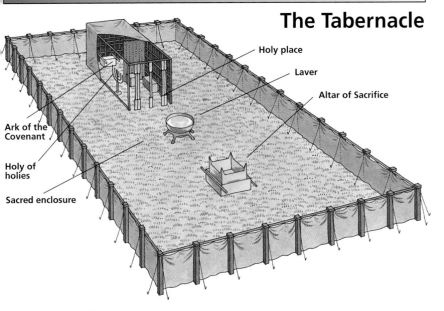

Holy place

Laver

Altar of Sacrifice

Ark of the Covenant

Holy of holies

Sacred enclosure

Artist's impression of the tabernacle, with part cut away to show the interior arrangement.

tabernacle. Bezalel and Oholiab, the principal craftsmen, were again singled out and their God-given talents for the work again noted, 35:30-35. **36:8-39:43. The tabernacle made.** These chapters record the material and furniture of the tabernacle collected and made according to the directions given in ch. 25-31.

40. The tabernacle set up
1-33. Built and furnished.
34-38. Divinely accepted. God blessed Moses and the people with His presence as the tent was filled with God's glory. So great was the splendor, Moses was not able to minister. A mob

of miserable slaves in Egypt marks the beginning of Exodus. An emancipated nation in fellowship with God and on its way to Canaan ends it. This is truly "the book of redemption."

Leviticus
The book of atonement

Nature of the book. Leviticus is the book of atonement and a holy walk. Leviticus says, "*Get right with God*" (the message of the five offerings: burnt offering, grain offering, fellowship offering, sin offering, guilt offering, ch. 1-7). Leviticus also says, "*Keep right with God*" (the message of the seven feasts: Passover, Unleavened Bread, Firstfruits, Pentecost, Trumpets, Atonement, Tabernacles, ch. 23).

Leviticus is the book of *holiness*. (This keynote idea occurs 87 times.) God says to the redeemed, "Be holy, because I am holy" (11:44-45; 19:2; 20:7, 26). A walk with God is on the basis of holiness, which is by *sacrifice* and *separation*.

Name of the book. The name *Leviticus* describes the contents of the book, as the law of the priests, the sons of Levi.

The sacrificial system
Origin of the sacrifices. Abel, Noah, Jacob, Job, and God's people down to the eve of the Exodus knew the way of access to God and practiced sacrifice (Ex. 10:25).

When Moses led Israel out of Egypt, the

Ceremonial washing of hands. Leviticus is the book of atonement and a holy walk.

sacrificial system was given fresh meaning in the light of experienced redemption. It was organized, codified, and written down by inspiration in the sacrificial codes of Exodus and Leviticus.

Meaning of the sacrifices for the OT worshipper

Basic meaning. The fundamental idea of the sacrifices to the Hebrew worshiper was that they were a *means of approach to God.* The Hebrew term for "sacrifice" (*qorban* from the root *qrb,*) is "to draw near or approach." Sinful, guilty mankind needed some way to draw near to the infinitely holy God with assurance of acceptance. This was divinely provided in a sacrificial system presided over by the Levitical priesthood.

Further significance. Besides the basic idea of the sacrifices as a means of his approach to God, the OT believer had other important aspects of worship in mind as he presented prescribed sacrifices. These included: (1) *Self-dedication to God,* in the burnt offering (Lev. 1; cf. Rom. 12:1-2). (2) *Generosity in giving,* in the grain offering (Lev. 2). (3) *Thanksgiving, praise, fellowship,* and *communion* of the worshiper because God accepted his offering. (4) *Expiation by substitution,* in the sin offering (Lev. 4). (5) *Expiation and restitution* in the guilt offering (Lev. 5).

Classification of the sacrifices. A twofold division is possible: (1) sacrifices used to approach God for the purpose of restoring broken fellowship—the sin offering (Lev. 4) and the guilt offering (Lev. 5); (2) sacrifices used to approach God for the purpose of maintaining

Outline

1-16	The way to God
1-7	By sacrifice
8-9	By priestly consecration
10	By avoiding priestly violation
11-15	By observing purification laws
16	By annual atonement
17-27	The way of fellowship with God
17-22	By separation from sin
23	By observing religious festivals
24	By obedience in worship and true reverence
25	By observing the sabbatic year and jubilee
26	By heeding God's promises and warnings
27	By keeping vows and paying tithes.

fellowship—the burnt offering (Lev. 1), the grain offering (Lev. 2), and the fellowship offering (Lev. 3).

The typological meaning of the sacrifices. For the NT believer the OT sacrificial system is particularly instructive through its illustrations of NT redemption. Many of the Levitical prescriptions are typical, i.e., they were symbolically *predictive,* expressing a need that they could not satisfy, but which the coming promised Redeemer would fulfill (1 Cor. 10:11; Eph. 5:2; Heb. 9:14). Others serve as principles that can be applied to the NT dispensation, while yet others illustrate facets of God's interaction with mankind that are timeless in their application.

Leviticus

procuring peace for the sinner (Rom. 5:1; Eph. 2:17; Col. 1:20).

4:1-5:13. The sin offering
4:1-12. The sin offering for the high priest. The sin offering pictures our Lord as the bearer of the sins of His people.
13-26. The sin offering. Regardless of who sinned among the Israelites, including leaders, 22-26, the sin could be atoned for by offering the specified sacrifice.
27-35. The sin offering for a member of the community.
5:1-13. Sin offering for special offenses.

5:14-6:7. The guilt offering
5:14-19. Sin against the Lord. This offering portrays Christ atoning for the harmful effects of sin, that is, injury done.
6:1-7. Sin against man. In injury done either to God or man, restitution had to be made along with an additional fifth (20 percent or a double tithe). In the case of wrong done to the Lord a 20 percent restitution was given to the priest; in the case of wrong done to man, it was given to the man defrauded.

6:8-7:38. The laws of the offerings
6:8-13. Law of the burnt offering. This continual burnt offering with the fire that never went out portrays Christ constantly offering Himself in God's presence on our behalf.
14-23. Law of the grain offering. The part of this offering eaten by the Aaronic priests shows the privilege of feeding upon Christ (John 6:53).
24-30. Law of the sin offering. The sin offering had to be killed in the place where the burnt offering was killed, showing the inseparable

1. The burnt offering
1-9. The young bull. The offerer of the sacrifice puts his hand on the head of the burnt offering; this illustrates the identification of the believer with his offerings. The antitype is the believer's faith in identifying himself with Christ (Rom. 4:5; 6:3-11), who died as his sin offering (2 Cor. 5:21; 1 Peter 2:24).
10-17. Animal and bird sacrifices. Sheep or goats, 10-13, and doves or young pigeons were used, 14-17, for sacrifices. The sheep (lamb) portrays our Lord in willing yieldedness to the death of the cross (Isa. 53:7; 1 John 2:2-9).

2. The grain offering
1-3 General meaning. Aaron and his sons shared this offering, 3, symbolizing our feeding on Christ (John 6:50-55).
4-11. The grain offering baked. The unleavened bread, which is first baked and then broken into small pieces, pictures the scene of the Last Supper.
12-16. The offering of the firstfruits. This offering connects Christ's sinless humanity with resurrection (cf. Lev. 23:9-14; 1 Cor. 15:20-23).

3. The fellowship offering
1-17. Two offerings. Offering from the herd, 1-5, and offering from the flock, 6-17, present Christ's work on the cross in the aspect of

connection between substitutionary atonement and the sinless perfection of the Substitute.

7:1-10. Law of the guilt offering. The guilt offering was also "most holy," 1, like the sin offering, and depended upon shed blood.

11-38. Law of the fellowship offering. All the details of this blessed offering center in Christ.

8. The consecration of the priesthood

1-13. The consecration. Three things were done to the priests. First, they were *washed*, 6, symbolizing regeneration (John 13:2-11; Titus 3:5; Heb. 10:22). Second, they were *clothed*, 7-9 (see Ex. 28). Third, they were *anointed,* 10-13 (see Ex. 29:5-25).

14-30. The offerings of consecration. All the offerings stressed the fact that priestly function depended upon a finished redemption.

31-36. The sacrificial feast. The eating of the sacrifices and the bread, so frequently seen in the Levitical ritual, illustrates the necessity of believers feeding on Christ (John 6:50-55).

9. The priests' minister

1-22. Inaugurating the ministry. The week of priestly ordination (ch. 8), symbolic of the priestly position of believers of this age, was followed on the eighth day by a series of new offerings of the priests in which the future priesthood of converted Israel, as a high priestly nation, may be portrayed.

23-24. The manifested glory. After Aaron and Moses came out of the tabernacle, the glory of the Lord fell and consumed the sacrifice.

10. Unauthorized fire of Nadab and Abihu

1-11. Sacrilege disciplined. By offering the "unauthorized fire," 1, to the Lord, Nadab and Abihu burned it in self-will without seeking or obeying God's directive in the matter. The seriousness of their sin is emphasized by the command not to mourn for them, 6.

12-15. New instructions were given the priests concerning eating the sacrifices.

16-20. Eleazar and Ithamar. Aaron explained that his two living sons were not sufficiently free of sin to deserve to eat the sin offering.

11. A holy people—their food

1-23. Clean and unclean food. Under the Christian dispensation distinctions between clean and unclean food have fulfilled their symbolic significance and have been abrogated, as in the case of Peter's vision when the gospel was released to Gentiles (Acts 10:9-15).

24-47. Defilement by a dead body. Death, illustrative of that which is purely in the natural realm and has no place in the experience of one who serves a *living* God (cf. Heb. 9:14), defiled on touch and required cleansing.

12. A holy people—childbirth

1-8. Childbirth and uncleanness. The declaration of uncleanness fulfills a religious, symbolic, and hygienic role for Israel.

13-14. A holy people—leprosy

Ch 13. Leprosy. Leprosy refers not only to modern leprosy but also to various skin diseases.

14:1-32. Its purification. This ritual assumed that the leper had been healed. The actual healing, like the forgiveness of sin, could be effected by God alone.

14:33-57. Mildew in the house. This refers to

Some of the special Passover foods.

various molds, mildews, or rots that may affect the moist plaster inside a house. It illustrates how sin may contaminate a home.

15. A holy people —personal defilement
1-18. Man's uncleanness. The bodily secretions mentioned, both voluntary and involuntary, normal as well as pathological, symbolize the deep-seated sin inherent in human nature and the curse upon it.
19-33. Woman's uncleanness. Fallen human nature is defiled even in its secret involuntary operations.

16. In the holiest—national atonement
1-28. The ritual portraying the Lord's objective redemption. Yôm Kippurîm, the Day of Atonement, the fast (Acts 27:9), on the tenth day of the seventh month (Sept.-Oct.), marked the climax of access to God under the old covenant. It was the most solemn day of the year, when the high priest (a figure of Christ) entered the holy of holies to make annual atonement for the sins of the nation, 1-5

(cf. Ex. 30:10; Heb. 9:7-8; 10:19).
29-34. The ritual picturing man's acceptance of redemption. The rest, 29, prefigures the rest of redemption and Israel's national enjoyment of a finished atonement.

17. Reverence for blood
1-16. Slain animals and the eating of blood. The blood was to possess sanctity because it represented life that God the Creator made.

18. Unholy practices forbidden
1-5. A holy life demanded. The holiness of the Redeemer is the all compelling reason for the holiness of the redeemed.
6-23. Unholiness specified. Various unholy relationships, 6-18, render a believer unfit for worship.
24-30. Judgment threatened. The panorama of history has shown God's warning consummated in judgment, both for the Canaanites and for Israel.

19-20. Other prescriptions for holiness
Ch. 19. Social regulations. These include honoring God and parents, 1-8, and care of the poor, 9-10.
Ch. 20. Special sins. Worship of Molech (from melek, "king"), a detestable deity adored by the Ammonites with sacrifice of the firstborn, offers a particularly cruel and revolting aspect of ancient Semitic paganism.

21-22. Rules for priestly purity
21:1-16. Holiness of the priests. These special laws regulated the holiness of the priests, guaranteeing a ministry beyond reproach.
21:17-24. Physical disqualifications of a

priest. Disabilities barred one from priestly function but not from priestly position, 22.

22:1-16. Personal purity of a priest. He must regulate his own life discreetly.

22:17-33. Priestly sacrifices must be unblemished and physically perfect.

23. The holy feasts

1-3. The weekly sabbath. This is basic to the entire cycle of feasts.

4-5. The Passover (Hebrew *pesah,* "a passing over"). This memorialized redemption from Egypt, when the Lord passed over the blood-covered dwellings of Israel.

6-8. Unleavened bread. Communion with Christ, the unleavened Bread, will result in separation from evil (yeast).

9-14. Firstfruits. These typify Christ in resurrection (the firstfruits) and those who are saved at Christ's appearing (1 Cor. 15:23; 1 Thess. 4:13-18).

15-22. Pentecost. This occurred 50 days after the Feast of Firstfruits, 15-16.

23-25. Trumpets. The blowing of trumpets after the assembly's ingathering furnishes a picture of Israel's regathering from her long dispersion.

26-32. Day of Atonement. This solemn occasion prefigures the repentant sorrow of Israel at the time of her conversion at the second coming of Christ.

33-44. Tabernacles. This is the last and great harvest home festival of the Jewish year. It foreshadows Israel's kingdom rest after regathering and spiritual conversion.

24. Priestly duties; blasphemy

1-4. Oil for the tabernacle light (cf. Ex. 25:6).

5-9. The bread. (cf. Ex. 25:23-30). Priests were to follow God's commands to Moses concerning these elements of the tabernacle worship.

10-23. Blasphemy dealt with. Traditional Judaism superstitiously refuses to pronounce the holy name Jehovah (*Yahweh*), substituting *Adonai* on the strength of this passage.

25. Sabbatical year and jubilee

1-7. The sabbatical year. The sabbath of days was extended to a sabbath of years. Every seventh year was to be a year of rest for the land, 5.

8-55. The year of jubilee. The cycle of seven sabbatical years was followed by the fiftieth year, 8, ushered in by the blowing of the jubilee trumpet on the Day of Atonement, 9.

26. Conditions of blessing in the land

1-39. Obedience and disobedience. The blessings of obedience, 1-13, are contrasted with the curse of disobedience, 14-39.

40-46. The restoration. Despite disobedience to the Mosaic and Palestinian covenants, the unconditional Abrahamic covenant remains, and through grace a remnant will be restored to kingdom blessing.

27. Appendix: vows

1-25. People and things dedicated. These were voluntary obligations assumed before God, often on condition of some desired blessing, as Jacob's vow (Gen. 28:20-22).

26-34. Things intrinsically the Lord's. These included the firstborn of animals, 26-27; other things dedicated, 28-29; and all the tithe of the land, 30-34.

Numbers
Walk and service of God's people

Outline

1-10	Leaving Sinai
11-20	Wandering in the desert
21-36	Journeying to the Promised Land

Nature of the book. Numbers is the book of testing. Numbers (Latin *numeri,* Greek *arithmoi*) is so named because the Israelites were twice numbered (ch. 1 and 26). Numbers is a wilderness book covering the time span from the second month of the second year after the Exodus from Egypt to the tenth month of the fortieth year. But the years of unbelief and wandering are mostly passed over in silence.

Spiritual significance. The NT repeatedly alludes to or quotes the book of Numbers (cf. John 3:14 and Num. 21:9). Balaam (Num. 22-24) is referred to by Jude (Jude 11), Peter (2 Peter 2:15-16), and John (Rev. 2:14). Jude also refers to Korah's rebellion (Jude 11; cf. Num. 16; 27:3). Its spiritually illustrative contents are given deep meaning (1 Cor. 10:1-11).

Part of a replica of the Ark of the Covenant, showing the cherubim on top.

Numbers

1. The people numbered

1-46. The numbering. The count was for military purposes, 3, according to family lineage.
47-54. The Levites excluded, and separated to tabernacle service.

2. The tribes arranged

1-2. The command. The camp of God's people was divinely arranged and ordered, with the tabernacle in the center (showing that God's worship and service were to be central).
3-34. The ordered camp. Three tribes were placed at each point of the compass.

3-4. The Levites assigned their work

3:1-4. The priests. They are mentioned first, since the worship of God (sacrifice and intercession) was centered in them as representatives of the nation.
3:5-51. The Levites. Sovereign grace was exemplified in the choice of this tribe for holy tabernacle ministry (cf. Gen. 34:25-31; 49:5-7). The work of the Levites in general is specified. The sanctity of the Levites for the firstborn is stressed (40-51).
Ch. 4. Responsibilities of the Levite families. The Kohathites, 1-20; the Gershonites; 21-28; and the Merarites, 29-33, are all occupied with holy things of the tabernacle, illustrating our occupation with Christ in fellowship with God and holy service.

5. Separation from defilement

1-4. Separation from those unclean. This illustrates the necessity of judging and putting away sin, as it is a barrier to divine fellowship and service.
5-10. Restitution. This was for wrong committed in the camp. Unconfessed sin cannot be condoned among the Lord's people.
11-31. Separation from adultery. This simple ritual showed the Lord's power and exposed the adulteress, punishing this serious sin in order to purge it out from among God's people.

6. The Nazirite

1-8. The vow. This was a voluntary dedication of a person to the Lord, 2. It involved abstinence from wine, 3, and long hair, 5, which was the outward badge that the separated one was willing to identify himself as belonging to the Lord. It also entailed separation from ceremonial uncleanness contracted by contact with a dead body (6-8).
9-21. The cleansing of the Nazirite from defilement. Defilement of a dedicated saint is cleansed only by confession and forgiveness.
22-27. Priestly blessing of a cleansed and consecrated people. This is a beautiful threefold invocation of the Lord's providence, grace, and favor.

7. The gifts of the leaders

1-88. The leaders and their gifts. The chiefs of the tribes contributed wagons and oxen for transporting the tabernacle. Verses 84-88 give the total offering as 2400 silver shekels, 120 gold shekels, and 252 sacrificial animals.

89. The voice from the mercy seat manifested the Lord's pleasure in the leaders' offerings at the dedication of the altar.

8. The Levites consecrated

1-4. The lampstand lighted. The lighting of the seven-branched lampstand at the beginning of the wilderness journey focused attention upon the need of the Lord's people for the Holy Spirit (the oil in the seven branches) to shed His light upon them, 2, 4.

5-26. Purification of the Levites. The laying on of hands upon the Levites by the Israelites points to the latter's identification with the Levites, who represented them and served in their place, 9-10, as well as in place of their firstborn, 11-22. The Levitical charge is repeated, 23-26.

9. Guidance for the redeemed

1-14. The observance of the Passover. This second observance, held in the desert at Sinai as they journeyed toward Canaan, shows how necessary the feast of redemption with its atoning blood is to all in a walk for God.

15-23. Supernatural guidance provided. The pillar of cloud by day and the pillar of fire by night were provided to lead the people.

10. The silver trumpets; the camp moves

1-10. The two silver trumpets. They made known the mind of the Lord in an audible way, 1-7.

11-36. Departure from Sinai. Though God promised to lead Israel through the wilderness by the pillar of cloud and fire, Moses asked Hobab, 29-31, his brother-in-law, to serve as a guide. The principle of divine guidance does not exclude human agencies.

11. Failure at Taberah and Kibroth Hattaavah

1-3. Murmuring at Taberah. Punishment for God's people because of their complaining was a consuming fire. Therefore, the place was called Taberah ("a burning").

4-9. Rejection of the manna.

10-30. Moses' complaint and the appointment of 70 elders. God directed in the appointment of 70 helpers for Moses in civil administration, and put a portion of the Spirit that rested upon Moses upon them.

31-35. Quails and the plague. There was abundance of quails "about three feet above the ground," 31, meaning within easy reach of people to catch. The craving of the Israelites was punished by a great plague, 33, the place being called Kibroth Hattaavah ("graves of craving"), 34-35.

12. Miriam's and Aaron's criticism of Moses

1-10. The mutiny of Miriam and Aaron. The general cause for this mutiny was jealousy of Moses' prominence, and the immediate occasion the marriage of Moses to an Ethiopian woman. Miriam, the prophetess, was the leader of this mutiny.

11-16. Aaron's repentance and Moses' intercession. Miriam was restored to fellowship with the nation through the intercession of her brothers.

13. Kadesh-Barnea:
The evil report of the spies
1-25. The scouts sent out. Spies were sent out to explore the Promised Land, 1-3. At Eschol ("cluster") they procured a huge bunch of grapes, 23. The Hebron region is famous for its grapes.

26-33. The report of unbelief. The land was truly all God said it was, 26-27. Caleb was vocal in his faith, 30, but general unbelief drowned out his advice, 31.

14. Kadesh: The tragedy of unbelief
1-10. The rebellion of the people. Joshua's and Caleb's exhortations enraged the people to the point of murder, 6-10.

11-25. Moses' intercession. God heard, spared the people, and announced eventual kingdom blessing, 21. The people's ten temptations of the Lord are mentioned, 22 (cf. Ex. 14:11-12; 15:23-24; 16:2; 16:20; 16:27; 17:1-3; 32:1-10; Num. 11:1; 11:4; 14:2).

26-39. The divine sentence. Death in the wilderness wanderings, a year for every day they spied out the land, was the penalty.

40-45. A new sin—presumption. They engaged in conflict without God's help and purely in their own power. Their disgraceful defeat was inevitable.

15. Various laws
1-31. Concerning offerings in the land. Two divine communications concerning offering, 1, 17, are remarkable in that they were given when the people were turning in unbelief from the land of promise.

32-36. The Sabbath breaker. This was a case of presumptuous sin mentioned in 30-31, giving an example of the severity of the Mosaic law.

37-41. The tassel of blue. On the corners of the garments was to be a memento to Israel that they were to be holy.

16. Korah's rebellion
1-19. The rebellion. Korah's sin was the rejection of the authority of Moses as God's mouthpiece and flagrant intrusion into the priest's office.

20-50. The punishment. Provision was made for a memorial of this event as a permanent warning by hammering out a covering for the altar from the bronze censers the rebels had used, 36-40.

17. Aaron's rod that budded
1-6. The divine command. This was further proof of the Lord's irrevocable choice of the Levites as ministers and the Aaronites as priests.

7-13. The sign. The Lord caused life to spring up in Aaron's rod alone, which became a picture of Christ in resurrection, acknowledged by God as High Priest.

18. The importance
of the Levitical priesthood
1-7. It was to bear iniquity. The Levitical priests were to execute every divine regulation meticulously and make atonement for the sinfulness pertaining to the tabernacle and its priesthood.

8-32. It was to be properly recompensed. Neither the priests nor the Levites were to have any land inheritance in Israel, thus avoiding a wealthy priestly caste. The priests, however, were to receive a large part of the offerings.

Spiritual significance of Kadesh

The people had faith to apply the redemption blood (Ex. 12:28) and to leave Egypt (the world), but lacked faith to enter their Canaan rest, enjoy conquest over enemies, and gain victorious possession of a land flowing with milk and honey (Heb. 3-4). They failed to enter into spiritual conquest and victory.

19. The red heifer ordinance

1-10. The ordinance. This ordinance is unique to Numbers and to the wilderness wandering. It was instituted because of wholesale contact with the death of so many Israelites who perished during the 40-year period in the desert (cf. 1 Cor. 10:5, 8-9). The use of the ashes of an animal in water for purification purposes is here invested with unique significance as it is introduced to Israel's faith.

11-22. The meaning. The red heifer beautifully illustrates the sacrifice of Christ as *the basis* of the cleansing of a believer from sinful defilement contracted in his pilgrim walk (1 John 1:7-2:2; cf. John 13:3-10).

20. Moses' sin; death of Aaron

1-13. Moses' sin. This chapter opens with death (Miriam's) and closes with death (Aaron's) and between recounts the failure of Moses, which consisted of *presumptuous disobedience,* 10-11, and *self-exaltation,* 10, "Must *we* bring you water?"

14-22. Futile negotiations with Edom. The descendants of Esau denied passage to the Israelites.

23-29. Death of Aaron. His son Eleazar succeeded him.

21. The bronze serpent

1-3. Victory over the Canaanites. King Arad in the Negev, the waterless district south of Beersheba extending south and southwest beyond Kadesh, was defeated and his towns placed under the ban of complete destruction.

4-9. The bronze serpent. The bronze serpent that Moses was instructed to make and hang on a pole, to which the people bitten were to look, prefigures Christ "made . . . sin for us" (John 3:14-15; 2 Cor. 5:21), bearing on the tree the judgment of our sin (Rom. 8:3).

10-35. Joyful journey to Transjordan. After healing, joyful singing is heard, 17.

22. Balaam the mercenary prophet

1-20. Balak calls Balaam. Balak, king of Moab, fearful of Israel passing by on the way to Canaan, sent for Balaam, originally a pagan diviner from Pethor, a city of Mesopotamia.

21-35. Balaam goes to Balak. The case of the speaking donkey is an instance of the omnipotence of God, and is not to be explained away by unbelief.

36-41. Balaam with Balak. Balaam is the type of a mercenary prophet, ambitious to exploit his gift financially. This is "the *way* of Balaam" (2 Peter 2:15).

23. Balaam's first two prophetic parables

1-12. The first parable and sequel. It was impossible for Balaam to curse or denounce Israel whom God had blessed, 8-9.

13-30. The second parable and sequel. God's

decreed blessing could not be revoked by Balaam, 20, nor indeed by all the sinister power of heathen occultism, 23.

24. Balaam's last two prophetic parables

1-14. The third parable and sequel. Introductory to the third parable, 2-9, was the account of Balaam's forsaking omens and the Spirit of God coming upon him in a vision, 4, to prophesy in beautiful figures concerning Israel's future kingdom glory, 5-7.

15-25. The last parable and sequel. This is the most remarkable of the four parables, containing a magnificent messianic prophecy of "a star . . . out of Jacob" and a "scepter . . . out of Israel," which shall "crush the foreheads of Moab" and destroy "all the sons of Seth," 17. Although the royal symbols "star" and "scepter" prefigure the Davidic dynasty, whose empire encompassed the Promised Land (Gen. 49:10), yet they find their ultimate fulfillment only in the greater David when at the Second Coming the kingdom is restored to Israel (Acts 1:6).

25. Israel's sin with Baal of Peor

1-3. The sin. This grievous sin of fornication and idolatry was the result of Balaam's teaching (Num. 31:16; Rev. 2:14; James 4:4). Although Balaam as an instrument of Satan could not turn the Lord against Israel, he could turn Israel from the Lord.

4-9. The punishment. There was a great slaughter of 24,000 people.

10-18. Phinehas's reward. Phinehas's zeal saved the people from further judgment, 11, and was rewarded by a covenant of peace and an everlasting priesthood, 12-13.

26. The second numbering

1-51. The command and its execution. The new census was taken after the plague and the events of the wilderness.

52-65. A fair method of dividing the land. The new revision of the military lists provided figures for a more equitable division of the land by lot-drawing.

27. Zelophehad's daughters; Moses' death announced

1-11. A question of inheritance. Daughters were to receive the right of inheritance, but were to marry only within their own tribe (cf. Num. 36:8).

12-23. Appointment of Moses' successor. Moses' death being announced, and the reason for it, 12-14, the great leader demonstrated his humility and meek selflessness in thinking only of the interests of God's people, 15-17.

28-29. The offerings for festal seasons

28:1-29:11. The portion the Lord was to receive. The key is 28:2: "Give this command to the Israelites and say to them: 'See that you present to me at the appointed time the food for *my* offerings made by fire, as an aroma pleasing to *me.*' "

29:12-40. Prominence given to the Feast of Tabernacles and its offerings. The seven days of this feast look forward to Israel's Kingdom Age and its worship, commemorating a finished redemption, while the eighth day of solemn rest, 35, points to the eternal state.

30. Laws regulating vows

1-2. Vows of a man. The man who keeps his word, who performs all he vowed, illustrates the sanctity and importance of the vow in ancient Israel.

3-16. Vows of a woman. These injunctions involved vows or pledges made by women in which men were involved as the heads of households, and were exceptions to the general rule that anyone who made a vow must perform it.

31. War against Midian

1-12. The divine command. Vengeance upon Midian was designed to show how uncompromising God's servants must always be against idolatrous apostasy and apostate prophets like Balaam, 8.

13-54. Cleansing, spoil gathering, and offerings. God gave complete victory. Israel was enriched by rooting out the danger of apostasy and thankfully offered to God the spoils of conquest.

32. The portion of Reuben, Gad, and Manasseh

1-24. Their request and dispute with Moses. The request was a selfish one, characterized by worldly convenience, 1-5.

25-42. The final arrangement. The tribes of Reuben and Gad and the half tribe of Manasseh, 33, obtained the rich grazing lands of Transjordan, but their choice was comparable to Lot's selfish decision (Gen. 13:5-11), and manifested similar results of unbelief and worldly conformity (2 Kings 15:29; 1 Chron. 5:25-26).

33. Summary of the journey from Egypt

1-49. The four stages. The first stage was from Egypt to Sinai, 1-15; the second, from Sinai to Hazeroth, 16-17; the third, from Hazeroth to Kadesh, 18-36, the 38 years of wilderness wandering; and the fourth, from Kadesh to the Plain of Moab, 37-49.

50-56. Directions to exterminate the Canaanites. Idolaters and every trace of their idolatry were to be rooted out.

34. Directions for the conquest and allotment of Canaan

1-29. The land divided. The boundaries of the land are given, 1-12, and the names of the men who would assign them, 13-29.

35. Levitical cities and cities of refuge

1-8. The Levitical cities. The cities were set apart because the Levites were not entitled to a tribal inheritance.

9-34. The cities of refuge. The six cities of refuge are described (Deut. 4:41-43; 19:1-13). They restrained the tribal law of blood revenge so that a suspected murderer might receive a trial, 12. Murder and manslaughter are distinguished, 16-34.

36. Laws of female inheritance

1-4. The request of the tribe of Manasseh. This plea asked that tribal inheritance involving women be kept in the tribe.

5-13. Moses' response. Moses approved the request.

Deuteronomy
The book of obedience

Outline

1-4	Moses' first discourse—historical
5-26	His second discourse—legal
27-30	His third discourse—prophetic
31-34	Historical appendixes

Name of the book. Deuteronomy is called by the Jews the "five-fifths of the law," since it completes the five books of Moses. Deuteronomy rehearses the law to the new generation that had come out of the wilderness and was looking toward the conquest of Canaan. The name "Deuteronomy" ("second law," the inexact rendering in Greek of 17:18) should be rendered, "This is the copy [or repetition] of the law."

Nature of the book. This is distinctly a book of *obedience*. Blessing is the reward of obedience; the curse, the result of disobedience. It is a book of *remembrance* and *retrospect*. It looks back to redemption out of Egypt and discipline and punishment in the wilderness, beholding both the goodness and severity of God. It is also a book of *hope* and *prospect*, looking to the future in Canaan and the prophetic forecast of Israel's future. Deuteronomy may have been our Lord's favorite book, as the book of obedience reflecting His own perfect obedience to the Father. Significantly, He quoted from this great book in repelling the disobedience suggested by the tempter (Matt. 4:1-11; cf. Deut. 8:3; 6:16; 6:13; and 10:20).

Boundary stones were set up to mark field limits.

Deuteronomy

1-4. Historical review: Summary of events in the wilderness

1:1-5. Introduction. An 11 days' journey by faith was changed to 40 years' wandering by unbelief.

1:6-46. Review of the journey from Sinai to Kadesh. A recapitulation of the wilderness wanderings is given. This is vital to clarify to the new generation the moral judgment of God upon Israel's unbelief and failure in these events.

2:1-15. Thirty-eight years of wandering are merely glimpsed, and stress is laid on not offending the Edomites or the Moabites.

2:16-3:29. New period of faith and advance. Joshua takes his place as Moses' successor, 3:21-29.

4:1-40. Moses' earnest exhortation to obedience. This speech strikes the keynote of the book (cf. 11:26-28).

4:41-43. Transitional statement. Cities of refuge were set apart.

4:44-49. Introduction to Moses' second discourse. The summary of the first discourse, 44-45, declares Mosaic authorship of this material.

5. Reiteration of the Ten Commandments

1-21. The Decalogue repeated. These ten commandments, together with the "judgments," governing the social life of Israel (Ex. 21:1-24:8), and the "ordinances," regulating the religious life (Ex. 24:12-31:18), form "the law" (Matt. 5:17-18), or Mosaic covenant.

22-33. The meaning of the events at Sinai stressed. The aged Moses recalled the fire, cloud, and darkness, 22, and notably God's voice, 23. The people were deeply moved, 27-29, and Moses' role of mediator was indicated, 31.

6. Exposition of the First Commandment

1-3. Summary and exhortation to obedience. This section relates to the content of ch. 5.

4. The first commandment. This is the most significant verse for orthodox Jews, who call it *Shema* after the first word, "Hear!" This command means that "the Eternally Existing One is our God and He is the unique and *only* Eternally Existing One."

5-25. Duties resulting from the first commandment. Since He is the unique and *only* Lord God, Israel is to love Him, obey, and serve Him supremely, 5-25 (cf. Matt. 22:37). The basis for this is gratitude for redemption and safe passage into the Promised Land.

7. Possession of the land and separation from sin

1-11. Command to destroy idolatry. The Canaanites were to be exterminated, 1-4, because their immorality was infectious and their iniquity full (cf. Gen. 15:16; 1 Cor. 10:14).

12-26. Promise of blessed assistance. Victory, numerical increase, and general prosperity would attend godly separation from idolatrous contamination.

8-10. Warnings to obedience
Ch. 8. Remember the past, and anticipate the future.
9:1-10:11. Warning in the light of former failure. The warning, 9:1-6, was in view of past unbelief, 7-24. Moses' intercession on behalf of the people was recounted, 25-29, and the results of former disobedience, 10:1-11, presented to the new generation.
10:12-22. The Lord's love for His people and their responsibility.

11-12. The blessing of obedience; the curse of disobedience
11:1-21. Israel's supreme duty was to love the Lord and to show that love by keeping the commandments.
11:22-32. The blessing and the curse. The key word "obedience" in Deuteronomy is further elucidated.
Ch. 12. Conditions of blessing in the promised land. True worship of the Lord had to be maintained in a central sanctuary that the Lord would choose, 5-14.

13. False prophets and their doom
1-5. Punishment of the false prophet.
6-11. Punishment of blood relatives who tempt to idolatry. So terrible is the snare of idolatry that even the nearest of kin found guilty were not to be spared.
12-18. Punishment of an apostate city.

14. Separation of God's people
1-2. Basis of separation. Relationship to God is to be the basis of separation from the sinful customs of the heathen.
3-21. Separation and distinctions in food. Boiling a kid in its mother's milk was a pagan custom, 21, the milk later being poured out as a charm to guarantee fertility of the soil.
22-29. Separation and pure religion. Once in three years the householder's tithe went to the Levites who were in the outlying villages (Deut. 18:6-8), the poor, the foreigners in Israelite employment, and orphans and widows, 28-29.

15-16. Sabbatical year and principal feasts
15:1-11. The Sabbatical year. The seventh year brought rest to the land and release from debts and obligations.
15:12-18. Liberation of Hebrew slaves.
15:19-23. Sanctification of the firstborn of the flock. The eating of the unblemished sacrifice at the central sanctuary prefigures the believer's feeding upon the spotless Lamb of God in the presence of God the Father.
16:1-17. Principal annual feasts. These were Passover, 1-8; Feast of Weeks, 9-12; and Feast of Tabernacles, 13-17.
16:18-22. Justice assured by legal provisions.

17. Civil government in the land
1-13. Legal decisions. Judges were to administer civil justice, idolaters being condemned to death by the testimony of at least two witnesses, who would be the first to throw stones (cf. John 8:7).
14-20. Anticipation of a king. The Spirit of God in Moses foresaw the eventual rejection of the

theocracy and the choice of a king in the time of Samuel.

18. Prophecy of the great prophet
1-8. The Levites' and the priests' portion. How the people were to minister to those who were dependent upon the Lord and closely identified with them is revealed.

9-14. Interdict against idolatry, divination, and the occult. That demonism is the source and dynamic of pagan idolatry is here revealed (cf. 1 Cor. 10:19-20; 1 Tim. 4:1-2; 1 John 4:1-6; Rev. 16:13-16).

15-22. The great prophet to come. This is a wonderful prediction of our Lord as *the Prophet* (cf. John 1:21-45). The test of false and true prophets is given, 20-22.

19-20. Laws for the nation in Palestine
19:1-13. The cities of refuge. Mercy was prescribed for the accidental manslayer but none for the willful killer.

19:14-21. Other laws.

Ch. 20. Future wars of the nation. Since the Israelites were the Lord's people, they were to be fearless, 1-4.

21. Various laws and instructions
1-9. The expiation of an unknown murder. Bloodguiltiness of this sort had to be atoned for by killing a heifer in a deserted valley, and by the elders and Levites washing their hands over the dead animal.

10-21. Family regulations. The case of a rebellious and unrepentant son and his punishment is given, 18-21.

22-23. The burial of a criminal. See Joshua 8:29. Paul quotes verse 23 in Galatians 3:13.

22. Exposition of laws from the second table
1-8. Duty of neighborliness and humanity. Love for one's neighbor is shown by guarding and preserving his property, 1-4.

9-12. Laws emphasizing separation from evil.

13-30. Laws against adultery, incest, and fornication. These were given to protect the home and family.

23. The holiness of the congregation of the Lord
1-8. Constitution of the congregation of the Lord. The congregation, "assembly of the Lord," 1, like the NT church, was to be separated from everyone and everything unclean or defiling (2 Cor. 6:11-7:1), because it was the Lord's assembly.

9-14. Cleanness of the camp in war.

15-18. The law of the escaped slave and the religious prostitute. How gracious that the poor escaped slave found a refuge in the assembly of the Lord, 15, and was not to be oppressed, 16. Sexual perversions under the guise of religion are abominable in the extreme, 17-18.

19-25. Other regulations of the congregation of the Lord. Taking of interest was not to be practiced between brothers in the Lord's congregation, only among foreigners, 19-20.

24. Divorce and other laws of mercy
1-4. Mosaic concession on divorce. This was *not a commandment,* as the Pharisees who encountered Jesus erroneously concluded (Matt. 19:7-8), but merely a concession.

5-22. Other regulations. A newly wed man was free from war or business for one year to make his wife happy, 5. Nothing necessary to a man's very existence, such as a millstone for grinding his food, was to be taken as security for a debt, 6.

25. Various laws continued
1-3. Corporal punishment.

4. The ox. As the ox was to be allowed to eat when treading out the grain, so the toiling servant of the Lord is worthy of remuneration (cf. 1 Cor. 9:9; 1 Tim. 5:18).

5-10. The brother-in-law's marriage. This custom of levirate marriage was pre-Mosaic (Gen. 38:8-11) and finds its outworking in the kinsman-redeemer theme in the book of Ruth. Taking off the shoe, 9 (cf. Ruth 4:7), arose from the custom of walking on the soil as a symbol of declaring one's right of acquired possession.

11-16. Other laws.

17-19. Doom upon Amalek. Amalek, the opposer of the people of God, was to perish forever (Num. 24:20).

26. Offering of firstfruits and prayer
1-11. The basket of firstfruits. The lovely confession, "My father was a wandering Aramean," 5, is a reference to Jacob's semi-nomadic life in contrast to Israel's anticipated settlement in the land.

12-19. Obedience and prayer result in blessing.

27. Laws on stone: blessings and curses
1-26. Dramatization of Israel's covenant responsibilities. Gerizim speaks of the grace of God. Ebal speaks of the curse of the law (Gal. 3:10).

A Bar mitzvah at Jerusalem's Western Wall.

28. Blessings and curses prophesied
1-14. The blessing promised.

15-68. The prophesied curses. A prophetic glimpse of the history of Israel's tragic career of unbelief and sin is here outlined.

29. The Palestinian covenant and the curse
1-15. The covenant introduced. This was the "Palestinian" covenant governing Israel's tenure of the Promised Land distinct from the Mosaic covenant given at Horeb, 1.

6-29. The curse reiterated. Warning against apostasy was again given, 16-21. All the nations would know these punishments were because Israel forsook her covenant, 22-29.

30. The Palestinian covenant defined
1-10. The terms of the covenant. The Palestinian covenant is here defined in seven prophetic declarations: (1) *Dispersion of Israel for disobedience and apostasy*, 1. (2) *Israel's future conversion while in the dispersion*, 2.

(3) *The second coming of Christ,* 3. (4) *Restoration of the land,* 5. (5) *Israel's future national conversion,* 6. (6) *The judgment of the nations,* 7. (7) *National prosperity of the millennial nation,* 9.

11-20. Final ominous warning against violation of the covenant. This is one of the most eloquent statements in the Scripture that sets forth the choice between obedience and disobedience and the resultant blessings and curses that God promises to those who choose good or evil.

31. Moses' final charge and a solemn prophecy

1-8. Moses' final charge.

9-13. The law written and delivered to the priests for safekeeping. Instructions were set down for its being read every seventh year at the Feast of Tabernacles.

14-23. The Lord's prophetic disclosure. Israel would apostatize, 15-21.

24-30. Moses instructs the Levites. The law written by Moses and delivered to the Levites was to be deposited in the ark.

32. The Song of Moses

1-3. Introductory appeal. This magnificent prophetic ode spans the history of Israel—past, present, and future. It is a great mountain peak of prophetic poetry.

4-6. Integrity of the Lord's ways vs. Israel's perversity. The Lord is "the Rock," 4, an ancient name for God, 15, 18, speaking of stability and dependability.

7-14. The Lord's love for Israel. The Lord encircled, cared for, prospered, and blessed Israel, 10-14.

15-18. Israel's apostasy. Israel took five steps downward: she forsook God, 15; scoffed at the Rock of her salvation, Messiah; served strange gods, 16; sacrificed to demons, 17; was unmindful of the Rock, 18.

19-33. Results of Israel's apostasy. Again history is prewritten. The sufferings of the Babylonian captivity, 587 B.C., and the worldwide woes from A.D. 70 to the Second Coming are reflected here.

34-42. The Lord's final dealing with Israel. The judgment, 40-42, is that which will fall upon the nations at the second coming of the Lord.

43. The final consummation.

44-47. The song of Moses taught to Israel.

48-52. Moses' death announced.

33. The blessing of Moses

1-5. The Lord's manifestation in glory. This, the basis of all blessing to Israel and the earth, is a prophetic picture of the Second Coming.

6-25. The tribes blessed.

26-29. The future joy of Israel. God is Israel's dwelling place, 27; deliverer, 28; and Savior, 29.

34. The death of Moses

1-7. Moses dies and is buried. Although Moses did not enter the Promised Land prior to his death, the next time he is seen is on the Mount of Transfiguration with Jesus and Elijah (Matt. 17:3), inside the Promised Land.

8-9. Israel mourns, and Joshua takes over.

10-12. Moses as a prophet. Moses was the greatest of Israel's prophets (Num. 12:6-8; Deut. 18:15-22, Hos. 12:13).

Joshua
The book of conflict and conquest

Outline

1-12	Entrance into Canaan and the conflicts
13-22	Division and settlement of the land
23-24	Joshua's final words and death

Place and nature of the book. Joshua is the first book in the second part of the Hebrew canon called the Prophets. Among the Prophets, Joshua heads up the Former Prophets, usually referred to in English Bibles as the historical books. This book takes its name from the great religious and military leader whose exploits it depicts. The name Joshua, or Jehoshua, means "the Lord saves or delivers."

Excavations at the Tell of ancient Jericho.

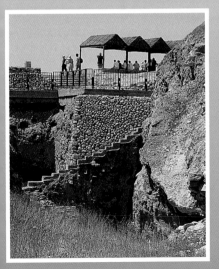

Spiritual meaning of the book. *Anticipation* marks the book of Deuteronomy, *realization* the book of Joshua. Redemption *out* of *Egypt* under Moses gave the Israelites a redeemed *position*. Redemption *into the Promised Land* under Joshua gave them a redemption *experience* of victory and conquest in possessing their possessions. Two factors, *position* and *experience,* are inseparable in salvation. Salvation is basically a position or status, but it is also an experience of the blessings involved in possessing that position. In a spiritual sense the book of Joshua is the Ephesians of the OT. "The heavenly realms" of Eph. 1:3; 6:12 are illustrated by the land of Canaan, which is a picture of the *experience* of victory and conquest belonging to those who are redeemed.

Joshua

1. Joshua assumes command

1-9. Joshua's commission. Moses' successor was commanded to lead God's people into their inheritance. He was given assurance of divine presence and success, conditional on obedience. Joshua prefigures Christ as the Captain of our salvation (Heb. 2:10-11), leading His people in the power of His Spirit.

10-18. Joshua takes charge. He addressed the people, 10-15, who promised obedience, 16-18.

2.The spies and Rahab's faith

1. The spies and Jericho. Joshua acted wisely in sending out the spies to learn the strategy of the enemy.

2-14. Rahab's faith. The harlot is an apt illustration of the power of the gospel of grace to save a sinner (cf. Heb. 11:31; James 2:25).

15-24. The scarlet line. Bound by Rahab to the window, this line by which she let the spies escape becomes a beautiful symbol of salvation.

3.The Jordan crossed

1-6. The ark of the Lord leads the way. The ark (Ex. 25:1-22), one of the most inclusive object lessons of Christ, led on and made a way through Jordan.

7-8. Joshua begins to be magnified. When the Lord's people enter into the *experience* of their position in Christ, portrayed by Israel crossing Jordan, they begin to exalt and obey the divine Joshua.

9-13. Joshua directs the crossing. Joshua's message to the people assured them that "the living God" would prove His presence among them by driving out the Canaanites, 10. The ark of the covenant is that "of the *Lord of all the earth,"* 11, 13, a title that Zechariah employed of the time when Israel will be established in the kingdom (Zech. 4:14) after all her enemies have been judged.

14-17. The crossing is made. It is wholly the result of a miracle, whether or not an earthquake dammed up the stream above the crossing at Adam, 16.

4. The memorial stones

1-24. The two memorials. The twelve stones taken out of Jordan and erected as a monument at Gilgal, 1-8, 20, speak of redemption for Israel into the land and into a sphere and experience of victory and conquest. The stones left in the swirling Jordan are mementos of Christ's death under judgment in the believer's place (Pss. 22:1-18; 42:7; 88:7; John 12:31-33).

5. Israel at Gilgal

1. Israel's terror-stricken enemies. A redeemed and victorious people always disheartens the enemy.

2-8. The new generation circumcised. From this time they bore the visible token of belonging to the Lord and the Lord, in turn, being in gracious covenant relation with them.

9-10. Reproach of Egypt rolled away. "The reproach of Egypt," which Joshua said he rolled

The River Jordan near Jericho.

away at Gilgal (Gilgal means "a rolling") when he circumcised the people, was their bondage to Pharaoh in Egypt.

11-12. Manna and the produce of the land. The Israelites appropriated the blessings of their privileged possession.

13-15. Joshua's vision of the divine captain of the Lord's army. The man with the drawn sword before Jericho was the Lord, the preincarnate Christ in visible form, who appeared to show Joshua that He who marshals the armies of heaven was fighting for Israel.

6. Jericho taken

1-21. Divine instructions followed. The city was to be taken in faith and obedience to God's word, and not by human wisdom. The miracle of its tumbling walls was the miracle of faith (cf. Heb. 11:30).

22-25. Rahab remembered. The scarlet line, doubtless an object of ridicule, saved Rahab and her house, while the entire city was devoted to destruction.

26-27. Curse on Jericho. Jericho was never to be rebuilt, except under the penalty of a curse, 26 (cf. 1 Kings 16:34).

7. Achan's sin

1-15. Defeat of Israel and the reason. The sin of one involves all. The specific sin of Achan was disobedience to the command of separation from the "devoted things" (Josh. 6:17-18), that is, from Jericho (the world), under the sentence of judgment, 1, 11 (cf. James 4:4; 1 John 2:15-17).
16-26. The sin judged. "I saw . . . I coveted . . . and took," 21, is the story of temptation and fall.

8. Ai taken

1-17. Joshua's strategy. The ruse of the ambush was by divine direction, not Joshua's brilliance, 3-8.
18-27. The capture of Ai.
28-29. The destruction of the city. "Joshua burned Ai and made it a permanent heap," 28.
30-35. The altar at Ebal was erected in the scenic Shechem area in the heart of the land as a commemoration of victories at Jericho and Ai and as an act of obedience to Moses' command (Deut. 27:2-8).

9. The deception of the Gibeonites

1-2. The confederacy of the enemy. "All the kings west of the Jordan" united to fight Israel.
3-15. The ruse of the Gibeonites. Their lie, that their wineskins had become old and worn on the long journey, their bread moldy, and their sandals worn, completely deceived the

Israelites, who made a treaty with the enemy.
16-27. The mistake discovered. The Gibeonites were found to be neighbors and enemies, among those who should have been eradicated, 16-17 (cf. 2 Cor. 11:14).

10. Southern Canaan taken
1-6. Adoni-Zedek and his alliance.
7-15. The war and the miracle. The Lord performed a tremendous miracle, 12-14, to aid Joshua in the victory over the southern confederacy. The hailstones, 11, caused more deaths than the Israelite army. The uniqueness of the miracle is stressed, 14, and hence may be considered scientifically inexplicable.
16-43. The great victory and subsequent conquests. The five kings were executed, 22-27, and further conquests brought about the subjugation of all southern Palestine.

11-12. Further conquests of Canaan
11:1-15. Conquest of northern Canaan. Joshua was divinely directed to hamstring the horses and burn the chariots, 6, 9, so that he might trust in the Lord and not in these means of warfare.
11:16-12:24. A review of the conquest.

13. Joshua instructed to apportion the land
1-7. The Lord's message to Joshua. "There are still very large areas of land to be taken over," 1, is the sad story of Israel, and of many believers who fail to claim their full spiritual possessions.
8-33. The inheritance of Reuben, Gad, and the half tribe of Manasseh is restated and confirmed.

14. Caleb's request and inheritance
1-5. Summary of the apportionment of the land.
6-15. Caleb's request. Caleb presented his testimony of the Lord's faithfulness, 6-12, and received Hebron, 13-15 (cf. Num. 13:6; 14:24, 30).

15-16. Judah's and Ephraim's portions
Ch. 15. The portion of Judah.
Ch. 16. The portion of Ephraim. Ephraim received its territory, 5-9, but failed to expel the Canaanites from Gezer, 10. The city remained under Canaanite control until Solomon's time (1 Kings 9:16).

17. Manasseh's portion
1-13. The names and boundaries.
14-18. Manasseh's complaint and Joshua's reply. The complainers' weakness and unbelief offered a striking contrast to Caleb's faithful courage. Joshua encouraged them, 17-18.

18-19. The portion of the other tribes
18:1. Tabernacle erected at Shiloh. Shiloh became the focal point of the 12 tribes till the destruction of the city by the Philistines and the capture of the ark (1 Sam. 4:11).
18:2-10. Failure of the seven tribes to claim their possession.
18:11-28. Portion of Benjamin. This was a small but influential tribe located in mountainous terrain.
Ch. 19. Portions of the remaining tribes.

20. The cities of refuge
1-6. Repetition of the provision, according to

Israelite citadel at Hazor, north of Galilee.

the law of Deuteronomy 19:1-13.

7-9. The cities specified. The three cities in the land are Kedesh, Shechem, and Hebron; those outside the land are Bezer, Ramoth, and Golan.

21. The Levites' portion

1-42. The portion of the Levites. Although true in a sense of all the tribes, the Lord was the particular inheritance of the tribe of Levi (cf. Num. 18:30; Deut. 10:9; Josh. 13:14, 33; 14:3-4).

43-45. The Lord's faithfulness was renewed. Nothing He promised did He fail to keep (Num. 23:19).

22. Return of the Transjordan tribes

1-9. Joshua sends the tribes home.

10-29. The great altar and the controversy. The departing tribes built an altar, which was interpreted as a violation of the law of the central sanctuary (Deut. 12:13-14) and therefore an act of rebellion against Israel and the Lord. A delegation headed by Phinehas examined the matter. The explanation given was that the monument was not a real altar, but merely a memorial, a "witness," 21-29.

30-34. The controversy settled. It was a testimony that the 12 tribes, though separated by Jordan, were *one* people.

23. Joshua's farewell admonitions

1-13. Exhortations of faithfulness to the Lord. Israel's great spiritual leader and military general, advanced in age, 1, exhorts Israel to obey the Mosaic law, 6-11.

14-16. Concluding appeal.

24. Covenant at Shechem; Joshua's death

1-15. Historical retrospect and Joshua's eloquent challenge. All Israel at Shechem heard the review of the Lord's dealings from Abraham to the conquest, 1-13, as the basis for the challenge to serve the Lord only, 14-15.

16-28. Covenant accepted. Israel accepted Joshua's challenge, 16-18, and asserted her loyalty to the Lord and the covenant.

29-33. Joshua's death. It is also recorded that Joseph's bones, "which the Israelites had brought up from Egypt, were buried at Shechem," 32.

Judges
The monotony and misery of sin

The name of the book. Judges takes its name from the 12 Spirit-anointed military and civil leaders the Lord raised up to deliver the nation. As a loose confederacy around the central shrine at Shiloh, the young nation had no stable central government, and, forsaking the Lord, it became an easy prey for enemy invasion. The judges first delivered the people, then ruled over them.

The nature of the book. Judges is a record of the dark ages of the decline and apostasy of

The book of Judges vs. the book of Joshua

JOSHUA	JUDGES
Victory	**Defeat**
Freedom	**Servitude**
Faith	**Unbelief**
Progress	**Declension**
Spiritual vision	**Earthly emphasis**
Fidelity to the Lord	**Apostasy from the Lord**
Joy	**Sorrow**
Strength	**Weakness**
Sense of unity	**Declension, anarchy**
Sin judged	**Sin lightly regarded**

Outline

1:1-2:5	Introduction to period of the Judges
1:1-36	Political conditions (from Joshua to the Judges)
2:1-5	Israel weeps in failure
2:6-16:31	The period of the Judges
2:6-3:6	Religious character of the period
3:7-16:31	List of the Judges
17:1-21:25	The double appendix
17:1-18:31	Idolatry of Micah and the Danites
19:1-21:25	The crime of Gibeah and its punishment

The Jezreel Plain, also known as Esdraelon.

Israel in the land. The people forsook the Lord (2:13); the Lord forsook the people (2:23). The key verse is: "In those days Israel had no king; everyone did as he saw fit," 17:6; 21:25. The record covers about 350 years, from Joshua to Saul.

Judges

1. Israel's failure to drive out the Canaanites

1-4. The question of confronting the tribes.
The Israelites "asked the Lord" by consulting the sacred lots, 1: "Who will be the first to go up and fight for us against the Canaanites?" The Lord directed Judah, 2.

5-20. Incomplete victory of Judah.

21. Incomplete victory of Benjamin. The Jebusites were not dislodged from the fortress of Jerusalem.

22-36. Failures of the other tribes. Manasseh failed to drive the Canaanites out of the valley of Esdraelon. Israel disobeyed by enslaving rather than driving out the Canaanites, 28.

The Ugaritic religious literature of Ras Shamra reveals the moral depravity of Canaanite religion. Failure to exterminate this immoral people led to Israel's apostasies and defeats in the era of the Judges.

2:1-3:4. Results of Israel's failure

2:1-5. The angel of Bokim. This was the Lord Himself who redeemed the Israelites from Egypt and brought them into the land, 1.

2:6-15. Israel's earlier obedience contrasted to present apostasy. The nation had been obedient to the Lord under Joshua and the elders who outlived him, 6-9.

2:16-19. Résumé of Israelite history under

Part of the reconstructed city gate at Dan.

the Judges. The Lord raised up "judges," i.e., military heroes, who by virtue of their successes were entrusted with government administration during their lifetime, 16. But as soon as the Spirit-anointed (charismatic) leader died, the people turned away from God and were taken over by an invader, 17-19.

2:20-3:4. Nations left to prove Israel. The nations left in the land had a double divine purpose: (1) to punish Israel for disobedience, 2:20-21; (2) to test and prove the faithful and instruct them in warfare, 2:22-3:4.

3:5-31. Judges Othniel, Ehud, and Shamgar

5-11. First apostasy, servitude, and judge (Othniel). The story of the decline is told, 5-7: compromise, intermarriage with idolaters, finally idolatry itself, serving the gods and goddesses of

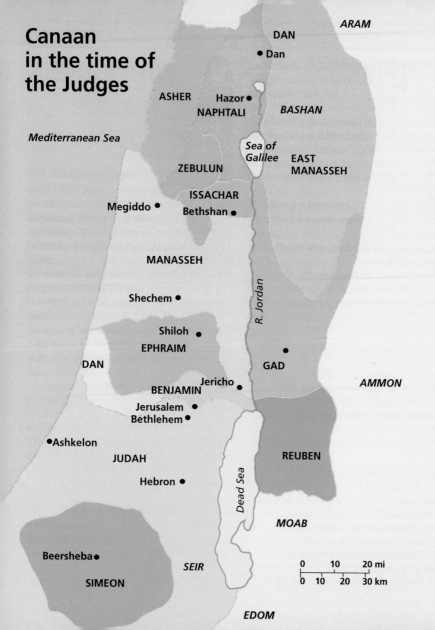

Canaan in the time of the Judges

ARAM

DAN

● Dan

ASHER

Hazor ●

NAPHTALI

BASHAN

Mediterranean Sea

Sea of Galilee

EAST MANASSEH

ZEBULUN

ISSACHAR

Megiddo ●

Bethshan ●

MANASSEH

Shechem ●

R. Jordan

Shiloh ●

EPHRAIM

DAN

GAD

AMMON

Jericho ●

BENJAMIN

Jerusalem ●

Bethlehem ●

● Ashkelon

JUDAH

Dead Sea

REUBEN

Hebron ●

MOAB

0   10   20 mi

Beersheba ●

SEIR

0 10   20   30 km

SIMEON

EDOM

Crucial battles occurred near Mount Tabor.

the Canaanites—Baals and Asherahs —worshiping the various images of these deities. Punishment was meted out in Israel's being sold to Cushan-Rishathaim for eight years. Othniel of Judah was raised up to deliver the Lord's people.

12-30. Second apostasy, servitude, and judge (Ehud). Ehud's deliverance from Moab was followed by an 80-year period of peace.

31. Shamgar slew 600 Philistines with an ox goad.

4-5. Deborah and her exploits

4:1-3. Third apostasy, servitude, and judge (Deborah). Iron chariots put the Canaanites ahead of the Hebrews, who were not familiar with the art of iron smelting (Josh. 17:16; 1 Sam. 13:19-22).

4-24. Deborah and Barak and their victory. Sisera was killed by Jael. This episode shows the rough morality of the period.

5:1-31. The song of Deborah. This is a spirited poetic version of ch. 4.

6. Gideon and the Midianite oppression

1-24. Fourth apostasy, servitude, and judge (Gideon). The Midianites and the other peoples were Bedouin raiders. Their camels enabled them to take waterless journeys of several days. Gideon was called to be a deliverer as he was beating out wheat in the winepress, instead of the usual place on the hilltop, to hide from the marauding invaders, 11-24.

25-40. Gideon's initial exploits. Gideon, charismatically anointed, mustered an army, 34-35, and was given the assurance of the sign of the fleece of wool, 36-40.

7. The victory of Gideon's three hundred

1-8. The reduction of the army. Gideon ("hewer down"), now called also Jerub-Baal ("let Baal contend," 1) because he tore down Baal's altar, sifted his army of 32,000 to 10,000, and finally to 300. Spiritual quality and not numbers is important if God is to work and be glorified.

9-14. The Midianite's dream. The loaf of barley bread, 13, represented the Israelite farmers, and the tent that the barley loaf flattened, the nomadic invaders.

15-25. The victory of faith.

8. Gideon's failure

1-3. Jealousy of the Ephraimites. The victory soon brought internal strife. Gideon's gracious reply, 2, illustrated his strength of character.

4-21. Complete victory over the invader. The people of Succoth and Peniel, 5-8, taunted Gideon and refused him aid, demonstrating that they were really secret allies of Midian.

22-32. Gideon's failure. Gideon made an ephod (probably some kind of image or memorial), 24-27, and placed it in his hometown of Ophrah.

33-35. The fifth apostasy. After Gideon's death Israel served Baal-Berith (lord of the covenant), a perversion of Jehovah's covenant relationship with Israel.

9. Abimelech and his wickedness

1-5. The murder of Gideon's sons.

6-57. Abimelech's pretensions and end. Jotham's parable, 7-21, incisively shows the base worthlessness of Abimelech (a worthless "thornbush," 14).

10. Tola, Jair, and the sixth apostasy

1-5. Tola and Jair. No record of achievement is given for Tola and little for Jair.

6-18. The sixth apostasy and servitude. A very serious departure, 6, brought the Philistine and Ammonite scourge, 7-9.

11. Jephthah delivers from the Ammonites

1-11. Jephthah rejected but called to be leader.

12-28. Jephthah's negotiations with Ammon. This showed tact, wisdom, and diplomatic skill, but was unsuccessful in averting war.

29-40. Jephthah's vow and its fulfillment. On the eve of the battle, 29, Jephthah made a vow that whoever came from his house first to meet him on his victorious return, 30, would be the Lord's and he would "sacrifice it as a burnt offering," 31.

12. Jephthah's war with Ephraim

1-7. The quarrelsome Ephraimites punished. In contrast to Gideon, Jephthah exhibited the selfish, proud attitude of sectarianism. "*I* and my people," 2; "*I* called," 2; "*I* saw," 3; "*I* took my life in my hands," 3. The result was strife and war among brothers.

8-15. The Judges Ibzan, Elon, and Abdon. These so-called minor judges never performed military exploits like the other judges.

13. Philistine domination; birth of Samson

1. The seventh apostasy. Israel was delivered into the power of the Philistines for 40 years. There was no cry to the Lord or record of repentance. This was the last and evidently the deepest apostasy. The Philistines were intensely religious, often carrying their gods into battle (2 Sam. 5:21).

2-23. Philistinism vs. Naziritism. The deliverer was to be a Nazirite, or "separated one." The Angel of the Lord, 3-23, was the preincarnate Christ, who appeared to Moses in the bush (Ex. 3:1-8) and Joshua outside Jericho (Josh. 5:13-15).

24-25. Samson's birth.

14. Samson's early exploits

1-7. Samson kills the lion. By virtue of Samson's Nazirite status, the Spirit of God came upon him mightily, as He always operates through a holy vessel set apart for God.

8-9. Honey in the lion's skeleton. The Nazirite vow forbade contact with a carcass.

10-20. Exploits despite compromise. Samson's betrothed wife nagged and deceived him, and the Philistines outwitted him.

15. Samson in conflict with the Philistines

1-8. Samson's revenge. The marriage was of the ancient type in which the husband came only periodically to visit his wife. The 300 foxes with torches tied to their tails let loose in the grain and vineyards of the Philistines was an act of pure revenge, not led of the Spirit of God.

9-13. Bound by his own. His own Israelite brothers, out of fear, bound Samson to deliver him to the Philistines.

14-17. The exploit with the donkey's jawbone.

18-20. Samson's prayer and its answer. This incident illustrates God's provision for His servant who called on Him in his need.

16. Samson and Delilah; his death

1-3. Samson at Gaza. Three Philistine women plagued the Nazirite Samson, and stripped him of spiritual power—the Timnite woman, 14:1-4; the harlot at Gaza, 16:1-3; and Delilah, 16:4-20.

4-19. Samson and Delilah. When Samson's locks, the badge of his Nazirite separation, were shaved off, his strength departed.

20-25. Results of Samson's violation of his separation. He was ignorant of his lack of spiritual power, 20.

26-31. Samson's death. In a tragic irony, Samson killed "many more when he died than while he lived," 30.

17-18. Idolatry of Micah and the Danites

Ch. 17. Micah and the Levite. Micah had an idolatrous shrine, and had made an ephod (an image) and "some idols," and in the spirit of that lawless age installed one of his sons as priest, 5-6.

Ch. 18. The Danite migration. The aim of the entire appendix of the book of Judges, ch. 17-21, is to show Israel's deep internal corruption.

19-21. Gibeah's crime and its punishment

Ch. 19. The deed of lust and violence. This chapter faithfully catalogs the horrible results of departure from God (cf. Rom. 1:26-32; 2 Tim. 3:1-5).

Ch. 20. The harvest of war and bloodshed. Because the Benjamites refused to surrender the criminals, a horrible civil war ensued in which thousands perished.

Ch. 21. Repentance concerning Benjamin. Benjamin was restored as a tribe.

Ruth
The rendezvous of romance and redemption

Outline

1   Ruth deciding by faith
2   Ruth gleaning under grace
3   Ruth communing in fellowship
4   Ruth resting in redemption

Place in the canon. This beautiful love story of redemption is closely associated with the book of Judges. Its place in the Hebrew Bible is in the third division of the threefold canon among the five shorter books called Megilloth or Scrolls (Song, Ruth, Lamentations, Ecclesiastes, Esther).

Typology. The rich underlying typology of this idyll makes the book of Ruth more than a pastoral story of love. It is an important link in the unfolding account of redemption, presenting in figure our Lord as the great Kinsman-Redeemer in general, but particularly as that aspect of His glorious character *will affect Israel,* His covenant people, in their future restoration.

The town of Bethlehem from the nearby hills.

Ruth

'Boaz's Fields' Bethlehem.

1. Ruth deciding by faith

1-5. Naomi and her misfortunes. Naomi ("pleasant one") reflects Israel, the chosen people. Her happiness in Bethlehem married to Elimelech pictures Israel's prosperity in the land, married to the Lord, faithful to Him, and enjoying His favor and blessing. The sorrows that came upon Naomi as a result of the famine speak of spiritual failure and punishment in the land.

6-18. Ruth and her decision. Ruth, clinging to Naomi, beautifully portrays the believing remnant of the nation, which will trust in God's provision.

19-22. Naomi and Ruth in the land.

2. Ruth gleaning under grace

1-17. Ruth gleaning in the field of Boaz. Boaz's coming from Bethlehem, 4; his kindness to Ruth, 5-9; his words of grace to her, 11-12; and his provision for her, 13-17, show the concern of Israel's Kinsman-Redeemer for the believing remnant of the nation.

18-23. Ruth learns about Boaz.

3. Ruth communing in fellowship

1-13. Boaz guarantees Ruth's redemption. Boaz's winnowing barley, 2, foretells the work of Christ (Matt. 3:12) when at His second coming He makes a separation among His people, and the believing remnant, like Ruth, seeks the place of rest at the feet of its Redeemer.

14-18. Ruth reported to Naomi and looked for the promised redemption.

4. Ruth resting in redemption

1-8. The nearer kinsman renounces his right. At the gate, 1 (Gen. 23:10, 18), the normal place for transacting business, Boaz told the nearer kinsman that he could not legally redeem the property without also marrying Ruth. The shoe symbolized the right of the owner to set foot on the land (Ps. 60:8).

9-17. Boaz's redemption and the marriage of Ruth. Ruth the Moabitess was officially accepted in Israel.

18-22. Messianic genealogy. Through a simple story is interwoven God's plan for the redemption of the world and the restoration of His people Israel.

1 Samuel
From the judges to the kings

Outline

1-8	Samuel as judge
1-3	Samuel's childhood and call
4-6	The capture and return of the ark
7	Samuel as judge
8	Israel's demand for a king
9-31	Saul's reign
9-15	The rise of Saul
16-31	The rise of David and the decline of Saul

Nature of the book. Treated as one book in the Hebrew, 1 and 2 Samuel constitute some of the finest historical writing in all literature. They are written largely as historical biography, the events themselves being stressed, and the moral and spiritual repercussions of these books have eminent ethical and didactic value. From a prophetic viewpoint they are also important in that they tell of the founding of Israel's kingdom under David. These events foreshadow the coming of Israel's kingdom under David. They also foreshadow the coming of Israel's true King (cf. Num. 24:17-19 and 1 Sam. 2:10) and the establishment of the kingdom under the Messiah (Acts 1:6).

The site of Shiloh, where Samuel was called to be a prophet.

1 Samuel

1. Samuel's birth and boyhood

1-18. Hannah's prayer and vow. The ancestry of Samuel is given, 1-2. God's sovereign working is seen in the child's birth.

19-28. Samuel born and given to God. The name Samuel ("requested of God") was given to the child as a token of the Lord's faithfulness in answering Hannah's prayer.

2. The failure of Eli's house

1-11. Hannah's ode. This is an inspired song of praise to the Lord, 1-3, celebrating His power and grace in deliverance, 4-8, with a prophetic glimpse into the future day of the Lord preceding Israel's true King and the establishment of His kingdom, 9-10.

12-36. Failure of Eli's house. The moral decline and lawlessness of the period of the judges were reflected in the disciplinary weakness of Eli and the flagrant wickedness of his sons, Hophni and Phinehas, 12-17.

3. Samuel's call

1-18. The call. Because of sin among God's people, "the word of the Lord was rare; there were not many visions," 1.

19-21. Samuel's prophetic ministry. From Dan on the northern boundary of Israel to Beersheba on the southern border, all Israel became aware of God's chosen human instrument of revelation.

4. Judgment of Eli's house

1-22. The death of Eli and his sons. Israel trusted in the ark rather than in Him of whom the ark spoke. Substitution of ritualism for spiritual reality led to domination by the Philistines with its dire results.

5-6. The ark among the Philistines and its return

5:1-5. The ark in Dagon's temple. Dagon was venerated in Palestine as god of the harvest. The spiritual blindness of the Philistines is seen in their superstitious veneration of Dagon.

5:6-6:21. The Lord's punishment of the Philistines. Malignant tumors and a plague of field mice (cf. 6:4, 11, 18) were the judgments visited on the enemies of the Lord and His people.

7. Samuel as judge

1-8. Samuel's message. The Baals were images of the Semitic fertility deity Baal ("lord"), and the Ashtoreth were replicas of Astarte, goddess of sexual love and fertility, 3-4.

9-17. Victory at Ebenezer. Repentance and faith in the Lord's redemption always bring a manifestation of the Lord as Ebenezer ("the stone of help").

8. Israel's demand for a king

1-3. Failure of the judges.

4-22. Demand for a king. The evils of having kings were pointed out by Samuel, 10-18. Unbelief and self-will were the basis of the rejection of the theocracy, 19-22.

9-11. Saul and his anointing
9:1-10:16. Saul's anointing. Saul is anointed king by the prophet Samuel, 10:1-16.

10:17-27. Saul's good start. Saul's initial humility, 21-22, imposing appearance, and commanding physique made him a promising choice, 23-24.

Ch. 11. Saul's initial victories. Saul was anointed by the Spirit to deliver Israel in the manner of the earlier judges, 6.

12. Samuel's farewell address
1-15. Samuel officially proclaims the kingdom. The people's reasons for choosing a king were wrong, 12. The kingship would expose them to many dangerous temptations. Obedience to the theocratic ideal alone could save them from the consequences, 13-15.

16-25. The Lord's sign of Israel's sin in asking for a king. Thunder and rain in the wheat harvest were so rare as to be miraculous.

13. Saul's first great failure
1-10. Saul's self-will. Saul showed flagrant unbelief and disobedience in taking upon himself the priest's office at Gilgal (cf. Num. 16:1-3, 32-40).

Archaeological light

The Philistines had a monopoly on iron (1 Sam. 13:19-22), which gave them military advantage. They apparently obtained the secret of smelting from the Hittites. Saul and David by their conquests broke their monopoly. The iron age extended from 1200 to 300 B.C.

11-23. The Lord's rejection of Saul announced. The prophet Samuel announced Saul's unfitness and rejection as king, 13-14.

14. Jonathan's heroism
1-23. Jonathan's great victory. He is one of the finest characters in sacred history, a glowing contrast to his father, a picture of genuine victorious faith, 6.

24-45. Saul's foolish impetuosity. This episode shows how unreliable Saul was to be king over the Lord's people.

46-52. Saul's successes and his family. Despite the king's unworthiness, God nevertheless granted victories for the sake of His people, 46-48.

15. Saul's second great failure
1-8. Saul's commission to exterminate Amalek. Saul's incomplete obedience was highlighted, 4-8, his stubborn self-will again becoming evident.

9-31. Saul's disobedience and rejection. He spared "the best" and "everything that was good," 9, forgetting that *nothing* of the flesh is good or can please God (Rom. 8:8).

32-33. Destruction of Agag.

34-35. Samuel separates from Saul. Samuel did not visit Saul again in any official capacity.

16. David anointed king
1-13. David's anointing. The rejection of the king after the people's heart was followed by the choice of the king after God's own heart, 1-2, whose exile and sufferings are told in ch. 16-31.

14-23. Saul's decline. The Spirit of God departed from Saul and an evil spirit from the Lord, 14, i.e., by the Lord's permission, began to

Archaeological light

Slings in OT warfare. The shepherd's sling was a formidable weapon in OT times. Judges 20:16 reports that the Benjamites could sling a stone within a hair's breadth. Sling stones have been excavated at Tell Bit Mirsim and Megiddo that averaged approximately four inches in diameter and weighed more than two pounds. Modern shepherds in the Middle East have demonstrated that the sling has a maximum range of 600 feet and that the stones can be propelled over 100 M.P.H.

torment him. After the young shepherd-king had soothed the troubled monarch, by playing the lyre, and was no longer needed, he returned to his father's sheep.

17. David and Goliath

1-11. Defiance of Goliath. This Philistine giant furnishes an illustration of Satan as he defied and terrified God's people through Philistine doctrines and practices.

12-30. David appears on the scene. David's being sent by his father Jesse, 12-19; his obedience, 20-27; his being misunderstood and unfairly accused by his own brothers, 28-30, tell of Him whom the Father sent into the world and of His treatment by His own.

31-54. David's victory. David went out to fight the giant with the confidence of faith and the shrewdness of wise preparation.

55-58. Saul's question.

18-20. David's flight from Saul

Ch. 18. Jonathan's love for David. This noble friendship, 1-4, was beautifully silhouetted against the dark background of Saul's demonic jealousy, 5-16.

Ch. 19. Saul's renewed attempt to kill David. Michal by a ruse, 11-17, saved David's life, and David fled to Samuel, 18-19. The grace of God dealt with Saul, 20-24, but his disobedience was his ruin.

Ch. 20. Jonathan protects David. The heir to the throne, far from being jealous or envious of David, loved him as himself (1 Sam. 18:1). Jonathan was himself a hero, but he had mastered the lesson that God's will is best, and that God had ordained David to be king. To this he bowed with admirable self-effacement.

21. David's flight to Nob and to Gath

1-9. David at Nob. After leaving Jonathan, David fled to Nob not far north of Jerusalem, where Ahimelech, son of Ahitub, great grandson of Eli, was high priest.

10-15. David at Gath. David feigned insanity among the enemies of God's people.

22. David at Adullam; Saul's vengeance

1-5. David gains followers. His headquarters at Adullam, southwest of Bethlehem, became a stronghold, 4.

6-23. Saul's desperate violence. Saul cruelly wiped out the entire priestly community at Nob, Abiathar alone escaping to inform David, 11-19.

23. David delivers Keilah

1-15. David delivers Keilah. Abiathar had brought an ephod (a priestly garment containing the sacred lots) with him. By its use David was assured of divine help in rescuing Keilah.

16-29. David is hunted by Saul. David was a fugitive in Ziph, a rocky, remote area south of Hebron, where he was nobly visited by Jonathan, 16-17.

24. David spares Saul's life
1-15. David spares Saul in the wilderness of En Gedi. David refused to kill "the Lord's anointed," 4-7, merely cutting off the corner of Saul's robe, 4. He acted in faith, allowing God to deal with his enemy.
16-22. Saul's reply to David. Saul was broken, but essentially unrepentant, 16-19.

25. David, Nabal, and Abigail
1. Samuel's obituary.
2-42. David obtains Abigail as his wife. Abigail acted wisely, asking for David's mercy, 23-31. Nabal was struck by God and died, 36-38. Abigail became David's wife, 39-42.
43-44. David also takes Ahinoam as his wife.

26. David spares Saul a second time
1-4. The Ziphites again inform against David. The Ziphites doggedly persisted in trying to hand over David to Saul.
5-16. Second reprieve of Saul's life. David amusingly taunted Abner, 13-16. Even today the Bedouins shout across great distance in this way.
17-25. Meeting between David and Saul. Saul's declaration to David, 25, was prophetic.

27. David's lapse of faith
1-7. Unbelief and discouragement. David's complaint, 1, is understandable on the human level in the light of his long and grueling hounding by Saul.

8-12. Deceit and deception. To court Achish's trust, David lied about the object of his military raids, 10.

28. Saul and the spiritistic medium
1-7. Saul's desperate straits. Heaven was closed, so to speak, to the rejected, disobedient monarch.
8-19. Saul resorts to spiritism. Samuel's spirit was brought back, but this was accomplished by God, not by the medium. The medium's fright proves this. This is a once-and-for-all exposé of the fraud and wickedness of necromancy and all occultism.
20-25. Saul takes food.

29. David's defection to the Philistines
1-5. Results of David's lapse of faith. David not only found himself among the enemies of the Lord's people, but put in the deplorable situation of fighting against the Lord's people.
6-11. Achish dismisses David. Achish showed his great respect for David, 6, by swearing by David's God and pronouncing him blameless in his sight "as an angel of God," 9.

30. David's chastening and restoration
1-6. The plundering of Ziklag. David was hard pressed and the embittered people were ready to stone him, 6. But the backslider was restored by discipline and "found strength in the Lord his God," 6.
7-20. The enemy defeated. David consulted Abiathar's ephod, and received the "go" sign to pursue the Amalekites, 8.
21-31. The spoil divided equitably.

A view of the Judean Hills, near the Dead Sea. David hid from Saul in this barren landscape.

31. Saul's death

1-7. Saul's suicide. The wounded Saul pressed his armor bearer to kill him, but committed suicide when the armor bearer refused, 4-6.

8-10. Saul's body dishonored. The victorious Philistines beheaded Saul's corpse, and hung up his body and his sons' bodies in ignominy on the walls of Beth Shan.

11-13. The men of Jabesh Gilead recover the bodies. They had now the chance to show their thanks to Saul for what he had done for them (1 Sam. 11). They not only recovered the bodies of Saul and his sons, but gave them honorable burial and proper mourning.

2 Samuel
David king over Judah and all Israel

Outline

1-4	David, king of Judah
5-10	David, king of Israel
11-20	David's sin and punishment
21-24	Historical appendix

Theme of the book. In 2 Samuel the restoration of order follows the enthroning of God's king with the establishment of Jerusalem as the nation's political center (2 Sam. 5:6-12) and Zion (2 Sam. 5:7; 6:1-17) as the religious center. Following this arrangement the great Davidic covenant was established by the Lord (2 Sam. 7:8-17.)

A twisted tree on top of the ruins of ancient Beth Shan reminds us that Saul's body was displayed here.

2 Samuel

1. David's lament for Saul and Jonathan

1-16. The Amalekite's report of Saul's death. David's allegiance to Saul showed his magnanimity of character and noble statesmanship.

17-27. David's lament. It is great lyric poetry from a skilled musician (1 Sam. 16:23) and talented poet.

2. David made king of Judah; Abner's revolt

1-7. David anointed king over Judah. Judah was evidently living a separate existence from the other tribes. David's first official royal act in thanking the men of Jabesh Gilead for their service rendered in burying Saul was a foretaste of David's brilliant diplomacy and political wisdom, 5-7.

8-32. Abner sets up Ish-Bosheth as king. An attempt was made by Saul's army commander to perpetuate the Saul dynasty, 8-11. David's forces were victorious, 29-32.

3. Abner's defection to David and his death

1-11. Quarrel with Ish-Bosheth. To attempt to procure a royal concubine in this way was tantamount to treason (2 Sam. 16:21-22; 1 Kings 2:22).

12-30. Abner goes over to David. Abner's reception by David, 20-21, motivated him to campaign for David all over Israel. However, he was murdered by Joab in the blood feud occasioned by Abner's killing of Asahel, 23-30.

31-39. David's lament over Abner.

4. Ish-Bosheth's death

1-7. Ish-Bosheth's assassination. Baanah and Recab, two army officers, murdered Ish-Bosheth, 2-7.

8-12. David's punishment of the murderers. David continued to honor Saul's house and to punish anyone who would harm it (cf. 2 Sam. 1:14-16; 3:28-39).

5. David made king over Israel; captures Zion

1-5. God's king comes into his own. David's stirring coronation foreshadows that day when Israel's long-rejected King, the Messiah, the son of David (Matt. 1:1), returns in glory to be the Shepherd-King of Israel.

6-25. David's conquest of Zion and other victories. Jerusalem's capture was politically important because it rooted out the last vestige of Canaanite power in the region and provided the kingdom with a neutral capital situated between Judah and Israel, but belonging to neither.

6. The ark brought to Zion

1-11. The sin of Uzzah. The Levites alone were commissioned to transport (i.e. "touch") the ark (Num. 4:15; 1 Chron. 13:9). Uzzah's sin broke this divine regulation.

12-19. The ark brought to David's city. This was done in the Mosaically prescribed manner

(1 Chron. 15:1-28), and blessing followed.

20-23. Michal's mockery. She is called not "wife of the king" but "daughter of Saul" and she displayed the pride of her father.

7. The Davidic covenant
1-3. David desires to build the temple. This worthy ambition to build the Lord a house furnished the revelation through Nathan the prophet that the Lord would build David a house.

4-17. The Davidic covenant. This great covenant of kingship centering in Christ provided: (1) a Davidic "house," 11, or family through which the Messiah would be born (Matt. 1:1, 16; Luke 3:23); (2) a perpetual kingdom, 12, and a throne, 13.

18-29. David worshiped, in holy humility and awe.

8. David's kingdom established
1-14. David's conquests. The kingly covenant in ch. 7 is followed by the account of David's great conquests.

15-18. David's reign. His rule of justice and equity, 15, prefigures the Messiah's administration of righteousness. David's sons were not priests but administrators (cf. 1 Chron. 18:17).

9. David's kindness to Mephibosheth
1-6. Mephibosheth brought to David. A helpless cripple (cf. 2 Sam. 4:4) who was carried into the king's presence, Mephibosheth is an illustration of the sinner made helpless by the Fall, but a candidate for God's grace, 3.

7-13. David's mercy to Mephibosheth. David, for Jonathan's sake (cf. 1 Sam. 18:1-4), lifted the poor cripple to a place at the king's table as one

of the king's sons.

10-11. David's great sin
Ch. 10. Prelude to the sin. The Ammonite-Aramean War triggered by Hanun's insult to David, 1-5, furnished the background of David's sin.

Ch. 11. The terrible sin itself. David committed adultery with Bathsheba, wife of one of his army officers, Uriah the Hittite, 1-5. Then David sent for Uriah, 6-13, and when subterfuge failed to hide his sin, he had Uriah murdered, 14-25, and then took Bathsheba as his wife, 26-27.

12. David's confession
1-13. The confession elicited. The Lord's rebuke came through the message of the prophet Nathan, 1-4, showing the king's hypocrisy and guilt, 5-6, and bringing the denunciation, "You are the man!" 7-9.

14-31. The punishment begins, in the death of the child and David's grief, 14-23. The Lord's grace spared David physical death but not severe chastening.

13-14. Amnon murdered by Absalom
13:1-22. Amnon's sin against Tamar. Lust and lawlessness ruled, and Amnon violated Tamar, full sister of Absalom.

13:23-29. Absalom murders Amnon and flees. Incest and violence in his own family were the beginning of David's punishments. Absalom not only avenged the wrong done to his sister, but doubtless knew he was removing the heir apparent to the throne at the same time, 23-26.

Ch. 14. Absalom's recall by Joab's craftiness. Joab was powerful as well as subtle, and secured Absalom's return through the ruse

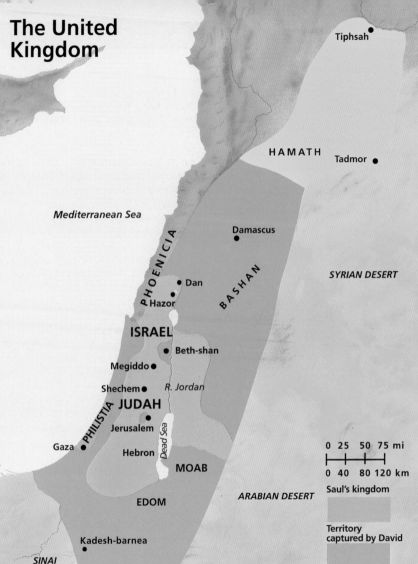

The United Kingdom

Tiphsah ●

HAMATH

Tadmor ●

Mediterranean Sea

Damascus ●

P H O E N I C I A

● Dan

● Hazor

BASHAN

SYRIAN DESERT

ISRAEL

● Beth-shan

Megiddo ●

R. Jordan

Shechem ●

P H I L I S T I A

JUDAH

Jerusalem ●

Dead Sea

Gaza ●

Hebron ●

MOAB

EDOM

ARABIAN DESERT

Kadesh-barnea ●

SINAI

Ezion-geber ●

```
0    25    50   75 mi
├────┼─────┼────┤

0    40    80  120 km
├────┼─────┼────┤
```

Saul's kingdom

Territory
captured by David

Area under Solomon's
economic control

of the woman of Tekoa. Absalom was partially forgiven, 21-24, and finally fully reinstated to the king's favor, 25-33.

15. Absalom's revolt

1-12. Absalom's conspiracy. By flattery Absalom stole the hearts of the Israelites, 1-6. It took him four years to plan his uprising, 7.

13-37. David flees from Jerusalem. David apparently decided that a showdown over the loyalty of his professed followers would be better accomplished by this move.

16. David in flight; Absalom in Jerusalem

1-14. David meets Ziba and Shimei. Strangely, David believed the wily falsehood of Ziba concerning Mephibosheth, 1-4, but acted with wisdom and restraint in the case of the cursing Shimei, 5-14.

15-23. Absalom follows Ahithophel's wicked counsel. Absalom's shameful public violation of his father's harem (royal property) was the final and irrevocable step in assuming the kingship (cf. 15:16; 1 Kings 2:17-25).

17. Ahithopel and Hushai

1-26. Ahithophel's counsel vs. Hushai's. Ahithophel's advice was to aim only at the life of David, 1-4, while Hushai advocated a prepared attack taking time, 5-13.

27-29. David's friends minister to him.

18. Absalom's death

1-8. The battle in the woods of Ephraim. Absalom's hastily recruited troops were no match for David's army.

9-18. Absalom's death. His head, not his hair, is said to have been caught in the oak, 9. The tradition that Absalom's hair was caught comes from Josephus (Jos 7.10.2).

19-33. David's lament. A touching scene of paternal love for his son, though Absalom probably deserved his fate.

19. David returns as king

1-15. Judah calls David back as king. Joab jolted David out of his excessive grief, 1-8.

16-40. Shimei, Mephibosheth, and Barzillai. David showed mercy to Shimei, 16-23. Mephibosheth's genuine joy, 24-30, at David's return was proof enough of Ziba's treachery.

41-43. Antagonism between Judah and Israel again broke out. This deep rift was prominent in the final disruption after Solomon's death (1 Kings 12:16-20).

20. Sheba revolts; Joab murders Amasa

1-22. Joab regains his position. Joab again proved his cruel thoroughness by hunting down the rebel and using the woman of Abel Beth Maacah to accomplish Sheba's death. A mother city, 19, is one with dependent villages or "daughters" (Num. 21:25; Josh. 15:45; Judg. 11:26).

23-26. A list of David's officials.

21. Famine and Philistine wars

The last four chapters of 2 Samuel are an appendix.

1-14. The famine and the Gibeonites. A three-year famine is traced to bloodguiltiness upon the land for Saul's murder of the Gibeonites, who were under a covenant of protection (Josh. 9:25-27) in the Lord's name, which Saul had violated.

David fled from his son Absalom via the Kidron Valley, which is today a lonely place.

15-22. Memoirs of the Philistine wars.

22. David's great prophetic psalm

1-28. Praise to the Lord for His intervention. This great ode of deliverance was placed here and also as Psalm 18 in the book of Psalms. It is prophetic and looks beyond the sufferings and triumphs of David to David's son and Lord, Jesus Christ.

29-51. Praise to the Lord for exaltation over foes. The judgment of enemies, 29-43, and exaltation over adversaries, 44-49, will be realized only by Him into whose hands is committed all judgment (John 5:22).

23. David's last words: his heroes

1-7. His last words. Verses 3 and 4 picture the clear morning of the Kingdom Age.

8-39. David's mighty men.

24. David's failure in the census

1-17. The sin and its punishment. The Lord allowed Satan to move in David's heart through pride, 1-9. David's confession, 10-14, was followed by the plague, 15-17.

18-25. The altar and atonement. Araunah's threshing floor, where Abraham had offered Isaac and where the temple was to be set, was a fitting spot for mercy upon Israel.

1 Kings
Solomon's reign and the divided kingdom

Outline

1:1-2:11	David's decease
2:12-11:43	Solomon's reign
12:1-16:34	The kingdom divided
17:1-22:53	Elijah's ministry

Name and purpose: 1 and 2 Kings, originally one book, record the history of the undivided kingdom from David's death through Solomon's and Rehoboam's reigns and the divided kingdom till Israel's fall in 722 B.C. and Judah's captivity in 586 B.C.

Remains of what have been called "Ahab's Stables" at the important ancient stronghold of Megiddo.

1 Kings

1-2. David's decease
1:1-27. Adonijah's bid to be king. Adonijah, David's oldest living son, put himself forward and said, "I will be king," 5. Nathan's and Bathsheba's plot, 10-14, resulted in David proclaiming Solomon king, 15-27.
1:28-53. Solomon crowned. Solomon's anointing, 28-40, resulted in Adonijah's fear and submission, 41-53.
2:1-11. David's charge and death. David charged Solomon to follow the law of Moses (cf. Deut. 4:40; 5:1; 11:1-12:32; 17:14-20).
2:12-46. Solomon eliminates his enemies.

3. Solomon's prayer for wisdom
1-3. Solomon marries an Egyptian princess. Undoubtedly she was a daughter of one of the pharaohs of the twenty-first dynasty, since Sheshonk (Shishak), founder of the twenty-second dynasty, did all in his power to weaken Solomon.
4-28. Solomon prays for wisdom. The "high places" were hilltop shrines. Gibeon was one of the most famous of these shrines (2 Chron. 1:2-6).

4. Solomon's government
1-34. His administration. His new administration ignored the old tribal divisions.

5-8. Solomon's temple
Ch. 5. Preparations to build. Hiram I of Tyre (c. 969-936 B.C.) bore the title of "King of the Sidonians."
Ch. 6-8. Description of the temple. Besides the temple, Solomon built his palace and administration complexes, 7:1-51. The purpose of the two pillars, Jakin and Boaz, 7:21, is uncertain, but W. F. Albright suggested that they were huge incense stands with oil bowls at the top, which served to illuminate the facade of the temple.

9. Solomon's second vision and splendor
1-9. Solomon's warning against apostasy.
10-28. Solomon's splendor. His foreign diplomacy and intermarriage designed to produce peaceful relations with his neighbors are described (3:1-3; 11:1-8). His buildings at Gezer, Hazor, and Megiddo are known, especially at the latter, which was the headquarters of Solomon's fifth administrative district. His navy was a refinery fleet, which brought smelted copper from the colonial mines of the Phoenicians in Sardinia and Spain, Tarshish denoting a copper-refining port.

10. Solomon and the Queen of Sheba
1-13. The queen's visit.
14-29. Solomon's revenues. His great wealth, 14-15; his famous shields, 16-17; his ivory throne, 18-20; his opulence in gold and silver, 21-22; and his horse and chariot trade, 27-29, are mentioned. Solomon acted as middleman for the horse and chariot trade between Egypt and Asia Minor.

Dynasties of Israel and Judah

Dynasty of Israel: Nine dynasties with 19 kings. Total reign 201 years, with average reign just over 10 years. All these kings were bad, with Ahab and his queen, Jezebel, the worst.

Dynasty of Judah: 20 kings, but only one dynasty, the Davidic, interrupted only by Athaliah, the usurper, who invaded the Davidic line by marriage for five years. Total reigns 335 years, with 16 average years per reign. The good kings included Asa, Jehoshaphat, Amaziah, Uzziah, Jotham, Hezekiah, and Josiah.

Site of Jeroboam's shrine at Dan in the north.

11. Solomon's failure

1-43. Solomon's sin and punishment. His sin was apostasy and idolatry because of the numerous pagan marriages entered into on grounds of security, 1-13.

12. Rehoboam and the revolt

1-24. The secession of the northern tribes. The folly of Rehoboam is almost unimaginable. But sin makes fools of its victims.

25-33. Jeroboam's evil plans. To stop people from going to Jerusalem and making sacrifices there, and giving their allegiance to King Rehoboam, Jeroboam built two shrines to the Lord, one at Bethel, and the other at Dan, in the north.

13-14. Jeroboam's and Rehoboam's reigns

Ch. 13. God sends a prophet to condemn Jeroboam's plan. The remarkable prophecy, 1-3, uttered by an unknown prophet, that Josiah

would burn the bones of the priests on Jeroboam's false altar was fulfilled in 621 B.C. (2 Kings 23:16-17).

14:1-20. Jeroboam's punishment. God's disciplining hand of judgment fell on the king's son, his most precious possession.

14:21-31. Rehoboam's reign over Judah. This son of Solomon was a fool, driving the ten tribes to secede.

Archaeological light

In Rehoboam's fifth year, Shishak (cf. 2 Chron. 12:2-4) invaded Judah, and Israel as well. Archaeology shows Shishak is Sheshonk I of Egypt (c. 945-924 B.C.), founder of the twenty-second dynasty, whose gold-masked body was discovered at Tanis in 1938-39. His triumphal Karnak (Thebes) inscription lists towns taken in Judah as well as in Israel and Gilead. Part of his stele was excavated at Megiddo, showing that he actually took this city, as the Karnak relief shows.

15:1-24. Abijah's and Asa's reigns

1-8. Abijah had an unworthy reign of three years.

9-24. Asa's rule. Asa cleansed the land of idolatry—pagan pillars, sun images, Asherah poles, and male cult prostitutes.

15:25-16:28. Kings of Israel: Baasha to Omri

15:25-31. Nadab's reign over Israel. His was a short-lived, unworthy rule of two years.

15:32-16:7. Baasha was cursed because of his idolatry and sin.

16:8-14. Elah was a drunkard.

16:15-20. Zimri was burned to death in his own house after a seven-day reign.

16:21-28. Tibni and Omri. After Zimri's death the people were divided, half following Tibni and half Omri.

Archaeological light

Omri's reign (c. 880-874 B.C.) ushered in a new era of Israelite power. He was an astute politician, cementing ties with Phoenicia to offset the Aramean commercial monopoly. This resulted in his son marrying Jezebel, daughter of Ethbaal, king of the Sidonians (18:18). The Moabite Stone from Dibon discloses that it was Omri who conquered north Moab. Omri's brilliant capital, Samaria, has been excavated. Periods 1 and 2 belong to Omri and Ahab.

Omri's fame in the world of his day is attested by the Assyrians' reference to him on the Black Obelisk of Shalmaneser III more than a century later in connection with King Jehu of Israel.

16:29-34. Ahab, king of Israel

29-34. Ahab. Ahab was wise and effective as a ruler, but wicked and idolatrous. He erected an altar to Baal, the great northwest Semitic fertility god, in the Baal temple that he dared to build in Samaria, 32. He also made an Asherah, 33, a wooden pole symbolic of the Canaanite fertility goddess Asherah, known from the Ugaritic tablets discovered at Ras Shamra in northern Syria, 1929-37. This Canaanite goddess, mentioned some 40 times in the OT, was a snare to the Israelites, for her cult was viciously depraved. Jezebel was a pagan princess and daughter of Ethbaal, "king of the Sidonians," 31.

17. Elijah before Ahab

1-4. Elijah's message to Ahab. Baal, the Phoenician storm god, was held by Ahab, Jezebel, and his other devotees to control the rain. Elijah ("my God is the Lord") abruptly announced to Ahab that Jehovah would be proved to be the one who does so.

5-24. Elijah and the widow. At Zarephath, beyond Ahab's jurisdiction, Elijah was miraculously fed by the ravens and then by the widow, during the three and a half years of drought.

18. Elijah on Carmel

1-19. The question. The terrible years of drought were about to end. Who withheld and would send the rain? "Baal of the heavens" or the Lord? Elijah met Ahab and called for the contest on Carmel, 17-19. The Baals were the local representatives of the great sky-god, 19. Asherah, Baal's consort, had 400 prophets and Baal 450, showing the tremendous gain of Canaanite paganism under Ahab.

20-46. The contest. Elijah's faith was superb. He staked everything on Jehovah's answering by fire and rain, and both came. Elijah ran 17 miles to Jezreel, 46, Ahab's secondary capital, to herald complete victory of the worship of Jehovah over Baalism (cf. Isa. 40:30-31).

19. Elijah at Horeb

1-14. Elijah's flight and despondency. Here the man of God demonstrated his fallibility by fleeing the wrath of Jezebel to Beersheba, 130 miles south of Jezreel, well into the territory of Judah and out of Jezebel's jurisdiction, 1-3. By divine assistance he reached Horeb, 4-8, also called Sinai, some 200 miles further south.

Tell Beer-sheba—ancient Beersheba.

15-21. The Lord's message. The Lord directed Elijah to finish his ministry, 15-16.

20. Ahab's wars with Damascus

1-34. The siege of Samaria. Ahab's brilliant strategy defeated Ben-Hadad's sudden attack on Samaria.

35-43. The prophet's warning was focused on Ahab's foolish release of his enemy.

Archaeological light

The Monolith Inscription of Shalmaneser III (859-824 B.C.), now in the British Museum, records Assyria's clash with a Syrian-Palestinian coalition at Qarqar, north of Hamath in the Orontes Valley, in 853 B.C. "I crossed the Euphrates; at Qarqar I destroyed 1,200 chariots, 1,200 horsemen, and 20,000 men of Benhadad, and 2,000 chariots and 10,000 men of Ahab, the Israelite . . ."

---

21. Ahab and Naboth's vineyard

1-16. Ahab murders Naboth. Naboth was religiously and legally right in keeping his ancestral property (cf. Lev. 25:10-17, 23-24, 34). Ahab realized this.

17-29. Elijah's pronouncement of judgment. The dogs would lick Ahab's blood at the place he had Naboth murdered, 19 (cf. 22:38).

22. Ahab's death

1-28. Ahab and Jehoshaphat go up to Ramoth Gilead. They disregarded Micaiah's prophecy and listened to the "lying spirit" of the false prophets, 23.

29-40. Ahab's death.

41-53. Jehoshaphat and Ahaziah.

2 Kings
The kingdom to the exiles

Ministries of the prophets

During this period Hosea and Amos prophesied in Israel. Joel, Micah, Isaiah, Obadiah, Nahum, Habakkuk, Zephaniah, and Jeremiah prophesied in Judah.

Outline

1:1-2:11	Elijah's final ministry
2:12-9:10	Elisha's ministry
9:11-17:41	From Jehu to fall in 722 B.C. to the Exile
18:1-25:30	Judah from 722 B.C. to the Exile

Period covered. About the middle of the ninth to nearly the middle of the sixth century B.C.

Chronology of the Dual Kingdoms

Israel

Jeroboam	931-910
Nadab	910-909
Bausha	909-886
Elah	886-885
Zimri	885
Tibni	885-880
Omri	880-874
Aha b	874-853
Ahaziah	853-852
Joram (Jehoram)	852-841
Jehu	841-814
Jehoahaz	814-798
Joash (Jehoash)	798-782
Jeroboam II	782-753
Zachariah	753/752
Shallum	752
Menahem	752-742
Pekahiah	742-740
Pekah	740-732
Hoshea	732-722
Fall of Samaria	722

Judah

Rehoboam	931-913
Abijam (Abijah)	913-911
Asa	911-870
Jehoshaphat	873-848
Jehoram (Joram)	853-841
Ahaziah (Azariah, Jehoahaz)	841
Athaliah	841-835
Joash (Jehoash)	835-796
Amaziah	796-767
Uzziah (Azariah)	791-740
Jotham	750-736
Ahaz	736-716
Hezekiah	716-687
Manasseh	696-642
Amon	642-640
Josiah	640-608
Jehoahaz (Shallum)	608
Jehoiakim	608-597
Jehoiachin (Coniah, Jeconiah)	597
Zedekiah	597-586
Fall of Jerusalem	586

2 Kings

Archaeological light

The famous Moabite Stone, a Louvre treasure, discovered in 1868, set up by King Mesha of Moab at Dibon, discloses the prominence of Chemosh, the national god of Moab. "I am Mesha, son of Chemosh . . . king of Moab, the Dibonite. . . . Omri, king of Israel . . . oppressed Moab many days because Chemosh was angry with his land. And his son succeeded him, and he said, I will oppress Moab."

1. Elijah and Ahaziah

1-17a. Ahaziah's sickness and death. Coregent with his father, a Baal devotee, Ahaziah preferred Baal to the Lord. Baal-zebub ("lord of flies") was a manifestation of the great Canaanite Baal, as worshiped at Philistine Ekron.

17b-18. Joram's accession. This last king of the Omride dynasty must not be confused with Jehoram, the son of Jehoshaphat, king of Judah (8:16-18, 25-27).

2. Elisha and the translation of Elijah

1-11. Translation of Elijah. The prophet of fire (1 Kings 18:38; 2 Kings 1:10, 12) was translated to heaven by a "chariot of fire and horses of fire," 11-12. Enoch (Gen. 5:24; Heb. 11:5) and Elijah (Matt. 17:3-4) were the only two men to be translated without dying.

12-25. Double portion upon Elisha. "A double portion of your spirit," 9, indicates the role of spiritual heir.

3. Elisha and Joram

1-20. Revolt of Moab. In Joram's reign Moab revolted and refused to pay tribute in lambs and wool, 1-8. Joram's plan required Judah's aid and that of its vassal Edom, as the plan was to attack Moab from the rear.

21-27. Defeat of Moab. The dry streambed, 16, separating Edom from Moab, filled with pools and reflecting the rising sun and the red sandstone of Edom, was taken for blood. Mesha's sacrifice of his eldest son to Chemosh on the wall in plain sight of Israel, 26-27, filled the attackers with such horror that they returned to their own land without exploiting to the full their victory.

4. Four miracles of Elisha

1-7. The widow's oil increased. This section, 4:1-8:6, constitutes an interlude dealing with Elisha's miracle-working ministry.

8-37. The Shunammite woman's son raised from the dead. Not only did the woman who lived in Shunem conceive a son late in life, according to God's word through Elisha, 8-17, but the lad was raised from the dead, 18-37.

38-41. The poisonous stew healed.

42-44. Bread multiplied finds its striking parallel in our Lord's ministry (Matt. 14:13-21; 15:32-38).

5. Elisha and Naaman

1-19. Naaman's healing. Naaman appears as a proud man, hurt by Elisha's curt directions to

1 and 2 Kings in Contrast

1 Kings	2 Kings
Begins with King David	Ends with the king of Babylon
Opens with Solomon's glory	Closes with Jehoiachin's shame
Begins with the blessings of obedience	Ends with the curse of disobedience
Opens with the building of the temple	Closes with the burning of the temple
Traces the progress of apostasy	Describes the consequences of apostasy
How kings failed to rule God's people	Consequences of that failure
Prophet Elijah introduced	Prophet Elisha presented
The long-suffering of the Lord	The Lord's sure punishment of sin

wash seven times in muddy Jordan, 8-12. His compliance is parallel to the proud sinner who accepts God's self-humbling way of salvation by grace and is cleansed of sin, 13-14, and saved, 15-19. Naaman had the wrong idea that a god could not be worshiped apart from his own land. **20-27. Gehazi's sin and punishment.** Covetousness earned Gehazi the leprosy from which grace had delivered the Syrian Gentile.

6-7. Elisha and other miracles
6:1-7. The floating ax head.
6:8-23. The Syrian army blinded and captured by Elisha's prayers.
6:24-7:20. Repulse of the Syrian siege of Samaria by Elisha's prophecy was fulfilled by the Lord's intervention.

8. Elisha and Hazael
1-6. Elisha again aids the woman of Shunem. The woman's land was restored to her through Elisha's influence.
7-15. Elisha's prediction of Ben-Hadad's death and Hazael's usurpation. Hazael was

Archaeological light

Ben-Hadad I's long and energetic reign ended in 842 B.C. 841 Hazael had usurped the throne. On a pavement slab from Nimrud is Shalmaneser's record of his attack on Hazael of Damascus. Another text from Asshur says: "Adadidri forsook his land. Hazael, son of nobody, seized the throne."

divinely chosen to punish Israel for her sins, so Elisha wept, 11. Hazael became king of Syria as predicted.
16-29. Jehoram's and Ahaziah's reigns in Judah. The "lamp," 19, was symbolic of the permanence of the Davidic dynasty (cf. 2 Sam. 21:17; 1 Kings 11:36; 15:4).

9-10. Jehu's reign
Ch. 9. Elisha has Jehu anointed. Jehu was anointed as the rough instrument for the bloody task of exterminating the house of Ahab and Baalism.
Ch. 10. Jehu's purge continued. By

Archaeological light

Like Hazael (see ch. 8), Jehu was a usurper. The Black Obelisk of Shalmaneser III, which Layard found in the palace at Nimrud, shows Jehu kneeling before the Assyrian emperor. Following the prostrate king come Israelites bearing gifts. The inscription reads: "Tribute of Iaua (Jehu), son of Omri. Silver, gold, and a golden bowl, a golden beaker, golden goblets, pitchers of gold, lead staves for the bed of the king, javelins I received from him."

cleverness and ruthlessness Jehu wiped out the entire house of Ahab, "seventy sons," 1. The Recabites were a simple-living people who strictly maintained the desert lifestyle, avoiding the corruption of urban living (1 Chron. 2:25; Jer. 35).

11. Athaliah's reign in Judah

1-16. Athaliah's usurpation and death.
Jehoiada led the revolt, crowning Joash king, 4-12, and ordering Athaliah killed, 13-16. The "Carites," 4, 19, were foreign mercenaries.
17-21. Jehoiada's revival. The common people, loyal to Jehovah, destroyed the temple of Baal, 17-18.

12. Joash king of Judah

1-16. Repair of the temple. Joash had a controversy with the priests over the repair of the temple, 4-8.
17-21. Joash's decline and death. Joash bought off Hazael by despoiling the temple of Baal, 17-18.

13. Jehoahaz and Jehoash, kings of Israel

1-9. Jehoahaz's reign. Jehoahaz was weak and Israel was brought very low by Hazael of Syria.
10-25. Jehoash's reign. He reestablished Israel as a real power for his son Jeroboam II.

14. Amaziah of Judah and Jeroboam II

1-22. Reign of Amaziah of Judah.
23-29. Jeroboam II of Israel advanced the power of Israel against Damascus, lifting the northern kingdom to the height of its strength and prosperity.

15. Uzziah and Jotham; Zechariah to Pekah

1-7. Azariah (Uzziah) of Judah. When he became a leper because of his intrusion into the priesthood, his son Jotham became regent, 5.
8-22. Zechariah, Shallum, and Menahem in Israel. Menahem murdered Shallum, 13-22, just one month after Shallum had assassinated Zechariah.

Archaeological light

Excavations at Samaria have confirmed the splendor of Jeroboam II's capital. Jeroboam refortified the city with a double wall. The jasper seal of "Shema, servant of Jeroboam" with its magnificently executed lion, shows the effervescence of art at this era.

Ahab's "ivory palace" (so-called because of the abundance of ivory inlays used in the decoration) was imitated by many of the wealthy as ivory finds at Megiddo and other sites attest.

23-26. Pekahiah's reign lasted only two years.
27-31. Pekah's reign. Tiglath-Pileser, who overran northern Galilee, refers to Pekah, Israel's king, in his records.
32-38. Jotham's reign.

16. Ahaz's reign
1-4. Ahaz's idolatries. Ahaz revived Canaanite idolatry, including the horrible practice of child sacrifice, 3.
5-8. His appeal to Assyria. Ahaz appealed to Assyria for help despite God's promise of assistance.
9-20. His trip to Damascus, to pay homage to Tiglath-Pileser III, further showed his idolatrous folly.

17. Fall of the Northern Kingdom
1-23. Hoshea's reign. The last king of Israel (732-722 B.C.), Hoshea was imprisoned for conspiracy with Egypt, his capital Samaria was besieged, and its citizens taken into captivity, 722 B.C.
24-41. Assyria repopulates Israel. Sargon's own records substantiate v. 24. "[The cities] I set up again and made more populous than before. People from the lands which I had taken I settled

Archaeological light
Tiglath-Pileser III (745-727 B.C.), to whom Menahem paid tribute, 19-20, is mentioned in Tiglath-Pileser's Annals: "As for Menahem, terror overwhelmed him. Like a bird, alone he fled and submitted to me. To his palace I brought him back and . . . silver, colored woolen garments, linen garments . . . I received as his tribute."

Archaeological light
The Taylor Prism in the British Museum describes Sennacherib's attack on Hezekiah's realm: "As for Hezekiah, the Jew, who did not submit to my yoke, 46 of his strong walled cities . . . I besieged and took. . . . Himself, like a caged bird, I shut up in Jerusalem, his royal city. . . . As for Hezekiah, the terrifying splendor of my majesty overcame him."

The destruction of the Assyrian army, 35, has been connected by some with a plague carried by field mice. Herodotus mentions such an onslaught in which the Assyrians suffered defeat on the borders of Egypt because the mice chewed up their bowstrings and leather equipment.

there." The country became known as Samaria (not Israel), its mixed population Samaritans, 29. Its worship became a syncretism of foreign cults, 39-40.

18. Hezekiah and Sennacherib's invasion
1-12. Hezekiah's reforms. Hezekiah destroyed the Asherim or wooden poles symbolic of the Canaanite fertility goddess Asherah and the bronze serpent.
13-37. Sennacherib's attack. Aramaic was the language of Syria, 26, which in Palestine largely superseded Hebrew after the Exile.

19-20. Hezekiah consults Isaiah
Ch. 19. Hezekiah consults Isaiah. See Isaiah 37. Sennacherib was finally assassinated by his sons, 37.
Ch. 20. Hezekiah's sickness.

See Isaiah 38-39.

21. Manasseh's and Amon's reigns

1-18. Manasseh's idolatrous orgy. Snake worship, male and female prostitutes, planetary worship, human sacrifices, and all kinds of demon-inspired pagan occultism constituted features of this horrible apostasy.

19-26. Amon's reign. Wicked like his father, Amon was murdered.

22-23. Josiah's reign

Ch. 22. Repairing the temple and finding the book of the law. Unlimited metal was collected to repair the temple. The outstanding event of Josiah's reign was the discovery of the book of the law, 8-10, precipitating great reformation and revival, 22:11-23:37. It was customary in ancient times to deposit documents in foundations of buildings.

23:1-30. Reforms and death of Josiah. The

Babylonian Chronicle shows that Neco went to the Assyrians' aid.

23:31-37. Jehoahaz and Jehoiakim. Both were evil and were dominated by Pharaoh-Neco of Egypt.

24. Jehoiachin and Zedekiah

1-17. Fall of Jerusalem and the first deportation. On March 16, 597 B.C., in Nebuchadnezzar's seventh year (Jer. 52:28), Jehoiachin surrendered to the Babylonian monarch.

18-20. Zedekiah made king, ruling 597-586 B.C. He was Jehoiachin's uncle Mattaniah; later called Zedekiah in token of servitude.

25. Jerusalem's destruction and the Babylonian exile

1-21. Zedekiah's rebellion. Jerusalem was laid under terrible siege and fell in 586 B.C. after frightful famine. The city was burned and the inhabitants deported or slain (cf. Jer. 52:29).

22-26. Gedaliah's governorship. His murder brought chaos and ruin (Jer. 40-42).

27-30. Jehoiachin's release. After being a political prisoner for 37 years in Babylon, Jehoiachin was set free by Nebuchadnezzar II's successor, Evil-Merodach.

Archaeological light

Hezekiah's pool and conduit, 20, the rockhewn conduit from the Gihon Spring to the Siloam Reservoir, 1,777 feet long, is one of the most amazing devices for water supply in the biblical period. In addition, Hezekiah built a new and larger reservoir called the Pool of Siloam (John 9:7-11). The Siloam inscription, discovered in 1880, is a six-line inscription in classical Hebrew cut on the wall of the conduit about 19 feet from the Siloam end of the aqueduct. It recounts the completion of the engineering feat, as workmen with wedge, hammer, and pickax, digging from opposite ends, finally met.

Assyria

Shalmaneser V (726-722 B.C.) was the Assyrian emperor who began the siege of Samaria.

Sargon II (722-705 B.C.) actually took Samaria in the opening months of 722 B.C. after Shalmaneser's death. "At the beginning of my rule, in my first year of reign . . . Samerinai [the people of Samaria] . . . 27,290 . . . who lived therein, I carried away."

Asshur and Assyria's beginning. Located 60 miles south of Nineveh on the west bank of the Tigris River, this site was the original center of Assyrian power (c. 3000 B.C.).

Named after Asshur, the national god of Assyria, the capital became the hub of the later Assyrian Empire and gave its name to the "giant among the Semites." Assyrian cruelty was proverbial, and the Hebrews suffered severely at the hands of the Assyrian kings.

Relief of a lion hunt at Ashurbanipal's Palace, Nineveh.

1 Chronicles
The reign of David

Outline

1-9	The genealogies
10	Saul's end
11-21	David's kingdom
22-29	David's temple ritual

Name and author. The name "Chronicles" is from the Vulgate *Liber Chronicorum* ("book of Chronicles"). The author is unknown, but may have been Ezra.

Chronicles and Kings compared. The books of Kings were written before the Captivity, the books of Chronicles after that event (1 Chron. 6:15). Kings traces the history from the *prophetic* viewpoint, Chronicles from the *priestly* approach, emphasizing the temple ritual. The blessing and grace of God toward David, as the establisher of the temple worship, and his successors on the throne of Judah are set out in Chronicles down to the Exile. The kings of Israel are ignored and treated only as necessity dictates, in contrast to 1 and 2 Kings, which interweave the history of the dual kingdom.

The city of Jerusalem viewed from the summit of the Mount of Olives.

1 Chronicles

1-9. The genealogies

Ch. 1. From Adam to the Edomites. The genealogies of ch. 1-9 show that the Chronicles are dealing with the true Chosen People, descended through Abraham, and destined to be the line through whom the Messiah was to come.

2:1-4:23. Genealogies of Judah. David's line to Zedekiah is traced, 3:1-24.

4:24-5:26. Simeon, Reuben, Gad, and half of Manasseh.

Ch. 6. Levi. Mentioned are the high priestly line, 1-15, 49-53; Levitical lists, 16-30; chief musicians of David, 31-48; and territories assigned, 54-81.

Ch. 7. Issachar, Naphtali, half of Manasseh, Ephraim, Asher.

Ch. 8. Benjamin. Sons of Benjamin are mentioned, 1-28, as well as the house of Saul, 29-40.

Ch. 9. People in Jerusalem after the return are listed, 1-34, followed by the genealogy of Saul, 35-44.

10. Saul's overthrow and death

1-12. Death and burial of Saul. The chronicler uses the downfall of Saul and his sons as the springboard to introduce the Lord's true king, David.

13-14. The reason for Saul's failure. His disobedience and unfaithfulness to the Lord are brought into final focus by his recourse to occultism (1 Sam. 28).

11. David's accession as king

1-9. The king and his capital. David was anointed king at Hebron, 1-3. He conquered Jebus and made it his capital, 4-9.

10-47. List of David's warriors.

12. David's warriors

1-22. The Benjamite warriors at Ziklag and others.

23-40. Those who came to crown him king.

13. David brings the ark from Kirjath Jearim

1-8. A praiseworthy thing performed wrongly. The ark, mentioned 46 times in 1 and 2 Chronicles, was to be carried on the shoulders of the Levites (Num. 4:5, 15), not in a Philistine expedient, a cart.

9-14. The punishment. Only Levites were to touch the ark (cf. 2 Sam. 6:1-10).

14. David's increase and success

1-7. His family.

8-17. His victories over the Philistines.

15-16. David brings the ark to Jerusalem

Ch. 15. The right way of doing it (cf. 1 Chron. 13 with Num. 4:5, 15 and 2 Sam. 6:1-10).

Ch. 16. The service of dedication. Described are David's sacrifices, 1-3; his choir, 4-6; his great psalm of thanksgiving, 7-36; and his appointment of the tabernacle ritual and music, 37-43.

Remains of David's citadel, Jerusalem.

17. The Davidic Covenant

1-6. David's desire to build the temple.
7-15. The Davidic Covenant. Only in Christ, David's son and Lord (Ps. 110:1), will this great covenant be fulfilled.
16-27. David's praise and prayer.

18-20. David's wars

Ch. 18. David's victories. Full establishment of his kingdom (cf. 2 Sam. 8:1-15).
Ch. 19. Defeat of Ammonites and Aramean allies.
Ch. 20. Other military successes. David and Joab took Rabbah, 1-3, and defeated the Philistines, 4-8.

21. David's sin in the census

1-7. Joab's protest. David's pride was apparently the cause.
8. The plague. The chronicler highlights David's ecclesiastical and ritualistic activities in accordance with the purpose of 1 and 2 Chronicles.

22-27. David's temple ritual

22:1. The purchase of a site for the sanctuary.
22:2-19. Preparation and charge to Solomon. All the leaders of Israel are ordered to help Solomon, 17-19.
Ch. 23-24. Preparation of the Levites and priests. The priests were divided into 24 orders, 24:1-19.
Ch. 25. Preparation of singers and musicians. They were also divided into 24 divisions.
Ch. 26-27. Preparation of other temple officers. Gatekeepers, treasurers, and other officials were organized, 26:1-32, including officers over military and civil affairs, 27:1-34.

28-29. Last acts of David and his death

Ch. 28. David's address to the assembly and to Solomon.
Ch. 29. David's final words and death. He reviewed his plans and preparations for building the temple, 1-19, and invested Solomon as king, 20-25. David's death is recounted, 26-30.

2 Chronicles
Judah's history to the exile

Outline

1:1-9:31	Solomon's reign
10:1-19	The division of the kingdom
11:1-36:14	History of Judah to the exile
36:15-23	Captivity and epilogue

Scope of 2 Chronicles. Solomon is presented second only to David in importance in connection with the temple and its service, ch. 1-9. The bulk of the book, ch. 10-36, concerns the period of the dual monarchy, but centers in the Lord's gracious dealing with the Davidic house. The northern kingdom is referred to as summarily as possible. It was regarded as not representing true Israel and hence not important. Judah's apostasy from the Deuteronomic law is given as the reason for the disaster that overtook Judah.

An artist's impression of Solomon's Temple, with part of the walls and roof cut away to reveal the interior.

Solomon's Temple

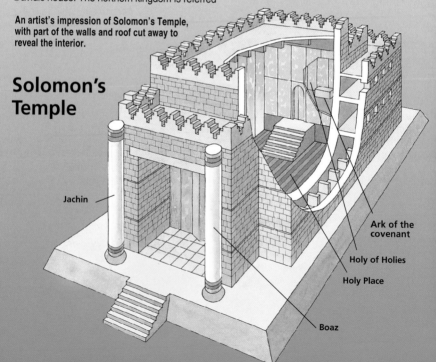

Jachin

Ark of the covenant

Holy of Holies

Holy Place

Boaz

2 Chronicles

1. Beginning of Solomon's reign
1-13. His vision at Gibeon. The tabernacle had been set up at Gibeon, about six miles northwest of Jerusalem, after Saul had destroyed Nob, and it stayed there until Solomon built the temple.
14-17. Summary of Solomon's splendor and wealth.

2-4. Solomon's building of the temple
Ch. 2. Solomon prepares to build. The timber from Lebanon was to be floated in rafts by sea to Joppa, 16, about 30 miles northwest of Jerusalem. Foreigners were conscripted for forced labor, 17-18.
Ch. 3. Details of the building operation. The cherubim, 10-13, were human-headed winged lions.
Ch. 4. The temple furnishings. The "Sea" was a huge basin built on 12 oxen, with the capacity of 3,000 baths (14,500 gallons) for ritual washings, 2-6.

5-7. Solomon dedicates the temple
Ch. 5. The ark brought in. The chronicler adds the account of the priests and singers, 11-13.
Ch. 6. Solomon's prayer of dedication.
Ch. 7. The Lord's presence consecrates the temple.

8. Solomon's prosperity
1-11. His building activities. His campaign, 3, is otherwise unknown.
12-18. His religious activities. Solomon's copper smelting establishment has been excavated at Ezion Geber.

9. The Queen of Sheba and Solomon's death
1-12. The queen's visit. The chronicler presents Solomon's good traits, as he did with David.
13-28. Solomon's wealth and splendor.
29-31. Solomon's death.

10. Secession of the ten tribes
1-15. Rehoboam's folly.
16-19. The sad result. The kingdom was divided.

11-12. Rehoboam's reign
Ch. 11. Beginning of Rehoboam's reign. He greatly fortified his kingdom, 5-12, and protected the priests and Levites, 13-17. He was obedient to the Lord for three years.
Ch. 12. Rehoboam's sin and its punishment. Apostasy resulted in Shishak's invasion, but repentance averted complete destruction, 5-12.

13-16. Abijah and Asa
Ch. 13. Reign of Abijah. The chronicler shows that the true worship of the Lord was conducted in the Jerusalem temple, 1-12.
Ch. 14-16. Asa's reign. Asa's prayer, 14:11, breathed the freshness of faith. Asa led a religious reformation, after being warned by the prophet Azariah, 15:1-7, but this did not prevent his apostasy, 16:1-14.

The Chaldean Empire

Old Babylonian period (1830-1550 B.C.) Babylon dates from prehistoric times but did not become the capital of a great empire until this period. Hammurabi (1728-1686 B.C.), of the first dynasty of Babylon, lifted it to the height of power.

The Chaldean Empire (605-539 B.C.) This Neo-Babylonian Empire was coterminous with Judah's captivity.

Nabopolassar (625-605 B.C.), father of Nebuchadnezzar II, threw off the Assyrian yoke and destroyed Nineveh, 612 B.C.

Nebuchadnezzar II (605-562 B.C.) His first deportation of Judah (Dan. 1:2) came in 605 B.C., the second in 597 B.C., and the third in 586 B.C., when he destroyed Jerusalem. He also besieged Tyre; desolated Moab, Ammon, Edom, and Lebanon; and invaded Egypt. He was one of the most autocratic and splendid rulers of the ancient world, whose capital city, Babylon, was immortalized for its magnificence (cf. Dan. 4:30).

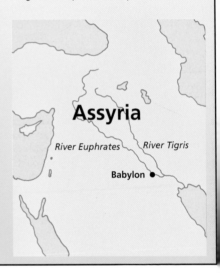

17-20. Jehoshaphat's reformation
Ch. 17. Godliness and prosperity of his early reign.
Ch. 18-19. His mistake. Jehoshaphat's alliance with Ahab (1 Kings 22:1-40) was a serious compromise and blunder, deserving the stinging rebuke of the prophet Jehu, 19:1-3. This was effective.
Ch. 20. His deliverance from an invasion. The Moab-Ammon invasion, 1-2, in answer to Jehoshaphat's prayer, 3-13, was repulsed, 14-25.

21-22. Jehoram, Ahaziah, Athaliah
Ch. 21. Jehoram's wicked reign. His doom was pronounced by a letter that had been written by Elijah, 12-15, doubtless delivered by Elisha. His end was disastrous, 16-20.
22:1-9. Ahaziah's wicked reign.
22:10-12. Athaliah's usurpation.

23-24. Joash's reform and eventual apostasy
23:1-11. Joash became king.
23:12-15. Athaliah executed.
23:16-21. Revival through Jehoiada.
Ch. 24. Joash's reign. A synopsis of his rule is given, 1-2. The repair of the temple, 4-14; the death of Jehoiada, 15-16; and the apostasy of the officials and king, 17-19, are mentioned, climaxing in the stoning of Jehoiada's son, Zechariah, 20-22, and the invasion of the

Arameans of Damascus, 23-24.

25-26. Amaziah and Uzziah

Ch. 25. Amaziah's reign. His campaign against Edom, 5-13, and his idolatry, 14, resulted in divine wrath against him, 15-16.

Ch. 26. Uzziah's reign. The reign of Uzziah (also called Azariah) was long and prosperous (c. 791-740 B.C.). He intruded into the priest's office by offering incense and was struck with leprosy.

27-28. Jotham and Ahaz

Ch. 27. Jotham's reign. "Jotham grew powerful because he walked steadfastly before the Lord," 6.

Ch. 28. Ahaz's great wickedness. His idolatries, 1-4, brought punishment at the hands of Rezin, king of Syria, and Pekah, king of Israel, 5-8.

29-32. Hezekiah's reformation

Ch. 29-30. Hezekiah's reign. He effected a great revival, 29:1-19, restoring temple worship, 20-36, and celebrating the Passover, 30:1-27.

Ch. 31. Other reforms.

32:1-23. Sennacherib's invasion.

32:24-33. Hezekiah's sickness, recovery, and envoys from Babylon.

33. Manasseh's and Amon's idolatry

1-10. Manasseh's orgy of wickedness.

11-13. His captivity and restoration.

14-20. His reforms and death.

21-25. Amon's rule. He was evil like his father.

34-35. Josiah's great reformation

34:1-7. Early reforms. Josiah, one of Judah's

The City of Babylon

Dazzling buildings. The Ishtar Gate led through a massive double wall of fortification decorated with bull dragon motifs in enameled colored bricks. The Great Processional Street led from the Ishtar Gate. A dominating building was the royal ziggurat or temple tower rising to eight stages. Marduk's temple stood nearby. The famous hanging gardens were constructed in terraces and constituted one of the seven wonders of the world. Most of the bricks found carry Nebuchadnezzar's stamp.

---

best kings, fought against Canaanite Baal cults.

34:8-35:19. Great revival. This was the result of finding the Mosaic law lost in Manasseh's reign of terror.

35:20-27. Josiah's death.

36:1-14. Jehoahaz to Zedekiah: the end

1-10. Jehoahaz deposed, Jehoiakim's and Jehoiachin's reigns.

11-14. Zedekiah. He reigned until the fall of Jerusalem, 586 B.C.

36:15-23. Captivity and Cyrus's decree

15-21. Fall of Jerusalem and the exile. The chronicler reviews the Lord's grace and patience and gives the reason for the exile.

22-23. Decree of Cyrus.

Ezra

Return from Babylon

Outline

1-6	Return under Zerubbabel
	Temple rebuilt
7-10	Return under Ezra
	His reformation

Chronology of the return

605-536 B.C.	General period of captivity
605, 597, 586 B.C.	Leading Judean citizens deported, including Daniel and Ezekiel
538 B.C.	Edict of Cyrus permitting the return
536 B.C.	Return of 49,897 from Babylon to Jerusalem
536 B.C.	Altar rebuilt, sacrifice offered in seventh month
535 B.C.	Temple begun, but stopped
535-520 B.C.	Economic and political struggle
520 B.C.	Ministry of Haggai
520-515 B.C.	Ministry of Zechariah
515 B.C.	Temple completed
458 B.C.	Ezra returned
445 B.C.	Nehemiah rebuilt the walls

Cylinder recounting Cyrus' capture of Babylon.

Ezra

1. The edict of Cyrus

1-4. The proclamation. Prophecies by Isaiah (44:28-45:3) and Jeremiah (Jer. 29:10) were divinely fulfilled in Cyrus, by means of the Persian monarch's decree, 2-4.

5-11. Gifts provided. These included the holy vessels appropriated by Nebuchadnezzar (2 Kings 25:13-16).

2. The returning exiles

1-65. Register of those who returned. Enumerated are the people in general, 1-35; the priests, 36-39; the Levites, 40-54; the descendants of Solomon's servants, 55-60; and other priests, 61-63, totaling 49,897.

66-70. The property and gifts of those who returned.

3. The temple begun

1-7. The altar erected. The altar of burnt offering was set up, 2, the first step in rebuilding the temple and reestablishing the nation.

8-13. Foundation of the temple laid.

Archaeological light

Esarhaddon's annals on a cuneiform cylinder now in the British Museum recount the deportation of Israelites and the settlement of colonists in their place.

4. Work on the temple stopped

1-5. Enemies try to hinder the building of the temple. The offer of help from the Samaritans soon proved to be a snare because it entailed a compromising union with semi-idolaters, 3.

6-24. Continued opposition. Tattenai and Shethar-bozenai succeeded in delaying the building of the temple until Darius's second year (520 B.C.).

5-6. The temple work resumed and completed

Ch. 5. Haggai's and Zechariah's ministry. Through the kindness of Darius and the prophetic ministry of Haggai and Zechariah (Hag. 1:1-4; 2:1-4; Zech. 4:9; 6:15), the work was resumed.

Ch. 6. The temple finished. The temple was finished, 14-15, and dedicated, 16-18; and the Passover and Feast of Unleavened Bread were kept, 19-22.

7-8. The arrival of Ezra

Ch. 7. Ezra went to Jerusalem in the reign of Artaxerxes I (465-424 B.C.) to teach the law of God, 6, 10.

Ch. 8. Ezra's mission. The treasure was committed to 12 priests, 24-30, and delivered to the temple storehouses ("chambers"), 29.

9-10. Ezra's reform

Ch. 9. Loss of separation. Ezra sat down "appalled," 4, at the news of mixed marriages with semi-idolaters.

Ch. 10. Separation restored. The people repented and put away the foreign wives, 1-17.

Nehemiah
Rebuilding Jerusalem's walls

Outline

1-7 Nehemiah's restoration of the walls
8-13 Ezra's and Nehemiah's reforms

Name and purpose of the book. Nehemiah takes its name from its principal character and traditional author (1:1). The rebuilding of Jerusalem as a fortified city, the establishment of civil authority under Nehemiah, and his governorship are recounted. More civil and secular than the book of Ezra, it is nevertheless also written from the priestly viewpoint. Ezra-Nehemiah, until 1448 one book called the book of Ezra, demonstrates God's faithfulness in restoring His exiled people. The divine working is seen through great Gentile monarchs—Cyrus, Darius, and Artaxerxes. It is also seen in the Jews' own anointed leaders—Haggai, Zechariah, Zerubbabel, Joshua, Ezra, and Nehemiah.

The walls of the Old City of Jerusalem.

The Persian Empire (539-331 B.C.). The Persian kings constituted a humane line of world rulers who permitted the Jews to return and rebuild their temple and city. Persia reversed the cruel policy of Assyria and Chaldean by repatriating displaced peoples. Under the two-century beneficent Persian regime, Judah was a tiny province in the Fifth Persian Satrap.

Cyrus (539-530 B.C.) permitted the return of the Jews to Palestine (Ezra 1:1-4; 2 Chron. 36:22-23).

Darius I the Great (522-486 B.C.). His decree allowed the rebuilding of the temple in Jerusalem to continue (Ezra 6:13-15).

Nehemiah

1-2. Nehemiah's call

Ch. 1. Nehemiah's concern for Jerusalem.
Nehemiah, the king's cupbearer (royal butler),
11, heard of the sorry state of Jerusalem, 1-3,
and showed his great sorrow in prayer, 4-11.
Ch. 2. Nehemiah's mission. King Artaxerxes
sent Nehemiah to rebuild Jerusalem, 1-8.

3. Jerusalem's gates and walls repaired

1-2. Builders of the Sheep Gate. Through the
Sheep Gate sacrificial animals were led to the
altar.
3-32. Builders of the other gates are
mentioned along with the builders of the walls
between.

4-5. Opposition to the work

4:1-9. Opposition by ridicule and anger.
Ridicule was answered by prayer, 1-6.
4:10-23. Opposition by discouragement.
Ch. 5. Opposition by selfishness.
Covetousness, 1-5, had a remedy in restitution,
6-13, reinforced by Nehemiah's personal
example of unselfishness during his 12-year
term as governor, 14-19.

6. The walls completed

1-14. Opposition by craftiness. Unsuccessful
in luring Nehemiah away from the work,
Sanballat, Tobiah, and Geshem then tried to
intimidate him by threatening to report him to the
king.
15-19. Wall completed.

7. Register of Zerubbabel's return

1-4. Provisions for the defense of the city.
5-73. The census of the first return. The
genealogy is recorded, 5-65; the whole number
given, 66-69; and gifts for the work described,
70-73.

8. Public reading of the law

1-8. The law read before the Water Gate. The
law of Moses, written in Hebrew, was interpreted
in the common Aramaic by Ezra, 7-8.
9-18. Effect of the Word. Revival and keeping
of the Feasts of Tabernacles were the results.

9. Spiritual revival

1-5. The public confession. Reading, hearing,
believing, and obeying the Word always brings
spiritual revival with humiliation, self-judgment,
confession, and true worship.
6-38. The great confession and prayer.

10. The covenant renewed

**1-28. The commitment to support God's
house.**
29-39. The obligations of the covenant. These
included the duty not to intermarry with Gentiles,
28-30; to observe the Sabbath, 31; to support
the temple ritual, 32-36; and to pay tithes and
priestly dues, 37-39.

11-12. The dedication of the walls

Ch. 11. Faithful workers. Registers of people
who lived in Jerusalem and outside Jerusalem

Jerusalem under Nehemiah

Temple area

Wall of Old City today

Ophel

Hezekiah's tunnel

Pool of Siloam

Probable city wall under Nehemiah

are given.

12:1-26. Other faithful people. Named are priests and Levites of the first return, 1-9; descendants of Joshua the high priest, 10-11; heads of priestly houses, 12-21; and heads of Levitical houses, 22-26.

12:27-47. Dedication of the walls and provisions for temple personnel.

13. Evils corrected

1-9. Separation enforced from "all who were of foreign descent," 3, and from unholy alliances, 4-9.

10-29. Nehemiah corrects other evils.

30-31. His testimony concerning his work was characterized by modesty and piety.

Esther
Divine providence at work in history

Outline

1	Vashti deposed
2	Esther made queen
3	Haman's plot
4-7	Esther's courage
8	Vengeance executed
9	Purim kept
10	Epilogue

Nature of the book. The book describes the origin of the festival of Purim ("lots"). This solemnity was celebrated on the 14th or 15th of Adar (Feb.-Mar.). Thus Esther is the Purim scroll (roll).

Griffin, from a glazed-brick relief at Susa.

Esther

1. Vashti deposed
1-9. Xerxes's feast. Ahasuerus (KJV), probably Xerxes I (486-465 B.C.), laid on a seven-day-long banquet to impress his guests.
10-22. Queen Vashti deposed. The all-powerful king, "in high spirits from wine," 10, was in no mood to be disobeyed.

2. Esther made queen
1-4. Search for Vashti's successor.
5-23. Mordecai and Esther. Mordecai was Esther's foster father (having adopted her as a child), as well as her cousin, 5-7.

3. Haman's plot
1-6. Haman's promotion. He was elevated to a seat of honor higher than all the other officials, 1. All lesser officials had to kneel before him and pay him honor, 2. Mordecai's faith prevented him from paying homage to any but the true God.
7-15. Haman's plot to exterminate the Jews.

Archeological light
Shushan (Susa) was the winter capital of Persia. The palace had three courts with multitudinous rooms decorated with warriors, winged bulls, and griffins. The famous Code of Hammurabi was found here in the excavated area.

Haman offered 10,000 talents to the king to bribe him to massacre the Jews. The royal signet ring, 10, 12, stamped the order of annihilation with authority.

4-5. Esther's intercession before the king
Ch. 4. Esther's decision to go before the king. Esther was informed of the edict, and she agreed to go before the king, 4-17.
Ch. 5. The king received Esther and indicated that he would grant her petition, 1-8. Haman determined to liquidate Mordecai, 9-14.

Darius I.

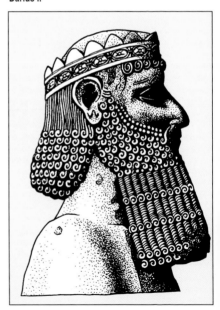

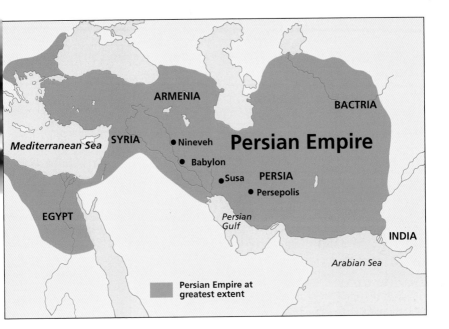

Persian Empire at greatest extent

6-7. Mordecai honored; Haman hanged

Ch. 6. Mordecai honored by the king. The king, sleepless, had "the book of the chronicles," 1, read, in which Mordecai's exposé of a plot against the king's life was told, 1-3.
Ch. 7. Haman hanged.

8. The edict of deliverance

1-2. Mordecai's exaltation. The signet ring given to Mordecai signified his exaltation to Haman's prime ministership.
3-17. Revocation of the edict. Mordecai was authorized to make a decree that the Jews could defend themselves.

9. Origin of the Feast of Purim

1-16. The triumph of the Jews.
17-32. Institution of Purim. In later times the book of Esther was read on these festal days.

10. Ch. 10. Epilogue: Mordecai's greatness

The continual greatness of Xerxes and the power of Mordecai are recounted.

Job
Why the righteous suffer

Outline

1:1-2:13	Prologue: Job's test
3:1-31:40	False comfort from his three friends
32:1-37:24	Elihu's speeches
38:1-42:6	God's discourses
42:7-17	Epilogue: Job's restoration

The book of Job and Hebrew poetry. Hebrew poetry does not possess meter or rhyme. Its basic structure is *parallelism* or thought arrangements, rather than word arrangements. Common types of such parallelism are (1) *synonymous parallelism,* where the second

Why do righteous people suffer?

line reiterates the first line (cf. Job 3:11-12; 4:17); (2) *antithetic parallelism,* in which the second line presents a contrasting thought to emphasize the first (Job 42:5); (3) *synthetic parallelism,* in which the second and succeeding lines add a progressive flow of thought to develop the first (Job 4:19-21). In addition, Hebrew poetry possesses rhythm or pulsating beats. It is also highly figurative, rich in imagery, simile, metaphor, metonymy, personification, and alliteration.

The theme of the book. It treats a perplexing, profound subject: Why do righteous people suffer? Job's three friends offered the same answer, ch. 3-31. Suffering is the outcome of sin. A fourth adviser, Elihu, then declares that afflictions are often a means of purifying the righteous. By God's speech, out of the storm, ch. 38-41, Job was humbly led to detest himself in relation to the divine majesty of God, 42:1-6. His self-renunciation and spiritual refining were the entrée to his restoration and blessing, 42:7-17.

Job

1-2. Prologue: Job's testing

1:1-5. Job's testing and integrity. Job was "blameless," 1, not sinless or perfect. He was a historical person (Ezek. 14:14, 20; James 5:11).

1:6-12. Satan's accusation. Satan appears here, as often in Scripture, as the "accuser of our brothers" (Rev. 12:10).

1:13-2:13. Job's affliction. Severe testing came. Possessions and family were wiped out, 1:13-22. Job's health was taken away, 2:1-8. His wife turned against him, 2:9-10.

3-14. The first cycle of speeches

Ch. 3. Job's first speech. He cursed the day he was born, 1-9, and longed to die, 10-26.

Ch. 4-5. Eliphaz's first speech. He rebuked Job, 4:1-6, and insisted the righteous are not cut off, 4:7-11.

Ch. 6-7. Job's reply.

Ch. 8. Bildad's first speech. God was punishing Job for his sins, 1-7.

Ch. 9-10. Job answers Bildad.

Ch. 11. Zophar's first speech. He tells Job to repent and so be restored, 13-20.

Ch. 12-14. Job's reply to Zophar. Denouncing his friends, he appealed to God.

15-21. Second cycle of speeches

Ch. 15. Eliphaz's second speech. Eliphaz assumed Job's guilt and told him that he stood self-condemned, 1-6.

Ch. 16-17. Job's reply to Eliphaz. Job branded his "friends" as "miserable comforters," 16:2.

Ch. 18. Bildad's second speech. He tries to frighten Job with a description of the doom of the wicked, 5-21.

Ch. 19. Job's reply to Bildad includes one of the most superlative statements of faith in all the OT, 25-27.

Ch. 20. Zophar's second speech. He mistakenly classified Job with the wicked and their fate, 4-29.

Ch. 21. Job's reply.

22-31. Third cycle of speeches

Ch. 22. Eliphaz's third speech. He accused Job of greed and cruelty, 6-11.

Ch. 23-24. Job's reply. He groped for God, proving he was not defiantly wicked, 23:1-9.

Ch. 25. Bildad's third speech. He presented a forceful description of what God is, 1-3, and what man is, 4-6.

Ch. 26. Job's reply. With great feeling, he described God's greatness, 5-14.

Ch. 27-31. Job's closing words of self-vindication. Job concluded by saying in a word: "*I am clean!*" The next time he spoke, he declared in essence, "*Behold, I am vile*" (42:6). The reason for the change is recorded in the rest of the book.

32-37. Elihu's speeches

Ch. 32-33. Elihu's first speech. God instructs mankind through affliction.

Ch. 34. Elihu's second speech. Job has yet to learn the purpose of suffering, 31-37.

Ch. 35. Elihu's third speech, the advantages of piety.

Ch. 36-37. Elihu's fourth speech. Elihu's concluding words, 37:17-24, stress mankind's sinful frailty before God, clearing the way for the Almighty to speak.

38:1-42:6. God's discourses to Job

38:1-40:5. God's first discourse to Job. Creation proclaims God's omnipotence.

40:6-42:6. God's second discourse to Job. God's power and human frailty are contrasted. Job was silenced as a contender and faultfinder with God, but not chastised as a sinner.

Job's reply to God, 42:1-6, *solves the problem* of suffering. Affliction is God-permitted to refine mankind so that they may see God, 42:5, in all His greatness and splendor and their own sin, so that they may "repent in dust and ashes," 42:6.

42:7-17. God rebukes Job's friends and restores Job

7-9. The Lord's vindication of Job against his friends. God's grace forgave Job's sin, and Job prayed for his erring friends.

10-17. Job's fortunes restored.

Afflictions are often a means of purifying the righteous.

Psalms
Prayer book and hymnal of God's people

Nature of the Psalms. The Hebrew title for the Psalter is "Book of Praises." Our English word "Psalms," from the Septuagint *Psalmoi,* means "songs" accompanied by string instruments. Praise, worship, confession, and the outpouring of prayer characterize the Psalms. The Psalter was the hymn book of the Jewish people and is the prayer and praise manual of the Christian church.

Themes of the Psalms
1. The spiritual conflicts and triumphs of saints under the old dispensation constitute the basic theme, but these reflect the conflicts of God's people in every age.
2. Great prophetic themes run through the book, concerning the Messiah (Pss. 2, 8, 16, 22, 45, 69, 72, 89, 110, 118, 132); the trials of the godly (Pss. 52, 58, 59, 69, 109, 140); and future glories for redeemed Israel, the earth, and all creation (Pss. 72, 110).

Classification

Five books: Book 1, Psalms 1-41; Book 2, Psalms 42-72; Book 3, Psalms 73-89; Book 4, Psalms 90-106; Book 5, Psalms 107-150.

Royal Psalms. 2, 18, 20, 21, 45, 72, 89, 101, 110, 144. They anticipate Christ as King.

Alphabetic Psalms. 9, 10, 25, 34, 37, 111, 112, 119, 145. They use some arrangement based on the Hebrew alphabet.

Penitential Psalms. 6, 25, 32, 38, 39, 40, 51, 102, 130. These psalms breathe deep contrition for sin committed.

Messianic Psalms. 2, 8, 16, 22, 45, 69, 72, 89, 110, 118, 132. They preview the person and work of the coming Messiah.

Imprecatory Psalms. 52, 58, 59, 109, 140. All of these implore God's vindication of His own people against godless persecutors.

Hallelujah Psalms. 111-113, 115-117, 146-150. These psalms employ the term Hallelujah, meaning "Praise Jah (Jehovah)."

Elohistic Psalms. 42-83. They use the name *Elohim* for God. Others use the name of Jehovah.

Ascent Psalms. 120-134. They were recited or sung as the pilgrims went up to Jerusalem to celebrate the feasts.

Psalms

a little lower than angels (Matt. 21:1-6; 1 Cor. 15:27; Heb. 2:6-9), and is now crowned with glory and honor, 1-5.

1. The godly vs. the ungodly

A wisdom psalm introduces the Psalter, contrasting the godly happy person, 1-3, with the ungodly person, 4-6.

2. Messiah's kingship and kingdom

This previews Christ's present rejection, 1-3 (cf. Acts 4:25-28), which continues throughout this age and culminates in the abysmal apostasy of the Great Tribulation.

3-7. Trials of the godly

Psalm 3. Peaceful trust in God. In time of deep anguish when Absalom rebelled against him, 1-2, David found God his glory, as his shield and encourager, 2-3, the One who answered his prayers, 4, and the One who gave him peace and deliverance, 5-8.

Psalm 4. Evening prayer sustaining faith results in enlargement of heart, 1.

Psalm 5. Morning prayer giving courage, 1-3, bestows a sense of God's goodness and justice, guidance, protection, and blessing.

Psalm 6. Heart cry of one distressed.

Psalm 7. Cry for protection against cruel enemies.

8. The sovereignty of the Son of Man (Messianic)

As Son of Man, Christ appears in humiliation,

9-15. The godly and the Wicked One

Psalm 9. The godly praise the Most High, 1-2, for His kingdom blessings and glories, 3-12, with prayer for the Lord's intervention in the judgments preceding the establishment of the kingdom, 13-20.

Psalm 10. Supplication of the godly.

Psalm 11. Faith's resources are for the day of trouble, when "the foundations are being destroyed" in that dark hour of universal apostasy, 1-3. The Lord will reward the righteous, 4-7.

Psalm 12. The arrogance of sinners, 1-3, is described, but God is about to judge them, 4-6.

Psalm 13. The faith of the godly, 1-4, ends in victory, 5-6.

Psalm 14. Human apostasy and depravity are described, 1-3.

Psalm 15. The character of the godly.

16-24. Prophetic vistas of Christ

These nine psalms reflect the character of the godly but find their *ultimate* fulfillment in Christ, starting in Psalm 16 with our Lord in His obedience on earth, climaxing in His Second Coming manifestation as "the King of glory" (Ps. 24).

Psalm 16. Christ, the Obedient One, is resurrected.

Psalm 17. Christ the Intercessor.

Psalm 18. God's power preserved Christ. David as prophet (Acts 2:30) here predicts Christ's experience of death, 1-6; glory, 7-27; subduing His enemies, 28-42; and being made

A shepherd with his flock on a hillside outside Bethlehem.

"Head of the nations," 45-50.

Psalm 19. Christ in creation and revelation.

Psalm 20. Christ and His salvation. Celebration of Christ's glorious salvation, 4-8, is climaxed by a cry of the godly in the time of trouble, 9.

Psalm 21. Christ's kingly glory is anticipated.

Psalm 22. Christ's sufferings and coming glory. The sufferings, 1-21, are a graphic portrayal of crucifixion (cf. Matt. 27:27-50), and are followed by the glory, 22-31.

Psalm 23. Christ the Great Shepherd.

Psalm 24. Christ the Chief Shepherd, the "King of Glory," appearing to reward His sheep (1 Peter 5:4).

25-39. Soul exercise of the godly

Psalm 25. Petition for deliverance.

Psalm 26. Prayer for vindication against an unjust charge is presented, 1-3, with protestations of innocence, 4-7, dramatized by a liturgical ceremony, 6, concluding with a prayer for help, 8-12.

Psalm 27. Prayer for spiritual orientation, toward God, 1-3, toward life, 4-6, toward self, 7-14.

Psalm 28. Prayer for deliverance, followed by thanksgiving for the answer, 6-9.

Psalm 29. The storm of judgment.

Psalm 30. Praise for healing. The recovery is noted, 1-3, and praise is offered, 4-12.

Psalm 31. Victory over enemies.

Psalm 32. The blessing of being justified. This is the first of 13 Mescal psalms, i.e., psalms of spiritual instruction. The justifier, 1-5, is also a hiding place, 6-7, and a Guide and a Preserver,

8-10, in whom the saint is to rejoice, 11.

Psalm 33. Praise to the Lord.

Psalm 34. Full praise of God's redeemed is sung for deliverance, 1-10, for instruction, 11-14, for redemption, 15-22. Verse 20 was fulfilled in John 19:36.

Psalm 35. Cry for help in distress. Like other imprecatory psalms, this psalm must be understood as the prayers of the godly in a day of abysmal apostasy and violence. The Spirit of God prays through them for the destruction of the wicked. God's holiness demands judgment when grace is rejected.

Psalm 36. Contrast of the wicked and the Lord.

Psalm 37. The righteous and the wicked contrasted.

Psalm 38. The suffering saint and sin. When the suffering saint, 1-8, looks to the Lord, 9-15, confession of sin and prayer result, 16-22.

Psalm 39. Human frailty.

40-41. David's experiences foreshadow Christ's

Psalm 40. The obedient Christ (cf. Heb. 10:5-7). His path of obedience, 4-12, is prefaced by the Redeemer's resurrection song, 1-3. The fruit of the Redeemer's work is outlined, 13-17, as He prays as the Sin-Bearer of His people.

Psalm 41. Messiah betrayed. David's experience, 9, foreshadows Christ's (John 13:18-19).

42-49. Through tribulation to kingdom blessing

These psalms open Book 2 of the Psalter, which begins with the oppression of the godly Hebrew remnant of the last days and ends with Psalm

72, the great Kingdom Psalm of the Psalter. The first group (42-49) presents aspects of this troubled scene and final deliverance.

Psalm 42. Longing for God in deep distress, 1-6, is described with the tonic of faith and the comfort of hope, 7-11.

Psalm 43. Cry to God against enemies.

Psalm 44. Increased cry for help.

Psalm 45. The answer: King Messiah's coming in glory. His majesty and power, 1-5, His dominion and glory, 6-8, and those who share His kingdom, 9-17, are foreseen (cf. Heb. 1:8-9 and Isa. 11:1-2).

Psalm 46. Deliverance from tribulation and the sequel. "Selah" is a liturgical direction of some sort.

Psalm 47. Messiah King in His kingdom is seen among His redeemed, 1-5, the object of the praise of His ransomed people, 6-9.

Psalm 48. Nations judged, the kingdom established.

Psalm 49. Transiency of the wicked and their wealth. Contrast is made to the lot of the righteous who trust in the Lord.

50-51. The righteous God and His penitent people

Psalm 50. God's demands for holiness.

Psalm 51. The sinner in deep penitence. This is the greatest of the penitential psalms. David's sin of adultery and murder is confessed before God and forgiven.

52-55. Israel's time of trouble

These four psalms are Mescal (instruction) odes reflecting the affliction David went through.

Psalm 52. The wicked tyrant and his destruction.

Replica of an ancient harp.

Psalm 53. An age of apostasy. This psalm is almost identical to Psalm 14, but uses *Elohim* instead of *Jehovah*.

Psalm 54. Petitions of the godly. David's betrayal by the Ziphites (1 Sam. 23:19-27) furnishes the historical occasion for this psalm.

Psalm 55. In the vortex of great distress. The defection of Ahithophel, David's trusted counselor, to the traitor Absalom (2 Sam. 15:12-17:23) causes the psalmist's deep distress, 3.

56-60. Trials of the saints before blessing

Psalm 56. Praise for anticipated deliverance. David was hemmed in by his own people and by the Philistines.

Psalm 57. Deliverance in distress. David cries to God for deliverance from Saul in a cave at Adullam (1 Sam. 22:1; 24:3).

Psalm 58. Judgment upon the wicked

Psalm 59. The hatred of the wicked for the righteous. This cruel animosity is reflected in David's lament when Saul tried to trap him in his home (1 Sam. 19:10-17).

Psalm 60. A national lament.

61-68. Through sufferings to kingdom blessing

Psalm 61. Prayer for the king.

Psalm 62. The saints' waiting and trusting for deliverance. David's waiting in faith, 1-4, has its expectation in God alone, 5-8, not in the vanity of man, 9-12.

Psalm 63. The saints' thirst for God. David's burning desire for fellowship with God despite his trials in the wilderness, 1-8, prefigures the heart exercise of every true saint in trouble.

Psalm 64. The fate of the wicked.

Psalm 65. Millennial restitution of the earth. Spiritual blessings are realized, 1-5, as well as temporal and material benefits, 6-13.

Psalm 66. Worship and praise in the kingdom.

Psalm 67. Full kingdom joy and blessing. The nations know and praise God, 1-4, and worldwide prosperity ensues, 5-6.

Psalm 68. Consummation of redemption.

69-72. Christ rejected and exalted

Psalm 69. The sufferings of the rejected Messiah. This remarkable psalm illustrates the deep prophetic strain running through the Psalms (cf. Luke 24:44).

Psalm 70. Israel's prayer for deliverance.

Psalm 71. Israel's paean of hope. The psalmist declares his faith, 1-18, resulting in spiritual victory, 19-24.

Psalm 72. The great kingdom psalm.

73-83. Psalms of Asaph concerning the sanctuary

Book 3 of the Psalter, Psalms 73-89, deals with the holiness of the Lord's sanctuary.

Psalm 73. Problem of the prosperity of the

wicked. God's justice and the holiness of the sanctuary prove an answer to the psalmist, 15-28.

Psalm 74. Desecration of the sanctuary by the enemy. The sight of the enemy in the sanctuary, 1-9, will be fully realized in the Antichrist of the end-time (Matt. 24:15). Prayer is made for divine intervention, 10-23.

Psalm 75. Divine intervention on behalf of the sanctuary.

Psalm 76. Divine government set up. The Lord reigns in Zion, 1-3, as a result of the judgments on the wicked, 4-12.

Psalm 77. The troubled saint.

Psalm 78. God is seen in Israel's history, 1-55, despite continued provocation by His people, 56-64. Grace appears to David, 65-72.

Psalm 79. Prayer for judgment upon Jerusalem's enemies.

Psalm 80. Cry for restoration of the nation Israel.

Psalm 81. Israel's regathering. The blowing of the trumpets foreshadows Israel's age-end regathering, 1-5. The restoration is against the background of deliverance from Egypt, 6-10, and the nation's subsequent disobedience and punishment, 11-16.

Psalm 82. Pre-kingdom judgment.

Psalm 83. Israel's enemies overthrown. The nation's foes of the writer's day, 1-8, foreshadow the final coalition and its complete overthrow, 9-18 (cf. Isa. 10:28-34; Dan. 11:36-42; Joel 2:1-11; Zech. 12:2).

84-89. Prayer issuing in kingdom glory

Psalm 84. Spiritual vitality of the kingdom.

Psalm 85. Promised blessing in the kingdom.

The benefits, 1-3, realized by prayer, 4-9, include righteousness and millennial peace, 10-13.

Psalm 86. A prayer, 1-9, and praise, 10-17, find full realization in the Kingdom Age, as 9 shows.

Psalm 87. Zion attains glory in the kingdom.

Psalm 88. Soul cry of distress, 1-7, with no apparent answer, 8-18, pictures the dark experiences of the godly in Israel.

Psalm 89. God's faithfulness.

90-93. From sinful wandering to redemption rest

Book 4 of the Psalter, Psalms 90-106, contains many psalms describing the time when the wilderness experiences of God's people end with glory for Israel and the nations.

Psalm 90. Mankind's fallen condition.

Psalm 91. The redeemed in fellowship with God. The psalmist's dependence on God, 1-2, is seen as he walks "in the shelter of the Most High." Satan realized the application of this psalm to Jesus, 11-12 (cf. Matt. 4:6).

Psalm 92. Song of praise for ultimate rest (Song for the Sabbath Day).

Psalm 93. The Lord's millennial reign. The Lord begins His reign over the earth in holiness, 5.

94-100. Judgment and the glories of the coming age

Psalm 94. Judgment of the wicked. Prayer is made for divine vengeance on the wicked, 1-13. The righteous are comforted, 14-23, as their enemies and God's enemies are destroyed.

Psalm 95. Worship and joy in prospect of the coming of Israel's Savior-King.

Psalm 96. The Second Coming. The Lord is supreme, 1-6. Creation celebrates, 7-13.

Psalm 97. The King reigns, 1-5.

Psalm 98. The new song of triumph. All creation is summoned to celebrate the establishment of the Lord's kingship in the earth with a new song, 1-9.

Psalm 99. The Lord's earthly kingship. He is ruler of the earth, 1-3. "He is holy" is the refrain, 5, 9. His rule will be just, 4-5; His dealings faithful, 6-9.

Psalm 100. Israel's kingdom praise.

101-106. The righteous king in humiliation and glory

Psalm 101. The righteous King and His rule.

Psalm 102. Christ the King in His rejection. The reference to verses 25-27 in Hebrews 1:10-12 demonstrates that this ode predicts the sorrow and anguish of the God-man.

Psalm 103. Israel's kingdom praise is given for blessings of full salvation, 1-7; for the Lord's gracious character, 8-18; and for His established kingdom, 19-22.

Psalm 104. Creation's praise to the Creator, Messiah-Christ, 1-9, for His creation shows His kindness and greatness, 10-35.

Psalms 105-106. Historical retrospect.

107-108. Israel's deliverances and praise to God

Book 5 of the Psalter, Psalms 107-150, sets out God's dealings with Israel culminating in deliverance for them, the nation, and all creation.

Psalm 107. God's mercies to Israel.

Psalm 108. Israel's praise, 1-4, for her inheritance, 5-9, through the Lord, 10-13, is offered.

109-113. Christ in rejection, exaltation, and coming glory

Psalm 109. Prediction of Christ's rejection. David as prophet sees the despised and rejected One, 1-5, His accusers and their doom, 6-20. The voice of the rejected One echoes in 21-25, and merges into the voice of the final remnant, 26-31, identified with Him.

Psalm 110. Christ as King-Priest. Christ, David's son and Lord, is exalted in resurrection and ascension, 1, and waiting till His enemies are put down. His Second Coming is described (Heb. 5:6; 6:20; 7:21).

Psalms 111-113. Three hallelujah psalms. Hallelujah! The King-Priest on his throne, 111; Hallelujah! The righteous are rewarded by the King-Priest on his throne, 112; and, Hallelujah! Praise the Lord, 113.

114-117. Past deliverances and future praise

Psalm 114. The Egyptian deliverance in retrospect. Future deliverance is implicit in prospect (cf. Jer. 16:14-15).

Psalm 115. Israel's God.

Psalm 116. Israel's praise of God for deliverance from death, 1-9.

Psalm 117. Universal praise in the kingdom. The praise, 1, is followed by the reason for it, 2.

118-119. Messiah and the Word of God exalted

Psalm 118. Messiah exalted as the Chief Cornerstone. This great hallelujah psalm was sung along with Psalms 114-117 and 136 by our Lord and His disciples in observing the Passover the night He was betrayed (Matt. 26:30). He applied verses 22-23 to Himself (Matt. 21:42).

Psalm 119. The Word of God exalted.
Although applicable to all generations this
magnificent alphabetic acrostic (each of the 22
letters of the Hebrew alphabet occurs eight
times in the 22 sections) will be finally fulfilled
when Israel, under the new covenant, will have
the law written "on their hearts" (Jer. 31:31-33).

120-134. The psalms of ascent
Apparently these psalms were sung as pilgrims
went up to Jerusalem to the sacred feasts.
Psalm 120. Suffering of the godly.
Psalm 121. Israel's keeper and preserver. He
never fails His own.
Psalm 122. Prayer for Jerusalem's peace.
Psalm 123. Cry for mercy in distress. Humble
dependence upon God, 1-2, and a plea for
mercy is made, 3-4, in the face of contempt from
the proud and the worldly.
Psalm 124. Answer of prayer for mercy.
**Psalm 125. Reward of the righteous and
punishment of the wicked.**
Psalm 126. Song of the returned captives.
The joy of past favors, 1-3, inspires prayer for
final restoration, 4-6.
**Psalm 127. Praise God from whom all
blessings flow.** The gift of many male children
is a blessing to an Oriental father.
Psalm 128. Blessings out of Zion are to be
fully realized when the Lord reigns.
Psalm 129. The Lord, Israel's preserver, has
protected His people in the past, 1-4. Prayer is
offered that Israel's enemies may not triumph
over her, 5-8.
**Psalm 130. The Lord, Israel's faithful
redeemer.**
Psalm 131. The Lord, Israel's hope.
Psalm 132. Messiah, David's son, enthroned.

David's concern for God's house, 1-10, is
rewarded by the Davidic covenant, 11-12. It will
be realized in King-Messiah at His Second
Coming, 13-18.
**Psalm 133. The blessings of fraternal
harmony.**
Psalm 134. Blessed worship. The priests are
called to praise the Lord, 1, and to bless the
congregation, 2-3.

135-136. Restored Israel
in praise and worship
Psalm 135. The cleansed nation worships.
**Psalm 136. The redeemed nation's praise of
God's mercy.** This psalm is called the "Great
Hallel" (cf. Pss. 114-118) in Jewish Passover
liturgy and may have been sung by Christ and
His disciples after the Last Supper (Matt. 26:30).

137-139. The experiences of God's
people in the light of their God
Psalm 137. The experience of the exile looks
through the Babylonian Captivity to the final age-
end restoration when Israel's foes are punished,
8-9 (cf. Isa. 13:16; 47:6).
Psalm 138. Praise the Lord.
Psalm 139. Israel's Creator-Redeemer is all-
knowing, 1-6; present everywhere, 7-12; worthy
of all praise, 13-18; righteous and holy to punish
sin and sinners, 19-24.

140-143. Trials and troubles
of God's people
**Psalms 140-143. Prayer for deliverance from
enemies.** These reflect David's various
experiences of suffering. He cries for vindication
in his distress and prays for deliverance and
restoration to spiritual prosperity.

Psalm 146. Hallelujah! The God of Jacob, 1-2. This is the name of the One who loves the helpless sinner in redemptive compassion, 3-4, yet who is the mighty Creator, faithful, and righteous, 5-7, the glorious Savior and Protector, 8-9, and the eternal King, 10.

Psalm 147. Hallelujah! For His power and providential care, 1-11, especially toward Israel, 12-20.

Psalm 148. Hallelujah! Let all creatures praise Him in heaven, 1-6, and on earth, 7-14.

Psalm 149. Hallelujah! Sing the new song of redemption.

Psalm 150. Hallelujah! Climactic crescendo of universal praise. The ultimate purpose of creation is the praise of the Creator. God alone is worthy. Hallelujah!

Psalms were sung as pilgrims went up to Jerusalem to the sacred feasts.

144-145. David's experiences a mirror of Israel's future

Psalm 144. Prayer for manifestation of the Lord's power.

Psalm 145. The glory of King-Messiah and His kingdom. This is an alphabetic acrostic of personal praise, 1-3, of the Lord's wonderful works, 4-7; of His love, 8-9; of His millennial kingdom, 10-13; and of His providential care for His creatures, 14-21.

146-150. The grand hallelujah finale

Each of these five psalms opens and closes with Hallelujah, "Praise the Lord."

Proverbs
Compendium of moral and spiritual instruction

Outline

1:1-9:18	Book 1. Proverbs of Solomon
10:1-22:16	Book 2. Various sayings of Solomon
22:17-24:34	Book 3. Words of the wise
25:1-29:27	Book 4. Proverbs copied by Hezekiah's scribes
30:1-33	Agur's words
31:1-9	Queen mother's counsel to her son
31:10-31	The virtuous wife

Nature of the book. Among the OT books, Proverbs is most typical of ancient Near Eastern wisdom literature. It is a library of moral and spiritual instruction for the young to ensure a godly, happy life here and reward in the life to come. A proverb is a short precept *regulating* or *governing* conduct and life, often taking the form of a resemblance parable. Many proverbs are condensed parables.

Authorship. Many of the proverbs stem from Solomon (1:1; 10:1; 25:1; cf. 1 Kings 4:32; 2 Chron. 1:10; Eccl. 12:9); some are from Agur (30:1) and Lemuel (31:1), who are unknown people.

The pursuit of wisdom brings a knowledge of God.

Proverbs

1. Purpose of the book of Proverbs
1-7. To promote wisdom and godly living.
Verse 7 strikes the theme of the entire book.
Reverence toward God is the essential prelude
to all wisdom and successful living.
8-19. Home discipline is a moral safeguard
against a life of crime.
20-33. Wisdom personified as a prophetess
and teacher.

2-3. Results of the pursuit of wisdom
Ch. 2. The promise of wisdom. The pursuit of
wisdom brings a knowledge of God, 5.
Ch. 3. The precepts of wisdom make for
physical and spiritual well-being, 1-10.

4. The primacy of wisdom
1-19. In both teacher and student
20-27. Wisdom practiced is productive for life,
health, and personal integrity.

5-7. Moral restraint of wisdom
Ch. 5. Restraint against sexual sins is urged,
1-14, and unfaithfulness in marriage is warned
against, 15-23.
Ch. 6. Warning against various sins.
Ch. 7. Warning against the adulteress.

8. Remarkable revelation of wisdom's identity
1-21. Personified wisdom. Her call, 1-5, is
followed by announcement of her worth, 6-11,
her authority, 12-16, and her rewards, 17-21.
22-31. Wisdom's identity. Wisdom as a person
is revealed to be the preincarnate Christ. This
magnificent passage anticipates 1 Cor. 1:30;
John 1:1-3; Hebrews 1:1-3.
32-36. Renewed appeal.

9. Contrast between wisdom and folly
1-12. Wisdom's invitation (Matt. 11:28-29;
cf. Luke 14:15-24).
13-18. Folly's enticement. Folly is personified
as a foolish woman, and those who choose her
instead of our Lord court death and hell.

10:1-22:16. The godly and ungodly contrasted and other maxims
**Ch. 10-11. Contrast in life and conduct is
made** in matters of work, diligence, ambition,
speech, truth, stability, honesty, integrity, fidelity,
guidance, graciousness, kindness, etc.
**Ch. 12. Contrast is made in relation to
various conditions,** in thought, words,
domestic relationships, etc.
**Ch. 13. Contrast in relation to advantage and
disadvantage.**
**Ch. 14. Contrast between the wise and
foolish, the rich and poor.**
**Ch. 15. The better course of wisdom and
serving God.**
**Ch. 16. The better way of life through serving
the Lord.**
**Ch. 17-18. Various maxims regulating good
conduct.**
19:1-22:16. Various proverbs regulating

> **Numerical Proverbs.** Hebrew poetry often has the formula, x, x+1 (e.g., for three . . . for four). This parallel structure signifies completion (cf. Job 33:14; Amos 1:3-2:16).

personal conduct.

22:17-24:34. The words of the wise
This section, Book 3, is a teacher's instructions to his student ("son").
22:17-21. Introduction.
22:22-29. Various social injunctions.
Ch. 23. Various admonitions are given. These concern being a guest, 1-8; speaking, 9; removing a boundary stone, 10-11, etc.
Ch. 24. Various admonitions are added. These concern envy, 1-2; wisdom, etc.

25-29. Proverbs copied by Hezekiah's scribes
These make up Book 4 and consist of separate proverbs guiding moral conduct.
Ch. 25. Wise conduct is enjoined.
Ch. 26. Other sins. Singled out are the fool, 1-12; the sluggard, 13-16; the meddler, 17-20, 22-23; the contentious, 21; the hater, 24-26; and the liar, 28.
Ch. 27-29. Various other maxims.

30. Agur's words
1-10. God's power, truth and centrality so overwhelm Agur of Massa that he abases himself and owns his ignorance, 1-3. Such a God must have first place in Agur's life.
11-17. Exposé of rogues and extortioners.
18-20. Exposé of the shameless adulteress.
21-33. Exposé of the arrogant, the foolish,

An eastern weaver at her loom.

the indolent, the disorderly, and the cowardly.

31:1-9. A queen mother's counsel to her son
1. Words of Lemuel are a twofold lesson taught him by his mother.
2-9. The maternal warning is given negatively to avoid lust, 3, and strong drink, 4-7; and positively to rule righteously and impartially, 8-9.

31:10-31. The virtues of an ideal wife
This noble acrostic poem (each verse beginning with a letter of the Hebrew alphabet) is a choice gem of wisdom literature.
10-28. The character of the ideal wife.
29-31. Writer's appraisal of her. She is superlative, 29.

Ecclesiastes
The futile thinking and living of the natural man

Outline

1:1-3	The theme: The supreme emptiness of godless living
1:4-3:22	The theme proved
4:1-12:8	The theme expanded
12:9-14	The conclusion reached

Difficulty of the book. Many people find Ecclesiastes the most perplexing book of the Bible because of (1) its spirit of hopeless despair, depicting the emptiness and disappointment of life; (2) its lack of a note of praise or peace; (3) its seeming sanction of conduct at variance with the rest of Scripture.

Nature and purpose of the book. The difficulties can be resolved only by a correct view of the nature and purpose of the book. (1) It must be understood as the *book of the natural man*—his thinking and actions apart from the Spirit of God and divine revelation (cf. 1 Cor. 2:14). This is the meaning of the characteristic phrase "under the sun," occurring 29 times. This is why the covenant name "Lord" (Jehovah) is not used, only Elohim as Creator. (2) The purpose of the book must be seen to demonstrate to the natural man the complete emptiness of what is "under the sun" apart from what is *above* the sun, i.e., God's revelation and salvation.

"A time to be born and a time to die" (Eccles 3:2).

Ecclesiastes

1:1-3. The theme of the book

"Meaningless! Meaningless!" is a Hebrew expression meaning the supreme "vanity" or "emptiness" ("breath").

1:4-3:22. The theme of the emptiness of life proved

1:4-11. By the transitoriness of things. Generations pass on, nature continues in the same round, but nothing new results.

1:12-18. By the futility of human endeavor.

Ch. 2. By the emptiness of pleasure, wealth, and work.

Ch. 3. By the certainty of death. People are helpless to understand or alter the predetermined pattern of their lives, 1-15.

4:1-12:8. The theme of the emptiness of life expanded

Ch. 4. In view of the inequalities of life. The folly of wasting life through envy or avarice is noted, 1-6.

Ch. 5. In view of religious insincerity and wealth.

Ch. 6. In view of mankind's end.

Ch. 7. In view of sin. The person "under the sun," the natural mind unilluminated by God's Spirit, sees no advantage in being righteous, 13-21.

Ch. 8-9. In view of life's uncertainties.

"A time to plant a time to uproot" (Eccles. 3:2).

Ch. 10. In view of life's disorders. Only divine revelation can give symmetry and meaning to life.

Ch. 11. In view of youth. Ecclesiastes mirrors the heart of the unregenerate and points to their need of salvation in Christ.

12:1-8. In view of old age. Symbols of old age are set forth, 2-6.

12:9-14. Conclusion reached —practical piety in view of judgment

"Fear [revere] God and keep his commandments." This is the whole duty of the *redeemed*. But Ecclesiastes does not say how people are to be redeemed.

Song of Songs
Sanctity of wedded love

Outline

1:1-3:5	Bride muses in the bridegroom's palace
3:6-5:1	Bride accepts the bridegroom's invitation
5:2-6:3	Bride dreams of separation from the bridegroom
6:4-8:14	Bride and bridegroom express ardent love for each other

The purpose of the book.

1. In a general sense to honor marriage and the joys of wedded love. The key word is "lover" (32 times), and the theme is the love of the bridegroom for the bride.

2. The poem may be interpreted allegorically, proclaiming the Lord's love for Israel (Hos. 2:19-20) and Christ's love for the church (2 Cor. 11:2; Eph. 5:25-33; Rev. 19:7-9).

"Descend from . . . the summit of Hermon" (Song of Songs 4:8).

Song of Songs

1:1-3:5. Musings of the bride in the bridegroom's palace

Ch. 1. She muses on her first love for Solomon. The Song begins with the bride's recollection of her first intense longings for her beloved, 2-3; how she had first voiced her love for him, 4; and her first meeting with her lover (Solomon), 7.

2:1-3:5. The bride's musings on the blossoming romance. The bride remembers past meetings with Solomon and her intense satisfaction in his companionship. Her first dream, 3:1-4, is recalled in which she pictures herself separated from her beloved at Jerusalem. After finding him, she dreamed she had led him to her humble home in the north.

3:6-5:1. The bride accepts the bridegroom's invitation

3:6-11. Solomon brings his bride to Jerusalem. Solomon comes for his bride and takes her from her rural home to Jerusalem.

4:1-15. The bridegroom praises the bride.

4:16-5:1. Anticipation of the joys of married love, signifying the blessings of the Lord's redeemed in manifested union and glory with Him (1 John 3:3; Rev. 19:5-7; 20:6).

5:2-6:3. The bride dreams of separation from the bridegroom but finds him

5:2-8. The bride's second dream.

5:9-6:3. In praising him to others, she claims him as her own. Her dream shows how much she loves him and misses him.

6:4-8:14. The bride and bridegroom express their ardent love for each other

6:4-10. He praises her loveliness. His praise of her beauty recalls his ardent praise in 4:1-15.

6:11-13. Her experience in the nut orchard.

Ch. 7-8. Mutual praise and devotion. They both express their praise of and devotion to each other, 7:1-8:4, asserting their unquenchable love, 8:5-14.

An Eastern bride.

The Prophets

Outline

1:1-3	The theme: The supreme emptiness of godless living
1:4-3:22	The theme proved
4:1-12:8	The theme expanded
12:9-14	The conclusion reached

The prophets' messages. These were primarily moral and spiritual in their purpose. Israel's prophets were rugged reformers, divinely raised up to call the nation from sin and idolatry in its periods of decline. They thundered warnings of impending doom in the centuries preceding the fall of Israel in 722 B.C. and the fall of Judah in 586 B.C. Their weighty messages of woe, however, were frequently the vehicle for far-reaching messianic prophecies. Daniel and Ezekiel ministered hope and comfort to the exiles. Haggai and Zechariah encouraged the weak remnant that returned. Malachi sounded a somber note of warning and repentance illuminated by brilliant messianic flashes.

The Prophets and Their Message

Isaiah to Malachi Period c. 800-400 B.C,

To Israel before the fall of the northern kingdom, 722 B.C.	To Judah during her declining years.	To Judah in her last years, 634-606 B.C.	To exiles in Babylon, 606-538 B.C.	To restored community, 538-400 B.C.
Amos Divine punishment follows persistent sin.	**Joel*** The Day of the Lord and judgment of nations.	**Jeremiah** Jerusalem's judgment and coming glory.	**Daniel** The times of the Gentiles and Israel's kingdom.	**Haggai** Restoration of temple and kingdom foretold.
Hosea God's love for Israel.	**Obadiah*** Doom upon Edom.	**Nahum** Doom of Nineveh and Assyria.	**Ezekiel** Future restoration of Israel and the land.	**Zechariah** Messiah the Branch and King-Priest.
Jonah Nineveh, repent! God's concern for Gentiles.	**Isaiah** The coming Savior and Israel's King.	**Habakkuk** The Lord's kingdom and people will triumph.		**Malachi** Final judgment and warning to the nation.
	Micah Bethlehem's King and kingdom.	**Zephaniah** Remnant rescued for blessing.		

* Since these prophets do not specifically date their ministries, opinions vary as to where they should be placed.

Isaiah
Prophecy of the coming Savior and Israel's King

Writer. Isaiah ("Jehovah is salvation") is the great messianic prophet of the OT. For splendor of diction, brilliance of imagery, beauty of style, profundity and breadth of prophetic vision, he is without equal.

Messianic character of the book. Every glory of our Lord and every aspect of His life on earth are set out in this prophecy: His deity, eternity, pre-existence, creatorship, omnipotence, omnipresence, omniscience, incomparableness (40:12-18; 51:13); His incarnation (7:14; 9:6); His lowliness and youth in Nazareth (7:15; 9:2; 11:1); His appearance as the Servant of the Lord, anointed as such (11:2), and chosen and delighted in as such (42:1); His mild manner (42:2); His tender kindness (42:3; Matt. 12:18-20); His obedience (50:5); His message (61:1-2); His miracles (35:5-6); His sufferings (50:6; 52:13-15); His rejection (53:3); His shame (53:4-6); His death for others (53:8); His burial and resurrection (53:9-10); His ascension (52:13); His present high priestly ministry (53:12); His future glory (52:13; 53:12).

Outline

1-35	Prophecies from the standpoint of Isaiah's day
1-6	Vol. I Book of reproof and promise
7-12	Vol. II Book of Immanuel
13-23	Vol. III God's oracle of judgment on the nations
24-27	Vol. IV Book of judgment and promise
28-35	Vol. V Book of woes preceding restoration glories
36-39	Vol. VI Historical parenthesis: Historical interlude
40-66	Vol. VII Book of comfort: Prophecies from the standpoint of the exile
40	Comfort in the message of redemption
41	Comfort in the Lord's vindication
42	Comfort in the Lord's servant
43-45	Comfort in the national restoration
46-48	Comfort in the downfall of idolatry
49-57	Comfort in the prophecy of Messiah-Redeemer
58-66	Comfort in the prospect of Israel's future glory

Isaiah

Vol. I. Book of reproof and promise, 1:1-6:13

1. The Lord's case against Judah

1. Isaiah's preface. The prophet gives his name; the nature of the prophecy ("a vision," implying a supernatural revelation); the time, c. 750-680 B.C.; and the subject, concerning Judah and Jerusalem, since Isaiah was a prophet of the southern kingdom.

2-6. The Lord's accusation. The charge takes the form of a courtroom scene in which the whole universe, 2, is called upon to witness the twofold accusation of base ingratitude, 2-3, and rebellious apostasy, 4, illustrated by the figure of a diseased body, 5-6.

7-9. The Lord's punishment.

10-15. The Lord's rejection of their religious externalism.

16-20. The Lord's call to repentance and reformation.

21-23. The Lord's challenge to contrast Jerusalem, past and present.

24-31. The Lord's promised restoration of Jerusalem. Though a foretaste of the fulfillment is seen in the return from exile, the force of the prophecy indicates that the total fulfillment is yet future.

2. Jerusalem and the Day of the Lord

1-5. Jerusalem the center of the earth in the kingdom age. The vision refers to the time when Israel is converted and restored to Palestine. Jerusalem's exaltation to the center of government will be made possible by the Messiah as the ruling King-Judge.

6-22. The Day of the Lord. This is the time when the Lord visibly judges sinners on the earth (Rev. 4:1-19:16), preparatory to the kingdom as outlined in 1-5.

3. Judgment on Jerusalem and Judah

1-15. All classes of Judah's society are to be punished for their sin.

16-26. The Lord's judgment. The sins of the prophet's day demand the judgments of the Day of the Lord before national blessing can come.

4. The glory awaiting the redeemed remnant

1. The remnant survives the judgment of the Day of the Lord.

2. The remnant accepts the Messiah as the branch of the Lord.

3-4. The remnant is cleansed and converted, and hence is called "holy."

5-6. The remnant is sheltered and protected, by a pillar of cloud by day and a pillar of fire by night, recalling Israel's wilderness experience (Ex. 13:21-22).

5. God's people shown their sin and its result

1-7. By a parable. The nation Israel is represented under the figure of the vineyard of the Lord, 7.

8-23. By a list of their sins. Greed would be punished by famine, 8-10; drunkenness, 11-12, 22, by the miseries of the Captivity.

24-30. By a threat of captivity, with general desolation, 24-25, and foreign invasion, 26-30.

6. Isaiah's call and commission

1-4. The prophet sees God, i.e., "Jesus' glory" (John 12:41), in the year of Uzziah's death, 1.

5-7. The prophet sees himself and his sin, 5, and is cleansed, fire being the symbol of cleansing, 6-7.

8-10. The prophet is commissioned. The prophet accepts God's commission, 8, which involves a hardening and blinding judgment on the nation (Matt. 13:14-15).

11-13. The prophet is told the outcome of the commission.

Vol. II. Book of Immanuel, 7:1-12:6

7. The great messianic sign concerning Immanuel

1-2. Historical circumstances calling forth the sign. About 735 B.C. Ahaz faced the coalition of Rezin, king of Syria, and Pekah, king of Israel. They advanced against Jerusalem to punish Ahaz for not aligning himself with them to check the growing power of Assyria.

3-9. A message of encouragement. The prophet was sent to Ahaz to persuade him to trust in God instead of Assyria.

10-13. God's sign to confirm the prophet's message.

14-16. The great messianic sign itself. The NT plainly testifies that the ultimate fulfillment of the sign is the virgin birth of Christ (Matt. 1:22-23).

17-25. Threatened punishment of Ahaz. The severity of the punishment is told, 17.

8:1-9:7. Present deliverance a precursor to a future deliverer

8:1-4. The fall of Damascus and Samaria prefigured.

8:5-8. The choice of unbelief and its results. The people followed Ahaz and chose Assyria rather than God's guidance and help, which was symbolized by the gentle waters of the pool of Shiloah.

8:9-15. The challenge of God's grace. The Lord encouraged and instructed Isaiah and His faithful followers not to be frightened by the popular charge of conspiracy or treason, 12, hurled against them because of their opposition to an Assyrian alliance against the northern coalition.

8:16-20. The challenge to trust God's grace alone. The faithful prophet declared his own steadfast testimony, 18-19, and warned that those who claim inspiration from demon-controlled religion will be deprived of spiritual light, 19-20.

8:21-22. The alternative to trusting God would be the indescribable anguish of Assyrian invasion and deportation.

9:1-2. Prophecy of Immanuel as the great light.

9:3-5. Prophecy of Immanuel as the great liberator. He would liberate the nation from all its oppressors and foes, supernaturally, but in terrible final conflict, 5.

9:6-7. Prophecy of Immanuel as the great Lord. The humanity ("a child is born") as well as the deity ("Mighty God") of Immanuel are foretold.

9:8-10:4. Proud Samaria is doomed

9:8-21. Israel's pride and presumption would be punished by Syrian and Philistine invasion, 11-12.

10:1-4. Captivity was imminent.

10:5-34. The Assyrian invades Immanuel's land

5-19. Assyria, God's instrument for judging His people, will in turn be judged.

20-23. The return of a faithful remnant. The remnant will, like Isaiah and his followers, reject this false ruler and "truly rely on the Lord, the Holy One of Israel," 20.

24-34. Therefore Assyria is not to be feared by those who trust in the Lord, 24-27, even in her fearful advance on Immanuel's land, 28-32, for the Lord will make a sudden end of the Assyrian, 33-34.

11. Immanuel-King and His kingdom

1. Immanuel-King's Davidic descent. He is here prefigured as "a shoot" from the truncated "stump of Jesse," showing His obscurity and lowliness, the house of David being poor and unknown at the time of Christ's nativity.

2. Immanuel-King's enduement. The general enduement is "the Spirit of the Lord," which is the necessary qualification for righteous government.

3-5. Immanuel-King's equitable government. His belt will be righteousness and faithfulness, 5.

6-9. Immanuel-King's peaceful kingdom. All people, everywhere, will be completely dedicated to God's will, 9.

10. Immanuel-King will bring the Gentiles into the kingdom.

11-16. Immanuel-King will regather the Jews when His kingdom is set up, 11. This will be a second (final) regathering of a remnant from a worldwide dispersion, 11-12, consummated by divine power.

12. The remnant's song of redemption

1-3. The believer's song of redemption, a triumphant chorus of praise to Immanuel-Redeemer because divine anger is turned away and comfort abounds, 1; because God is the singer's salvation, 2; and because He is his strength and song, 2.

4-6. The remnant's united song of redemption.

Vol. III. God's oracles of judgment on the nations, 13:1-23:18

13. The judgment of Babylon

1-16. The confusion of the nations before destruction. Babel ("confusion") here appears symbolically to portray the political and governmental disorder that characterizes the earth during the times of the Gentiles (Luke 21:24).

17-22. Prophecy of Babylon's destruction in Isaiah's day.

14. Babylon's fall and Israel's restoration

1-3. Prophecy of Israel's restoration anticipates Babylon's fall.

4-11. Israel's song of triumph over Babylon's last king. This is not simply Nebuchadnezzar II nor Belshazzar, but the last-day political head of the restored Roman Empire (Rev. 13), "the man of lawlessness, the man doomed to destruction" (2 Thess. 2:3-4), "the little horn" (Dan. 7:8, 24-27; 11:36-45). He is seen in Sheol (cf. Rev. 19:20, where he is cast into Gehenna).

12-17. Satan addressed as empowering Babylon's last king.

18-27. Future destruction of the satanic

world system. This passage goes beyond the destruction of literal Babylon, 18-24, and of the Assyria of that day, 25, and includes "the whole world," 26, in preparation for God's order in the kingdom He has planned, 27.

28-32. Prophecy against the Philistines.

15-16. Judgment on Moab

Her arrogance and pride would be humbled by terrible devastation from Assyria, 16:10-14.

17. Judgment on Damascus and Samaria

Damascus and Ephraim (the northern kingdom) would be desolated, 1-3, but eventually Samaria would yield a remnant of true believers who would disavow idolatry, 3-8.

18. Judgment on Ethiopia

The prophet tells Ethiopian ambassadors that birds of prey will feed on their corpses rotting in a field of battle, 1-6.

19-20. Judgment on Egypt

Egypt will yet be terrified by the land of Judah because of God's purpose through it against Egypt, 19:16-18.

21. Judgment on Babylon, Edom, Arabia

1-10. The judgment of the desert by the sea. The "Desert by the Sea," 1, was Babylon (cf. 9). **11-12. Judgment on Edom.** "Dumah," 11 ("silence"), is a wordplay on "Edom." **13-17. Judgment on Arabia.** The northwestern tribes along the Red Sea, called Dedanites, noted for their flocks (Isa. 60:7) and their black tents, were to be driven into flight by conquering

> These chapters form a continuous prophecy on the subject of judgment in the Day of the Lord, followed by blessing. They have been called Isaiah's Apocalypse.

Assyrians and Chaldeans.

22. Judgment on Jerusalem

The world-renowned city, 1-4, invaded by armies, 5-7, was to suffer siege and calamity, 8-14. It is called the "Valley of Vision," 1, 5, for God revealed Himself on the hill of Zion, which was surrounded by valleys with higher hills beyond.

23. Judgment on Tyre

Isaiah foresaw the downfall of this commercial center of the world, 1-7. God had decreed this calamity because of their pride, 8-12.

Vol. IV. Book of judgment and promise, 24:1-27:13

24. The Day of the Lord and millennial blessing

1-13. The judgments of the Day of the Lord. The apocalyptic desolations are described, 3-13, and the reason for them specified, 5.
14-16. Interlude: the preservation and song of the remnant. Singing begins "in that day" and is heard because of God's deliverance through the Great Tribulation (Rev. 7:1-8; 14:1-5).
17-22. The judgment of the Day of the Lord continued. It will concentrate on the earth and wicked earth dwellers, and on Satan and demons, 21.
23. The millennial reign of Christ. It will be so

glorious that the sun and moon will be confounded when the Messiah "will reign on Mount Zion" in Jerusalem.

25. Israel's praise for kingdom blessing

1-5. Israel praises her Lord for His miraculous deliverances, 1.

6-8. Blessings for all nations described. The eternal state blends with this millennial scene.

9. Israel's reward for waiting.

10-12. Israel's enemies judged, including Moab.

26. Judah's millennial song

1-6. Praise the Lord's faithfulness and mercies. Jerusalem is celebrated as a saved city opening its gates to welcome the righteous, 1-2.

7-11. Experiences of waiting during the night.

12-18. Assurances of peace and deliverance. Israel restored and converted, enjoying the blessing of the land, expresses her worship of the Lord in glad praise and testimony.

19. Assurance of bodily resurrection of righteous OT saints. Although the restoration of Israel as a nation is symbolized by the figure of resurrection (Ezek. 37:1-11), this passage evidently has in mind physical resurrection.

20-21. Glimpse of the divine indignation in the Day of the Lord.

27. Punishment of Israel's enemies and kingdom triumph

1. Destruction of Israel's enemies.

2-9. The Lord's care for His own even in punishing is indicated under the figure of a vineyard (cf. Isa. 5:1-7), with Israel hereafter

flourishing, 6, after the punishment is over, 8-9.

10-11. Israel's enemies are destroyed—totally and finally.

12-13. The return of the remnant. This last word in this volume of judgment and promise tells of Israel's final regathering under the blowing of the trumpet (cf. Matt. 24:31) and future worship in Jerusalem (cf. 2:1-5).

Vol. V. Book of woes preceding restoration glories, 28:1-35:10

28. Woe against Ephraim

1-13. Judgment upon the ten tribes. Their threatened punishment by Assyrian invasion is foretold, 2-4. Nevertheless, a remnant will be preserved to confess the Lord as a "glorious crown" and "beautiful wreath" in the kingdom, 5.

14-29. Fate of Ephraim a warning to Judah. The scoffing rulers of Jerusalem have made "a covenant with death," 14-15, but all who trust in the false covenant rather than in God's deliverance through the Stone (Messiah), 16, will be swept away in judgment, 17-29.

29. Woe against Ariel (Jerusalem)

1-4. Jerusalem's last siege. Despite her sacred character as Ariel ("the lion of God"), associated with David, 1, a type of Jerusalem's great Deliverer ("the Lion of the tribe of Judah," Rev. 5:5), the Lord Himself through His instruments of punishment will encamp against her.

5-10. The Lord will then deal with Jerusalem's enemies.

11-12. This prophecy is for the end time. It is to be sealed because neither Sennacherib's siege nor the siege by the Romans fully accomplished it. Its fulfillment is still in the future.

13-16. The condition of the people is one of religious blindness and empty formalism.
17-24. Blessing for a redeemed remnant.

30-31. Warning against alliance with Egypt
30:1-14. The wickedness of the pro-Egypt party. They fostered a foolish cause, 1-7, by resisting God's word, 8-11, and calamity was to result from following their advice, 12-14.
30:15-33. Advice to trust in the Lord.
Ch. 31. The woe of trusting Egypt again outlined. A repeated condemnation of the Egyptian alliance is indicated, 1-3. The Lord promises to rescue Jerusalem, 4-9.

32. Messiah-King and His kingdom
1-8. Israel's ultimate deliverance by Messiah-King. The King (Jesus Christ) is seen as "a shelter from the wind and a refuge from the storm," 1-2, and His earthly rule is described, 3-8.
9-14. Israel's interim sins and sufferings outlined.
15-20. Hope for the future—the outpoured Spirit and the result. Results of the outpouring of the Spirit are blessing on the land, 15; prevalence of justice and righteousness, 16; peace and security, 17-20.

33. Punishment of the Assyrian, triumph of Christ
1-12. The destruction of Assyria declared.
13-16. The plight of the godless in the face of the Assyrian menace. Their fearful trembling is the result of their sin and unbelief.
17-24. Salvation by seeing Messiah-King in His beauty. Jerusalem will be seen as a secure city, filled with the Lord's majesty and deliverance, 20-22, and the remnant will divide the spoil, 23-24.

34. Armageddon and the destruction of Gentile world power
1-7. The battle of Armageddon. All nations are to be gathered to battle, 1-3. Frightful carnage results as the Lord wreaks vengeance upon the armies of the Satanic world system, centering in Edom, 4-6 (cf. Rev. 19:11-21; Isa. 63:1-6).
8-15. Desolation following this disaster.
16-17. Divine guarantee that Israel will possess and inhabit the land.

35. The glory of the kingdom
1-2. The restoration of the land and the manifestation of the Lord. Palestine, physically and climatically changed to welcome its Redeemer and the redeemed at the Second Coming, is poetically personified. With lilting joy, the desert, Arabah, Lebanon, Carmel, and Sharon see "the glory of the Lord, the splendor of our God."
3-7. Retrospect on the tribulation preceding blessing.
8-10. Return of the redeemed remnant to Zion. This will be by an appointed way, a highway, a holy way, a plainly marked way, 8, a safe way, 9.

Vol. VI. Historical parenthesis, 36:1-39:8

36-37. Overthrow of the Assyrian army
Chapters 36-39 form a historical parenthesis connecting the first part of the book (ch. 1-35),

Relief of a dying lioness, from the palace of Ashurbanipal, Nineveh.

consisting of predictions of judgment and blessings springing out of the Assyrian period, with the second part of the book, composed of prophecies of comfort emanating from the Babylonian period. Hezekiah's name is mentioned some 35 times in this section, and it is sometimes called the Volume of Hezekiah. This section is almost identical to the text of 1 Kings 18:13-20:19. It is likely that Isaiah wrote the material that was later incorporated into the court history of Judah and ultimately into the Book of the Kings.

Ch. 36. The Assyrian blatantly challenges the Lord. The arrogant conqueror Sennacherib in 701 B.C. sent his Assyrian commander-in-chief from Lachish, the Judean fortress commanding the road to Egypt, to demand the unconditional surrender of Judah. The commander met with Hezekiah's delegation, 1-3, and in its presence taunted Judah for trust in Egypt, 4-6, and in

Hezekiah's God, 7-10. He continued his blasphemous taunts before all the people of Jerusalem, 11-22.

Ch. 37. The Lord's reply to the challenge. Hezekiah laid the matter before the Lord in the temple, 1, and sent a delegation to Isaiah for counsel and prayer, 2-5. He received from the prophet two assurances of deliverance, 6-7, 21-35.

38-39. Hezekiah's sickness and sin

Ch. 38. Hezekiah's deliverance from serious illness. Isaiah announced that Hezekiah's sickness would be fatal, 1. The monarch's prayer, 2-3, was answered, and God added 15 years to the king's life and confirmed His promise by the "sign," 4-8 (explainable only as a miracle).

Ch. 39. Hezekiah's foolish pride. Hezekiah's egotistical folly in displaying all his wealth and power, 2, drew a scathing rebuke from Isaiah and a warning of the Babylonian Captivity, 3-7.

Vol. VII. Book of comfort, 40:1-66:24

40. Comfort for delivered Israel

1-11. The call and circumstances of the promised comfort. A call is given to comfort Jerusalem, 1, because her suffering is foreseen as ended and her sin forgiven, 2.

12-26. The character of the Comforter. His power is limitless to comfort, 12. His wisdom is unsearchable, 13-14. His Being is incomparable, 15-17. His worship must be spiritual, 18-26.

27-31. The prescription for present comfort.

41. The Lord's case against idolatry

1-7. Idolaters are arraigned.

8-20. God's people are encouraged. The basis of this encouragement, 8-9, is the fact that they are God's servants, His elect people, Abraham's progeny, 8, and objects of former deliverance, 9.

21-24. The idols themselves are challenged.

25-29. The Lord Himself produces proof of His sole deity. He alone has irresistible power to effect Cyrus's rise, and infallible foresight to foretell it more than a century and a half in advance.

42. The Messiah-Servant of the Lord

1-4. God (the Father) presents the Servant in relation to Himself as His Servant, His elect, and His delight, 1.

5-9. The prophecy of the Servant's ministry. The ratification of the commission is assured, 8-9, by the deity and authority of the Commissioner, 8, and the integrity of His word, 9.

10-12. Expression of praise and worship to God for the coming Servant.

13-17. Prediction of the Servant's vengeance He will triumph as a warrior over His foes, 13. He will terminate His silence at His enemies' insults, 14-15. He will treat His friends with mercy, 16, but will shame idolaters, 17.

18-25. Exposure and reproof of Israel the unfaithful servant.

43:1-44:5. Assurance for the restored nation

43:1-7. Promise of comfort for the remnant. The basis of the promise is twofold: (1) the Lord is Creator, and (2) He is the Redeemer of the yet-to-be-restored nation.

43:8-13. Purpose of God in the nation. It was to be a witness to the pagan nations blinded by idolatry, 8-9, of the one true God and His Servant, 10-13.

43:14-21. God's sovereign power will be demonstrated by crushing the Chaldeans and restoring their captives.

43:22-28. The nation's punishments are the result of its ingratitude. This is manifested in prayerlessness, 22; religious indifference, 23; and sin, 24, all in the face of God's ready grace to forgive, 25, and to plead and reason with it, 26-28.

44:1-5. God's saving grace will be manifested in the conversion of the servant nation.

44:6-28. Israel a witness to the one true God

6-8. God's declaration of His sole deity.

9-20. Satire on the sheer folly of idolatry. It darkens the mind and blinds the eyes to spiritual truth.

21-23. God's nation Israel is to be a witness

against idolatry.
24-28. The Lord decrees the restoration of His people through Cyrus. He calls Cyrus "my shepherd" who shall "accomplish all that I please," 28 (cf. 41:2-4, 25-29; 46:11; 48:14).

45. Cyrus a type of Messiah
1-6. The Lord promises irresistible conquest to Cyrus as a type of Messiah.
7-25. The Lord's sovereignty is vindicated against human critics. His lordship is vindicated by what He has done, 7-12, by His raising up Cyrus as His servant, 13, by the prediction that the Gentiles are to be converted as well as Israel, 14-19, and by His open invitation to the "ends of the earth" to believe and be saved, 20-25.

46-47. Deliverance from Babylon and its lessons
Ch. 46. The helplessness of idols in contrast to the Lord's omnipotence. Bel (Marduk, Jer. 50:2, the patron god of Babylon) and Nebo (an influential Babylonian deity, patron of culture and learning) will be a burden to the beasts who cart them into humiliating captivity, 1-2. In contrast, God bears and carries His people from birth till old age, creating and redeeming them, 3-4.
47:1-7. The proud city of Babylon will fall because of its excessive cruelty to God's people.
47:8-15. The godless culture, philosophy, and religion of this world are doomed.

48. The Lord's dealing with disobedient Israel
1-8. The Lord presents the evidence of fulfilled prophecy. Idolatrous, hypocritical

Entrance to Hezekiah's tunnel, Jerusalem.

Jews, 1-2, are confronted with the truth of fulfilled prophecy as a manifestation of the omniscient power of God against any claim they might make for their idol.
9-11. God upholds His glory by means of Israel's punishment.
12-16. God will raise up a Gentile deliverer to liberate His people from Babylon.
17-19. He laments the tragedy of their disobedience. The purpose of His punishment is to teach them "what is best" and to lead them "in the way [they] should go," 17.
20-22. They are to advertise His redemption from Babylon.

49. The Messiah-Servant and His mission
1-4. The Servant's arresting exclamation.

Dramatically the Lord summoned the Gentiles and announced to them that His call is divine, 1.

5-13. The Lord's assurance of the unqualified success of His Servant.

14-26. The Lord encourages disheartened Israel. He has not forgotten His people; they are inscribed on the palms of His hands, 14-18. He will restore and bless them in their land, 19-23, punishing their enemies, 24-26.

50. Disobedient Israel versus the obedient Servant

1-3. The disobedient people presented.

4-9. The obedient Servant-Savior prophesied. He will come as the taught one, the docile one, the one obedient to suffering, rejection, and death, 4-6. The Servant will conquer as a courageous champion, 7-9.

10-11. His promise of salvation and threat of doom.

51. Encouragement for the faithful

1-3. The faithful are given a promise of Zion's future.

4-8. The faithful are assured of the fulfillment of the promise to Zion.

9-16. The faithful petition for a demonstration of the promise by deliverance. The prayer is presented, 9, and enforced by a recital of the wonders of past deliverance from Egypt, 9-11. It is answered, 12-16, with regard to the fearful, 12; the fettered, 14-15; and the faithful, 16.

17-20. Predicament of Jerusalem portrayed.

21-23. Prediction of Jerusalem's future redemption. The Lord assures her that He is her God and will speedily end her affliction, 22. He will make her persecuting foes drink the same cup as she had to drink, 23.

52. Jerusalem aroused to glory

1-2. Appeal to Jerusalem to prepare herself for glory. She is to arouse herself from the humiliation of her captivities, put on her high priestly apparel (cf. Zech. 3:1-8), separate herself from defilement, and assume her regal position, 2.

3-6. The case the Lord presents for His people's liberation.

7-10. Praise of prophet and people at Zion's liberation. The desolated city is commanded to rejoice, 9. The Lord is glorified and His worldwide salvation published, 10.

11-12. The importance of their repatriation demands speed and thorough separation from Babylon, 11, with an orderly return in dependence upon God, 12.

13-15. The preeminence of the Servant epitomized. He is exalted because the Lord God views the Servant as divinely commissioned and qualified, 13. He startles many nations and awes kings into silence as a result of His exaltation, 15.

53. Prophecy of the Messiah-Servant as sinbearer

1-3. The person of the Servant despised.

4-6. The passion of the Servant summarized. Although He died for mankind in general, this is the penitential confession of the future repentant nation. She will glimpse His vicarious bearing of her (and the world's) sins, as well as see His shame and misrepresentation, stripes and wounds.

7-10a. The perseverance of the Servant particularized. He suffered silently, 7; unjustly, for our good and in our place, 8; ignominiously, 9; and under the frowns of heaven, 10.

10b-12. The recompense of the Servant is realized. He is rewarded and justifies many, 11; obtains universal dominion, 12; and is given a high priestly ministry, 12.

54. The radiant joy of restored Israel
1-10. The blessings of the converted nation. Her restoration will be permanent, and God's covenant of peace will not depart from her, 7-10.
11-17. The radiant beauty of the restored nation. She is likened to a beautiful city, 11-12. Her citizens will become spiritually prosperous, 13-14, and be secure, 15-17.

55. Worldwide evangelistic invitation
1. The invitation offered. The salvation offered is priceless, having already been purchased by Christ's own blood (Isa. 53:1-8; 1 Peter 1:19).
2-7. The invitation enforced, 2-4, extended and defined, 5-7.
8-13. The invitation authorized and accepted. It is not authorized by any human being, 8-9, but by God Himself, 9-10, and this because of the certain fulfillment of His word, 10-11.

56:1-8. Gentiles included in kingdom blessing
1-2. Latter-day Israel admonished to maintain a godly witness. She is to preserve justice, do righteousness, keep the Sabbath, and refrain from doing evil, as the Lord's salvation is about to be revealed.
3-8. Blessing is promised to non-Israelites.

56:9-57:21. Condemnation of the wicked in Israel
56:9-12. The sins of wicked rulers in Israel denounced. These included spiritual blindness, covetousness, gluttony, and false optimism.

Relief of Arabs fleeing from Assyrians.

57:1-13. The sins of the wicked populace in Israel denounced. They pay no attention to the death of a righteous man, 1-2. They give themselves to idolatry, 3-10, but find no benefit, 11-13.
57:14-21. Mercy for the repentant, but judgment for the wicked.

58. False worship versus the true
1-5. Hypocritical worship and Israel's sins.
6-7. True worship outlined.
8-14. The promises for the repentant remnant. All the great future blessings of the converted remnant of Israel are set forth. It is the focus of the entire closing section of the book.

59. The coming of the Redeemer to Zion
1-8. Israel's unbelief and sin of the last days. The terrible catalog of the nation's depravity

Isaiah speaks of Jerusalem's glory in the kingdom age.

(cf. Rom. 3:10-18) shows what has separated her from God.

9-15. Israel's last-day confession.

16-19. The Lord's gracious intervention. He personally interposes on their behalf, 16, judging and punishing the wicked, 17-18.

20-21. The Second Coming of the Redeemer. Christ appears in person for the salvation of those who turn from sin (Rom. 11:26-27).

60. Jerusalem's glory in the kingdom age

1-2. Israel enlightened in the kingdom age. Messiah the Light shines on Jerusalem, and Jerusalem shines on the earth, 1.

3-14. Israel enlarged in the kingdom age. Gentiles are drawn to the Light, 3, and Jews return to the Light, 4.

15-22. Israel exalted in the kingdom age. Her humiliation gives way to exaltation, 15; her weakness to strength, 16; her poverty to wealth, 17; her troubles to salvation and safety, 18; her darkness to perpetual light, 19-20; her sin to righteousness, 21; and her insignificance to importance, 22.

61. Messiah's ministry for Israel and the world

1-2. Messiah's ministry in His first coming detailed.

2-3. Messiah's ministry in His second coming.

4-9. Results of Messiah's ministry at His second coming. Waste places are rebuilt, 4. Israel, lately enslaved, will be served, 5; lately abased, will be exalted, 6. Lately afflicted, she will be enriched and comforted, 7; lately scattered, will be divinely gathered, 8; lately reproached, will be fully vindicated, 9.

10-11. The joy of Messiah's ministry is depicted.

62. Jerusalem is praised

1. The divine concern for Zion.

2-5. The results of the divine concern for Zion. Zion will be honored by the nations, 2. She will be called by a new name, 2-4. The name will be given because the Lord's delight will be in her and she will be married, as illustrated in the simile in 5.

6-12. The concrete expression of the divine concern for Zion. The final end-time blessing is expressed in a fourfold name for the Lord's own—"the Holy People," "the Redeemed of the Lord," "Sought After," "the City No Longer Deserted," 12.

63:1-6. The Messiah-Avenger and the day of vengeance

"The year of the Lord's favor" is ended and fearful judgment sweeps the earth (Rev. 19:11-21).

1-2. Two rhetorical questions are asked: "Who is this coming from Edom?" and "Why are your garments red?"

3-6. Messiah the Avenger's answer. The brilliant red of His garments (Rev. 14:18-19) is explained as the result of treading the winepress of wrath against His enemies, 3-4.

63:7-64:12 The remnant's great prayer of intercession

63:7-19. The remnant remembers past deliverances. Isaiah, as the representative of the godly remnant, utters one of the greatest prayers in the Bible, to be prayed by the godly remnant in the Tribulation preceding the kingdom.

64:1-4. The remnant beseeches the Lord to assert His power over the nations.

64:5-7. The penitent confession of the believing remnant.

64:8-12. The appeal for pardon and restoration. The touching plea is from a chastened and yielded people, 8-9, reviewing their punishments, 10-11, and interceding for help, 12.

65. The Lord's answer—His mercy reserved for the remnant

1-7. The sins of latter-day apostate Israel.

8-10. The election and blessing of the righteous remnant.

11-12. The judgment of latter-day apostate Israel. Idolatry, covetousness, rebellion, and disobedience destine the apostates for slaughter.

13-16. The blessings of the remnant vs. the curses of apostate Israel.

17-25. The glories and blessings in store for God's own. The prophet glimpses the eternal sinless state, 17. In the kingdom he sees Jerusalem blessed, 18-19, longevity restored, 20, security and happiness prevailing, 21-23, prayer answered, 24, and the curse lifted, 25.

66. Synoptic finale; the entire prophecy in retrospect

1-4. Wicked worship of age-end apostate Israel. The final chapter restates the leading prophetic themes of the book. The apostate mass of the Jewish nation (Israel) restored in unbelief erects a temple in Jerusalem and resumes its ancient worship. This is a worship of unbelief and is an abomination to the Lord (cf. 2 Thess. 2:4; Dan. 9:27; Matt. 24:15; Rev. 11:1-2).

5. The remnant persecuted and encouraged.

6. The coming of the Lord.

7-9. Israel's national rebirth. A nation is regenerated in a moment (Rom. 11:26-27).

10-14. Jerusalem's millennial glory and exaltation.

15-17. Messiah the avenger and the day of vengeance.

18-21. Gentiles brought into the kingdom.

22. The perpetuity of Israel and the eternal state. The truth of the eternal state is used as a simile for the fact of Israel's perpetual existence.

23. Blessings for the righteous.

24. The destiny of the wicked. Eternal perdition is their portion (cf. Mark 9:44-48; Rev. 20:14-15).

Jeremiah
Death throes of a decadent nation

The world of Jeremiah. Jeremiah ministered when Assyria was tottering on the brink of ruin, and Babylon and Egypt were struggling to take over world control. He warned of Babylon's victory, but Judah failed to repent of her sin and accept his warnings. As a result Judah suffered destruction, but the prophet announced that she would be restored, and through Messiah would come into worldwide blessing.

Arrangement of book. The messages that are dated show that the book was not arranged in chronological order. For instance, messages in *Josiah's* reign are found in 1:2 and 3:6, while those in *Jehoiakim's* reign are in 22:18; 25:1; 26:1; 35:1; 36:1; 45:1. Those in *Zedekiah's* reign are in 21:1, 8; 27:2, 3, 12; 28:1; 29:3; 32:1; 34:2; 37:1-2; 38:5; 39:1; 49:34; 51:59. The lack of chronological order is evidently intentional. Probably the order is to be found in the arrangement of the subject matter by contrast, not by date of composition.

Outline

1-45	Prophecies against Judah and Jerusalem
1-20	Under Josiah and Jehoiakim
21-39	At various periods till Jerusalem's fall
40-45	After Jerusalem's fall
46-51	Prophecies against the nations
52	Historical appendix

Replica of the Ishtar Gate, Babylon.

Jeremiah

Kings of Judah in the time of Jeremiah

Manasseh 697-643
Jeremiah born under this wicked tyrant.

Amon 643-641
Doom of Judah threatened.

Josiah 641-609
This godly king began his reforms 627. Jeremiah's call 626.

Book of the law found, followed by Josiah's great reformation 621,(2 Kings 22-23).

Scythian invasion 620 (Jer. 4); growing power of Neo-Babylonia 625-605; fall of Nineveh. Josiah killed at Megiddo 609 by Pharaoh-Neco.

Jehoahaz 609
Reigned three months—carried to Egypt.

Jehoiakim 609-598
Wicked idolater.

Rise of Nebuchadnezzar II 605-562.

Jehoiachin 598-597
Reigned three months—carried to Babylon.

Zedekiah 597-586
Zedekiah visited Babylon 593.

Lachish Letters 589.

Jerusalem sacked 586.

Temporary end of Davidic dynasty.

1. Introduction

1-3. Superscription. Jeremiah's ministry, 2, extended from Josiah's thirteenth year (627 B.C.) to Zedekiah's eleventh year (586 B.C.).

4-19. Jeremiah's call. God's electing grace, 5, and the prophet's humility, 6, resulted in a definite commission to preach the unpopular message, "to uproot and tear down, to destroy and overthrow," as well as the positive ministry, "to build and to plant," 7-10. Jeremiah's encounter with God and commission were buttressed by the vision of the almond tree, 11, and the vision of the boiling pot, 13. The almond tree is the first harbinger of spring.

2:1-3:5. Sermon 1—Sin of the nation

2:1-19. A faithful Lord vs. an unfaithful people. The review of the Lord's goodness, 1-3, is followed by an exposé of the apostasy of the nation, 4-13.

2:20-37. The divine impeachment and expostulation. Israel had become like a stubborn ox, 20; a wild vine, 21; a lustful prostitute, 22-25; a disgraced thief, 26; a foolish idolater, 27-28; an ungrateful people, 29-32; an impudent transgressor, 33; and a blinded nation, 34-37.

3:1-5. The results of Israel's unfaithfulness.

3:6-6:30. Sermon 2
—Devastation from the north
3:6-25. Judah's apostasy greater than Israel's.

Ch. 4. The foe from the north. Jeremiah is apparently speaking of the imminent Babylonian invasion.

Ch. 5. Judgment and impending disaster. The weeping prophet of Anathoth bewailed the sins of Jerusalem, his moral sensitivity pained.

Ch. 6. Continued warning. A great destruction was coming on Jerusalem, 1-26. Jeremiah appeared as the Lord's tester to try the Lord's people, 27-30 (cf. Job 23:10).

7-10. Sermon 3—Threat of exile

This temple message, like the two preceding sermons, was a stern rebuke and warning, but centered in the religious conditions in Judah.

Ch. 7. Rebuke of apostate religiosity. The destruction of Shiloh (18 miles north of Jerusalem) should have been a lesson, 12-14. The Lord's anger burned at Jerusalem's idolatry, 15-19, and apostasy, 20-34.

Ch. 8. Further warnings of judgment. All classes of God's people were corrupted, prophets as well as priests, 10.

Ch. 9. Jeremiah weeps over sinners. The prophet was torn between pity for sinners and revulsion at their sin, 1, which could not be condoned, 2-26.

Ch. 10. The Lord and idolatry.

11-13. Sermon 4—The broken covenant; sign of the linen belt

Ch. 11-12. The broken covenant. The rebukes and warnings of this sermon were a result of the violation of the Palestinian covenant (Deut. 28:1-30:9).

Ch. 13. The parable of the linen belt. The pure white linen garment worn next to the skin symbolized the pristine purity of the nation in fellowship with the Lord. The wineskins, 12-14, filled to the top, symbolized the people's drunkenness and their ruin under divine judgment.

14-17. Sermon 5—The drought; sign of the unmarried prophet

Ch. 14. Drought and the nation's doom. This terrible calamity, 1-6, the empty ritualistic prayers of the nation, 7-9, and their rejection by the Lord, 10-12, are described.

Ch. 15. The Lord's answer to Jeremiah.

Ch. 16. The approaching disaster, the wages of sin. The inexorable fulfillment of God's word is shown by the Lord's denying marriage to the prophet, 1-4, and even denying him observance of funerals and festivities, 5-9, seen as signs of impending ordeals because of Judah's apostasies, 10-13.

Ch. 17. Judah's terrible sin. Sabbath desecration, an index of their disloyalty to the Lord, was warned against, 19-27.

18-20. Sermon 6
—Sign of the potter's house

Ch. 18. The prophet's visit to the potter. This episode furnished a lesson in God's sovereign molding of His people (Rom. 9:20-24).

Ch. 19. The broken clay jar was another sign that the Lord would smash the idolatry-ridden people. Topheth (see 7:31) was the center of the cruel Molech cult.

Ch. 20. Public punishment of Jeremiah. Jeremiah's severe testing produced momentary perplexity and complaint, but faith triumphed over unbelief in the prophet, 7-18.

21-24. Oracles concerning reigning kings

Ch. 21. Jeremiah's message to Zedekiah.
Ch. 22. Jeremiah's message concerning other kings of Judah. This was an introductory oracle warning the Davidic court, 1-9, and comforting Shallum (Jehoahaz), who reigned only three months and was carried to Egypt (608 B.C.), 11-12.
Ch. 23. Great messianic prophecy. The false shepherds (unworthy rulers) of Judah, 1-2, furnished the somber background for the bright prophecy of kingdom regathering and restoration, 3-4, under Messiah, the "righteous Branch," 5, "The Lord Our Righteousness," 6.
Ch. 24. Vision of the two baskets of figs directed against Zedekiah. The good figs symbolized the best of the people carried to Babylon with Jehoiachin (597 B.C.). The bad figs stood for the apostates who remained in Jerusalem to support the wicked Zedekiah.

25. Prediction of the 70-year captivity

1-11. The exile is declared, as a 70-year captivity, 8-11.
12-38. Judgment of the nations and the Day of the Lord. Babylon with its king was to be punished, 12-14, as well as "all the nations," 15-29.

26. Jeremiah faces threat of death

1-11. His prediction of the destruction of the temple. All classes rejected the truth and persecuted the prophet.
12-24. Jeremiah's deliverance. Uriah's martyrdom, under Jehoiakim, 20-23, is also described.

27-28. The sign of the yokes

Ch. 27. The divinely imposed yoke of Babylon. Jeremiah saddled himself with an ox yoke to symbolize how Babylon would put a yoke on the neck of Jerusalem and Judah.
Ch. 28. Opposition by false prophets.

29. Jeremiah comforts the exiles

1-23. His letter sent to Babylon. Jeremiah urged the people to be law-abiding, peaceful exiles and to multiply, 1-9, against the day of restoration after 70 years, 10.
24-32. Shemaiah's attack and Jeremiah's second letter.

30-31. Restoration and messianic promises

30:1-17. The time of trouble for Jacob. Jeremiah's dark warnings of judgment were relieved by a prophecy of the glorious future of the nation, ch. 30-31.
30:18-24. Israel's restoration to kingdom glory. They will be restored as the Lord's people, 22.
31:1-26. The nation's homegoing and salvation.
31:27-40. The new covenant and the everlasting nation. This restoration of the Lord's blessing is based on the new covenant, 31-34. The old covenant was the law covenant grounded in legal observance. The new covenant (Heb. 8:8-12) would be entirely on the basis of grace and the sacrificed blood of Christ, which would be the foundation of Israel's future inward restoration to God's favor.

Archaeological light

The Lachish Ostraca discovered at Lachish in 1935 belong to this exact time. Letter No. IV says, "We are watching for the fire signals of Lachish . . . for we no longer can see the signals of Azekah." The names, places, and circumstances of these 21 Hebrew inscribed tablets closely resemble the times of Jeremiah just before the fall of Lachish, Azekah, and Jerusalem, 589-586 B.C.

32.Jeremiah's faith in the restoration

1-25. The sign of the prophet's faith. He purchased land in Anathoth, early in 586 B.C., before the fall of Jerusalem. Storage of deeds, written on papyrus, in earthen jars is known from Elephantine in Egypt, 14.

26-44. The Lord's answer.

33. The great prophecy of the Davidic kingdom

1-5. Jerusalem's imminent overthrow. A call to prayer was issued, 1-3, as the siege of Jerusalem was begun. This picture of impending disaster furnished the dark background against which was flashed the future glory of the nation.

6-14. Future blessing and glory.

15-26. The Davidic king and his kingdom. "In those days" is the time of the second coming of Christ when He, the "righteous Branch" will come to sit on the throne of His father David (Luke 1:31-33; cf. 2 Sam. 7:8-16).

34. Jeremiah's warning to Zedekiah

1-7. The warning. The siege of the city impending, Jeremiah warned Zedekiah of its fall. Lachish, 7, the fortress city 23 miles southwest

of Jerusalem, and Azekah, 11 miles north of Lachish, are well known from the Lachish Letters.

8-22. Zedekiah's treachery. Zedekiah released all Hebrew slaves (Ex. 21:2) hoping to "buy" God's favor and provide more fighting men. When the siege was temporarily lifted, Zedekiah's reversal of this policy exposed his true intentions.

35. The loyalty of the Recabites

1-11. The command concerning them. A religious order inculcating the simplicity and purity of Bedouin life, the Recabites were founded by Jonadab, son of Recab, during Jehu's reign.

12-19. The lesson for the Jews. The Recabites refused to drink wine and were obedient to their ancestor Recab, 6, while the Jews were utterly disobedient to the Lord's command.

36. Jehoiakim's opposition to the Word of God

1-20. The reading of the scroll. The purpose of the scroll was to set before the people the evil coming on them, so they might turn from their sin.

21-26. Jehoiakim cuts and burns the scroll.

27-32. Indestructibility of God's Word. The Word moves on, but pronounces doom on its would-be destroyers.

37-38. Jeremiah's experiences during the siege

37:1-10. Jeremiah's response to Zedekiah's inquiry. Jeremiah warned that the Chaldeans would shortly return and burn the city, 6-10.

37:11-38:13. Jeremiah's arrest. Jeremiah was

charged with desertion and treason.

38:14-28. Jeremiah's final appeal to Zedekiah. His wise advice to surrender was again rejected.

39. The fall of Jerusalem

1-10. The burning of the city and fate of Zedekiah. The Word of God through Jeremiah was vindicated. The city was destroyed, Zedekiah's sons were killed, Zedekiah's eyes were put out, and he was carried in chains to Babylon.

11-18. Kind treatment of Jeremiah. He was given a choice to go to Babylon or stay in Palestine.

40-41. Murder of Gedaliah

40:1-8. Jeremiah chooses to cast his lot with Gedaliah. The Babylonians appointed Gedaliah as governor over the towns of Judah, 5. In 1935 a seal inscribed, "Belonging to Gedaliah, who is over the house," was found in ashes left by Nebuchadnezzar's fires at Lachish. Jeremiah went to Gedaliah and "stayed with him among the people who were left behind in the land," 6.

40:9-16. Plot against Gedaliah. His wise regime prospered, 9-12. But Ishmael was sent to assassinate him, 13-16.

Ch. 41. The crime perpetuated. Ishmael slew Gedaliah, 1-3, and fled to Ammon.

42-43. The remnant's flight to Egypt

Ch. 42. Jeremiah the intercessor. The remnant in dire perplexity appealed to Jeremiah to pray for them, 1-6, but when the answer came from the Lord that they should remain in the land, they refused God's word and decided to go down to Egypt anyway, 7-22.

43:1-7. Rebellion against Jeremiah and the trip to Egypt. The people took Jeremiah along to Egypt.

43:8-13. Jeremiah's prediction of Nebuchadnezzar's conquest of Egypt. This came true in 568 B.C. when Nebuchadnezzar, "my servant" (25:9; 27:6; cf. 43:10), invaded Egypt against Amasis (Ahmosis II) (cf. 46:13-20).

44. Jeremiah's final plea in Egypt

1-19. His admonition of the Jews in Egypt. The diaspora at Pathros impudently defied Jeremiah, 15-16, declaring they would continue adoration of the "Queen of Heaven," 17-19 (the Assyrian Ishtar, Canaanite Astarte, Greek Aphrodite, Roman Venus), a polluted cult.

20-30. The Lord's answer and sign. The sign given to confirm God's word through Jeremiah was Pharaoh Hophra, who was given "over to his enemies" and slain, 30. He was assassinated by Ahmosis II.

45. Jeremiah's message to Baruch recalled

1-3. Baruch's initial complaint. Baruch, as Jeremiah's secretary and associate, was told at the beginning of his ministry of the difficulties ahead.

4-5. The Lord's sustaining promise (cf. 39:15-18).

46. Prophecy against Egypt

This section of prophecies against foreign nations, ch. 46-51, compares with Isaiah 13-23 and Ezekiel 25-32.

1-12. Prediction concerning Pharaoh Neco. Neco II of Egypt, in June, 604 B.C., was routed at

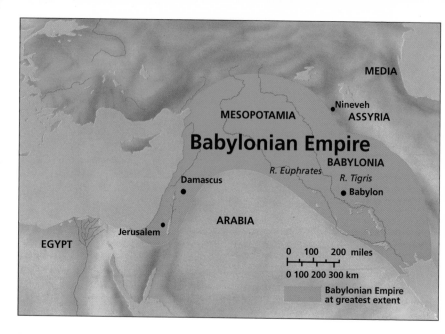

Carchemish. Victorious crown prince Nebuchadnezzar pursued his defeated foe to Egypt, 2-6.

13-26. Nebuchadnezzar's invasion of Egypt. This prophecy was fulfilled in 568 B.C. (see note on 43:8-13).

27-28. Promise of future blessing to Israel.

47. Prophecy against the Philistines

1-4. The advance of Nebuchadnezzar.

5-7. Results of Nebuchadnezzar's invasion. The Philistines were Indo-Europeans from Caphtor (Crete), the main wave of them settling in southwest Palestine in the 12th century B.C.

48. Prophecy against Moab

1-19. The overthrow of Moab.

20-47. Reason for the overthrow. Moab was to reap the harvest she had sown, 20-28, and was to be punished for her pride, 29-42. After terrible devastation Moab would be restored, 43-47.

49. Prophecy against various nations

1-6. Against Ammon. Ammon was the northern "brother" nation of Moab (Gen. 19:30-38).

7-22. Against Edom. Teman, 7, is modern Tawilan, some three miles east of Sela (Petra), the rock-cut city.

23-27. Against Damascus.

28-33. Against Kedar and Hazor.

34-39. Against Elam. Elam, with its capital at Susa, was overrun by Nebuchadnezzar in the winter of 596 B.C. "The bow of Elam" refers to the skill of Elamite archers, 35.

A fortified city under attack.

51. Prophecy against Babylon continued

1-5. Divine judgment upon Babylon. Babylon would be mowed down and winnowed like grain, a common threshing figure indicating judgment (Isa. 21:10).

6-10. Address to the remnant. The whole chapter is a forecast of the destruction of the satanic world system at the end-time before the kingdom-coming of Messiah.

11-19. Attack by the Medes. Media lay northeast of Babylonia.

20-33. Babylon's utter ruin. As a hammer ("war club"), 20-23, Babylon was God's instrument to punish His disobedient people. But Babylon would fall like Assyria, 24-26.

34-40. Israel's deliverance was again reviewed.

41-64. Babylon's fall continued. Sheshach, 41-43, was Babylon, which would be inundated by attackers.

52. Fall and captivity of Judah; Jehoiachin's liberation

1-30. The fall of the city. This final chapter is a historical appendix, largely a repetition of 2 Kings 24:18-25:30 (cf. also Jer. 39:1-10; 40:7-43:7). Three deportations are enumerated, 28-30, apparently connected with Jehoiachin's exile in 597 B.C. (2 Kings 24:12-16); the suppression of Zedekiah's revolt in 586 B.C; and the punishment for Gedaliah's assassination (40:7-41:18).

31-34. Jehoiachin's liberation. See 2 Kings 25:27-30.

50. Prophecy against Babylon

1-3. Fall to Persia. Two themes interlace: the fall of the historical Babylon of that day and the fall of the future Babylon (Rev. 17-18). The gods of Babylon were confounded by the prophecy of Babylon's fall—Bel (Baal) and Marduk, the two chief deities. The disaster came out of the "north," a reference to Cyrus the Persian who took Babylon in October, 539 B.C. (cf. Dan. 7:4-5).

4-7. Return of the exiles. This prediction included but went beyond the return from Babylon in 536 B.C. and embraced the final pre-kingdom regathering.

8-16. Fall of Babylon resumed.

17-20. Israel's restoration. Israel will be regenerated and regathered in the last day.

21-32. Divine judgment on Babylon.

33-34. Israel's deliverance repeated.

35-46. Babylon's downfall repeated. No nation can defy God with impunity.

Lamentations
Lament over Jerusalem's desolation

Outline

1   Desolated Jerusalem cries for pity
2   The Lord's chastening and its results
3   Heart cry of a chastened people
4   The horrors of the siege and fall of the city
5   ament and petition for restoration

Author. There is little doubt that Jeremiah was the author.

Literary form. Of the five poems, the first four are alphabetic acrostics. Poems (ch.) 1, 2, and 4 have 22 verses apiece, each beginning with one of the 22 letters of the Hebrew alphabet. Poem (ch.) 3 has three verses to each letter, totaling 66. Poem (ch.) 5 has 22 verses, but is not in alphabetic order. Dirge (*qinah*) meter, 3+2, prevails, with a lively three beat trailing away in a sad two beat.

Message. "The Lord is afflicted when His people die; He suffers when they suffer," is the theme of this book (cf. Ex. 3:7). It is because of His loving-kindness that His own are not "consumed" (3:22). "His compassions never fail. They are new every morning; great is your faithfulness" (3:22-23). Tradition has the suffering prophet weeping in a grotto outside Jerusalem's north wall under the knoll called Golgotha where the suffering Savior was to die. However that may be, the Spirit of Christ in the prophet made him in a real sense a prefigurement of our Lord (Jer. 13:17), as the Master likewise wept over the erring city (Matt. 23:36-38).

Praying at the Western Wall, Jerusalem.

Lamentations

Remains of an Israelite Tower, Jerusalem.

1. Desolated Jerusalem cries for pity

1-11. Her desolation is described. Only twice does the voice of the city, personified as a widow, speak in this section, 9b, 11b. The rest of the verses describe the misery of the ruined city. When she speaks, she breathes a prayer.

12-22. The personified city bewails her destruction.

2. The Lord's chastening and its results

1-8. The Lord's punishment of the city. Jerusalem's woe was not a piece of bad luck or a mere accident. "The Lord" occurs more than seven times in this section as the author of her calamity.

9-17. The results of the Lord's punishment. The city is desolated and spiritual darkness befalls its prophets and people, 9-10.

18-22. The prophet's exhortation to true repentance and his prayer.

3. Heart cry of a chastened people

1-24. A psalm of personal faith in God. The prophet Jeremiah identifies himself with the chastened people, and in agony pours out his heart to the Lord in faith.

25-51. Jeremiah advises repentance and submission to God.

52-66. Prayer for vindication against the enemy. Jeremiah recalls the Lord's faithful blessing in times past, and he pleads for the punishment of Jerusalem's destroyers.

4. Horrors of the siege and fall of the city

1-20. Jerusalem's disaster described. Terrible famine stalked the city, 3-9, accompanied by horrible cannibalism, 10.

21-22. Prediction of disaster on Edom.

5. Lament and petition for restoration

1-18. Lament over Judah's misery under Babylon's heel.

19-22. Intercession for divine mercy. These verses echo Psalms 74:12; 79:5-8; 80:1-7, and capture the plea of the faithful remnant for the establishment of the kingdom.

Ezekiel
Role of divine disciple

The prophet. Ezekiel ("God strengthens") was the son of a Zadokite priest. He was deported to Babylon in 597 B.C. with King Jehoiachin. The prophet's wife died the day the siege of Jerusalem began, 588 B.C. (24:1, 15-18).

Date. In the fifth year of Jehoiachin's exile, 593 B.C.., Ezekiel began his prophetic ministry (1:1-2), continuing till at least April, 571 B.C. (29:17), his last dated utterance.

Purpose. While Jeremiah in Palestine was prophesying the destruction of Jerusalem,

The site of the temple, Jerusalem.

Outline

1-3	The prophet's call
4-24	Prophecies against Jerusalem
25-32	Prophecies against the nations
33-48	Prophecies of the final restoration of Israel.

Ezekiel, his younger contemporary in Babylon, was declaring the same fate for the apostate city (ch. 1-24). Unlike Jeremiah, however, Ezekiel, ministering principally to the exiles, had a large note of consolation in his messages. He showed his suffering colleagues that the Lord was justified in sending His people into captivity (cf. 18:25, 29; 33:17, 20). His ministry centered in showing the preventive and corrective nature of God's chastenings that His people might "know that I am the Lord" (an expression occurring more than 30 times in the book from 6:7 to 39:28).

Ezekiel and the book of Revelation. Ezekiel's visions bear striking resemblances to the book of Revelation (cf. Ezek. 1 with Rev. 4-5; Ezek. 3:3 with Rev. 10:9-10; Ezek. 9 with Rev. 7; Ezek. 10 with Rev. 8:1-5). The prophet Daniel was already famous in Babylon when Ezekiel prophesied (Ezek. 14:14, 20; 28:3).

Ezekiel

1. Ezekiel's vision of God's glory

1-3. Introduction. "The thirtieth year," 1, probably means when Ezekiel was 30 years old. "The hand of the Lord was upon him" shows Ezekiel's contact with God, 3 (3:14, 22; 8:1; 33:22; 37:1; 40:1).

4-28. The vision of God's glory. This revelation of the Shekinah glory of God prepared Ezekiel for his great ministry (cf. Ex. 3:1-10; Isa. 6:1-10; Dan. 10:5-14; Rev. 1:12-19). The four wheels symbolize mobility in all directions. The Lord enthroned above His creatures, 26-28, compares with the Lord enthroned above the cherubim on the ark (Ex. 37:9; 1 Sam. 4:4).

2-3. Ezekiel's fivefold commission

Ch. 2. His commission as a prophet. More than 90 times the nonmessianic expression "son of man" (2:1) occurs in Ezekiel. This would remind Israel that she is but a small part of the entire human race for whom God is solicitous.

3:1-9. As a fearless denunciator. Ezekiel was to digest the Word of God, symbolized by eating a papyrus scroll inscribed with divine judgments, 1-3 (cf. Zech. 5:1-4; Rev. 10:8-11).

3:10-15. As God's mouthpiece to the exiles.

3:16-21. As a watchman. Ezekiel's doctrine of personal responsibility (cf. 18:1-32) is here applied to his prophetic ministry (33:6-16).

3:22-27. As a faithful herald. "The plain"

(valley) was the flat alluvial southern Tigris-Euphrates country. The prophet's protracted dumbness was a sign he was to be mute when God wanted him to be silent.

4-5. Symbolic prophecies of Jerusalem's siege

4:1-3. The sign of the brick. Jerusalem was outlined on a soft mud brick with the clay dried in the sun, so common in S. Babylonia. The captives were hoping for a speedy return to Jerusalem, but the prophet foretells Jerusalem's awful siege and fall.

4:4-8. Sign of the prophet's physical position. His discomfort for 390 days on his left side and 40 days on his right side (total 430 years, symbolically a year for a day) recalled the Egyptian servitude (Ex. 12:40-41).

4:9-17. Sign of famine. Hunger and cannibalism were to stalk besieged Jerusalem. Mixing of grains, 9, indicates scarcity.

Ch. 5. Sign of the shaved head and beard. Hair of the head and face cut with a sword, 1, spoke of the shameful military defeat of Jerusalem.

6. Judgment against the mountains of Israel

1-7. Judgment upon the idolatry of the high places. Figuratively, "the mountains of Israel," 2, stood for the high places, used as outdoor pagan sanctuaries.

8-14. The surviving remnant. The remnant (Rom. 11:5) would survive and learn the purpose of these terrible punishments, 10, 14 (cf. Isa. 6:10-13).

7. The end imminent
1-9. The doom of the city.
10-27. Horror in the city. The confusion and brutality in the fallen city are portrayed.

8-9. Vision of Jerusalem's sin
Ch. 8. Vision of idolatry. The renewed vision of God, 2-4, was a proper background for the judgment of false gods. Tammuz worship, 14-15, was the adoration of the Sumero-Akkadian god of vegetation.
Ch. 9. Vision of punishment for idolatry. The Lord's linen-clothed scribe, 2, signifying ritual cleanness, undoubtedly represented Deity.

10-11. Departure of the Lord from His temple
Ch. 10. The renewed vision of God's glory. The manifested glory of Israel's God was the background for the judgment of Israel's idolatry and horrible profanation of the temple. The linen-clothed person, 9:2-4; 10:2-4, who scattered coals from the fire between the cherubim (1:13) over the idolatry-ridden city, in the light of Revelation 5:1; 8:3-5 was apparently the preincarnate Christ, the Angel of the Presence, who appeared to Abraham, Isaac, Jacob, Moses, Joshua, Gideon, and Daniel (Dan. 10:5-6).
Ch. 11. Ichabod, the glory departs. A glimpse into the wicked political leaders is given, 1-13. A message of mercy, 14-21, precedes the departure of the Shekinah glory from the wicked city, 22-25.

12. The exile portrayed in symbol
1-20. Signs given through Ezekiel. Ezekiel was to enact the exiles' fate, 1-7.

21-28. Message of impending judgment. Unbelief in God's true prophets was the cause of judgment.

13-14. Condemnation of false prophetism
Ch. 13. Divine denunciation of false prophets. Those who proclaim, " 'Peace,' when there is no peace," are as useless as whitewash on a mud brick wall to protect it against a storm, 10-16.
Ch. 14. Depravity of the idol-loving elders.

15. Allegory of the vine
1-5. The allegory. The vine branch is no good for wood. It is used only to produce fruit. Even as fuel it is practically useless.
6-8. The meaning.

16. The allegory of the faithless wife
1-52. Israel's idolatry described figuratively as a homeless orphan, 1-7; as a maiden, 8-14; as a degenerate, 15-34; as a prostitute, 35-52.
53-63. Promise of gracious restoration. Even in this lurid setting the Lord pledged future blessing under the Palestinian covenant (Deut. 30:1-10) and the new covenant (Jer. 31:31-34; Heb. 8:8-12).

17. The allegory of the eagles and the cedar
1-21. The allegory of the eagles. The "great eagle," 3-6, was Nebuchadnezzar (Jer. 49:22).
22-24. The allegory of the cedar. The Lord will take a "shoot" (Messiah) from "the very top of a cedar" (Davidic house) and "a tender sprig" (Messiah), and plant it "on a high and lofty mountain" (Mt. Zion, Mic. 4:1).

18. Divine judgment and individual responsibility

1-13. False accusation against God and the divine answer. Sinners in their plight incline to blame God and their forebears for their troubles. The exiles in Babylon and the sinners in Jerusalem were doing this, 1-2. The Lord rebuked this shifting of blame, 3-4, and through Ezekiel stressed God's justice and individual responsibility for wrongdoing.

14-32. Ezekiel's doctrine of individual responsibility. The good or evil of one generation is not transferable to the next, 19-20. To deny this truth is to fail to comprehend God's justice, 25-29. Repentance was the only way to escape from terrible judgment, 30-32.

19. Lament for the princes of Israel

1-9. Lamentation for the princes. The princes were Jehoahaz, the first cub, 3-4, and Jehoiachin, the second cub, 5-9.

10-14. Lament for the land. The vine portrays Judah (Isa. 5:1-7; Jer. 2:21).

20. Rehearsal of divine mercy to Israel

1-8. Israel's sins in Egypt.

9-26. Israel's sins in the wilderness. A review is made of the wonderful redemption wrought for God's name's sake, 9, 10, 14; with the Sabbath given, 11-13; and grace shown, 14-26.

27-49. Israel's sins in the land.

21. Judgment by the sword

1-17. The Lord unsheathes His sword. The sword was a common symbol of divine judgment (14:21; Isa. 34:5; Jer. 14:12; Rev. 6:8).

18-32. The sword of Nebuchadnezzar. His sword would actually be God's means of

judgment, 18-19. His occultism, 21, would guide him to Jerusalem and slaughter. Divination was the pagan counterpart of prophecy.

22. Jerusalem's indictment

1-16. Jerusalem's violence and abomination.

17-31. The smelting furnace of God's wrath refined all classes of corrupt Jewish society. The purpose of the smelting, 17-22, and the dross, 23-31, are indicated.

23. Oholah and Oholibah

1-4. The allegory. Oholah is Samaria (the northern kingdom), and her sister Oholibah is Jerusalem (representing by metonymy the southern kingdom).

5-49. The meaning. Oholah, 5-10, politically and spiritually contaminated herself with Assyria by alliances and religious syncretism. Oholibah, 11-21, likewise sinned.

24. The cooking pot and the end

1-14. The allegory of the pot was symbolic of the imminent destruction of Jerusalem.

15-27. Death of Ezekiel's wife. He was not to mourn over his wife, who died the day the siege of Jerusalem began.

25. Prophecies against various nations

Ezekiel 25-32 corresponds to Isaiah 13-23 and Jeremiah 46-51. These nations were to be judged before Israel was restored (36:5-7).

1-14. Predictions against Ammon, Moab, and Edom. The nations of this chapter were immediate neighbors of Judah.

15-17. Predictions against Philistia.

26. Prophecy of Tyre's destruction
1-6. Judgment announced.

7-21. Judgment executed. The lament would be made by Tyre's commercial neighbors, "the princes of the seacoast," 15-18. The city would sink into the pit (Sheol), the realm of the dead, 19-21 (cf. Isa. 14:15; Zech. 9:3-4).

27. Lament over Tyre
1-24. Tyre symbolized as a ship. The Tyrian commercial empire is fittingly described as a goodly merchant vessel, 3, "perfect in beauty." The ship was made of fir trees from Senir, i.e., Mt. Hermon (Deut. 3:9).
25-36. Destruction of the ship.

28. Lament over the king of Tyre
1-10. The king of Tyre. The "prince" or ruler of the city at that time, Ittobaal II, headed up in himself the arrogance and pride of the city, claiming to be divine, 2, and "wiser than Daniel," 3.

11-19. The spiritual power behind the Tyrian king. This vast panoramic revelation, like Isaiah 14:12, reached beyond the human ruler to the spiritual power energizing him in the realm of human government. Satan and demons have a notable role in this sphere (cf. Dan. 10:13; Eph. 6:12).

20-26. Judgment of Sidon. The Sidonian worship of Baal served as "painful briers and sharp thorns" for Israel, as it led them into many apostasies (cf. 1 Kings 16:31-33; 18:17-40). Promise of restoration was made to Israel, 25-26, to be fulfilled after her enemies have been judged.

29-32. Judgment against Egypt
Egypt was to be reduced to a second-rate kingdom. This judgment was fulfilled after Nebuchadnezzar's invasion in 527 B.C. and 568 B.C.

29:1-16. Against Pharaoh Hophra. "From Migdol to Aswan," 10, is an expression indicating the northern extent (Migdol) and the southern limits (Aswan, at the first Nile cataract).

29:17-21. Conquest of Egypt. This is Ezekiel's last dated oracle, April, 571 B.C.

Ch. 30. Egypt's doom. This prefigures the day of the Lord in an eschatological sense (Isa. 2:12; Jer. 30:5-7).

Ch. 31. Lament over Pharaoh as a cedar.

Ch. 32. Lament over Pharaoh as a lion. The proud Egyptian ruler considered himself a kingly lion, but he was only a sea monster to be caught in a net.

33. Ezekiel's responsibility as watchman
Chapters 33-39 portray events preceding the restoration of the kingdom of Israel (cf. Acts 1:6), and ch. 40-48 give the description of the restoration.

1-20. A watchman and his responsibility. The prophet's commission included his being a "watchman."

21-33. News of Jerusalem's fall. Ezekiel's enforced silence (3:24-27) was lifted by news of Jerusalem's fall.

34. False shepherds and the true
1-19. Indictment of the faithless shepherds (rulers). The law of individual responsibility (3:16-21) is applied to the nation's leaders, metaphorically called "shepherds," who were

responsible for misusing God's flock (Jer. 23:13-17) and scattering them (Jer. 10:21; 23:1-4).

20-31. Restoration of Israel under Messiah, the true shepherd. This prophecy goes beyond Zerubbabel, the civil head of Judah at the restoration from Babylon in 536 B.C. , and refers to Messiah, David's son and Lord, David's name being used typically (Isa. 9:6-7; 55:3-4; Jer. 23:5-6; Hos. 3:5).

35. The judgment of Edom
1-10. Edom's evil design. With Israel and Judah in exile, Edom planned to possess their land, 10 (cf. Obadiah).
11-15. Edom's ruin.

36. Restoration to the land
Ezekiel 36-48 is yet unfulfilled and envisions the future restoration of the land and the people of Israel.

1-7. Future judgment of Israel's enemies. The judgment of enemy nations (Matt. 25:31-46) must precede Israel's restoration (Joel 3:11-16; Rev. 16:12-16).

8-38. Promised return to the land. The land is to be restored to its former fertility, 11. The regathering, 22-24, goes far beyond the small return from Babylon.

37. Vision of the dry bones
1-14. Scope of the vision. The most satisfactory view of this passage sees it as setting out the national and spiritual reinstatement of God's chosen people Israel in kingdom blessing. The method of the restoration will be by divine power, 3, by the divine Word, 4-6, and by the divine life, 7-10.
15-28. The extent of the restoration. It

embraces the entire house of Israel (the 12 tribes), comprising the union of both Judah and Israel into one nation, 15-17.

38-39.Destruction of Israel's last foes
38:1-6. The great last-day northern confederacy. Gog is the leader of the coalition, 2; Magog his land.
38:7-23. Attack on Israel. The Lord personally undertakes and gives triumph, 14-23.
39:1-24. Overthrow of Gog.
39:25-29. Vision of restored and converted Israel.

40.Description of the temple
Chapters 40-48 constitute Ezekiel's remarkable vision of restored Israel in the land during the Kingdom Age. Envisioned are the millennial temple, ch. 40-42, the millennial worship, ch. 43-46, and the millennial land, ch. 47-48.
1-4. The introduction. On April 28, 573 B.C., the twenty-fifth anniversary of the prophet's exile, Ezekiel was supernaturally transported in vision to Israel, 2, and prophesied from a future idealistic standpoint "on a very high mountain" (Isa. 2:2-3; Mic. 4:1).
5-49. The vision of the temple. There are various views about what this temple was. One view that seems to fit the context in Ezekiel, and the testimony of other Scripture, is that Ezekiel's temple is a literal future sanctuary to be constructed in Palestine during the coming Kingdom Age.

41. The arrangement of the temple
1-14. The house itself will be the dwelling place of the visible presence of the Lord in the kingdom.

15-26. Interior details. The face of a lion (kingly majesty) and that of a man looking on a palm tree describe the kingly role of the glorified Son of Man, the Lion of the tribe of Judah, ruling in regal splendor on David's throne.

42-43. The purpose of Ezekiel's temple
Ch. 42. To demonstrate God's holiness. This is the pervading theme of the entire book and especially so in the purpose and details of the kingdom temple (cf. 43:10). The holiness of the Lord is further emphasized by the principle of *separation*. At the outset the wall separating the courts and temple from all that is defiling is introduced (40:5).

43:1-17. To provide a dwelling place for the divine glory. Ezekiel sees the return of the glory to take up residence in the temple's holy of holies during the Kingdom Age. The temple provides a center for the divine government, 7 (cf. Isa. 2:2-3).

43:18-27. To perpetuate the memorial of sacrifice.

44-46. Worship in the Kingdom Age
Ch. 44. Concerning the priests and the prince. Matters concerning the priesthood (Zadokites) are given, 15-27, with a statement of the priests' inheritance, 28-31.

Ch. 45. Portions of other groups.

46:1-18. The worship of the prince. His personal worship, 1-8, and other institutions for worship are given, 9-15.

46:19-24. A final description of places in the temple.

Figure of winged genius from Babylon.

47-48. The millennial land
47:1-12. The river of the sanctuary (cf. Zech. 14:8-9; Rev. 22:1). The reality of this river is of one piece with the vision of the temple, the land and the people of Israel. It must be a literal river, and the blessed healing it accomplishes must also be literal. It constitutes part of the topographical changes in Palestine when the covenants and promises made to Israel are fulfilled and the curse is lifted.

47:13-23. The boundaries of the land.

48:1-29. The apportionment of the land. The general assignment by tribes, 1-9, is followed by the allotment for the priests and Levites, 10-20, and for the prince, 21-29.

48:30-35. Jerusalem in the Kingdom Age (cf. Rev. 21:10-27). Ezekiel sees the city as it will exist in the coming age. Jerusalem's kingdom name is "the Lord is there," 35.

Daniel
Prophecies of the times of the Gentiles

Relief from ancient Babylon.

Daniel the prophet. Daniel is called a prophet by our Lord (Matt. 24:15), and his predictions are of immense importance, constituting the indispensable introduction to NT prophecy. Daniel was contemporaneous with Jeremiah, Ezekiel (a fellow exile—Ezek. 14:20), and Joshua and Zerubbabel of the restoration. His long career extended from Nebuchadnezzar (605 B.C.) to Cyrus (530 B.C.).

The message of the book. The book is the key to all biblical prophecy. Jesus' great Olivet Discourse (Matt. 24-25), as well as 2 Thessalonians 2 and the entire book of Revelation, can be unlocked only through an understanding of the prophecies of Daniel. The great themes of NT prophecy, the manifestation of the Antichrist (the man of sin), the Great Tribulation, the Second Coming of the Messiah, the times of the Gentiles, and the resurrections and judgments are all treated in Daniel.

Outline

1-6   Daniel's prophetic career in Babylon from Nebuchadnezzar's reign to Cyrus
7-12   Daniel's great visions under Belshazzar, Darius, and Cyrus

Daniel

1. Daniel the man and his character

1-2. Beginning of Judah's exile. Daniel's deportation to Babylon "in the third year of the reign of Jehoiakim," 1 (605 B.C.), marks the beginning of the times of the Gentiles (Luke 21:24), the prophetic period when Jerusalem is under Gentile control. It is plain from 2 Kings 24:1-4 and 2 Chronicles 36:6 that Judah from this moment on was subservient to Gentile rule.

3-21. Daniel's great moral decision. Daniel was of royal birth, highly gifted, and with great promise. His moral faith and spiritual courage were proved in his decision for godly separation from the defilement of Babylon.

2. Nebuchadnezzar's colossus vision

1-28. The forgotten dream. To recall a forgotten dream was a matter beyond human or demonic ability, 10-16. Daniel and his friends prayed and received help from "the God of heaven," 17-23, and Daniel stood before the king, 24-28.

29-45. The revelation and interpretation of the dream. The large statue or colossus, as interpreted by Daniel, symbolizes the entire period known in prophecy as the times of the Gentiles (Luke 21:24). This is the long era when Jerusalem is politically subservient to the nations, among whom the chosen people are not to be reckoned (Num. 23:9). It began with Judah's initial captivity to Babylon in 605 B.C. , and will extend to the Second Coming of the Messiah, the Smiting Stone, 34-35, who will destroy the Gentile world system catastrophically.

The four metals symbolize four empires—Babylon, Media-Persia, Macedonian Greece, and Rome, 37-40. The fourth kingdom (Rome), 40-44 (cf. 7:7), is envisioned panoramically, as it would exist in its ancient imperial glory, as divided into Eastern and Western empires in A.D. 364 (the two legs).

46-49. Daniel's promotion. It was customary to give Babylonian names to conquered peoples who served in the civil administrations.

3. The fiery furnace

1-7. The image of gold. Nebuchadnezzar's pride manifested in this act of idolatry and deification of man marks the spirit that prevails in the times of the Gentiles.

8-25. The faithful three and their deliverance. The fourth person walking unscathed in the fiery furnace "like a son of the gods," 25, was evidently the preincarnate Christ.

26-30. The king's confession and decree. The king gradually apprehends God's sovereign power (cf. 2:47; 3:28; 4:34-35).

4. Nebuchadnezzar's insanity

1-3. The king's greeting.

4-27. The tree vision and its interpretation. Nebuchadnezzar sees a great tree, 4-18, a symbol of his pride and imperial self-exaltation.

28-37. The vision fulfilled. The king was punished for his pride by temporary mental derangement (lycanthropy), in which the victim imagined himself to be a wild beast.

5. Belshazzar's feast

1-9. Belshazzar's licentious and blasphemous celebration. The holy vessels from the Jerusalem temple were desecrated by drunkenness, debauchery, and idolatry. The mysterious writing on the wall, 5-9, turned the feast into a nightmare.

10-28. The forgotten Daniel and his message of doom. Daniel, the aged saint, was called in. The writing, "Mene, Mene, Tekel, Parsin," 25, means literally: "numbered, numbered," i.e., "thoroughly numbered," where the repetition emphasizes the thought; "weighed," "and divided." *Peres,* past participle of *parsin,* "divided," is a word play on *Parus* ("Persia") or *perasin* ("Persians"). The riddle means that the Chaldean Empire was completely numbered, weighed, and divided among the Medes and Persians. For the figure of weighing in a balance, see Job 31:6; Psalm 62:9; Proverbs 16:2.

29-31. The reward of Daniel and Belshazzar's death.

6. Daniel in the den of lions

1-28. Darius the Mede and Daniel. Daniel was now over 80 years old. This signal demonstration that the Lord of the captive Hebrews was really God had a great effect upon Darius, as is seen in his decree, 25-27, and doubtless it also affected Cyrus favorably to issue his decree a few years later to permit the Jews to return to Jerusalem.

7. Daniel's four-beast vision

1-8. The vision of the beasts. The four beasts trace the same four world empires as in the image of 2:37-45, with this difference, that the colossus presents the outward dazzling brilliance of world governments in their political, economic, social aspects, while ch. 7 gives their intrinsic selfish and beastlike character.

9-14. The vision of Messiah's second coming. This is the OT counterpart of Revelation 19:11-16. "The Ancient of Days," 9, 13, is God. "One like a son of man," 13, is Christ invested with the kingdom and returning to earth as King of kings and Lord of lords (Rev. 19:16).

15-28. The interpretation of the vision. "The saints of the Most High" who "receive the kingdom," 18, 22, 25, 27, are the saved Jewish remnant who pass through the Great Tribulation and inherit the kingdom and the covenants and promises made to Israel in connection with it.

8. The ram, the goat, and the small horn

1-14. The vision. The ram, 3-4, with two horns (Media and Persia) is the Medo-Persian Empire, 539-331 B.C.. The goat is Macedonian Greece in its lightninglike conquests under Alexander the Great, "the prominent horn" of the goat, 5. Alexander's conquest of the Persian Empire is prophetically symbolized, 6-7. His untimely death in Babylon (323 B.C.) and the division of his world empire among his four generals are prefigured, 8. This resulted in three great Hellenistic empires by 275 B.C.: Macedonia, Egypt (Ptolemies) and Syria (Seleucides). The career of Antiochus Epiphanes (175-163 B.C.) is prophetically outlined, 9-14.

15-27. The interpretation of the vision. The angel Gabriel's interpretation shows that the vision of Antiochus Epiphanes is a foreshadowing of the future tribulation.

Alexander the Great.

9. The prophecy of the seventy weeks

1-19. Daniel's prayer. Daniel was stirred to intercession for the restoration of his people by reading Jeremiah's prophecies of the 70 years (Jer. 25:11-12; 29:10).

20-27. The answer—the prophecy of the seventy weeks. Jeremiah's prophecy of the 70-year Babylonian captivity is made the basis of a newly revealed panoramic prediction of the entire history of Daniel's people, the Jews, from the rebuilding of Jerusalem's walls until the ultimate establishment of Messiah's earthly kingdom.

10. The role of demonic powers in governments

1-14. The vision. This chapter is the prologue for the vision of ch. 11, while ch. 12 is the epilogue. "The prince of the Persian kingdom" was the evil spirit of government working in and through Cyrus (not Cyrus himself), to hinder him in his good intention to repatriate the Jews.

15-21. The meaning of the vision. The world governments of the times of the Gentiles (Luke 21:24) are operated by unseen evil spirits or demons in the satanic world system. These tried to hinder Daniel's prayer for God's people.

11. Kings of the north and south

1-35. The wars of the Ptolemies and Seleucids. History has minutely verified these prophecies fulfilled by Persian kings, 2; Alexander the Great, 3-4; the Ptolemies of Egypt, 5; "the king of the South" and the Seleucids of Syria, "the king of the North," 6-35.

36-45. The end-time and the man of sin. The willful king of these verses is the Antichrist of the last days, the man of lawlessness of 2 Thessalonians 2:3-4, the lawless one of Revelation 13:1-10, foreshadowed by Antiochus Epiphanes.

12. The great Tribulation and Israel's deliverance

1. The great end-time period of trouble. "At that time" (twice in v. 1) is the time of the end, the last half of Daniel's seventieth week, the terrible period of "trouble for Jacob" (Jer. 30:5-7) preceding the return of Christ.

2-3. Israel's resurrection. This resurrection is predicted of Israel, and the idea of a general resurrection of all the dead is excluded.

4-13. The final consummation. Verses 11 and 12 give the time of the setting up of Antichrist's image (9:27) in the Jerusalem temple (2 Thess. 2:3-4) and the duration of the great time of wrath.

Hosea
The love of God for His erring people

Outline

1-3   Israel's rejection as an unfaithful wife; her future reception and restoration

4-14   Messages of judgment mingled with pleadings of love and mercy

The prophet and his times. Hosea began his ministry toward the latter part of the prosperous and morally declining era of Jeroboam II of Israel (782-753 B.C.) and continued after the fall of Samaria (722 B.C..) into the troubled reigns of Jotham, Ahaz, and Hezekiah (1:1). With the brokenness and passion of Jeremiah, Hosea had a sensitivity of heart that made him the apostle of love in the OT. Although the theme of judgment for apostasy runs through the book, it is interwoven by the golden strand of mercy and love. And Hosea's exposure of sin and impending judgment is not the fiery denunciations of Amos, but a mournful, solemn elegy that breathes the deep love of the Lord for His sinning people.

In Hosea's time there was probably a pagan shrine on Mount Tabor.

Hosea

1. The prophet's marriage illustrates Israel's sin

1. Introduction.

2-9. Hosea divinely commanded to marry a harlot. Hosea took the prostitute Gomer, and she bore him children. He gave them names, 2-9, which were historically and prophetically meaningful.

10-11. Future restoration of Israel. Cf. Romans 9:23-26 for the divine commentary on God's sovereignty and Israel's reinstatement.

2. Israel's suffering for her harlotry

1-13. Appeal and warning.

14-23. Israel to be restored. She who has immorally taken Baal as her husband shall return to the Lord (*Ishi*, "my husband") and no longer call Baal that detestable name *Baali* ("my Baal," Lord), 16.

3. Israel's future restoration

1-3. Israel's past symbolized. "As the Lord loves the Israelites, though they turn to other gods," 1, expresses the central theme of Hosea's prophecy—God's undying love for His covenant people.

4-5. Israel's present and future.

Cities of the prophets

Gath-hepher
Jonah

Great Sea

Abel-meholah
Elisha

ISRAEL

Anathoth
Jeremiah
Jerusalem
Isaiah, Ezekiel

Tekoa
Amos

PHILISTINES

Moresheth-gath
Micah

JUDAH

0   10   20 mi

0 10 20 30 km

4. Ephraim's attachment to idolatry

1-11. Fruits of idolatry. The sins, 1-5, are augmented by willful ignorance, 6-11.

12-19. Description of Ephraim's idolatry. Beth Aven ("house of wickedness or vanity"), 15, is apparently a derogatory name for Bethel (5:8; cf. 10:8), a center of Canaanite idolatrous pollution (cf. 10:5, "calf-idol of Beth Aven").

5-6. Message of rebuke and future mercy

5:1-14. The favor of the Lord withdrawn. Israel's leaders (priests and civil rulers), 1, had been a trap to the people and judgment was due.

5:15-6:3. Future return and blessing. "The third day," 2, is Israel's day of spiritual resurrection (regeneration) and consequent spiritual blessing (Joel 2:28-29).

6:4-11. The Lord's reply.

7-13. The Lord's indictment of Israel

7:1-16. Her moral depravity. The horrible harvest of her idolatry, 1-7, in mixing with the polluted paganism of the surrounding nations, 8-16, is denounced.

8:1-9:9. Judgment on her apostasy.

9:10-11:11. Retrospect on the nation's sin and woe.

11:12-13:13. Ephraim's indictment. The Lord has had to turn against her as a lion, 13:7; as a leopard, 13:7; and as a bear robbed of her cubs, 13:8. Israel's ruin is in the fact that she is against the Lord, who is her help, 13:9-11.

13:14-16. Israel's future resurrection.

14. Kingdom restoration of Israel

1-3. Call to return. God's Spirit through the prophet calls apostate Ephraim to come back to the Lord in repentance and faith.

4-8. The Lord's gracious response. The olive (cf. Rom. 11:16-24) is a symbol of Israel in her spiritual blessing.

9. Concluding statement. The spiritually wise will understand these things, but not sinners.

The Minor Prophets and Their Message

Hosea
The Lord loves Israel despite her sin. 755-715

Joel
Judgment precedes Israel's future spiritual revival. 835-796*

Amos
God is just and must judge sin. 765-750

Obadiah
Sure retribution must overtake merciless pride. 848*

Jonah
Divine grace is universal in its sweep. 780-750

Micah
Bethlehem-born Messiah will be mankind's Deliverer. 740-690

Nahum
Doom is to descend on wicked Nineveh. 630-612

Habakkuk
Justification by faith is God's way of salvation. 625 or earlier

Zephaniah
The Day of the Lord must precede kingdom blessing. 625-610

Haggai
The Lord's temple and interests deserve top priority. 520

Zechariah
The Lord will remember His people Israel. 520-515; Ch.9-14 after 500

Malachi
Let the wicked be warned by the certainty of judgment. 433-400

* The text does not specifically date these prophets. As a result difference of opinion exists concerning the time of their ministries.

Joel
The great Day of the Lord

Outline

1:1-20	The locust plague—the Day of the Lord
2:1-32	Events of the Day of the Lord
3:1-16	The judgment of the nations
3:17-21	Kingdom blessing

Author. Joel means "the Lord (*Yahweh*) is God." The name of his father is given, but merely to distinguish him from others of the same name.

Site of a Chalcolithic Temple at Megiddo—site of Armageddon (Joel 2).

Joel

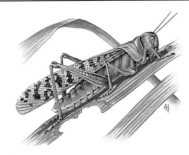

A locust.

1. The locust plague —the Day of the Lord

1-7. The desolation of the land. Four names are given to the locusts portraying their decimating destruction. "The leavings of the *gnawer* the *multiplier* ate, and the leavings of the *licker* the *devourer* ate" (Keil and Delitzsch), 4. The locusts form a prophetic picture of a greater disaster. They prefigure an invading army, 6-7, and its desolation of the land.

8-13. Appeal to lament the plague.

14. Call to self-humiliation and repentance.

15-20. The plague a prophetic symbol of the Day of the Lord.

2. Events of the Day of the Lord

1-10. The invading army from the north. Joel 2 conducts us at once to the closing times of the Gentiles and the historical enactment of the Day of the Lord, 1.

11. The Lord's army appears. This involves the Second Coming, and is a phase of the titanic struggle at Armageddon (Rev. 16:14).

12-17. The repentant remnant.

18-27. The Lord's response to the repentant Jews in the land.

28-32. The promise of the outpoured Spirit. Peter's use of this prophecy at Pentecost (Acts 2:15-21) was illustrative of what the Spirit of God can do. Its final fulfillment awaits the introduction of the Kingdom Age. The kingdom outpouring is to be universal, 28-29, and connected to the climactic phase of the "Day of the Lord," 30-31.

3. The judgment of the nations

1. Israel's end-time restoration. The nations that have persecuted Israel must be judged before Israel can be brought into safety and blessing (cf. Zech. 6:1-8; Matt. 25:31-46; Rom. 11:25-27; Rev. 16:14).

2-16. The nations judged. The Lord Himself is the speaker, 2-8. He announces what He will do to Israel's enemies when He restores His people. The sin of the nations has been their mistreatment of the Jew (cf. Ps. 79; Isa. 29:1-8; Jer. 25:13-17; Zech. 1:14-15).

17-21. Full kingdom blessing. At last unbelieving Israel receives the Messiah, the true basis of their holiness, 17. "My holy hill" is Moriah, the temple hill (cf. Ps. 2:6; Dan. 11:45; Obad. 16; Zech. 8:3). The kingdom prosperity of Palestine, 18, is a common prophetic theme of the prophets.

Amos
Impending judgment

Outline

1:1-2:16	Judgment on Israel, Judah, and surrounding nations
3:1-9:10	The Lord's indictment of the whole house of Jacob
3:1-6:14	Four condemnatory sermons
7:1-9:10	Five symbolic predictions of punishment
9:11-15	Kingdom blessing for restored Israel

The times of Amos. Amos's ministry occurred in the latter part of the reign of Jeroboam II (c. 793-753 B.C.). It was an age of economic prosperity with luxurious living, moral corruption, and rampant idolatry. Amos directed his fiery oratory against these sins.

The prophet. Amos was a shepherd and dresser of sycamore fruit (7:14) from Tekoa, a hill country town about 10 miles south of Jerusalem. He was called to be a prophet chiefly to the northern kingdom (7:14-15) at the main sanctuary at Bethel (7:10). He met the opposition of the high priest Amaziah, who reported the fearless preacher to Jeroboam II.

Amos was a shepherd and dresser of sycamore fruit.

Amos

> ## Arrangement of the oracles
> Geographically, the judgments surround Israel in an ever-tightening noose that focuses God's wrath on His sinful people.

1:1-2:3 Superscription and judgment upon surrounding nations
1:1-2 Superscription.
1:3-2:3. Judgment upon six nations.
"For three sins . . . even for four," 3, 9, 11, 13; 2:1, 4, 6, means sin multiplied on sin, more than enough. The numerical sequence *x, x+1* is a common device in Hebrew poetry (cf. Prov. 3:18, 21, 29; Job 33:14), here designating fullness or completion.

2:4-16. Judgment upon Judah and Israel
Israel's judgment was more detailed because she had enjoyed great light.

3. Israel's greater privilege and guilt
1-11. Because of her greater privilege. She
was a nationally elect nation, redeemed out of Egypt and under covenant responsibility, and so her failure would be severely judged, 1-2.
12-15. The thoroughness of the divine judgment.
"Houses adorned with ivory," 15 (cf. 1 Kings 22:39), were so called because they were lavishly decorated with ivory inlays.

4. Prepare to meet your God, O Israel
1-3. Indictment of the wealthy women of Samaria.
These greedy, vain women (cf. Isa. 3:16-26) were called "cows of Bashan," 1 (cf.

Ps. 22:12). Bashan, a fertile area east of the Sea of Galilee, was known for its sleek, fat cattle.
4-5. Israel's abominable ritualism. Bethel was
the idol-ridden royal sanctuary and Gilgal was another polluted shrine.
6-13. Israel must face God's judgment.

5. Seek the Lord and live
1-3. A lament for the fallen and forsaken nation.
4-17. Seek the Lord. The only way Israel could
be spared from national death was to seek the Lord rather than the idols of Bethel, Gilgal, and Beersheba.
18-20. Be warned of the Day of the Lord.
21-27. The Lord's hatred of their empty religiosity.
To avert disaster, justice must "roll on like a river, righteousness like a never-failing stream," 24—the essence of Amos's message.

6. Calamity upon the self-secure
1-7. Warning to self-indulgent sinners. The
dissipating indulgence, 4-5, and spiritual unconcern, 6, of the carnal rich in Samaria would result in early captivity to Assyria.
8-14. Punishment is inevitable.

7. The locust plague, the drought, and the plumb line
Amos presents five symbolic predictions of punishment, 7:1-9:10.

Amos uses the image of a fruit basket. The fruit market in Nazareth.

1-3. The locust plague.
4-6. The drought.
7-9. The plumb line.
10-17. **Amos and Amaziah.** Amos's bold prediction against the house of Jeroboam of the Jehu dynasty, 9, aroused the official priest of the royal sanctuary at Bethel to report Amos to the king.

8. The fruit basket
1-3. **The basket of ripe produce.**
4-14. **The reason for the end.** Crooked businessmen chafed at the sacred festal seasons and at the Sabbath, because those days caused a lull in the dishonest money-making activities, 4-5, and their oppression of the poor, 6.

Dan and Beersheba were pagan shrines in the farthest northern and southern limits of the land, 14.

9:1-10. The Lord at the altar
1-6. **The Lord at the altar.**
7-10. **The Lord and sinful Israel.** The Lord would destroy every sinful kingdom, Israel not excepted.

9:11-15. Future kingdom blessing
11-15. **Messiah's return and reign.** David's tent is the Davidic dynasty the Lord will raise up (cf. Acts 15:15-17). After the Lord has called out a people for His name in this present age, He will return and reestablish the Davidic dynasty in Christ, 11-12; and millennial prosperity, 13, will result in a restored Israel, 14-15.

Obadiah
God's retributive justice

Obadiah

Nature of the book. This is the shortest prophecy and the smallest book of the OT. Its author was Obadiah, whose name means "the servant of the Lord." The prophecy is wholly taken up with the condemnation of Edom for its treachery toward Judah, with a prophecy of its utter destruction and Judah's salvation in the Day of the Lord.

Outline

1-9   Edom's destruction foretold
10-14   Cause of Edom's fall
15-21   The Day of the Lord

Part of the "broad wall" built by Hezekiah to protect Jerusalem.

1-9. Edom's destruction foretold
1-4. Dislodged from her mountain fortress. Obadiah is unknown, identifiable with none of the dozen or so men in the OT who bore the same name. Edom ("the red region") was Israel's neighbor on the southeast.
5-9. Plundered and deserted completely. Esau, 6 (Gen. 25:30; 36:1), was the progenitor of the Edomites. Esau's treasure was enormous wealth from iron and copper mines, and caravan trade, 6. Edom was famous for her wise men (Jer. 49:7).

10-14. Cause of Edom's fall
Edom joined in the attack against Jerusalem.

15-21. The Day of the Lord
The prophet links the future with the past in a prediction still unfulfilled, "The Day of the Lord is near for all nations," 15. All nations will be judged as to their treatment of Israel, as Edom was.

Jonah
Israel's mission to the nations

Outline

1-2 Jonah's commission and disobedience

3-4 Jonah's renewed commission and its result

Jonah the man. Jonah ("dove") was the son of Amittai, who came from Gath-hepher some three miles northeast of Nazareth.

The book. This book is more than biographical history. It is *predictive typical history.* It prefigures Christ as the Sent One, suffering death, being buried, and, after being raised, ministering salvation to the Gentiles (Matt. 12:39-41; Luke 11:29-32).

Jaffa—Joppa—on the Mediterrranean coast of Israel.

Jonah

The Minor Prophets

The 12 so-called Minor Prophets are distinguished from the Major Prophets—Isaiah, Jeremiah, Ezekiel and Daniel. In the Hebrew canon the Minor Prophets are grouped together as *one* book called the Twelve, and with the first three Major Prophets make *four* books, known as the Latter Prophets. The Former Prophets are also reckoned four in number—Joshua, Judges, Samuel, Kings. From Augustine's time (late fourth century) the Latin church has used the term Minor Prophets because of their brevity (not their unimportance) as compared with the Major Prophets.

1. Jonah's call and disobedience

1-3. The divine call and attempted escape. "The great city of Nineveh," 2, is aptly designated. At this period it was the capital of the Assyrian Empire at its height and was the greatest city of the time.

Jonah's proposed flight to Tarshish, 3, in open rebellion against the Lord, 3-4, represents the most distant point the disobedient prophet could go. It was probably Tartessus in southern Spain.

4-7. The storm at sea. Disobedience to God's word always brings spiritual torpor and frequently results in rebuke from the unsaved.

8-17. Jonah's witness and fate. Five "greats" occur in the book: a *great* city, 1:2; the *great* refusal, 1:3; the *great* fish, 1:17; a *great* jealousy, 4:1; and a *great* God, 4:2b.

2. Jonah's prayer and deliverance

1-9. His prayer of thanksgiving. Remarkably this prayer is not petition of desperate entreaty but thankful praise for escape from physical death.

Archaeological light

Excavations have revealed that "greater" Nineveh was a district of 30 to 60 miles across, agreeing well with the text of Jonah.

10. His deliverance. When he learned his lesson, he was delivered to do God's will.

3. Jonah's renewed commission

1-4. Jonah's obedience. To go around the complex of suburbs that made up the great metropolis of Nineveh required three days, 3.

5-10. Nineveh repents. Sackcloth, 5, rough goat's hair worn over the naked body, was a garb of mourning. Nineveh was spared, 10 (cf. Nahum 1-2).

4. Jonah's reaction to the revival

1-5. Jonah is angered.

6-11. The prophet rebuked. He must be shown that God loves all His creatures, not only sinful Ninevites but even dumb cattle.

Micah
Personal and social righteousness

Outline

1-3	General prediction of judgment
4-5	The coming messianic Kingdom
6-7	The Lord's controversy with His people and final mercy

Micah the poet and Isaiah. Micah's prophecy is a beautiful and moving example of classical Hebrew poetry. Like his contemporary, Isaiah, Micah possessed great literary power. While Isaiah was a court poet—a voice to kings, Micah was a rustic from an obscure village—a herald for God to the common people. Isaiah was a statesman; Micah, an evangelist and social reformer.

Great emphases of Micah: (1) Back to Bethlehem (5:2), back to David, back to Messiah, David's son and Lord. (2) Back to ethical righteousness (6:8), the practice of justice, kindness, compassion, mercy, and humility. (3) Back to the coming Prince of Peace (4:3), the man who will be "their peace" (5:5), the world's only hope of permanent peace.

Capture of an ancient city, such as Nineveh.

Micah

to be regathered into the kingdom, 6-8, the Babylonian Captivity, 9-10, intervening and typifying the final regathering, culminating in the battle of Armageddon, 11-13.

5. The first and second comings of the Messiah

1. Prospect and retrospect.

2. His first coming and rejection. Verse 2 tells who the "smitten ruler" of 1 is. He is the Bethlehem-born preexistent, eternal One (cf. Isa. 9:6-7).

3. Interval between the comings.

4-6. The Second Coming. The rejected One now becomes the Shepherd of Israel, standing and feeding in "the strength of the Lord," 4, for He is the Lord.

7-15. The blessed remnant and the kingdom. The remnant will be a spiritual witness and blessing, 7, and an avenger of wrongs, 8-9.

1. Judgment upon Samaria and Judah

1. Introduction.

2-7. Judgment upon Samaria. This splendid city, whose brilliance has been revealed by archaeology, became a heap of rubble and her stones rolled down the hill of Shemer upon which she was built. This happened in 722 B.C., when Sargon of Assyria took the city.

8-16. Lamentation over Samaria and Judah. As a sign of the impending Assyrian invasion, Micah went naked, predicting the judgment of enemy invasion up to the very gates of Jerusalem, 8-9.

2-3. Judgment upon various classes

2:1-11. The leaders of Samaria and Jerusalem mislead.

2:12-13. Mercy upon the remnant.

Ch. 3. Denunciation of various classes. The oppressors of the poor are indicated, 1-4. Mercenary priests and prophets were identified and judgment was focused on Jerusalem, 9-12, fulfilled in the fall of the city in 586 B.C.

6-7. Final controversy and mercy

6:1-7:6. The people's ingratitude and sin. The Lord's controversy was with His people, 6:1-8, because they had forgotten His mercies of old and the practice of common piety.

7:7-20. Confession, petition, and thanksgiving. Those in Israel who kept faith had an unquenchable trust in the Lord's faithfulness to restore the nation eventually in fulfillment of all His promises.

4. The establishment of Messiah's kingdom

1-5. Character of the kingdom. Chapters 4 and 5 present Israel's glorious future and the restoration of the Davidic kingdom.

6-13. Establishment of the kingdom. Israel is

Nahum

Outline

1 A psalm of God's majesty
2-3 Prophecy of Nineveh's fall

periodically from 850 B.C.. till its fall in 612 B.C. Nahum's ministry was exercised between the conquest of No-amon (Thebes) in Egypt (3:8) in 661 B.C. and Nineveh's fall in 612 B.C. The book is a classic of Hebrew poetry, with exceptionally fine and vivid descriptions.

God's holiness vindicated in judgment Nahum's throne. The prophet has one theme, judgment upon Nineveh, the capital of the mighty Assyrian Empire, and hence on Assyria. Its tyrannical cruelty scourged the ancient world

Assyrian Empire at greatest extent (c 660B.C.)

Nahum

1. God's majestic holiness

1. Superscription. Nahum ("comforter")
prophesies judgment upon wicked Nineveh, and
his indication of God's mercy to His own
constitutes him a "consoler" to those who do
good.

2-11. Character of God in judgment. On the
one hand God is jealous, the source of His
passion being in His love for His people, 2. Yet
on the other hand He is also infinitely holy and
must show His vengeance against those who
wrong His people. He must punish the
wicked, 3.

12-15. The fall of Nineveh announced.

2. Siege and destruction of Nineveh

**1-12. The overthrow of Nineveh predicted
and described.** In superb poetry Nahum
dramatically portrays the city's siege.

13. The reason for Nineveh's destruction.
The Lord was *against* her.

3. Nineveh an example
of God's judgment

1-17. Her sins reap their harvest. The case of
Thebes, the great Egyptian city, was a warning
when it fell in 661 B.C. 8-10.

18-19. Lament over the king of Assyria.
Dramatically he was addressed directly. His

The Babylonian Chronicle tablet includes an
account of the fall of Nineveh.

destruction was declared, 18, and the joy it
would cause is outlined, 19.

Habakkuk
The just shall live by faith

The prophet and his message. Practically nothing is known of the prophet Habakkuk. His theme centers in the theological question of how God's patience with evil can square with His holiness. The answer the prophet received is valued for all time. A sovereign God has the incontestable prerogative of dealing with the wicked in His own time and way. "But the righteous will live by his faith" (2:4).

Outline

1. Judah's judgment through the Chaldeans announced
2. Ultimate judgment upon the Chaldeans predicted
3. The prophet's vision of the coming king

Literary beauty. Habakkuk, like Nahum and Isaiah, is couched in sublime poetry, reflecting the classical era of Hebrew prophecy. The magnificent lyric ode of ch. 3 contains one of the greatest descriptions of the theophany in relation to the coming of the Lord that has been given by the Holy Spirit, awaiting fulfillment in the Day of the Lord (cf. 2 Thess. 1:7-10).

Assyrians cross a river on inflated skins to attack a walled city.

Habakkuk

Deportation of prisoners by Assyria.

1. Judah's judgment by the Chaldeans

1-4. Problem: why the Lord had not judged Judah's sin. How can a holy God toierate the sin of His own people Judah, 1-4?

5-11. The divine solution. The Chaldeans would judge Judah. According to Acts 13:37-41, verse 5 anticipates the redemptive work of Christ. The Chaldeans ruled the ancient near East 612-539 B.C.. They were aggressive Semitic-Aramean nomads who gradually settled in southern Babylonia. Nobopolassar was the founder of the Chaldean Empire, inherited by his son Nebuchadnezzar II. Verse 10 accurately portrays the military practice of the Chaldeans in throwing up earthen ramparts to take fortresses.

12-17. Problem: why the wicked Chaldeans were used to punish Judah. How could the Lord employ people more wicked than His own sinning people as a rod of punishment?

2. The Lord's solution —judgment of the Chaldeans

1-5. A righteous remnant to be preserved. Those not upright in soul, 4, shall fall, "but the righteous will live by his faith" (the godly remnant).

6-19. The Chaldeans themselves shall be punished. In the midst of these five woes the prophet catches a glimpse of the future Kingdom Age, 14, when all these evils will be eradicated.

20. The sovereign Lord is ruling. This is part of the Lord's answer. God's presence demands that the entire globe be silent before Him because His sovereign power and righteousness are operative in *all* the earth.

3. Vision of the Lord's coming and kingdom

1-2. The prophet's prayer.
3-15. The coming of the Lord as judge and warrior.
16-19. The effect of the theophany on Habakkuk. His reaction and quiet trust reflect the attitude of the future godly remnant during the Great Tribulation, 16. He professes his deep faith in God, despite outward sufferings to be endured, 17-19.

Zephaniah
A warning of judgment

Zephaniah

Date. Zephaniah, a contemporary of Jeremiah, exercised his ministry during the reign of Josiah (641-609 B.C.). Zephaniah had access to the royal court and had an influence on King Josiah's policies.

Outline

1:1-18	Judah's coming doom
2:1-3:8	Judgment upon surrounding nations
3:9-20	Israel in kingdom blessing

The Mediterranean Sea at Ashkelon, the ancient Philistine city.

1. Judah's doom and the Day of the Lord

1-3. Judgment of the whole earth. The scope of these verses embraces a worldwide judgment of the Day of the Lord (cf. 1:17; 2:11, 14, 15).

4-13. Judgment of Judah and Jerusalem. Molech, 5, was the chief Ammonite deity.

14-18. The Day of the Lord. The imminent invasion of the Chaldeans under Nebuchadnezzar is treated as a prefiguration of the apocalyptic Day of the Lord in which all earth judgments culminate (cf. Joel 1-2).

2:1-3:8. The judgment of the nations

2:1-3. The call to repentance.

2:4-7. Judgment upon the Philistines.

2:8-15. Judgment upon Moab and Ammon, and other nations.

3:1-8. Judgment upon Jerusalem. Four charges are made against the city: disobedience, opposition to correction, unbelief, and godlessness.

3:9-20. Israel in kingdom blessing

9-13. Salvation and deliverance in the kingdom. The gift of a pure speech removes the curse of Babel (Gen. 11:1-9) and anticipates the great outpouring of the Spirit (Joel 2:28-32), of which Pentecost (Acts 2:1-21) was the firstfruits.

14-20. Praise in the kingdom.

Haggai
Call to complete the unfinished temple

Outline

1:1-15	Call to rebuild the temple
2:1-19	Prophecy of the millennial temple
2:20-23	Prophecy of the destruction of Gentile world power

Historical background. Cyrus's decree (538 B.C.) permitted the Jews to return home and rebuild their temple at Jerusalem (Ezra 1:1-4). The remnant laid the foundation (Ezra 3:1-3, 8-10), but from c. 535 B.C. to 520 B.C. failed to complete the building. Through Haggai's and Zechariah's combined ministry (520 B.C., the temple was completed (520-515 B.C.). The circumstances of the construction of the temple gave rise to panoramic messianic predictions by the two prophets, especially Zechariah.

Relief of Darius giving an audience.

Haggai

The barren Judean Hills.

1. Call to rebuild the temple

1-6. Call to face sinful neglect. The rulers and the people at large were faced with their failure, 1-6.

7-11. Declaration of the Lord's judgment. Economic stress, drought, and unemployment were directly traceable to neglect in building the temple, 9.

12-15. The people's response. Haggai gave a word of encouragement from the Lord, 13, and the people resumed building the temple.

2:1-19. Prophecy of the millennial temple

1-9. The prediction of the temple. Human disparagement of the modest plans for the second temple engendered pessimism and discouragement, 1-3. Haggai gave assurance of the divine presence and success of the venture, 4-5. The restoration of the temple furnished the background for the far-reaching prophecy of the kingdom temple, 7-9.

10-19. Promise of present blessing. Being sanctified would bring the Lord's favor and a solution to their pressing economic problems, 15-19.

2:20-23. Destruction of Gentile world power

20-22. The shaking of the nations. The shaking of the heavens and the earth, 21, in the future tribulation, will destroy the throne of kingdoms, so that the kingdom of the Messiah may be set up.

23. The promised ruler. Zerubbabel, a son of David, typifies Christ, the son of David. In that day Christ will receive His Davidic throne and be made a signet ring—a mark of honor, a badge of royal authority possessed by kings and conferred on their administrative agents.

Zechariah
Israel, the nation God remembers

Nature of the prophecy. This book is unique in its messianic emphasis among the minor prophets and in its unfolding of events connected with the first and second comings of Christ. It has been called the most messianic, apocalyptic, and eschatological of all the writings of the OT.

Important messianic predictions. These predictions include: the Lord's Servant, the Branch (3:8); the Man, the Branch (6:12); the King-Priest (6:13); the True Shepherd (11:4-11); the True Shepherd vs. the false shepherd—the

Antichrist (11:15-17; 13:7); the betrayal of the Good Shepherd (11:12-13); His crucifixion (12:10); His sufferings (13:7); His second coming in glory (14:4).

Outline

Part one

1:1-6	Introduction
1:7-6:8	Eight night visions
6:9-15	Crowning the high priest
7:1-8:23	Question of facts

Part two
Oracle 1:

9:1-11:17	Messiah's first coming and rejection

Oracle 2:

12:1-14:21	Messiah's second coming and acceptance

A model of Herod's Temple. Zechariah looks forward to the restoration of Jerusalem.

Zechariah

1:1-17. Vision of the man among the myrtles

1. Preface.

2-6. The call to repentance. This is the spiritual keynote sounded so that the remnant of less than 50,000 might be spiritually prepared for the great visions given to them through the prophet.

7-17. The man among the myrtle trees. This vision signifies hope for scattered and down-trodden Israel. The red-horse rider is the Lord in theophanic form, 8 (cf. 13), the color red speaking of Him who wrought redemption at his first coming and will come to judge and make war at His second coming (Rev. 19:11). The myrtle trees symbolize Israel as the covenant people.

1:18-21. Vision of the four horns and four craftsmen

18-21. Israel triumphant over her foes. The prophet first sees four horns, 18-19. These represent hostile nations, i.e., the four great world powers of the times of the Gentiles, namely, Babylon, Medo-Persia, Greece, and Rome.

The Lord then shows the prophet four craftsmen, 20-21. These artisans symbolize kingdoms that the Lord used to cast down the persecutors of His people Israel.

2. Vision of the surveyor

1-3. The measuring line. This vision presents Jerusalem in millennial glory. The surveyor is probably the same divine Person as the red-horse rider of the first vision. His surveying activities intimate the growth and prosperity of Jerusalem, not only at that time, but ultimately to be fulfilled in the Kingdom Age, as 4-13 demonstrates.

4-13. Promises proceeding from the vision.

3. Vision of Joshua's cleansing

This vision sets forth the restoration of Israel as a high-priestly nation.

1-3. Israel as defiled and condemned is pictured under the representative figure of Joshua, the high priest.

4-5. Israel as pardoned and repositioned. This portrays the conversion of the nation at the Messiah's second coming.

6-7. Covenant of priesthood renewed with Joshua.

8-10. Prediction of restored Israel under the figure of Messiah, the Branch. Joshua and his colleagues were "symbolic," i.e., men who personally signified future events for Israel, 8. The "stone," a precious carved gem, portrays the Messiah in His glorious second coming when Israel will be converted, 12:10.

4. Vision of the golden lampstand

This vision portrays Israel as the light of the world under the Messiah King-Priest.

1-5. The symbolism of the vision. The lampstand of pure gold typifies Christ our Light (John 8:12). The seven-branched lampstand *in the midst* of Israel symbolizes the realization of

Israel's divine vocation to be a witness and testimony of God's salvation in Christ to the unbelieving nations around her.

6-10. The purpose of the vision. The temple was to be completed by divine power, 6, with every obstacle removed, 7. The word of God would be fulfilled, 9. God would be magnified, 10.

11-14. The prophet favored with a full explanation. The two olive trees portray the civil (kingly) and priestly office. The two olive branches represent the present incumbents, Zerubbabel and Joshua. The two golden pipes symbolize these two offices united in Christ as King-Priest. The gold (oil) is the work of the Holy Spirit through the King-Priest to the restored nation as lightbearer.

5. Visions of the flying scroll and the measuring basket

1-4. The flying scroll. The sixth vision, 1-2, portrays a flying scroll, illustrating the rod-of-iron rule of the kingdom. The scroll symbolizes the curse of God against sinners.

5-11. The measuring basket. This seventh vision portrays the removal of commercial and ecclesiastical wickedness from the earth. The woman sitting in the basket, 7, is personified wickedness.

6:1-8. Vision of the four chariots

This vision presents the judgment of the nations before the Messiah's reign. The findings of the scouts in the first vision are now executed.
1-3. The vision presented. The "two mountains" (Olivet and Zion) typify divine judgment. The four chariots are pictured with their horses, 2-3. The *red* horses portray war

and bloodshed (Rev. 6:4); the *black* horses, famine and starvation (Rev. 6:5-6); the *white* horses, victory and conquest (Rev. 6:2); the *dappled* horses portray death (Rev. 6:8).
4-8. The vision explained. Attention focuses on the horsed *chariots,* not the horses. The interpretative key is given in 5. These horsed chariots represent "the four spirits" (angelic ministers) who are the celestial agents executing judgment against the nations.

6:9-15. Crowning the high priest

The eight visions have ended. Now follows an actual historical event—Joshua's coronation—for which the eight visions were preparatory. This symbolic event was the summary and climax of these visions.
9-11. The historical event and the prophetic symbolism. The significance of this event is that the crown was to be placed upon the head of the high priest Joshua, *not* Zerubbabel, despite the rigid separation of the priestly and kingly offices in Israel. The reason was that *all* eight night visions pointed to the kingdom restored to Israel under Messiah King-Priest.
12-13, 15. Messianic import of the prophetic symbolism. The Messiah will combine the two offices in perfect harmony, 13, binding together both Jew and Gentile, 15.
14. Provision for a permanent memorial. The crown, as a prophetic symbolism, is to be kept as a memorial.

7. The question of the fasts

1-3. The question raised. The city of Bethel sent a delegation to Jerusalem to ask about observing certain fasts.
4-7. The motive of selfishness exposed. The

A menorah or seven-branched candlestick.

prophet rebuked meaningless ritualism, 4-6, and urged obedience to the word of God, 7.
8-14. Call to repentance proclaimed.

8. When the fasts become joyful feasts

1-8. Present partial restoration is a harbinger of an eventual full restoration of Israel. This full restoration is guaranteed by God's word and God's electing love, 1-2.
9-17. Encouragement amid the hardships of the present partial restoration.
18-23. Prediction of the full millennial restoration. Fasts will one day give way to feasts, 18-19. The Jew will enjoy special divine favor, 23.

9:1-10:1. Human world ruler vs. divine prince of peace

9:1-8. Sudden rise of Alexander the Great. Tyre's siege and fall to the conqueror are graphically predicted, 3-4, and dramatically fulfilled in Alexander's conquest of the city after an eight-month siege.
9:9. First coming of Israel's humble king and savior. He is to be righteous and lowly, shown by His riding a humble beast, which no king at that period would ever ride.
9:10-10:1. Second coming of Israel's glorious king. He establishes peace, 10. Suffering Israel is encouraged in the light of the nation's future hope, 11-12.

10:2-12. Divine prince of peace and deliverer

2-4. The Second Coming and the cure of the nation's deception. The cure of the nation's deception, 4, is in the Messiah's coming as "cornerstone" (Isa. 28:15-16), "tent peg" (Isa. 22:15-25), and "battle bow" (cf. Ps. 45:5; Rev. 19:11).
5-12. The Second Coming and the nation's triumph over its foes. The Lord promises that He will gather Israel out of her present worldwide dispersion, 8-9, to her own land, 10-12.

11. Israel's rejection of the good shepherd

1-3. Impending devastation of the land.
4-14. Prediction of the rejection of the good shepherd. The two rods "Favor" and "Union" symbolize the Lord's final efforts to reclaim apostate Christ-rejecting Israel, 7-8.
15-17. Prediction of the acceptance of the bad shepherd. The rejection of the good

The Golden Gate, Jerusalem. Tradition says it will not be opened until Messiah comes in glory.

shepherd is connected with the first coming, as the acceptance of the evil shepherd is with the second coming (John 5:43; Rev. 19:20; 20:10).

12. Israel's deliverance and national conversion

1-9. Future siege of Jerusalem.
10-14. Vision of the crucified Messiah and the result. The appearance of "the one they pierced" will produce a great outpouring of the Spirit, 10 (cf. Joel 2:28-32; Ezek. 39:29).

13. Israel's national cleansing

1-6. Prophecy of Israel's national cleansing.
This is illustrated in the extermination of idolatry and false prophecy, 2-5.
7. Provision for Israel's national conversion.
Here appears the divine-human person of our Lord in the OT—deity united to humanity in one unique Person.
8. Prelude to Israel's national conversion.
9. The appropriation of the provisions for cleansing. The remnant calls on the Lord, is delivered, and testifies to salvation, 9.

14. Messiah's second coming in glory

1-3. Last enemy siege against Jerusalem.
The Lord intervenes in deliverance, 3.
4-7. Personal coming of the Messiah. The place, result, purpose, manner, and time of the Second Coming are described.
8-21. Messianic kingdom established over Israel. Millennial worship and government, with Jerusalem as the religious and political capital of the earth, 16-19, are predicted. The prophecy closes with Israel's holiness as a high-priestly nation.

Malachi
The Lord's love for His sinning people

Outline

1:1-5	Preamble: the Lord's love for Israel
1:6-2:9	Oracle against the priests
2:10-4:3	Oracles against Jewish laymen
4:4-6	Concluding warnings

Message of Malachi. The last prophetic voice of the OT rings out over the years intervening till the coming of the forerunner, John the Baptist, and the King at His first coming. But Malachi's prophetic emphasis is on the Day of the Lord with its judgment of the wicked and the deliverance of a righteous remnant. These vast themes connect Malachi with the great stream of Hebrew prophecy. His immediate message deals with the sins of the priests and the people of his day. These sins form the background for his prophecies of judgment certain to fall in the future.

Malachi prophesied Messiah's forerunner, John, who baptized in the Jordan River.

Malachi

Malachi prophesied that Elijah will appear at the end-times.

1:1-5. The Lord's love for Israel
1-2. Declaration of that love. The message to Israel, God's ancient chosen nation, is, "I have loved you," 2 (cf. Deut. 10:15; 33:3; Hos. 2:18-20; Amos 3:2).
3-5. Contrast to Esau (Edomites).

1:6-2:16. Oracle against the priests and people
1:6-14. The impenitence of the priests. The conduct of the priests was utterly reprehensible in the light of who the Lord is and His reputation among the nations, 14.
2:1-9. Their impenitence to be punished.
2:10-16. First oracle against the people. The results of that treachery against men, 10, and God, 11, were seen in divorce, unfaithfulness, and violence, 13-16.

2:17-4:6. Prophecy of Messiah's coming
2:17. The occasion of the prophecy.
3:1-6. The prophecy itself. "My messenger," 1, is a prediction of the forerunner of the Messiah, John the Baptist (cf. Matt. 11:10).
3:7-12. The people's sin of robbing God.
3:13-4:3. The people's sin of criticizing the Lord. The people said that it did not pay to serve God, 14.
4:4-6. Concluding warning. Malachi, in remonstrating with the priests and people of his day concerning their sins, has a message for us in our day when similar sins prevail. His messianic flashes (3:16; 4:2) prepare us for the NT revelation and focus our attention on Him who alone is the world's hope.

Bible Weights and Measures

Measures of length OT

Finger	0.72 in.
Handbreadth = 4 fingers	2.91 in.
Span = 3 handbreadths	8.74 in.
Cubit = 2 spans	17.49 in.
Ezekiel's cubit = 7 handbreadths	20.37 in

Weights OT

Gerah	8.81 grains.
Bekah 10 gerahs =	88.10 grains.
Shekel 2 bekahs =	176.20 grains.
Maneh = 50 shekels =	20.148 oz.
Talent = 60 manehs =	75.558 lbs.

Measures of capacity OT

Dry measures

Kab	1.159 qts.
Omer = 1 4/5 kabs	2.087 qts.
Seah = 3 1/3 omers	6.959 qts.
Ephah = 3 seahs	20.878 qts.
Lethech = 5 ephahs	3.262 bu.
Kor/homer = 2 lethechs	6.524 bu.

Measures of capacity OT

Liquid measures

Log	0.674 pts.
Kab = 4 logs	1.349 qts.
Hin = 3 kabs	1.012 gals.
Bath = 6 hins	6.073 gals.
Kor = 10 baths	60.738 gals.

Weights NT

Shekel (silver) =	4 Rom. denarii
	(4 Gr.drachma.)
Shekel (gold)	= 15 silver shekels.
Mina (silver) =	50 silver shekels.
Mina (gold) =	50 gold shekels.
Talent (gold) =	3,000 shekels.
Litra	1 Rom. pound (12 oz).
	(John 12:3; 19:39)

Measures of capacity NT

Dry measures

Choinex	0.98 qts.
Modios Lat. modius	7.68 qts.
Saton Hebrew seah	12.18 qts.
Koros Hebrew kor	6.52 bu.
Cubit pechus	about 1.5 ft.
Fathom orguia	about 72.4 in.
Furlong stadion	about 606 ft.
Mile milion	about 4,879 ft.
Sabbath day's journey	about 3/5 mile.

Measures of capacity NT

Liquid measures

Xestes (Lat. sextarius)	1.12 pts.
Batos (Hebrew bath)	6.07 gals.
Metretes (John 2:6)	10.3 gals.
Koros (Hebrew kor)	60.73 gals

Between the Testaments

The four hundred silent years

From Malachi (c. 400 B.C.), the last prophetic voice of the OT, to the coming of Jesus, divine revelation as it developed in the production of canonical Scripture was in abeyance. The result was the completion of the Hebrew canon. According to Josephus, a Jewish historian of the second half of the first century A.D., this took place in the reign of Artaxerxes I Longimanus, 465-424 B.C.

Importance of intertestamental period

During this 400 year period the OT was translated into the Greek language. This version was produced c. 280-150 B.C. and was called the Septuagint. It released the great truths of OT Scripture from the restricted influence of the Hebrew language and people, and gave them to the Graeco-Roman world in the common speech of the day.

The Apocrypha

The Apocrypha is the name given to the 14 books that originated in the period between the OT and the NT *after* the OT canon had closed. These apocryphal books were *never* in the OT Hebrew canon. They were included in the Septuagint and the Latin Vulgate, being placed between the OT and NT. The Roman Catholic church accepts 11 of the 14 as so-called deutero-canonical books, declaring them to be an equal part of Scripture by the Council of Trent in A.D. 1546. Protestants deny the canonical status of these books on the basis both of internal and external evidence. They were never recognized as Scripture by the Jews, nor by Jesus, nor by the apostolic community.

The books of the Apocrypha are:

1 Esdras

2 Esdras

Tobit

Judith

The remainder of Esther

The Wisdom of Solomon

Ecclesiasticus

1 Maccabees

2 Maccabees

Baruch

The Song of the Three Children

Story of Susanna

Bel and the Dragon

The Prayer of Manasses

Preparation for the Greek New Testament

The interbiblical period witnessed the development of the various Greek dialects into a *lingua franca* of the Hellenistic world through the conquests of Alexander the Great. This universal language vitally affected the Jews of the diaspora and resulted in the translation of the OT into Greek (the Septuagint). This translation became an important factor in the formation of the NT, and with it constituted the Bible of early Christianity.

Introducing the New Testament

The OT constitutes the *preparation* for Christ and contains prophecies of His divine person and redemptive work. The NT is the account of the realization of these predictions in the *appearance* of the Redeemer and the provisions of His glorious gospel.

In the Gospels Christ is *manifested* to the world and His gospel *provided* in the death, resurrection, and ascension of the Redeemer. In the Acts Christ is *proclaimed* and His gospel *propagated* in the world. In the letters His gospel is *expounded* in its doctrinal and practical meaning. In the book of Revelation all the redemptive purposes of God in and through the Redeemer are *consummated* for time and eternity. The NT is thus the capstone and fulfillment of the prophetic and redemptive truths contained in the OT, the OT forming the foundation for the completed edifice of revealed truth found in the NT.

A scribe of Bible times.

Events of the Intertestamental Period

424-331
Malachi, last OT prophet.
Palestine a tiny province under rule of Persian governor.

359-332
Jews enjoyed comparative peace and prosperity under their Persian overlords.

338-323
Jews were torn between allegiance to Persian overlords and threat of Alexander's conquests.
Alexander swept into Syria taking Palestine, Tyre, Gaza. Jews submitted to Alexander and were treated well. Alexander conquered Egypt. Alexandria was founded.

323-277
Dissemination of Greek language, culture, and philosophy by Alexander's conquests.

Palestine under the Ptolemies (323-198)
Ptolemy I favored Jews and settled many in Alexandria, which he raised to economic and cultural heights.
Ptolemy II favored Jews. Began translation of OT into Greek (Septuagint).

Palestine under Seleucids (198-165)
198
Antiochus III, the Great, annexed Palestine to the Seleucid Empire.
Septuagint completed (c. 150).

167-165
Enforced Hellenization of Jews.
Antiochus IV sacked Jerusalem, profaned the temple, offered sacrifices to Olympian Zeus on altar of burnt offering.
Maccabean revolt led by aged priest Mattathias and his five sons.

Alexander conquered Egypt in 335 B.C.

Simon captured Joppa (modern Jaffa).

166-134
Palestine under the Hasmonaeans (166-163)
Judas (166-160) defeated Syrian armies, cleansed and rededicated the temple (166-165).
Jonathan (160-143) made great strides towards Jewish independence.
Simon (143-135) inaugurated period of Jewish independence (143-163). Expelled Syrian garrison from Jerusalem, conquered Gezer and Joppa.

134-104
John Hyrcanus (135-104), son of Simon, embarked on a career of conquest in Transjordan in Samaria, destroying the rival temple on Gerizim. Rise of the two great parties

in Judaism—Pharisees and Sadducees—as well as the Essenes.

104-169
Aristobulus I (104-103)
Alexander Jannaeus (103-76), ruthless conqueror, sealed fate of Hasmonaean dynasty by alienating Pharisees.
Alexandra (76-67), Alexander Jannaeus's wife. Golden age of Pharisaism.
Aristobulus II (67-63) Deposed and carried to Rome to grace Pompey's triumph.

63-41
Pompey brought Palestine under Roman control and organized the Decapolis league in Tansjordan to balance the power of Judea, which was reduced to its former smallness.

40-4
Palestine under the Romans (63 B.C.-A.D. 135)
Antipater the Idumaean ruled Palestine under Roman grant (55-43). Herod and Phasael, Antipater's sons, were tetrarchs (41).
Antigonus, Aristobulus's son, was high priest and king through the help of the Parthians (40-37).
Herod the Great was king of Judea by Roman senatorial grant (37-4).
Birth of John the Baptist and Jesus (c. 6 or 5).

Political background in New Testament times

Roman Emperors

Caesar Augustus
27 B.C.-A.D. 14

Birth of Jesus, boyhood at Nazareth

Tiberius Caesar 14-37 Public ministry, death, resurrection of Jesus

Caligula 37-41 Growth of church, conversion of Paul
Claudius 41-54 Early missionary labors of Paul

Nero 54-68 Paul's later labors; martyrdom at Rome

Galba, Otho, Vitellius 68-69 Jewish Roman war in Palestine
Vespasian 69-79 Fall and destruction of Jerusalem and the Jewish state; Jews scattered

Titus 79-81

Domitian 81-96 John's probable exile to Patmos; the book of Revelation

Herodian Rulers

Herod the Great 37-4 B.C King of Jews, great builder, Hellenizer.

Archelaus 4 B.C.-A.D. 6 Son of Herod, ethnarch of Judea, cruel.

Herod Antipas 4 B.C-A.D. 39 Tetrarch of Galilee and Perea. Killed John the Baptist.

Philip 4 B.C.-A.D. 34 Tetrarch of Iturea and Trachonitis.

Herod Agrippa I 37-44 Ruled tetrarchy of Philip, Judea, Perea, and Galilee (**41-44**)

Herod Agrippa II 50-100 Ruled former tetrarchy of Philip and Lysanias and parts of Galilee and Perea

Procurators

Pontius Pilate was Procurator of Judea and Palestine 26-36

The four gospels

What the Gospels are

The four gospels are neither histories of the life of Christ nor biographies. They are rather portraits of the person and work of the long-promised Messiah, Israel's King and the world's Savior. As portraits they present four different poses of *one* unique personality. Matthew by the Holy Spirit presents Christ as King, Mark as Servant, Luke as Man, and John as God. But all four writers present the one and same unique Person, the God-man, Servant of the Lord, King of Israel, humanity's Redeemer.

The meaning of the word "gospel"

As applied to the four portraits of Christ, the term "gospel" (cf. Mark 1:1) is used in the sense of the good news of salvation provided by the death, burial, and resurrection of Christ (cf. 1 Cor. 15:1-4). The Gospels are an account of the provision of the gospel for needy sinners in the person and work of Christ.

What the Gospels accomplish

Describing the eternal preexistence, human birth, death, resurrection, and ascension of Jesus the Christ, as well as His life and teachings, the four gospels present a living, dynamic, unique personality, God become man, to work out man's redemption from sin. These four portraits present Him as Lord and Savior, rather than describing all He did and in the precise order in which He did it. They introduce us to Him, rather than to His life as a whole.

The Gospels are designedly incomplete as a story, but marvelously complete and purposeful as a divine revelation of the Son of God our Savior!

The Gospels and humanity

The four gospels are directed toward the various classes of society that existed in the first century A.D.—Matthew toward the Jews, Mark toward the Romans, Luke toward the Greeks, and John toward believers on the Lord Jesus Christ.

Papyrus fragment of probably the earliest surviving document of the New Testament, dating to *c.* A.D. 130.

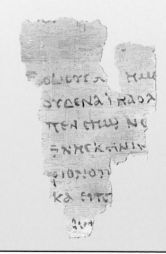

NEW TESTAMENT

Matthew
The Gospel of the Son of David

Outline

1-12	The King appears and His kingdom is rejected
13-25	The King's teaching and ministry
26-27	The King's passion and death
28	The King's resurrection and commission

The author. The writer of this gospel is anonymous, but from a very early period he has been identified as Matthew or Levi, the tax collector, a Galilean Jew who became one of Jesus' disciples. This would give a mid-first century date to the book.

Matthew's theme. Matthew is a Jewish gospel, rooted in OT prophecy relating to the coming of the Messiah-King and His kingdom. The Jews' rejection of Him as King is followed by His death as the son of Abraham and His resurrection as the Son of God.

The town of Bethlehem seen from the surrounding hills.

Matthew

1. The genealogy and birth of the King

1-17. A royal family tree. This genealogy proves that Jesus was born with legal right to be King of the Jews since He was the son of David, the son of Abraham. It is selective, having three divisions of fourteen generations each, David alone being designated as king. Jesus had no legal right to the throne as the virgin-born son of Mary. This had to come through Joseph.

18-25. His virgin birth. The account of His conception by the Holy Spirit in the womb of a virgin shows Jesus to be the Son of God, who became man, fulfilling Isaiah 7:14. Hence He had a sinless human nature joined to deity.

2. The infancy of the King

1-12. The magi's visit. This visit of believing Gentiles to worship the newborn King particularly fits this Gospel of the King and is recorded only here. Herod the Great, an able and cruel Idumaean, who even murdered some of his own family, ruled Judea as king by permission of the Roman senate from 37 to 4 B.C. The magi brought gold, symbolizing the King's deity; incense, indicating the fragrance of His life; and myrrh, used to embalm the dead, foreshadowing His death.

13-23. Flight into Egypt. Egypt, the site of Israel's great enslavement, now became the

The Star of Bethlehem

Various explanations for the appearance of the star—a supernova, a comet, or the triple conjunction of Saturn and Jupiter—should not obscure the its supernatural purpose. It was a sign of the birth of the King of kings.

The traditional site of Jesus' birth.

refuge of Israel's Deliverer and the world's Redeemer.

3. The King's herald and baptism

1-12. The King's herald. John the Baptist, predicted in the OT, 3, appears as the King's forerunner. His message, "Repent, for the kingdom of heaven is near," 2, announces the messianic kingdom, over which David's son and Lord is to reign.

John's baptism was not Christian baptism, but an outward act signifying the repentance of the candidate.

13-17. The King's baptism. The sinless one insisted on a ceremony that signified confession of sin and repentance "to fulfill all righteousness," 15, i.e., the righteous requirements of the Mosaic law. The Levitical law laid down that all priests should be consecrated by washing and anointing (Ex. 29:47; Lev. 8:6-36). Jesus' baptism (washing), 14-15, was followed by His anointing, when the heavens were opened, the Holy Spirit came on Him, 16, and the Father's voice was heard.

4. The testing of the King

1-11. Testing by the devil. The man of obedience conquered Satan by the Word of God in Deuteronomy, the book of obedience (cf. Deut. 8:3; 6:16; 10:20).

12-25. The King begins his public ministry. The King's message was, "Repent, for the kingdom of heaven is near," 17. "Near" or "has drawn near" meant that the King was then present and that a genuine offer of the kingdom was being made to Israel on the one condition of her repentance. Peter and Andrew, and James and John were called to be Jesus' disciples, 18-22. On Decapolis, 25, see note at Mark 7.

5-7. The Sermon on the Mount

5:1-16. Character of the citizens of the kingdom. The beatitudes, 1-12, give the character of those who inherit the kingdom.

5:17-48. The King and the Mosaic law. The King fulfilled the law, confirming and emphasizing its deeper spiritual meaning.

6:1-18. Heirs of the kingdom and prayer. Heirs of the kingdom are to be motivated by true inner righteousness. The Lord's Prayer, or "The Disciple's Prayer," is a timeless masterpiece that serves as a model for all prayer.

6:19-34. The world. How heirs of the kingdom are to act toward worldly wealth and cares is here outlined.

7:1-14. Censorious judging. Judgment of motives is here forbidden. "Dog" and "pig," 6, symbolize unregenerated externalists. The "golden rule," 12, summarizes proper human motives.

7:15-29. False teachers. False teachers are known by their fruit.

8-9. The manifestation of the King

8:1-17. The King's power over sickness. Miraculous signs demonstrated to Israel that the kingdom was at hand.

8:18-34. The King's power over nature and demons.

9:1-38. The King's power to forgive sin and other signs. The paralytic's healing showed the King's power to forgive sin.

10. The King's ambassadors

1-15. The Twelve and their commission. Their commission was to confirm the gospel of the kingdom with miraculous powers.

16-42. Resumption of the commission. Verses 24-42 give encouragement to true disciples of the King.

The reconstructed third-century synagogue at Capernaum, on the Sea of Galilee.

11. Rejection of the kingdom message

1-19. John the Baptist rejected. He that is least in the kingdom of heaven, 11, when it is established on earth, will be greater in position (not in moral grandeur) than John.

20-24. The King rejected. At Korazin, just two miles north of Capernaum, extensive ruins remain, including a synagogue. Bethsaida, meaning "houses of fishing," was the fishing quarter of Capernaum.

25-30. The new message of the King. Turning from the unrepentant nation, the King offered rest and service to individuals.

12. Rejection of the King

1-21. The King in rejection. The events of this chapter focus on the full rejection of the kingdom and mark the great turning point in Matthew's gospel.

22-45. The King and the unpardonable sin. The Pharisees, 24, committed the unpardonable sin of attributing the mighty works of the incarnate King to satanic power, rather than to the Holy Spirit, 25-32.

46-50. The King's new relationship. The King refused to see even His own family, symbolizing that He was cut off from His own nation.

13. The rejected King tells of the interim kingdom

1-2. The King at the seaside. The King began to teach in parables. These parables, reported in full only in Matthew, portray the mysteries of the kingdom of heaven.

3-52. The seven parables (secrets) of the kingdom. They are called "secrets" because they contain truth previously not revealed. The seven parables deal with the present age when

Israel, the vineyard, is untended (Isa. 5:1-7).
53-58. Further evidences of the King's rejection.

14. The martyrdom of the King's herald

1-14. John's martyrdom. Herod Antipas was denounced by John the Baptist for his incestuous marriage to his niece Herodias, former wife of his half-brother, Herod Philip.
15-36. Jesus' ministry of mercy.

15. Further ministry of the rejected King

1-20. His denunciation of the scribes and Pharisees. Jesus condemned their sin of setting aside the word of God by their traditions, 3-6.
21-28. He ministers to a Gentile. The rejected son of David ministered to a non-Israelite of Phoenicia, here called "the region of Tyre and Sidon" after its two principal seaports. The "dogs" were Gentiles, outside the sphere of Jewish spiritual privilege, referred to as "the children's bread," 26. This episode prefigured Gentile salvation in this age.
29-39. He ministers to the multitudes. Feeding the 4,000 showed the compassion of the King.

16. The rejected King predicts His death

1-12. The leaven of the scribes and Pharisees. The leaven of the Pharisees was hypocritical externalism, that of the Sadducees rationalistic belief. Both rejected the King and His kingdom.
13-19. Peter's confession. On Caesarea Philippi, 13, see note on Mark 8:27. Peter's confession involved the full deity of Jesus, "Christ, the Son of the living God," 16. The deity of Christ was to be the foundation of the church, 18, and not Peter himself: "You are Peter (*petros,* a stone), and on this rock (*petra,* great ledge of rock) I will build my church."
20-28. Christ foretells His death, resurrection, and return. Peter and the other disciples could not understand Christ's sudden prediction of His sufferings and death, 22-23, so they had to be instructed in the rigors of true discipleship, 24-26, and rewards at the Second Coming of the King, 27-28.

17. The rejected King and His coming glory

1-21. The transfiguration. Christ's transfiguration was a portrayal, in miniature, of His Second Coming in glory: Christ in glory, and Moses and Elijah glorified. Moses represents the redeemed who have entered the kingdom through death, and Elijah the redeemed who have entered by translation.
22-23. Jesus' repetition of His approaching death.
24-27. The temple tax. Our Lord was, in effect, saying, "This is a tax for supporting My Father's house. As His Son, then, this tax is not incumbent on Me. I am free."

18. Instructions of the rejected King —forgiveness

1-14. Character of citizens of the kingdom. The disciples were interested in holding office; Jesus stressed the importance, rather, of being a citizen of the kingdom by being converted, 2-3, and by showing the humility of a child, 4-5.
15-20. Discipline and prayer in the kingdom.

Jesus healed two blind men outside Jericho.

The church is here anticipated. Discipline is to take a certain pattern so that the injured member will know how to respond. This is the procedure of love and patience, bathed in prayer.

21-35. Forgiveness in the kingdom. Genuine forgiveness is beyond record-keeping.

19. Instructions of the rejected King —divorce

1-15. Divorce. Monogamy is God's standard, 4-6, but certain accommodations to human frailty were permitted by the Mosaic law, 7-8 (Deut. 24:1-4). Christ seems to allow only adultery as a ground for divorce, 9, but also takes into consideration men's weaknesses, 10-12.

16-26. The rich young man. Religious and moral but unsaved, this young man pictures the case of many in Christendom.

27-30. Rewards in the renewal (re-creation).

20. Instructions of the rejected King —the laborers

1-16. Parable of the laborers. This parable corrects Peter's self-occupation and bargaining spirit.

17-28. Jesus again predicts His death and resurrection. The request of the mother of James and John shows that she misunderstood the character of the promised kingdom.

29-34. Two blind men healed. They called on Jesus as "Son of David" and recognized His messianic authority.

21. The rejected King enters Jerusalem

1-11. The royal entry into Jerusalem. Jesus came to Jerusalem as King to fulfill the prophecy of Zechariah (Zech. 9:9). Although acclaimed superficially by excited mobs, He was still the rejected King, for the official representatives of the nations did not welcome Him.

12-32. Second cleansing of the temple and the fig tree cursed. The first cleansing of the temple was at the beginning of His ministry (John 2:13-17); this was at the end, 12-13. The barren fig tree, 18-22, is a type of Israel (Joel 1:7), here symbolized in national rejection.

33-46. Parable of the landowner. The landowner (God) planted a vineyard (Israel, Isa. 5:1-7). The servants were the prophets. God sent His Son and they put Him to death, 37-39.

22-23. The rejected King clashes with the leaders

22:1-14. Parable of the wedding banquet.
This parable portrays how the King and the kingdom were offered to the nation, 1-2, but were refused, 3. The wedding clothes, 11-14, are the righteousness of Christ.

22:15-46. The nation further shows its rejection.
The Herodians were Jews in external religious forms, and the Sadducees, 23-33, were the religious rationalists. Jesus confounded the Pharisees by asking them about Psalm 110:1, which refers to His own divine-human person, 41-46.

23:1-39. The doom pronounced and lament made over Jerusalem.

24-25. The rejected King's Mount of Olives discourse

24:1-3. Prophecy of the destruction of the temple.
The rejected King, as Prophet, predicted future events when He would resume dealing with Israel (cf. 23:39) just before His return to earth in glory.

24:4-26. Events of the Tribulation.
Verses 9-26 describe the events of the last half of the Tribulation after the world leader (Antichrist) has broken his covenant with Israel and forced idolatrous worship of himself (Dan. 9:27b; 2 Thess. 2:4; Rev. 13:15-18).

24:27-30. Second Coming of Messiah.
This follows immediately after the Tribulation, 29.

24:31. Regathering of Israel.

24:32-36. The certainty of the Messiah's coming.

24:36-51. Exhortations to watchfulness.
All three illustrations emphasize the unexpectedness of the Lord's coming.

25:1-30. The judgment of Israel.
The ten virgins, 1-13, represent Israel at the end of the Tribulation. Those without oil (a symbol of the Holy Spirit) will be shut out of the messianic kingdom.

In the parable of the talents, 14-30, the man going on a journey represents Christ during His absence from the earth.

25:31-46. The judgment of the nations.
The rejected King presented a picture of that for which Israel had been looking in His first coming, Messiah sitting on the Davidic throne of glory, 31.

26. Betrayal and arrest of the rejected King

1-16. His anointing for death.
Mary of Bethany alone seemed to have understood the meaning of the King's death.

17-35. The Passover and the Lord's supper.
The Passover, commemorative of Israel's deliverance out of Egypt by the blood of the slain lamb (Ex. 12), was to be fulfilled in Christ's death, as the true Paschal Lamb. At the last Passover, 17-25, the King introduced the new memorial, the Lord's Supper, with the new meaning, 26-30, "Do this in remembrance of me" (1 Cor. 11:24-25).

36-56. Christ's agony at Gethsemane.
This involved no fear of death, but the contact of His sinless soul with the sin of the whole world as its vicarious bearer and expiator through the death of the cross (Isa. 53:10; 2 Cor. 5:21).

57-68. The King before Caiaphas and the Sanhedrin.

69-75. Peter's denial.

The Citadel, Jerusalem, probable site of Jesus' trial before Pontius Pilate.

27. The trial and death of the rejected King

1-32. Jesus before Pilate. The Sanhedrin handed over Jesus to Pontius Pilate, the Roman procurator of Judea (A.D. 26-36), since Rome was the final authority. The choice of Barabbas, a notorious criminal, 15-23, highlighted Pilate's cowardice, as did his washing of his hands as a sign of his innocence. Flogging, 26, was pitiless lashing with a whip of leather thongs embedded with pieces of metal. It usually preceded capital punishment.

33-44. The crucifixion of the King. "Golgotha" is the Aramaic for "skull." Since 1842, when Otto Thenius of Dresden located Calvary on a rocky hill 250 yards northeast of the Damascus Gate, this spot has been popularly identified as the location of the crucifixion. Gall, 34, was a bitter and poisonous herb, offered to Jesus as a painkiller, but it was refused. See notes on "Passion Week" and "Trials of Jesus," Luke 23.)

45-50. The death of the King. The three-hour darkness was a supernatural phenomenon when the Father hid His face from the Son as He became sin for us and cried out, 46, the pitiable words of Psalm 22:1.

51-56. The end of the legal age. The supernatural tearing of the curtain that separated the holy place, into which priests might enter, from the holy place, which only the high priest could enter once a year on the day of atonement (Ex. 26:31; Lev. 16), signified that all believers could now go into God's presence through Christ's death (cf. Heb. 9:1-8; 10:19-22).

57-66. The burial of the King.

Matthew and Mark Compared

Matthew	Mark
Jesus as King	Jesus as Servant
Jews in mind	Gentiles in mind
Jesus the predicted miracle-working King	Jesus the miracle-working Servant
Rooted in OT prophecy	Much fewer OT prophetic references
Key in God's purposes for Israel	Key in God's purposes for the world
Deity of the King by birth, fulfilled prophecy, works	Deity of the Servant by mighty works
Events recorded concerning the King —His genealogy, birth in Bethlehem, visit of wise men, childhood in Nazareth	All these omitted as not appropriate to the Servant portrait
Sermon on Mount, spoken as King, giving the principles of the kingdom	Omitted
Many parables included which belong to this gospel of the King	Omits many of the parables
Presents the King of the Jews rejected	Presents the Servant of the Lord in life, death, resurrection, bringing salvation

28. The resurrection of the rejected King

1-10. The resurrection. The Sabbath (Saturday) ended at 6:00 p.m., and just before daybreak on Sunday, the first Easter (cf. John 20:1), the women came to the tomb to anoint Jesus' body. They thus showed much love but little faith in His resurrection (Mark 16:1, 11), being last at the cross and first at the tomb.

11-15. The false report of the Jews. If the Roman soldiers fell asleep, 13, they were liable to death. And if they did fall asleep, their testimony about the alleged theft would be worthless.

16-20. The great commission. The gospel ends with the promise of the Lord's continued presence with His own, 20b.

Mark
The gospel of the Servant of the Lord

Outline

1:1-13   The Servant's coming
1:14-13:37 The Servant's work
14:1-15:47 The Servant's death
16:1-20   The Servant's resurrection

Author. The early church ascribed the second gospel to John Mark, the son of a certain Mary of Jerusalem (Acts 12:12). He accompanied Paul and Barnabas on the first missionary journey but for some reason left them at Perga (Acts 13:13). Paul refused to have Mark on the second tour. Later Paul and Mark were reconciled (Col. 4:10-11).

Nature and purpose of Mark's gospel. This is the briefest of the four gospels. It is a narrative of dynamic movement and action, "straightway" and "immediately" being used more than 40 times in the KJV. It presents Jesus acting rather than speaking. It is directed not to the Jew as is Matthew, but to the Roman world, giving a portrait of Jesus as the powerful Son of God whose word was law in the natural as well as the supernatural realm. The paradox is that this strong Son of God is Servant of man, Savior, and Ransomer (Mark 10:45).

Galilee from near the Mount of Beatitudes.

Mark

1:1-13. The Servant's coming

1. The Servant's identity. He is "Jesus Christ [Messiah the Anointed One], the Son of God," i.e., Deity incarnate.

2-8. The Servant's coming promised and announced. Malachi ("the prophets," KJV) foretold His coming, 2 (Mal. 3:1), as well as Isaiah, 3 (Isa. 40:3); and John the Baptist, His forerunner, announced His coming.

9-11. The Servant's baptism. The Sinless One as Servant-Savior submitted to the baptism of sinners to identify Himself with them in their need.

12-13. The Servant's testing. This was a divine necessity, because His humanity had to be tried as a servant.

1:14-45. Ministry in Galilee

14-15. The Servant's message.

16-20. The Servant calls helpers. As a humble servant Himself, He called lowly fishermen, 16-20, to make them "fishers of men," 17.

21-28. The Servant casts out demons in Capernaum. The Servant's ministry was dynamic, not ritualistic, 21-22.

29-45. Other ministries of the Servant. These ministries included numerous healings, and further casting out demons; the Servant's prayer life, 35; His tour of Galilee, 36-39.

2. Further ministry in Capernaum

1-12. Healing the paralytic. Jesus' healing of the paralytic was proof of the deity of the Servant, for He alone could forgive sins, 5.

13-22. Calling Matthew. As a tax collector for Rome, Levi was despised and counted as a common sinner, 14.

23-28. The Servant and the Sabbath. As the redeeming Servant, by His death and resurrection He was to supplant the Sabbath by the Lord's Day.

3. The Servant further displays His deity

1-12. Man with the withered hand healed. By this miracle in the synagogue the Servant proved what He had said about the Sabbath in 2:27-28.

13-19. The choosing of the twelve.

Peter was a strange mixture of cowardice and courage, impulsiveness and fearlessness.

James, brother of John, suffered martyrdom under Herod (Acts 12:2).

John. See introduction to John's gospel.

Andrew led his brother Peter to Christ (John 1:40-42).

Philip brought Nathanael to Christ. With Peter and Andrew he came from Bethsaida.

Bartholomew, James the son of Alphaeus, Thaddeus. Little is known about them.

Matthew. See introduction to Matthew's gospel.

Thomas ("twin") displayed zeal (John 11:16), but also a spirit of skepticism about Christ's resurrection (John 20:24-25).

Simon the Zealot had been a member of an extremely nationalistic sect of Judaism.

Judas Iscariot betrayed Jesus (Matt. 26:46-50).

20-30. The unpardonable sin. See note on

Matthew 12:24-37.
31-35. The Servant's new relationship.
See note on Matthew 12:46-50.

4. The Servant's seaside teaching
1-29. The parable of the sower. The vivid contrast between mere profession and genuine possession of the Word may be noted

throughout the parable. The gospel must shine forth into testimony, 21-25, and grow in fruitfulness, 26-29.
30-34. The parable of the mustard seed. The rapid growth of the present kingdom of God is shown here, for the common mustard seed is extremely small but grows into a plant twelve feet high.
35-41. The Servant and the storm. Jesus' rebuke of the winds showed His power and deliverance, which are available for His own.

5:1-20. The Servant's power over Satan
See feature on Demonism opposite

5:21-43. The Servant's power over disease and death

6-7. The Servant's rejection
6:1-6. In his hometown. The people saw Jesus as Joseph's actual son, as a carpenter, 3, as a mere sinful man with brothers and sisters.
6:7-13. He sends out the Twelve.
6:14-29. John the Baptist's martyrdom described. See note on Matthew 14:1-14.
6:30-44. Miracle of the five thousand fed. See feature on Miracles in Mark 5.
6:45-52. Miracle of walking on the water. The Servant is the mighty Son of God.
6:53-56. Healings at Gennesaret.
7:1-23. The empty religionism of the Pharisees. The Pharisees were blinded in their rejection of and opposition to the Servant Son of God.
7:24-30. The Servant and the Syrophoenician woman. See note on Matthew 15:21-28.
7:31-37. The healing of the deaf and dumb man. See feature on Miracles in Mark 5.

Capernaum

This busy fishing port on the northwest shore of the Sea of Galilee was also a toll-collecting station (Matt. 9:9; 17:24-27), gathering tax revenue from caravans en route from Damascus to the Mediterranean coast and Egypt. Jesus' headquarters were located here. One of the finest white limestone synagogues in Palestine, dating back to the third century, has been excavated and restored here. It was probably built on the site of the synagogue in which Jesus ministered.

The restored synagogue, Capernaum.

8. The Servant predicts His death
1-9. Miracle of feeding the four thousand.
See feature on Miracles in Mark 5.
10-21. The wicked unbelief of the Pharisees.
22-26. The blind man healed at Bethsaida.
See feature on Miracles in Mark 5.
27-38. Peter's confession of faith.

Caesarea Philippi

Caesarea Philippi, i.e., Caesarea of Philip was rebuilt and enlarged by this son of Herod the Great. Its name had been Panias, in honor of the nature god Pan worshiped there, but was changed to Caesarea in honor of the then reigning Caesar Tiberius. At this center sacred to paganism it is significant that Jesus broached the subject of His deity.

Niches for images of Pan, Banias.

Demonism

Demons are evil or unclean spirits (cf. Mark 1:23 with Mark 1:32-34; Rev. 16:13-16), and are fallen angels, servants of Satan (Matt. 12:26-27; 25:41). There is only one devil, but myriads of demons serve the devil and make his power practically universal. A demoniac (Mark 5:1-20) is a person whose personality has been invaded by one or more demons, who at will can speak and act through their human victim, deranging both his mind and body (Matt. 12:22; 17:15-18; Luke 13:16).

Demons know the deity and lordship of Christ in the spirit world (Matt. 8:31-32; Mark 1:24; Acts 19:15; James 2:19) and realize their predestined fate (Matt. 8:29-32; Luke 8:31). They have a conspicuous role in the government of the satanic world system (Dan. 10:13; Eph. 6:12), in promoting false doctrine (1 Tim. 4:1-3), and in opposing God's program and God's people (1 John 4:1-6).

Prayer is the believer's resource against Satan and demons (Eph. 6:10-20).

Expulsion of demons Specific instances

Mark 1:21-28; Luke 4:31-37. Demoniac in the synagogue at Capernaum.

Matthew 9:32-34. Dumb demoniac.

Matthew 15:21-28; Mark 7:24-30. Daughter of the Syrophoenician woman.

Matthew 8:28-34; Mark 5:1-20; Luke 8:26-39. Gadarene demoniacs.

Matthew 12:22; Luke 11:14. Blind and mute demoniac.

Matthew 17:14-21; Mark 9:14-29; Luke 9:37-43. Epileptic child.

Miracles of physical healing

A leper	Matt. 8:2-4; Mark 1:40-45; Luke 5:12-15
A paralytic	Matt. 9:2-8; Mark 2:3-12; Luke 5:18-26
Fever (Peter's mother-in-law)	Matt. 8:14-17; Mark 1:29-31
Nobleman's son healed	John 4:46-53
Physical infirmity	John 5:1-9
A withered hand	Matt. 12:9-13; Mark 3:1-6; Luke 6:6-11
Deafness and dumbness	Mark 7:31-37
Blindness at Bethsaida	Mark 8:22-25
Blindness in Jerusalem	John 9
Bartimaeus	Mark 10:46-52
Ten lepers	Luke 17:11-19
Malchus's severed ear	Luke 22:47-51
Hemorrhage	Matt. 9:20-22; Mark 5:25-34; Luke 8:43-48
Dropsy	Luke 14:2-4

Miracles of resurrection

Jairus's daughter	Matt. 9:18-26; Mark 5:35-43; Luke 8:41-56
Widow's son	Luke 7:11-15
Lazarus of Bethany	John 11:1-44

Miracles of nature

Water converted to wine	John 2:1-11
Stilling of a storm	Matt. 8:23-27; Mark 4:35-41; Luke 8:22-25
Supernatural catch of fish	Luke 5:1-11; John 21:6
Multiplying food: 5,000 fed	Luke 9:11-17; John 6:1-14
Multiplying food: 4,000 fed	Matt. 15:32-39; Mark 8:1-9
Walking on water	Matt. 14:22-33; Mark 6:45-52; John 6:19
Money from a fish	Matt. 17:24-27
Fig tree dried up	Matt. 21:18-22; Mark 11:12-14

Method and purpose of the Servant's miracles

The purpose of the Servant's miracles was to authenticate the King (Matthew), the Servant (Mark), the Man (Luke), and God (John) as the Creator-Redeemer and the world's Savior. Jesus' miracles were outward demonstrations of His deity and messiahship. They were also the expression of His love for the human race.

Most of Jesus' miracles are unrecorded (cf. Matt. 4:24; 15:30-31; Mark 6:53-56; Luke 4:40; 6:17-19; John 21:25). Those that are recorded, as in John's gospel (cf. John 20:30-31), are selected for a specific purpose—to arouse faith in Jesus as "the Christ, the Son of God, and that by believing you may have life in his name."

9. The Servant's coming glory

1-13. The transfiguration. See notes on Matthew 17:1-21.

14-29. The demon-possessed boy. See feature on Miracles in Mark 5.

30-41. The Servant again predicts His death. The disciples' selfish bickering, 33-37, illustrated how little they understood the Lord's approaching death or its meaning, 31.

42-50. The Servant warns of hell. This is Gehenna, eternal hell, the "lake of fire" (Rev. 20:14-15), "the second death" (Rev. 21:8), signifying eternal separation from God. Gehenna was the rubbish pit for Jerusalem, where the worm (soul) never died and the fire never went out—a graphic picture of the eternal destiny of those who reject Christ.

10. The Servant's Perean ministry

1-16. Question of divorce. Jesus taught a monogamous standard on the subject of divorce, 6-8, teaching that God joins man and woman in marriage, 9, and that easy divorce is adultery, 10-12.

17-31. The rich young man. See note on Matthew 19:16-26.

32-34. The Servant again foretells His death.

35-45. James's and John's selfish ambition is contrasted with the Servant's aim to serve, 45. This verse is the key to Mark's presentation of the Son of God as Servant.

46-52. Bartimaeus receives his sight. See feature on Miracles in Mark 5.

11. The Servant's entry into Jerusalem

1-11. His presentation as King. This is in fulfillment of Zechariah 9:9.

12-14. The barren fig tree. See notes on

Jericho

Jericho of Jesus' day was Herod's winter palace. He and his son Archelaus beautified it with magnificent Hellenistic buildings—palace, theater, fortress, and hippodrome. Herodian Jericho was a splendid city 17 miles from Jerusalem, 1,000 feet below sea level in the Jordan Valley, with a delightful winter climate.

The site of Herod's palace, near Jericho.

Matthew 21:18-22.

15-21. The cleansing of the temple is another proof of the apostasy of the nation.

22-33. Faith contrasted with wicked unbelief. The prayer of faith, 22-26 (cf. James 5:15), starkly focused upon the unbelief of the scribes and elders who questioned Jesus' authority, 27-33, as further proof of their rejection of the King-Servant.

The Sea of Galilee

In Jesus' day this beautiful body of fresh water, 13 miles long and seven and a half miles wide, was dotted with populous towns, such as Capernaum, Bethsaida, Chorazin, Magdala, and Tiberias. The lake lies in a depressed cup 700 feet below sea level and enjoys a healthy semitropical climate. The lake was often subject to sudden and violent storms as the air from snowy Lebanon collided with the warmer air above the lake.

The lake abounds in fish, with fishing an important industry. The sunny climate, with the healthgiving sulfur springs near Tiberias, made it a mecca for the sick and a fruitful scene for Jesus' healing ministry (Mark 1:32-34).

Tiberias from the shore of the Sea of Galilee.

12. The Servant's teaching in Jerusalem

1-12. Parable giving a summary of Israel's spiritual history. See notes on Matthew 21:33-46.

13-17. Question of the tribute. The Pharisees and Herodians joined to trap the Servant. Jesus with omniscient wisdom declared the principle of the separation of church and state, and so silenced both groups.

18-27. The Servant silences the Sadducees. Jesus settles the question with one stroke—no marriage in heaven, but there is a resurrection, because Scripture so declares—and He quoted from the Pentateuch, which the Sadducees claimed to believe (cf. Ex. 3:6).

28-34. The great commandments. God is to be first in our affection, our neighbor second.

35-40. The Servant questions the Pharisees. Jesus silenced them and at the same time revealed their unbelief.

41-44. The widow's offering.

13. The Servant's Olivet discourse

1-4. Prediction concerning the temple. On Olivet in full view of Herod's resplendent edifice, Jesus predicted its destruction.

5-23. Events of the Tribulation. See notes on Matthew 24:4-26.

24-26. Second Coming of the Son of Man.

27. Regathering of Israel.

28-33. The certainty of Christ's coming. See note on "Time of the Second Coming" below.

34-37. Exhortations to watchfulness.

14. Events leading to the Servant's death

1-2. The plot.

Time of the Second Coming

Did the Son not know the time of His Second Coming? "No one knows about that day or hour, not even the angels in heaven, nor the Son, but only the Father" (Matt. 24:36; Mark 13:32). In Mark the Lord takes the place of complete humiliation as a Servant and the servant is properly presented as he who "does not know his master's business" (John 15:15). After his servantship was discharged in death and He was raised in glory, the glorified Son omnisciently knew all, having this particular disclosure given to Him (Rev. 1:1).

3-9. The Servant anointed for death. Mary of Bethany alone understood the full import of His approaching vicarious death.

10-11. Judas plans to betray Jesus.

12-26. The last Passover and the Lord's Supper. The Servant instituted the Lord's Supper, a memorial speaking of His death and second coming (1 Cor. 11:23-26), superseding and fulfilling the slain lamb typology of the Passover.

27-31. Peter's denial predicted.

32-42. Gethsemane's agony. See notes on Matthew 26:36-56.

43-52. Judas's betrayal and arrest of Jesus. Judas's base betrayal, 43-46, was followed by Peter's flashing ire and show of courage, 47-52.

53-65. Jesus before the Sanhedrin.

66-72. Peter's denial.

15. The Servant's death and burial

1-15. Jesus before Pilate. Jesus' silence before Pilate, the Roman procurator of Judea (A.D. 26-36), 5, fulfilled Isaiah 53:7.

Order of the events of the Crucifixion

Arrival at Golgotha (Calvary), Matt. 27:33; Mark 15:22; Luke 23:33; John 19:17
Offer of a benumbing drink, Matt. 27:34
The crucifixion, Matt. 27:35
First cry, "Father, forgive . . . ," Luke 23:34
The parting of Christ's garments, Matt. 27:35
Jesus is mocked, Matt. 27:39-44; Mark 15:29
The thieves rail on Him, but one believes, Matt. 27:44
Second cry, "Today you will be with me...," Luke 23:43
Third cry, "Dear woman, here is your son," John 19:26-27
The darkness, Matt. 27:45; Mark 15:33
Fourth cry, "My God, my God . . . ," Matt. 27:46-47; Mark 15:34-36
Fifth cry, "I am thirsty," John 19:28
Sixth cry, "It is finished," John 19:30
Seventh cry, "Father, into your hands . . . ," Luke 23:46
Jesus dismisses His spirit, Matt. 27:50; Mark 15:37

16-20. The king of the Jews mocked.

21-23. The road to the cross.

24-41. The crucifixion. See notes on Matthew 27:33-44.

42-47. The burial.

16. The Servant's resurrection

1-8. His resurrection. How gracious is the report of the angel of Jesus' resurrection, 6-7, with the appended note to Peter, who must have thought surely he was disowned—"But go, tell his disciples *and* Peter," 7.

9-20. His post-resurrection appearances.

Luke
The gospel of the Son of Man

Outline

1:1-4:13	Birth, childhood, early ministry
4:14-9:50	Galilean ministry
9:51-21:38	Journey to and ministry in Jerusalem
22:1-23:56	Rejection and death
24:1-53	Resurrection and ascension

The author. The author is "our dear friend Luke, the doctor" (cf. Col. 4:14; 2 Tim. 4:11; Philem. 24). He with Mark was a companion worker of Paul, shown by the "we" sections of Acts 16:10-11; 20:5ff.; 21:1ff.

The synoptic gospels. Matthew, Mark, and Luke constitute the synoptic gospels. Synoptic means "seeing the whole together at a glance." These three gospels, in contrast to John, present a common story and relate substantially the same incidents in the life of our Lord. The Holy Spirit presents through three different human writers, the *one* Messiah-King, Servant-Savior, God-Man. Each presents Him under a different aspect for a particular purpose, but the threefold presentation is of the one and same divine-human Person.

Characteristic Features of Luke's gospel

Luke compared with Matthew and Mark

Luke	Matthew	Mark
The human gospel	The kingly gospel	The servant gospel
Perfect manhood of Christ	Divine kingship of Christ	Divine servanthood of Christ
Basis of the saviorhood and present intercession Heb. 5:1-2	Basis of His offer of Himself to Israel and His coming kingdom Acts 1:6	Basis of His giving His life a ransom for many Mark 10:45
Moral perfections and tender sympathies of the perfect Man	Kingly power and humble grace of Israel's Savior-King	Miraculous power in service to mankind of the God-sent Servant
Our Lord in prayer stressing His dependency Appeal to Greek	Our Lord in kingly manifestation Appeal to Jew	Our Lord in Spirit-empowered service as a man Appeal to Roman

Luke

Mary and Joseph, living in Nazareth in Galilee, to fulfill the prophecy of Micah relating to the Messiah's birth in Bethlehem (Mic. 5:2).

1. Births of John and Jesus foretold

1-4. Introduction. "Theophilus" ("God-lover") connects this gospel as well as the book of Acts (Acts 1:1) with Luke as the author. He was Luke's literary patron, doubtless a high-ranking Roman Greek, since he is referred to as "most excellent."

5-25. Birth of John the Baptist foretold. John was to be born of a barren couple and was to minister in the spirit and power of Elijah (1 Kings 21:20; 2 Kings 1:8).

26-45. Birth of Jesus foretold. Gabriel visited Mary at Nazareth, 26-27, announcing the most glorious event of human history. Deity and humanity were to be united for the redemption of the fallen race.

46-56. Mary's ode of praise. Filled with OT Scripture and the Spirit of God, the virgin burst into praise (cf. 1 Sam. 2:1-10).

57-80. Birth of John and Zechariah's prophetic joy. Zechariah's prophecy was immersed in OT promises, which he saw would be fulfilled in the person and work of the coming King.

2:1-20. Birth of Jesus
1-3. Census of Quirinius.
4-20. Birth in Bethlehem. God's providence working through Caesar Augustus and the imperial enrollment decree made it possible for

Chronology of this period

6-5 B.C.
John's birth announced
to Zechariah — Luke 1:5-25

6 months later
Jesus' birth announced to Mary — Luke 1:26-38
Mary goes to see Elizabeth — Luke 1:39-56

3 months later
Mary returns to Nazareth — Luke 1:56
Joseph receives a message — Matt. 1:18-24
John born — Luke 1:57-80

5 B.C.
Jesus born — Matt. 1:25; Luke 2:1-7

8 days later
Jesus is circumcised — Luke 2:21

33 days later
Jesus presented in the temple — Luke 2:22-38

4 B.C.
Magi visit the King — Matt. 2:1-12
Flight to Egypt — Matt. 2:13-15
Murder of Bethlehem's
children — Matt. 2:16-18

3-2 B.C.
Return to Nazareth — Luke 2:39; Matt. 2:19-23

2:21-38. The infancy of Jesus

21-24. The circumcision and presentation.
These rites were prescribed in the Mosaic law
(Lev. 12:3; Ex. 13:12-13; Num. 8:17). They
demonstrated that the perfect Man "born of a
woman" was "born under law, to redeem those
under law" (Gal. 4:4-5).

25-38. Simeon's and Anna's prophecies.
These two elderly saints belonged to the faithful
remnant who believed the Word and waited for
Christ at His first coming. Anna, 36-38, is a
beautiful picture of devotion. She came in at the
glorious moment, 38, to see the Babe, her faith
in Him who could bring redemption being
rewarded.

2:39-52. The boyhood of Jesus

39-40. Synopsis of his boyhood years.
41-52. His visit to Jerusalem at twelve. This
incident is pivotal as our Lord's first self-witness
to His deity.

3:1-20. John's ministry

1-14. John's ministry. In a passage
remarkable for its accuracy and
comprehensiveness, 1-2, Luke pinpoints the

Date of Christmas

Our traditional date of December 25 as the
day of Christ's birth was set in the fourth
century by the Western church. The Eastern
church celebrates January 6. Actually the
day is unknown. The nativity is unlikely to
have occurred in the winter, since the
shepherds in Palestine do not stay in the
open with their flocks except from spring to
autumn.

Bethlehem

This ancient picturesque town, seven miles
south of Jerusalem, called Bethlehem-
Ephrathah in Micah 5:2, was the original
home of the Davidic family, called
Ephrathites (Ruth 1:2; 1 Sam. 17:12), since
they were residents of Ephrath, an early
suburb of the city. Under the ancient Church
of the Nativity, originally built in the fourth
century by Helena, mother of Constantine,
tradition points out the manger room. Just
east of the town is the Shepherds' Field
where the angels sang about the coming of
"a Savior . . . Christ the Lord," 11.

The market place in Bethlehem today.

beginning of John's ministry. The fifteenth year of Tiberias was c. A.D. 29. Pontius Pilate was procurator of Judea. John prepared the way for the Christian gospel by announcing the Messiah-Savior and His salvation.
15-20. John's testimony to Christ.

3:21-38. Baptism and genealogy of Jesus
21-22. The baptism of Jesus. Luke adds the detail that Jesus was praying when He was baptized and the heavens were opened, 21. Luke's Gospel of the perfect Man often portrays Jesus praying as the expression of human dependence on God.
23-38. The human genealogy of Jesus. In Luke we have Mary's genealogy in contrast to Matthew, where Joseph's genealogy is presented. In giving Mary's line Luke presents the blood line of Jesus, "who as to his human nature was a descendant of David" (Rom. 1:3).

Corrected calendar

In the sixth century A.D., when the Christian calendar, which reckoned time before and after the birth of Christ, replaced the old Roman calendar, which dated from the founding of Rome (753 B.C.), the monk Dionysius Exiguus made an error of at least four years. This mistake was not detected until long after the Christian calendar had been established in popular use. Dionysius reckoned 748 or 749 B.C. instead of 753 as the date of Rome's founding. Hence 5 or 4 B.C.. must be reckoned as the birth of Christ.

Jesus' prayers in Luke

Luke 3:21	At His baptism
Luke 5:16	In the wilderness
Luke 6:12-13	Before calling the Twelve
Luke 9:18	At Caesarea Philippi
Luke 9:28-29	Before the transfiguration
Luke 11:1-4	When He instructed in prayer
Luke 22:31-32	For Peter
Luke 22:41	In Gethsemane
Luke 23:34	On the cross
Luke 24:30	At Emmaus

4:1-13. Jesus' temptation
1-12. The temptation. Luke presents the *order* of the temptation as it affected Christ's human nature, body, soul, and spirit, in the perfect Man.
13. The devil routed. The accuser, however, left only temporarily.

4:14-44. Jesus begins His Galilean ministry
14-15. He begins the Galilean ministry.
16-30. Rejection at Nazareth. Jesus' preaching that divine grace is not confined to Israel, but will reach the Gentiles, filled the people with wrath, 28-29.
31-37. The demoniac healed. See feature on Demonism in Mark 5.
38-44. Peter's mother-in-law healed, 38-39, and others healed. See feature on Demonism in Mark 5.

5. Miracles and teaching in Galilee
1-11. The call of Peter, James, and John. The miraculous catch of fish demonstrates Jesus'

Nazareth

Nazareth was a small, little-known place (cf. John 1:46) until immortalized in the NT as the boyhood home of Jesus. It was just a small village of farmers and artisans, such as the carpenter Joseph. Situated at an altitude of 1150 feet, the view above the village commanded a majestic panorama of snow-capped Hermon on the north, nearby Tabor on the east, the extensive Plain of Esdraelon on the south, and Mt. Carmel and the blue Mediterranean on the west. At Nazareth Jesus received the regular training of a Jewish lad in home and synagogue (Luke 4:16).

The Church of the Annunciation, Nazareth, mid-distance.

lordship as the last Adam over the animal creation.

12-26. The leper and the paralytic healed. See feature on Miracles in Mark 5.

27-29. Call of Levi (Matthew).

30-39. Scribes and Pharisees answered.

6. The Twelve chosen; the Beatitudes

1-11. The Sabbath question. The healing of the atrophied hand showed our Lord transcended mere religious externalism.

12-16. Choosing the Twelve. The perfect Man spent the whole night in prayer to God, 12,

before this important task.

17-19. Healings. See features on Demonism and Miracles in Mark 5.

20-49. The Beatitudes. Many of the sayings echoed here are in the Sermon on the Mount (Matt. 5-7).

7:1-35. Miracles of mercy

1-10. The centurion's servant healed.

11-17. The widow of Nain's son raised. Nain is a Galilean town five miles south southeast of Nazareth.

18-35. Jesus' testimony to John. John's

and Miracles in Mark 5.

10-17. Feeding of the five thousand.
Bethsaida, 10 ("house or place of fishing"), was the hometown of Philip, Peter, and Andrew.

Roman centurion

The Roman centurion commanded about 100 men ("century") which was one-sixtieth of a Roman legion of 6,000 men. The centurion was the backbone of the Roman army and was required to be a good, brave, level-headed leader.

languishing in prison tested his faith, 19-20, but Jesus strengthened it with a marvelous demonstration of miracles of healing and demon expulsion.

7:36-50. Jesus anointed
36-50. The anointing by a sinful woman.
Guests reclined, so it was easy for the woman to wash Jesus' feet with her tears and anoint them.

8. Deliverances and instructions
1-3. Women who ministered to Christ. This is unique to Luke's gospel. The women were particularly demonstrative of their affection and devotion to the One who had delivered them.
4-15. Parable of the sower.
16-18. Parable of the lamp.
19-21. The new relationship.
22-25. Jesus stills the storm.
26-39. Demoniac of Gadara. See features on Demonism and Miracles in Mark 5.
40-56. A woman healed and Jairus's daughter raised.

9:1-17. The Twelve sent out
1-9. The ministry of the Twelve. They were given power "to drive out all demons" and "to cure diseases," 1. See features on Demonism

9:18-62. Prediction of death and coming glory
18-26. Peter's confession. Peter's confession of the perfect Man's deity, 20, did not settle his spiritual problem. So Jesus instructed in discipleship, 23, and its law of self-sacrifice and self-giving, 24-25, in the light of His approaching rejection and death, 22, 31, 44.
27-36. The transfiguration. Christ's glory showed the three disciples that the only way to glory for our Lord, as well as His disciples, was through self-giving to God's will and to others.
37-50. Demonstration of the futility of the self-saving attitude. The self-centered, powerless disciples, 37-43, are contrasted with the selfless, powerful Christ.
51-62. Journey toward Jerusalem.

10. The seventy-two sent; the good Samaritan
1-24. The seventy-two sent out. This sending of the 72 was in addition to Christ's sending out of the Twelve some nine months before.
25-29. The lawyer's question.
30-37. The good Samaritan. This superb parable, exclusive to Luke, reflects on our responsibility to care for others, whether friend or stranger. In a spiritual sense it pictures the saving ministry of our Lord—the Good Samaritan.
38-42. Mary vs. Martha. This is another Lukan exclusive, which shows the primacy of spiritual worship over service. Service if it is not to

degenerate into mere fleshly busyness spoiled by frustrations and tensions (Martha) must be grounded in true spiritual worship of Christ.

11:1-13. Jesus' doctrine of prayer
1. Jesus praying.
2-4. Jesus instructing in prayer. This is more correctly the disciples' prayer rather than the Lord's prayer.
5-13. The parable of the importunate friend teaches persistence in petition.

11:14-54. Demon expulsion and warnings
14-28. Jesus instructs in demonism. Beelzebub is another name of Satan. See features on Demonism and Miracles in Mark 5, and Satan in Luke 4.
29-32. The sign of Jonah. "The Queen of the South," 31, was the Queen of Sheba (1 Kings 10:1-13).
33-38. The lamp of the body.
39-44. The Pharisees denounced.
45-54. The lawyers denounced. "From the blood of Abel (cf. Gen. 4:8) to the blood of Zechariah" (2 Chron. 24:20-21), 51, follows the Hebrew order of the books of the Old Testament in which Chronicles is the last book.

12. Parables and warnings
1-12. Warning against false doctrine. Yeast represents corrupt teaching. For blasphemy against the Holy Spirit, 10, see note on Matthew 12:31-32.
13-34. Warning against covetousness.
35-48. Watching for the Second Coming.
49-59. Christ causes a division because He causes people to choose between good and evil.

13:1-21. Teachings and deliverances
1-5. Teaching on repentance and judging, exclusive to Luke.
6-9. The barren fig tree. The nation Israel was the fig tree. Because Israel showed no repentance the nation would be chopped down.
10-17. The woman delivered from infirmity. Satan is represented as having bound this Jewish woman.
18-21. Parables of the mustard seed and yeast.

13:22-35. Teachings on the way to Jerusalem
22-30. How many will be saved? The question, unique to Luke, was given a practical turn by the Savior, 24, to avoid presumption, 25-30.
31-33. Jesus warns of Herod Antipas. The expression "today and tomorrow," 32, describes Christ's healing and delivering ministry. The "third day" refers to His resurrection.
34-35. Jesus' lament over Jerusalem. The tender love of the perfect Man shines through.

14. The cost of discipleship
1-6. Healing on the Sabbath.
7-15. Parable of the ambitious guest. This teaches the wisdom of humility, 11.
16-24. Parable of the great banquet. The self-righteous (unbelieving Jews), especially the Pharisees, made excuses to avoid attending the great supper of salvation provided by God, 18-20.
25-35. Conditions of discipleship. Counting the cost of being Christ's disciple is illustrated by three short parables, 28-35.

Heaven and hell

Jesus lifted the curtain to the life hereafter, revealing the place of departed souls, both saved and unsaved, between death and the resurrection.

Hades (Greek, Hebrew "Sheol," "hell," 23) is the place all dead went in OT times. The righteous, however, went to "Abraham's side," 22, and were separated from the wicked OT dead by a "great chasm," 26.

The believing thief (Luke 23:43) was to be that day with Christ in paradise, which seems to indicate that since the ascension of Christ, paradise, or "Abraham's side," is the immediate presence of God (1 Cor. 15:53; 2 Cor. 5:2, 18; Phil. 1:23; 1 Thess. 4:13-18).

At the sinners' judgment (Rev. 20:11-15) the wicked dead are raised and cast into eternal hell. This is the "second death" or eternal separation from God (Rev. 20:14), the final state of the wicked.

15. Parables: Lost sheep, lost coin, lost son

1-2. Occasion of the parables.

3-7. The lost sheep. The ninety-nine sheep represented the carping Pharisees; the one lost sheep, the publicans and sinners the Son of man came to save. The parable severely rebuked the Pharisees' empty religiosity.

8-10. The lost coin.

11-32. The lost son. The prodigal, 11-22, represented the publicans; the elder son, 25-32, the Pharisees.

16. The shrewd manager; the rich man and Lazarus

1-15. The parable of the shrewd manager. In this illustration Jesus commended the manager's provident foresight, not his dishonesty.

16-18. Additional teaching.

19-31. The rich man and Lazarus. This parable also was aimed at the sneering, unbelieving, self-righteous Pharisees.

17. Forgiveness; Second Coming foretold

1-10. Instruction in forgiveness and service. Those who cause others, especially the young, to stumble are doomed to severe punishment, 1-2.

11-19. The cleansing of the ten lepers. The Samaritan was the only one who worshiped the Healer rather than the healing.

20-37. When the kingdom of God should come. Our Lord answered the Pharisees' question, 20, by declaring that the kingdom of God did not come with outward show but was among them, 21—i.e., in the person of the King.

18. Parables and instructions

1-8. Parable of the persistent widow.

9-14. The parable of the Pharisee and the tax collector. This parable was directed against the empty ritualistic self-righteousness of the Pharisees, 9. The Pharisee was filled with egotism. Five "I's" in this short prayer were directed to himself and not to God, 11-12.

15-17. Jesus blesses little children.

18-30. The rich ruler.

31-34. Jesus again predicts His death.

35-43. The blind man healed near Jericho.

19:1-27. Zacchaeus; parable of the pounds

1-10. Conversion of Zacchaeus. Zacchaeus's restitution, 8-9, proved the reality of his spiritual experience and admirably illustrates the fact that "the Son of Man came to seek and to save what was lost," 10, the golden text of the gospel of Luke.

11-27. The parable of the minas. This parable was given to correct the false notion that the kingdom of God would appear immediately, 11.

19:28-48. Triumphal entry; second cleansing of the temple

28-40. The triumphal entry. See comments on Matthew 21:1-9.

41-44. The perfect Man weeps over Jerusalem. His heart of compassion overflowed as He prophesied the destruction of the city.

45-48. Second purification of the temple. Contrast the first cleansing at the beginning of Christ's ministry.

20. Clash with the Jewish leaders

1-8. Jesus' authority questioned. Jesus exposed the empty hypocrisy and unbelief of the Jewish leaders by the test question concerning John's baptism, 4.

9-18. Parable of the tenants. See notes on Matthew 21:33-46. He on whom the stone falls will be crushed—a reference to the Smiting Stone of Daniel 2:34-35.

19-26. Question of the tribute. See notes on Mark 12:13-17.

27-47. Sadducees silenced and scribes interrogated.

21. The Olivet discourse

1-4. The widow's mite.

5-38. The Olivet discourse. Luke predicts the fall of Jerusalem (A.D. 70), 20-23, and the worldwide dispersion of the Jews during the period prior to Christ's second coming, called "the times of the Gentiles," 24.

22:1-23:26. Events prior to the crucifixion

22:1-6. Plot to kill Jesus and Judas's treachery.

7-13. Preparation for the Passover.

14-20. The last Passover and the Lord's Supper.

21-23. Announcement of the betrayal.

24-30. The apostles' place in the future kingdom.

31-38. Jesus' prediction of Peter's denial and warning of coming conflicts.

39-46. Jesus on the Mount of Olives.

47-65. The betrayal and arrest.

22:66-23:26. Before the Sanhedrin, Pilate, and Herod.

23:27-56. The crucifixion and burial

27-38. The crucifixion. The cross not only judged the world, but uncovered what the world is. The people in general just stared in indifference, 35; the religious leaders scoffed, 35; the brutal mocked, 36; the convicted sinner prayed, 42; the materialistic unbelievers gambled (Mark 15:24); the believing centurion glorified God, 47; the disciples stood afar off, 49.

39-43. The repentant robber. Here is the case of a deathbed repentance that was genuine.

44-45. The sun stops shining; curtain of the

The roof of the Church of the Holy Sepulchre, Jerusalem, by tradition the site of Jesus' burial.

temple torn in two.

46-49. Jesus dismisses His spirit, voluntarily performing an act of sovereign will, thereby differentiating the death of the God-Man from all other cases of physical death, 46.

50-56. Jesus' burial. "Waiting for the kingdom of God," 51, indicates Joseph's messianic expectation, according to the great promises of the OT.

24. Resurrection and ascension

1-12. The resurrection. See feature on "the resurrection authenticated" in John 20.

13-35. Post-resurrection ministry to the Emmaus disciples. "Moses," 27, refers to the Pentateuch, and "all the Prophets," 27, was the second part of the Hebrew Scriptures: Law,

Prophets, Writings.

36-43. Post-resurrection appearance to the eleven. See feature on "the resurrection authenticated" in John 20.

44-49. The worldwide commission. Luke's narrative ends on its note of universal proclamation—salvation offered to the whole world.

50-53. The ascension. Until they were clothed with power from on high they were to stay in the city (Jerusalem) and not attempt to fulfill their superhuman task by merely human means.

John
The gospel of the Son of God

The author. This gospel is traditionally ascribed to John, the beloved disciple. At the Last Supper John leaned against Jesus (John 13:23). At the cross he stood faithful and was entrusted with the care of Jesus' mother (John 19:26-27). At the tomb he was the first to believe in Jesus' resurrection (John 20:1-10). On Galilee's shore he was the first to recognize the Lord (John 21:7).

Outline

1	Introduction
2-12	Public ministry of the Son of God
13-17	Private ministry of the Son of God
18-20	Death and resurrection of the Son of God
21	Epilogue

John the beloved. Both John and his brother James were Galilean fishermen. They earned the epithet "sons of thunder" (Mark 3:17) for their fiery impetuosity. John was in the inner circle close to Jesus (Matt. 17:1; Mark 5:37; Luke 8:51).

John and his brother James were Galilean fishermen.

John

1:1-18. The prologue: The Word —who He was and what He became

1-13. The Word—who He was. These verses declare eight truths about our Lord Jesus Christ. (1) He was and is the Eternal One, 1. (2) He was and is a Person distinct from God the Father, 1. (3) He was and is God, 1. (4) He was co-existent with God from eternity, 2. (5) He was the Creator of the universe, 3. (6) He is the Source of all life and light, 4, 5, 9. (7) He is the self-revealing God to a fallen universe, 5. (8) He was ignored and rejected, 10-11; but those who receive Him are granted spiritual regeneration, 12-13.

14-18. The Word—who He became. Deity united Himself to humanity in one glorious Person and dwelt in a tabernacle of flesh among us, 14.

1:19-51. The testimony of John and of Jesus' first disciples

19-28. Testimony of John the Baptist. John declared he was merely "the voice" (Isa. 40:3) prophetically announcing the Messiah's coming, 23.

29-34. The baptism of Jesus. Jesus was the sacrificial Lamb of God, 29 (Ex. 12; Isa. 53:7; 1 Peter 1:19), outranking John because He existed before John, 30 (cf. 1-18).

35-51. Testimony of Jesus' first disciples.

2. Water turned to wine; the temple cleansed

1-12. The first miracle. "Signs," 11, are mighty works or miracles that symbolize spiritual truths. This sign illustrates the basic nature of the newness of life that Christ came to give.

13-25. The temple cleansed. This act of Jesus manifested His authority as the Son of God and fulfilled Psalm 69:9.

3. Nicodemus and the new birth

1-21. Discourse on regeneration. From John 2:23 to 17:26 the Son of God imparts eternal life and describes what it is and what it does. In Jesus' interview with Nicodemus, a rigid moralist and a Sanhedrin member, 1, Jesus showed the necessity of regeneration, 7.

22-36. John the Baptist's testimony. Verses 27-36 constitute John's keen insight into the person and work of the Messiah, who had the Spirit in immeasurable fullness upon His sinless humanity, 34.

4. The Samaritan woman and eternal life

1-45. Jesus and the Samaritans. The woman's testimony had a remarkable effect on the Samaritans, 27-39, and opened the way for Jesus' two-day ministry among them, 40-45.

46-54. The second sign. The healing illustrates faith as the condition for receiving eternal life.

5. Infirm man healed

1-9. The third sign in John's gospel—the invalid healed at Bethesda. This illustrates the divine power granted to live the new life.

10-18. Opposition of the Jews. The Jews saw clearly that Jesus was claiming to be God.

The Dead Sea Scrolls

Discovered since 1947, these documents have shown the NT to be Jewish in background. The recovery of the Essenic literature from Qumran, the site on the northwest shore of the Dead Sea demonstrates that John's gospel reflects the genuine Jewish background of John the Baptist and Jesus, and not the Gnostic background of the late second century A.D.

This is attested by the remarkable parallels to the conceptual imagery of the fourth gospel found in the Essenic literature from Qumran. These archaeological findings have discredited the rationalistic criticism that had removed John's gospel from the traditional date of the apostolic age (between A.D. 90-130) and thus treated it as essentially apocryphal.

The watch-tower, Qumran.

Two of the Dead Sea Scrolls.

19-47. Discourse on the source of eternal life. Christ presented four witnesses to Himself as the Source of eternal life, 33-47: (1) John the Baptist, 33-35; (2) His mighty signs or works, 36; (3) the Father, 37-38; (4) the Holy Scriptures, 39-47.

6. Five thousand fed; discourse on the bread of life

1-21. Feeding the five thousand. This gives the setting for the next great discourse.
22-59. Discourse on the bread of life. Christ announced Himself as the Divine One, the nourisher and sustainer of the eternal life which He gives.

60-71. Discipleship tested: Peter's confession.

7. The prophecy of the Spirit's coming

1-13. Jesus delays going to Jerusalem.
14-36. Jesus at the feast. The Feast of Tabernacles or Booths (Lev. 23:33-44) was the harvest memorial of redemption for Israel.
37-39. The prophecy concerning the Holy Spirit. The eighth and last day of the feast of Tabernacles was the climax of the whole festal cycle. During the seven days water was drawn from the pool of Siloam and then poured out, commemorating the water supplied to Israel in the desert. On the eighth day no water was

The doorway to "Lazarus' Tomb," Bethany.

poured out, signifying the enjoyment of the springs of water of the land. On the eighth day Jesus stood and offered the spiritual reality of the kingdom to believers, 37-39.

40-53. The people's confusion.

8. The adulterous woman; discourse on the light of the world

1-11. The woman taken in adultery. Many textual critics omit this incident (7:53-8:11) on evidence from the oldest manuscripts. Whether or not it appears in the earliest texts, the story is certainly authentic and it illustrates our Lord's tender compassion for the sinner.

12-30. Discourse on the light of the world, and faith. Many believed on Him, the true Object of faith, 30.

31-59. Discourse on spiritual freedom. The Jews proved their slavery to sin by their reaction to the Liberator from sin.

9. The blind man healed

1-34. The blind man restored to sight. The clay and spittle did not effect the healing, but symbolized what the creative power of Christ, the Creator-Redeemer, did, 6.

35-41. Jesus reveals Himself to the man.

10. Discourse on the good shepherd

1-21. The discourse itself. Israel, as the Lord's true elect OT people in covenant with Him, were His sheep and He their Shepherd (Pss. 23:1; 95:7; 100:3; Ezek. 34; Zech. 11:7-9; 13:7).

22-39. Discourse on the unity of the Godhead. The tenth discourse of John's gospel was delivered at the Feast of Dedication, 22. It commemorated the reconsecration of the Jerusalem temple by Judas Maccabeus in 165 B.C.

40-42. Jesus at the place where John had baptized.

11. The raising of Lazarus

1-44. The Son's power over death. This was the last and greatest of Jesus' public miracles recorded by John, proving His claim to be the resurrection and the life.

45-57. The effect of this climactic sign.

12. Supper at Bethany; acclaim at Jerusalem

1-11. The anointing by Mary. See notes on Matthew 26:6-13.

12-19. The triumphal entry. See notes on Matthew 21:4-9.

20-36. Discourse on the world's redeemer.
The sins of believers would be judged in the
person of Christ lifted up on Calvary, 32.
37-50. Jesus' final words. Notice the
prominence of Isaiah's prophecy in the
quotations in 38 (Isa. 53:1) and 40-41 (Isa. 6:10).

13. Washing the disciples' feet
1-20. The meaning of the Lord's action. The
Lord's washing of the disciples' feet illustrates
the believer's continual need of cleansing after
the once-for-all bath of regeneration.
21-35. Prophecy of the betrayal by Judas.
Jesus' choice of Judas was an instance of divine
overruling of evil for good.
36-38. Prophecy of Peter's denial. Impetuous
and well-meaning, Peter had to learn the hard
way to gauge his weakness.

14. The Second Coming and the Spirit's coming
1-6. Christ's return for His own. Jesus' return
here declared is His coming *for* His own
(1 Thess. 4:13-17), not His return in glory *with*
His own (Matt. 24:29-30).
7-15. Christ expounds His deity. The "greater
things," 12, are possible because our Lord in the
flesh was confined to one place at a time.
16-26. The promise of the Spirit. The coming
of the Spirit would make up for Christ's
departure, 18.
27-31. The bequest of peace.
cf. Philippians 4:7.

15. Union with Christ and fruit-bearing
1-17. Abiding and fruit-bearing. The believer's
relation to Christ is here prefigured as that of
union (position) and *abiding* (experience).

18-27. The believer and the world. The world
will hate and persecute the true disciple. This
refers to the evil satanic world system organized
under Satan's principles of greed, ambition, self-
will, and pleasure (Matt. 4:8-9; John 12:31;
14:30; Eph. 2:2; 6:12; 1 John 2:15-17).

16. The work of the promised Spirit
1-6. Disciples warned of suffering.
7-11. Threefold work of the coming Spirit.
The Spirit would convict sinners (1) "in regard to
sin, because men do not believe in me," 9, the
one damning sin of rejecting Christ as Savior;
(2) "in regard to righteousness," 10, because the
Son's return to the Father was the evidence of
the provision of a perfect righteousness for
sinners; (3) "in regard to judgment," 11, because
rejection of Christ results in the sinner sharing
Satan's doom (Matt. 25:41, 46).
12-15. Teaching ministry of the Spirit. This
embraces Christ's authentication in advance of
the NT Scriptures to be written, 12-13.
**16-33. Jesus predicts His death, resurrection,
and Second Coming.**

17. Christ's great high priestly prayer
1-26. The seven petitions. (1) That the Son
might be glorified, 1. This involved our salvation.
Our Lord defined salvation, 3. (2) Restoration to
His preincarnate glory in union with the Father,
5. (3) Safety of His own from the world, 11.
(4) Sanctification of believers, 17. (5) The
spiritual oneness of believers, 11, 20-21. (6)
That the world might believe, 21. (7) That
believers might be with Him in heaven to behold
and share His glory, 24.

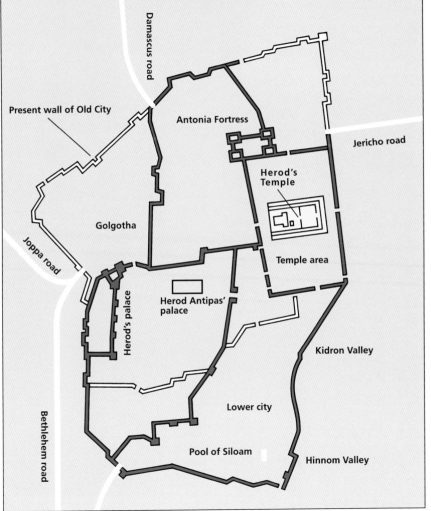

Jerusalem during the Time of Herod the Great

Damascus road

Present wall of Old City

Antonia Fortress

Jericho road

Herod's Temple

Golgotha

Temple area

Joppa road

Herod's palace

Herod Antipas' palace

Kidron Valley

Lower city

Bethlehem road

Pool of Siloam

Hinnom Valley

The resurrection authenticated

The open tomb, John 20:1-2
The recovered grave clothing,
John 20:3-8
The revelation of the risen Lord
1. To Mary of Magdala, Mark 16:9;
John 20:11-18
2. To women returning from the tomb,
Matt. 28:8-10
3. To Peter later in the day, Luke 24:34;
1 Cor. 15:5
4. To the Emmaus disciples, Luke 24:13-33
5. To the apostles—Thomas absent,
Luke 24:36-43; John 20:19-24
6. To the apostles—Thomas present,
John 20:26-29
7. To the seven by the Lake of Tiberias,
John 21:1-23
8. To a multitude of believers on a Galilean
mountain, 1 Cor. 15:6
9. To James, 1 Cor. 15:7
10. To the eleven, Matt. 28:16-20; Acts 1:3-12
11. At the ascension, Acts 1:3-12
12. To Stephen, Acts 7:55
13. To Paul near Damascus, Acts 9:3-6;
1 Cor. 15:8
14. To Paul in the temple,
Acts 22:17-21; 23:11
15. To John on Patmos, Rev. 1:10-19
Pilate's sealing and guarding the tomb,
Matt. 27:62-66
Removal of the stone by an angel,
Matt. 28:1-3
The terror of the Roman guards, Matt. 28:4
The message of the angel to the women,
Matt. 28:5-6
**The report of the guards to the chief
priests,** Matt. 28:11

**The chief priests' bribe to the Roman
guards,** Matt. 28:12-13
**The Roman guards spread the lie that
Jesus' body was stolen,** Matt. 28:15
The certainty of Christ's death,
John 19:34-42
The certainty of His burial,
Mark 15:42-47
The certainty His body was not stolen
1. If His enemies had done so (Matt. 28:4-15),
they would have produced it.
2. If His friends had done so they would not
have preached a lie or been willing to die for it
A hallucination? How could doubting
Thomas have a hallucination, or 500 people
imagine something at the same time?
A hoax? How does one then account for the
wonderful change in all the disciples from
deepest gloom to radiant joy, cowardice to
valor, timid disciples to powerful witnesses?
**The miracle of the Christian faith,
personal regeneration**
The conversion of Saul of Tarsus

The Garden Tomb, Jerusalem.

The blood and the water (John 19:34)

Jesus' death is thought by many to be due to heart rupture, i.e. a "broken" heart. The suffering and pressure of His sinless humanity in becoming an offering was too much for His physical body to stand, and so His heart ruptured, the blood collecting in the pericardium and separating in a sort of bloody clot and watery mass, 34.

18. The Son of God before His enemies

1-11. The arrest in Gethsemane. This gospel of Christ's deity describes the momentary out-flashing of deity of Him who was the great "I AM," 5-6 (cf. Ex. 3:13-14).

12-27. Trial before Annas and Caiaphas. Annas had been succeeded as high priest by his son-in-law Caiaphas, but Annas still wielded great influence, 12-13.

28-40. Trial before Pilate. Jesus was emphasizing the true nature of His kingdom in stark contrast to Rome and other world governments.

19. The Son of God condemned, crucified, buried

1-15. Pilate brings Jesus before the populace. The scourging was a pitiless Roman atrocity, often itself fatal, 1. The "Pavement" (Aramaic *Gabbatha*), 13, was an exquisite inlaid floor, 2,500 meters square, designed as a parade ground for Roman military pomp and as the approach to the procurator's judgment hall.

16-30. The crucifixion. Above the cross, as was customary when executing criminals, the accusation was written in Hebrew (Aramaic), Latin, and Greek, the three common languages of Palestine.

31-37. Fulfillment of Scripture. Breaking the criminal's legs was to hasten a horrible death that sometimes lingered for days.

38-42. Jesus' burial in a garden. The burial of Jesus by these wealthy friends shows the reality of Christ's death.

20. The resurrection

1-29. Evidence of the resurrection. This event is authenticated: (1) By the open tomb, 1-2; (2) by the grave clothes, 3-8; and (3) by the self-revelation of the Lord to Mary Magdalene, 11-18.

30-31. Purpose of John's gospel.

21. Epilogue: instruction in spiritual service

1-2. Post-resurrection appearance.

3-25. Peter instructed in spiritual service. After instructing Peter concerning his responsibilities as a leader of the flock, Christ spoke of his eventual martyrdom.

The synagogue

The synagogue (from the Greek *synagoge,* "a gathering" or "assembly") evidently had its origin in homes in Babylon (cf. Ezek. 8:1; 20:1-3). The "house synagogue," like the first Christian churches that met in homes, after the Exile gradually developed into formal assemblies for instruction, public worship, and prayer. They replaced the temple worship, which was no longer possible for the Jews who were scattered far beyond Palestine. Every town with a large number of Jews in the Graeco-Roman world of 300 B.C.-A.D. 300 had its synagogue for worship and instruction in the law and the prophets (cf. Luke 4:16-30).

The Sanhedrin
The Sanhedrin was an aristocratic body possessing judicial powers. By Jesus' day it had developed into the supreme court of the Jews and functioned in both civil and religious realms until the fall of Jerusalem (A.D. 70). It had seventy members and was presided over by the high priests.

The Pharisees
During the Maccabean period in the reign of John Hyrcanus (134-104 B.C.), the conflicting parties in Judaism—the Pharisees, Sadducees, the Essenes—came into existence. The Pharisees were apparently successors to the Hasidim ("the pious"), who stood true to the law under Antiochus Epiphanes's restriction of Judaism in 168 B.C. They were rigid legalistic separatists, with watchwords of prayer, repentance, and charitable giving. From an admirable beginning in the fires of Maccabean suffering, many of them gradually degenerated into empty, unprincipled religionists in Jesus' day.

The Sadducees
The Sadducees were chiefly aristocratic, worldly-minded priests, who obeyed the letter of the law but denied resurrection and future retribution. They welcomed hellenistic culture. Their deep rift with the Pharisees continued until Jesus' day.

The scribes and Essenes
The scribes were copyists of the Holy Scripture, intimately conversant with the Mosaic law, hence also called lawyers. During the interbiblical period they became influential and appear prominently in Jesus' day.

The Essenes were a monastic sect rather than a political religious party such as the Pharisees and Sadducees. Until the discovery in 1947 of the Dead Sea Scrolls, Philo, Josephus, and Pliny were the only sources on information on this communal monastic order. A similar if not identical group is now well known as a result of the excavation of its headquarters at Qumran on the northwest shore of the Dead Sea. The recovery of their book of rules and order has corroborated ancient sources and added to our knowledge of sectarian Judaism from about 200 B.C. to A.D. 70.

The synagogue at Chorazin in Galilee.

Acts
The gospel to the ends of the earth

Outline

1-7	From Jerusalem to all Judea
8	To Samaria
9-12	To the Gentiles
13-28	To the end of the earth

Author. The author of Acts is the same as the author of the gospel according to Luke, as is indicated by Luke 1:3-4 and Acts 1:1. The "former book" addressed to Theophilus (Acts 1:1; Luke 1:3) is the third gospel. Internal evidence, particularly the "we" passages of Acts (16:10-17; 20:5-15; 27:1-28:16), confirm Lukan authorship.

Scope and contents. The book of Acts, called the Acts of the Apostles since about the middle of the second century A.D., bridges the period between the four gospels and the later letters.

1. The book shows the progress of Christianity from Jerusalem, to all Judea, Samaria, and to the end of the earth (1:8).

2. The book continues the acts of the risen Lord through the Holy Spirit. In the first account (the gospel of Luke) Luke says he dealt with "all that Jesus began to do and to teach" (Acts 1:1). In the Acts he describes what Jesus *continued* to do and teach through His body (the church), brought into existence at Pentecost (Acts 2), and indwelt by the Holy Spirit. This activity of the risen Christ in heaven working through the Holy Spirit on earth suggests the name "The Acts of the Risen Christ" or "The Acts of the Holy Spirit," rather than merely "The Acts of the Apostles," who were only human agents. This truth of Christ in glory working on the earth through the believer indwelt by the Holy Spirit, seen in historical outworking in Acts, is the subject of doctrinal revelation in the Pauline letters.

The Arcadian Way, ancient Ephesus.

Acts

1. The forty days

1-8. Post-resurrection teaching. In verses 3-8 Luke presents a summary of our Lord's 40-day post-resurrection ministry in which He instructed His own concerning the kingdom of God, 3.

9-11. The ascension and promised return. The "cloud" which received Christ, 9, was evidently the cloud of the Shekinah glory, so often seen in the OT, and to be seen when He returns again (Matt. 26:64; Rev. 1:7).

12-14. The ten-day wait for the Spirit.

15-26. Choice of Matthias. This is not to be considered a mistake with Paul being regarded as the rightful twelfth apostle. The twelve had a ministry of witness to the entire Jewish nation. Not until Israel's final rejection of the testimony (Stephen's death) was Paul chosen as the apostle to the Gentiles.

2. The Spirit's coming —birth of the church

1-13. The coming of the Spirit. This is a pivotal chapter opening a new era, witnessed by wind, 2; fire, 3; and supernatural tongues, 4. Pentecost marked the giving and reception of the Holy Spirit and signaled the beginning of the church and the worldwide proclamation of the gospel of grace to every race.

14-47. The results of the coming of the Spirit. Three thousand were converted and became recipients of the blessings of the gift of the Spirit, 37-41.

3-4. The first miracle and its results

3:1-11. The healing of the lame man. This miracle witnessed to the fact that the Crucified One was risen and ascended to glory.

3:12-26. Peter's second sermon. Israel, as a nation, was called to repent, 19, of its crime of killing the Author of life, 15.

Ch. 4. The result. The nation rejected the message of the miracle and of Peter's appeal.

5. Discipline and persecution

1-11. Ananias and Sapphira's sin. Ananias and Sapphira sinned the "sin that leads to [physical] death" (1 Cor. 5:1-5; 1 John 5:16). It was a direct yielding to Satan in the sense of lying to the Holy Spirit, 3, and tempting Him who was operating in such fullness of power in giving witness to the power of a crucified and risen Christ.

12-42. Powerful witness to the Jewish nation. The place was prominent—Solomon's portico in the temple, 12. The results were so miraculous that even Peter's shadow effected cures, 12-16.

6. The first deacons

1-7. Choosing the seven. The deacon's office was to guard the calling of the pastor, presbyter, or bishop, from encroachment by other necessary functions of a minister of Christ.

8-15. Stephen's ministry and arrest.

7. Stephen's martyrdom

1-53. Stephen's sermon. Stephen, the accused, became the accuser of his judges, 51-53.

54-60. Stephen's martyrdom. Three manifestations of the glorified Christ are recorded: to Stephen (Acts 7:55-56); to Paul (Acts 9:3-6; cf. 7:58-8:1); and to John (Rev. 1:10, 12-16).

8. The Samaritans admitted to gospel privileges

1-17. Philip's ministry in Samaria. As Peter opened the gospel to the Jew (2:14) and to the Gentile (10:34), so in a similar sense he opened

Chronological chart of Acts

All dates are approximate

Events	Acts	Dates
Ascension	1:9-11	A.D. 30
Pentecost	2:1-41	A.D. 30
Early church	2:42-6:7	A.D. 30
First persecution	4:1-31	A.D. 31
Second persecution	5:17-42	A.D. 32
Third persecution; Stephen's martyrdom	6:8-8:4	A.D. 35-36
Philip's ministry in Samaria and to the Ethiopian	8:5-40	A.D. 36
Paul's conversion	9:1-21	A.D. 37
Paul in Damascus, Jerusalem, Tarsus	9:22-30	A.D. 38
Peter at Caesarea	10:1-11:18	A.D. 41
Founding of Gentile church at Antioch	11:19-24	A.D. 41
Paul in Antioch	11:25-26	A.D. 43
Martyrdom of James; Peter imprisoned	12:1-19	A.D. 44
First missionary journey	13:1-14:28	A.D. 45-47
Jerusalem council	15:1-29	A.D. 5
Second missionary journey	15:36-18:22	A.D. 51-54
Third missionary journey	18:23-21:19	A.D. 54-58
Paul arrested in Jerusalem	21:20-23:22	A.D. 58
Paul a prisoner at Caesarea	23:23-26:32	A.D. 58-60
Paul's journey and arrival in Rome	27:1-28:31	A.D. 60-61

the gospel privilege to the racially and religiously mongrel Samaritans, who were a bridge to the Gentiles. The episode was *not* a second experience after salvation, but marked the initial giving of the Holy Spirit to the Samaritans as an ethnic group.

18-25. Simon the magician. God's spiritual gifts are not to be bartered for in the hope of personal gain.

26-40. The Ethiopian eunuch. The eunuch's conversion illustrates the outgoing of gospel privilege beyond those racially and religiously related to the Jews and their religion.

9. Conversion of the apostle to the Gentiles

1-19. Saul's conversion. Saul saw the risen, ascended Christ, 3-8; was filled with the Spirit, 17; and was baptized to show his identification with Christ and His people, 18-19.

20-25. Damascus and the beginning of Saul's ministry. Saul's fearless preaching stirred Jewish persecution, 20-24, so that he had to be let down over the wall in a basket, 25.

26-31. Saul's return to Tarsus, preceded by a visit to Jerusalem, 26-29.

32-43. Peter prepared for Gentile evangelism. In Joppa Peter stayed with Simon the tanner, 36-43. Jewish law regarded a tanner as an outcast and his work defiling.

10. The Gentiles admitted to gospel privileges

1-33. Cornelius and Peter. The conversion of Cornelius, as a representative Gentile, 1-8, marked the giving of the Holy Spirit to the Gentiles.

34-48. Peter's last use of the keys. For the last

Caesarea

This brilliant capital of the Roman government in Judea was built (25-13 B.C.) by Herod the Great. He dedicated the city to Caesar Augustus in 12 B.C.), changing the name Straton's Tower to Caesarea in honor of the emperor.

Fine Graeco-Roman buildings included a forum, a stadium, and an amphitheater. The amphitheater, 300 feet by 200 feet, larger than the Colosseum at Rome, was the scene of bloody gladiatorial contests. Caesarea became the center of Graeco-Roman culture and customs in Palestine. Luke highlights Caesarea in his account of the outreach of the gospel.

The Graeco-Roman amphitheater, Caesarea.

recorded time Peter used the keys of the kingdom of heaven (Matt. 16:19), by his sermon opening the gospel and the gift of the Holy Spirit to the Gentiles.

Speaking in tongues

There are two aspects in the manifestation of tongues: first, the sign of tongues in Acts 2, 10, 19 (and probably in ch. 8); second, the gift of tongues in the early apostolic church. The gift under the second aspect evidently was not permanent (1 Cor. 13:9-13), nor given to every believer. It required the concomitant gift of interpretation (1 Cor. 12:10; 14:1-40). This sign gift with interpretation was meant to instruct the church before the completed NT Scriptures were given.

Under the first aspect tongues were a means by which the Spirit witnessed to Israel on the day of Pentecost (2:4-13). They were a sign of the truth that Jesus was the Messiah and an indication of the new age of the Spirit. The Jews were again challenged by the Samaritans' receiving the Holy Spirit (8:14-17). Nothing could have been more convincing to skeptical Peter and his Jewish colleagues than the fact that Cornelius spoke in supernatural languages (10:44-47) just as the Jews at Pentecost. The disciples of John the Baptist who received the Holy Spirit and spoke in languages they had never learned (Acts 19:6-10) were a similar witness to the strong Jewish community at Ephesus.

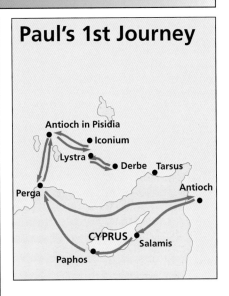

Paul's 1st Journey

11:1-18. Paul defends his ministry to Gentiles

1-18. Peter explains his ministry to Gentiles.
Peter recounted his experiences at Joppa and Caesarea, 4-14 (cf. 10:1-33). He declared that the gift of the Spirit granted to the Gentiles, which included supernatural languages (2:4; 10:46; 19:6), was identical with the gift given to Israel in Acts 2.

11:19-30 The church at Antioch

19-26. The disciples called Christians.
Believers were called Christians first at Antioch, 26. The term *Christiani* ("partisans of Christ") was probably an official name of Jesus' disciples by Roman officials at Antioch.

27-30. Relief sent to Jerusalem. Prophets like Agabus, possessing a supernatural gift of prediction, were common in the early church before a completed canon.

12. Herod's persecution and death

1-19. Arrest of Peter and his deliverance.
James the son of Zebedee was martyred.

20-25. Josephus relates how Herod was struck with a deadly illness after being hailed as divine.

Importance of the first church council

The immense significance of the first church council consists, first, in saving the gospel from Judaistic mixture, thereby setting Christianity on its own course as a universal spiritual movement transcending all social, racial, and religious barriers, offering spiritual regeneration to everyone who believes; second, in the revelation of God's gracious purposes for the present age and the age to come, 14-18.

13:1-12. First tour—Cyprus

1-3. Antioch the birthplace of foreign missions. From Antioch-on-the-Orontes in Syria, the third largest city in the Roman Empire in Paul's day, was launched the pivotal gospel witness in the West.

4-12. The tour of Cyprus, spring of A.D. 45.

13:13-52. First tour —Perga and Pisidian Antioch

13. From Paphos to Perga. Crossing the 180 miles of water from Paphos, Paul and Barnabas landed at Perga, chief city of Pamphylia in Asia Minor. At Perga John Mark decided to quit the tour, 13.

14-52. From Perga to Pisidian Antioch and Iconium. The 100-mile trip to Pisidian Antioch was through rugged robber-infested terrain. In bringing the gospel to Pisidian Antioch Paul and Barnabas were planting the gospel in the heart of Asia Minor.

14. First tour—Iconium, Derbe, Lystra

1-5. Iconium, one of the most important cities in the southern part of the Roman province of Galatia.

6-19. The work at Lystra. Driven out of Iconium by unbelieving Jews, the missionaries came to Lystra and Derbe, two other towns in the Roman province of Galatia. The superstitious nature of the Lycaonians, not Greeks or Romans, is illustrated by their viewing Barnabas as Zeus and Paul as Hermes.

20-28. Work at Derbe and the return to Antioch of Syria. Derbe was of strategic importance on the great east-west military and commercial artery.

15:1-35. The council at Jerusalem

1-12. The council and the issue. The question was whether Gentiles could be saved apart from circumcision and the legalism of the Mosaic system, 1, 5.

13-35. The council and the decision. The question of the first church council was happily settled in the form of the gospel of free grace,

Archaeology and Athens

The marketplace or Agora (Acts 17:17) was the hub of Athens's culture.

On the 512-foot Acropolis are the ruins of the splendid Parthenon, the Temple of Athena, Athens's patron goddess. The bronze statue of Athena, forged from the spoils of Marathon, towered above the Acropolis.

Below the Acropolis was the concert hall, the Odeion of Pericles, the theater of Dionysius, and the huge Temple of Olympian Zeus, 354 by 135 feet and 90 feet tall, one of the largest temples in antiquity.

which Paul had seen so signally authenticated. James summarized the council's decision, 19.

15:36-16:11. Second tour —Asia Minor and the call to Europe

15:36-41. Paul and Barnabas separate. This epoch-making tour, which was to bring the gospel to Europe, began in sharp dissension. Paul and Barnabas separated over John Mark (Acts 12:25; 13:13; 2 Tim. 4:11).

16:1-5. Paul finds Timothy as he revisits Derbe and Lystra. Timothy was chosen as Paul's

secretary and helper on this second tour.
16:6-11. The call to Europe. Careful leading by the Holy Spirit, 6-7, indicates the tremendous spiritual import of the gospel going west into Europe. Luke joined Paul's party, 10-17 (cf. 20:5-21:18; 27:1-28:16).

16:12-40. Second tour—Philippi

12-15. First European convert. This convert was a woman of ability and means, 14, a dealer in purple dye, a native of Thyatira, a thriving market for purple. Lydia's home became the first

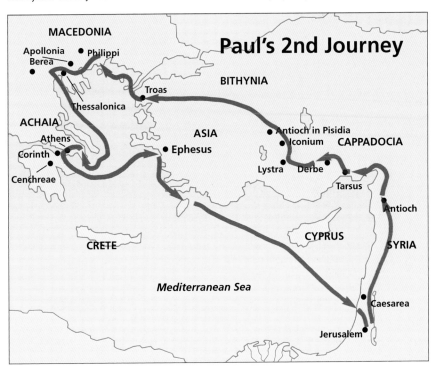

private home to be used as a meeting place for Christians in Europe.

16-18. Clash with demonism at Philippi. The young woman was a spiritistic medium with powers of oracular utterance, 16, not a fake. The real enemy was not the girl but the evil spirit that controlled her and gave her powers of divination.

19-40. Persecution at Philippi. Lethargic paganism was aroused when the promoters of the spiritistic medium saw their profit gone. The violation of the rights of Paul's Roman citizenship, 37, was a real cause for the magistrate's fear, 38. Paul used his citizenship not for selfish gain but to proclaim the gospel.

17:1-14. Second tour —Thessalonica, Berea

1-9. Paul at Thessalonica. Paul and Silas's labors resulted in a strong church in the city.

10-14. Paul at Berea, a refreshing contrast to the treatment from the Jews elsewhere, 11.

17:15-34. Second tour—Athens

15-18. Paul and Athenian idolatry. To the apostle the artistic magnificence and cultural refinements of the city were seriously tarnished by superstition and spiritual ignorance.

19-34. Paul's sermon to Areopagus. This court met on the 377-foot hill, the Areopagus, Hill of Ares (Mars), god of war, a little northwest of the Acropolis. Paul's sermon was a masterpiece of perceptive adaptability to the Greek mentality. Paul quoted one of the Greek poets, Aratus, a Stoic of the third century B.C., 28.

18:1-22. Second tour—Corinth

1-11. Founding the church. See 1 Corinthians 1-4 for Paul's own account. His ministry in this

Corinth in Paul's day

Corinth was a great emporium with two seaports—Cenchraea and Lechaeum. Materialism and lust were two vices that plagued the city. Its brisk commercialism fostered the former; the entrenched cult of Aphrodite fostered the latter. The goddess of love (lust) had her temple above the Acrocorinth, served by more than a thousand religious prostitutes, making Corinth a notorious center of immorality (cf. 1 Cor. 5:1-5).

The Temple of Apollo, Corinth.

dissolute thriving metropolis was begun in spiritual and financial testing. But Paul's encouraging vision from the Lord assured the success of the work in the city, 9-11.

12-17. Paul before Gallio. The Jewish charge against Paul, 13, was treated lightly by proconsul Gallio, 14-16. He was unconcerned in a Roman court about altercations over minutiae of Jewish practice, and his judicious decision saved Paul from the rage of Jewish bigotry.

18-22. End of second tour.

18:23-19:7. Third tour begun —John's disciples

18:23. Beginning the third tour. Paul visited and reported to his home church at Antioch the results of his second tour as he had done on the first trip (14:26-28), giving a permanent lesson for missionary method, 23.

18:24-28. Apollos at Ephesus. Apollos knew only John the Baptist's preparatory and introductory baptism, 25, and nothing about the baptism of the Holy Spirit that occurred at Pentecost. Aquila and Priscilla gave him precise teaching about the gift of the Holy Spirit, 26.

19:1-7. Apollos's disciples become Christians. The result of faith in the gospel was that "the Holy Spirit came on them," 6, which means that they were introduced to NT salvation.

19:8-41. Third tour—Ephesus

8-22. Paul's powerful Ephesian ministry. Paul first ministered in the synagogue, 8, then in the school of Tyrannus, 9, who apparently was a Greek rhetorician. Probably busy at his loom

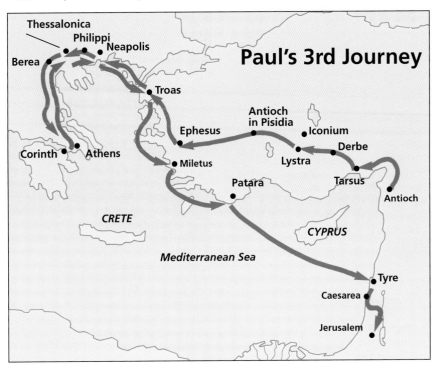

Paul's 3rd Journey

from dawn till about 11 A.M., Paul rented the lecture hall for the rest of the day.

23-41. Clash with the cult of Diana. The religious life of Ephesus centered around the worship of the fertility goddess Artemis or Diana, worshipped in a temple that was one of the seven wonders of the ancient world. Paul's success at Ephesus was so great that the cult of Artemis and its mighty temple were seriously affected, 25-27.

The "city clerk" is known from non-biblical sources to have been an important administrative official in the city, 35-41.

20. Third tour—Macedonia to Miletus

1-6. Last visit to Greece. After leaving Ephesus Paul returned first to Macedonia, revisiting the churches planted there, 1-2. He then went on to Greece, where he stayed three months.

7-16. From Troas to Miletus.

17-38. Farewell to the Ephesian elders at Miletus. Paul's touching speech to them and through them to the Ephesian church was his third discourse thus far reported by Luke. The first was addressed to Jews in the synagogue at Pisidian Antioch, 13:16-41, and the second to Gentiles in Athens, 17:22-31. Verse 35 is a quote from Jesus not found in the Gospels.

21. End of third tour —on to Jerusalem

1-14. From Miletus to Caesarea. Cos and Rhodes, 1, are islands in the southernmost Aegean Sea northeast of the island of Crete. Rhodes was both the name of the island and its capital city in the northeast extremity of the island where Paul gazed on one of the seven

The city of Ephesus

Ephesus in Paul's day was the metropolis of proconsular Asia and vied with Alexandria of Egypt and Antioch of Syria among the top three cities of the East.

Ephesus and the worship of Artemis
The worship of Artemis was the most distinctive source of Ephesus's prestige. The temple of Artemis was called the Artemesion. This vast edifice was 340 feet long, 160 feet wide and was decorated with 100 columns more than 55 feet high. Richly adorned with art treasures, the temple was also a bank, an asylum for fugitives, and the center of an elaborate cult.

Site of the temple of Artemis, Ephesus.

wonders of the world—the colossus of Helios, the sun-god, towering 105 feet above the fine harbor of the city.

15-40. Paul in Jerusalem. Paul conformed to Judaism, 23-26, to allay suspicions of Jewish believers zealous for the law. The result was disastrous.

22. Paul's defense before the populace

1-21. Paul gives his testimony.

22-30. Paul appeals to his Roman citizenship. The examination by scourging, 24, was not for punishment but to obtain evidence.

23. Paul's defense before the Sanhedrin

1-10. Before the Sanhedrin. Paul used wit and humor, 6-10, even though hard pressed. Sadducees were rational critics who denied the resurrection of the body.

11-22. Plot to kill Paul.

23-35. Paul sent to Caesarea. The large bodyguard for Paul, 23, shows the seriousness of the plot against him.

24. Paul before Felix

1-23. Before Felix the first time. "The Way," 14, 22, i.e., the true way of the Lord (John 14:6), was one of the first designations of Christianity (cf. 9:2).

24-27. Before Felix the second time. Paul had to languish in prison for two years on Felix's account, 27.

25-26. Paul before Festus and Agrippa

25:1-12. Before Festus. Paul, knowing the calamity of being turned over to a Jewish court,

Rome in Paul's day

Size of the city. In Paul's day Rome was the greatest city in the world. Most of its teeming millions lived in large tenement houses, multi-storied, called *insulae*.

Palaces and temples. The Forum was a maze of exquisite temples and altars. Among the innumerable temples that graced the city were those dedicated to Jupiter, Augustus, Saturn, and the Divine Julius.

Avenues and hills. Built on seven hills, the city was famous for its roads and scenic avenues, which interwove among the hills and along the Tiber. The Via Appia was among its well known roads.

Theaters and places of pleasure. The Rome of Paul's day was given to pleasure. "Bread and circuses" were the concern of the populace, according to Juvenal. Famous circuses included the mammoth Circus Maximus, enlarged to seat some 200,000 in Nero's day.

The ancient Forum, Rome.

Paul's life

Early life
Born in Tarsus (Acts 22:3), c. a.d. 10
Educated in Judaism (Acts 22:3), a.d. 20-30
Saw Stephen's death (Acts 7:58), c. A.D. 35
Persecuted Christians (Acts 9:1-2), A.D. 35-36
Conversion near Damascus (Acts 9:3-18), A.D. 37
Stay in Arabia (Gal. 1:17), A.D. 37-39
Visit to Jerusalem (Acts 9:26-29), A.D. 39
Return to Tarsus (Acts 9:30), A.D. 39
Brought to Antioch (Acts 11:25-26), A.D. 43

First tour
Cyprus crusade (Acts 13:4-12), A.D. 45
Perga (Acts 13:13)
Pisidian Antioch, Iconium, Lystra, Derbe
(Acts 13:14-14:20)
Return to Lystra, Iconium, Pisidian Antioch
(Acts 14:21-24), A.D. 47
Perga, Attalia (Acts 14:25), A.D. 47
Syrian Antioch (Acts 14:26-28), A.D. 47-50
Jerusalem council (Acts 15), A.D. 50

Second tour
Antioch by land through Syria and Cilicia
(Acts 15:41), A.D. 50
Derbe and Lystra (Acts 16:1-5)
Phrygia and Galatia (Acts 16:6)
Troas, Samothrace, Neapolis, Philippi
(Acts 16:8-40)
Thessalonica (Acts 17:1-9)
Berea (Acts 17:10-14)
Athens (Acts 17:15-34)
Corinth (Acts 18:1-17)
1 and 2 Thessalonians written
Ephesus, Caesarea, Jerusalem (Acts 18:18-22)
Return to Antioch (Acts 18:22), A.D. 53 or 54

Third tour
Galatia and Phrygia (Acts 18:23), A.D. 54
Ephesus (Acts 19:1-41), A.D. 54-57
1 and 2 Corinthians, Romans, Galatians written
Macedonia and Achaia (Acts 20:1-5), A.D. 57
Troas (Acts 20:6-12), A.D. 58
Miletus (Acts 20:13-38)
Journey to Jerusalem (Acts 21:1-17), A.D. 58
Arrested in Jerusalem (Acts 21:27-36), A.D. 58

Prisoner and death
Prisoner at Caesarea (Acts 23:23-26:32), A.D. 58-60
Journey to Rome (Acts 27), A.D. 60
Arrival in Rome (Acts 28:16), A.D. 61
First imprisonment, A.D. 61-63
Prison letters:
*Philemon, Colossians, Ephesians, Philippians
written*
Release, A.D. 64-67 (?)
1 Timothy, Titus written
Spain (?) Crete (Titus 1:5)
Asia (2 Tim. 4:13)
Macedonia (1 Tim. 1:3)
Greece (2 Tim. 4:20)
Second arrest (?), A.D. 67
2 Timothy written
Martyrdom, A.D. 68

**The Areopagus, Athens, where Paul preached a
famous sermon.**

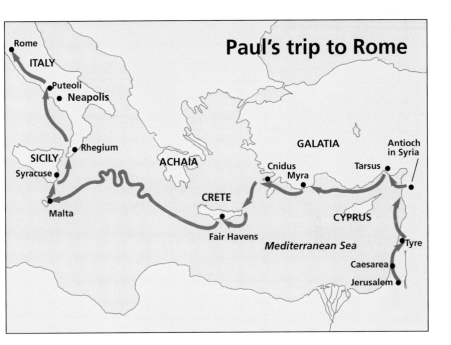

Paul's trip to Rome

chose Caesar's tribunal, 9-10.
25:13-26:32. Paul before Agrippa. Both Festus and Agrippa agreed Paul was guilty of no crime worthy of death or even imprisonment, 30-31.

27. Paul's journey to Rome
—Caesarea to Malta
1-12. From Caesarea to Crete.
13-44. The storm. This account is a classic of graphic precision and accuracy. Paul displayed faith and moral strength in the terrible ordeal, 21-26, and was strengthened by God through an angel.

28:1-16. Malta to Rome
1-10. Paul in Malta. Maltese fever, due to an organism in goat's milk, is a notorious sickness on the island.
11-16. Malta to Rome. The Forum of Appius and Three Taverns were both on the famous Appian Way.

28:17-31 Paul in Rome
17-22. Paul contacts the Jews. At last Paul was in the world's capital. Although a prisoner, he trusted for an open door to all parts of the Empire (cf. Rom. 15:23-28).
23-31. Final Jewish rejection of the gospel. This final appeal to Jews in the world's capital constituted a scene of immense importance. It was the signal that the new age was fully established and God's purpose for it, to visit the Gentiles, fully launched (cf. 15:14-15).

Romans
The revelation
of the gospel of God

Importance. Romans is the greatest and most influential of all Paul's letters, the first great work of Christian theology. The letter is for sinful humanity *as it is.* It points out how lost, helpless humanity can find deliverance in Christ and what this deliverance includes. All focuses on Christ's cross. Christ's redemption is shown to be humanity's *only* hope. But what a glorious, exhilarating hope!

Place and occasion of writing. The letter was apparently written from Corinth after Paul had completed collecting contributions for the Jerusalem church (Rom. 15:25-27, cf. 1 Cor. 16:3-5). Paul wrote his doctrinal masterpiece to the members of the church in the Imperial City to announce his intention to visit them and to enlist their prayer and interest in evangelizing the West.

Outline

1-8	Doctrinal
1:1-17	Introduction
1:18-3:20	The sin of humanity
3:21-5:21	Justification of the sinner
6:1-8:39	Sanctification of the believer
9-11	Dispensational (the case of Israel)
9:1-33	God's past purpose for Israel
10:1-21	God's present purpose for Israel
11:1-36	God's future purpose for Israel
12-16	Practical (duties and privileges of the believer)
12:1-13:14	The Christian's service
14:1-15:3	Christian service and questionable things
15:4-13	Christian service and God's worldwide glory
15:14-16:27	Christian service and fellowship

Vespasian's Arch, the Forum, Rome.

Romans

1:1-17. The theme
—the gospel of salvation

1-6. Paul and his gospel. The author of the letter presents himself as "servant" in his personal relation to Jesus Christ, "apostle" in his official relation to Him, and "set apart for the gospel of God" in relation to the message committed to him, 1

7-17. Paul and his readers. In Paul's statement of his theme, 16-17, the great words of the letter emerge—"the gospel," "power of God," "salvation," "faith" (believe), "revealed," "righteousness," and "live."

1:18-2:16. The revelation
of mankind's sin—the Gentile

1:18-32. God's wrath against mankind's sin revealed. This divine wrath is a revelation God has made. The divine arraignment of the fallen race is on two counts: mankind's guilty abandonment of God's glory, 18-23, and its progressive moral decline, 24-32.

2:1-16. The sin of the Gentile revealed. The Gentile begins to plead "not guilty" to God's indictment of his sin. This claim is refuted because unsaved people have no consistent morality.

2:17-3:20. The revelation
of mankind's sin—the Jew
2:17-3:8. The sin of the Jew revealed.
Immediately the Jew under the Mosaic law also begins to plead "not guilty," attempting to gloss over his sin with the claim of religion, boasting in his spiritual privileges, 17-20. Yet his unchanged life nullifies any such claim, 21-29.

3:9-20. The universality of sin. The final verdict, 19-20, is that all opposition is removed, 19, and the whole world is found guilty before God, 20.

3:21-31. Justification defined
21-23. Justification involves the revelation of God's righteousness. The righteousness that God's infinite holiness requires is apart from the law, 21; it is by grace.

24-28. Justification involves the imputation of God's righteousness. Justification is God's act of declaring the sinner righteous, so that the divine righteousness is judicially reckoned to his account. This divine transaction is on the basis of *grace*.

29-31. Objections to justification answered. Justification honors the law, 31. How it establishes the OT Scriptures is seen in ch. 4.

4. Justification illustrated
1-5. By God's dealings with Abraham. In defending justification from the OT Scriptures, the apostle shows it was a well-established principle in God's dealings with people as far back as Abraham.

6-8. By the case of David (parenthetical) (cf. Ps. 32:1-2).

9-25. Resumption of the case of Abraham. He was justified by faith, not by religious rites, 9-12, before he was circumcised, 9-10, or practiced legal observances, 13-25.

5:1-11. The results of justification
1-5. Our present possessions. We have "peace," 1, "access," and "hope," 2.
6-11. Our future security. "Saved from God's wrath," 9, expresses what we have been saved *from.* "Saved through his life," 10, expresses what we have been saved *to*—a life of holiness.

5:12-21. Justification summarized
The results of justification are seen in the contrast between what the sinner was in condemnation and what he becomes in justification.

6:1-11. Sanctification—the method
1-10. Positional sanctification by union with Christ. Divinely administered baptism of the Spirit, of which water baptism is an outward symbol, makes us one with Christ in a body that has passed through death, burial, and resurrection into new life, 4. Thus we are no longer in Adam but in Christ, united to Him.
11. Experiential sanctification by knowledge and faith. Justified believers *are* "dead to sin" and "alive to God" unchangeably in their position. They become so in their experience only as they momentarily count upon their position in faith. This requires yielding, 13, to God's will.

6:12-7:6. Sanctification by grace, legalism
6:12-23. Sanctification by grace dispenses with the problem of legalism. The gospel of grace which Paul expounds does not give license to sin, 12-14. Law says, "Do and live." Grace says, "Live and do," conferring blessed enablement so that deeds and fruit may follow.
7:1-6. Sanctification by grace delivers from the principle of legalism. The illustration of the law of marriage simply points out that death alone dissolves legal obligation. The believer "died" and so becomes released from the legal principle by incorporation into the body of Christ, 4. The believer is now free to be "married to another," (4, KJV), that is, to Christ, who is risen from the dead.

7:7-25. False sanctification—its defeat
7-14a. Sanctification by grace and the law. The law is blameless. It reveals sin to be sinful, 7-13. It is sin that is to blame.
14b-24. False sanctification by the self-effort of legalism. In these 11 verses the pronouns "I," "me" and "my" occur 35 times. "I" trying to sanctify itself is the reason for the dismal defeat here outlined.
25. True sanctification. Victory alone is "through Jesus Christ our Lord."

8:1-25. True sanctification—its victory
1-4. The new law. "Therefore" is cumulative of the truth presented in ch. 1-7. The new "law of the Spirit of life," 2, is the Holy Spirit operating in the believer's new position in Christ, overcoming the lower "law of sin and death," producing righteousness and life.
5-25. The new victory. The Holy Spirit takes over the conflict with sin, 5-13. The new victory brings a new realization of being God's children, 14-17. Being heirs of God and suffering for him, 17, we are now viewed in the light of the coming glory, 18-25.

Tombs along the Appian Way, Rome.

8:26-39. True sanctification —its power and assurance

26-27. True sanctification—its power in prayer. The Spirit's intercession *in* us on behalf of the saints according to God's will is made possible.

28-34. True sanctification—its assurance. True sanctification gives assurance, in the middle of life's providences, of God's unfailing purposes of good toward us. But the magic lens that enables us to see all things working together for our good is love.

35-39. True sanctification—its climactic triumph. Nothing in time or eternity can

Sanctification

The Bible teaching on sanctification
Largely misunderstood and abused, sanctification (a setting apart for God's worship and service), as taught by the Scripture, has three aspects: past, present, future.

Past aspect of sanctification
Positional (1 Cor. 1:2, 30): *All* believers were so sanctified as saints, the youngest as well as the oldest, the most carnal as well as the most spiritual.
Static, unalterable, inseparable from justification, and the result solely of our union with Christ.
As God sees us in Christ (1 Cor. 1:2, 30, with Phil. 1:1, etc.).

Present aspect of sanctification
Experiential, depends upon our knowledge of and faith in our position in Christ (Rom. 6:1-11), converting our position into experience.
Progressive, changeable, depends upon yielding to God's will (Rom. 6:13) and conformity to God's Word (Rom. 12:2).
As we are in our conduct (2 Thess. 2:13).

Future aspect of sanctification
Final: When we see the Lord and are made like Him—sinless, sickless, deathless (1 Cor. 4; 15:54; 1 John 3:2).
Eternal: Will result in our final state in eternity (Phil. 3:21).
As we shall be in glory (Rom. 8:29; 1 Cor. 15:49).

separate one from God's love manifested in Christ, 38-39. This is the summit where true sanctification leads.

9:1-13. God's past purpose in Israel —her position

Romans 9-11 is parenthetical. In the unfolding of the gospel of grace, what about the Jew? Are the covenants and promises God made with His ancient people empty words? Has God failed them because they failed Him?

1-5. Israel's national position. Paul's deep love and intense anguish of heart for Israel are expressed, 1-3. He follows with a statement that distinguished Israel from any other nation, 4-5.

6-13. Israel's spiritual election. God has not failed in Israel's unbelief. The spiritual remnant of the nation, 6-7, are the recipients of the promise, 8, descended from a supernaturally generated posterity through Isaac, 9.

9:14-33. God's past purpose in Israel—His sovereignty

14-29. An objection offered and answered— God's righteous sovereignty. The divine Potter can make from the clay that which He sees fit, 21-24. Moreover, the Potter had proclaimed His purpose through the prophets, 25-29, to show that the Gentiles were to become God's people.

30-33. Israel's rejection of God's righteousness. Israel stumbled through unbelief, seeking legalistic righteousness by works, 31-33.

10. God's present purpose for Israel

1-5. Israel's present condition. They are zealous, but ignorant of God's righteousness, 2-3.

6-21. Present salvation for both Jew and Gentile. The divine plan for bringing God's righteousness to everyone, 14-15, involves sending out preachers. This method of gospel propagation makes unbelief inexcusable, 16-21.

11. God's future purpose for Israel

1-10. Israel's national setting aside not final. God's faithfulness is guaranteed in a future restoration of the nation. The present setting aside of Israel in her national election is only temporary, 1.

11-24. Israel's present national rejection has a divine purpose. It has brought salvation to the Gentiles, 11, hence it has been beneficial to the world. The wild olive graft represents Gentiles brought into spiritual privilege.

25-36. Restoration of the nation certain. It is assured *by special revelation,* 25. A "mystery" is a truth once hidden but now revealed. The restoration of Israel will constitute a fulfillment of God's purpose, 30-32, and will contribute to God's glory, 33-36.

12. Practical Christian service

The last five chapters contain the practical part of the letter.

1-2. Christian service and self. Self is to be sacrificed. The body is to be presented to God the Father. This is a privilege.

3-8. Christian service and gifts. Our varied service is to be discharged as a gift from the Lord, 6-8.

9-21. Christian service and fellow believers, and unbelievers. General exhortations to kind conduct toward Christians are followed by special pleas to loving forbearance under provocation from unbelievers.

13. Christian service and government
1-7. The Christian and the state. Human government represents God's authority, 1-7.
8-14. The Christian and good citizenship. The essence of good citizenship is outlined, 14, involving putting on Christ as a garment, and putting off sinful desires as dirty clothes.

14:1-15:3. Christian service and questionable things
14:1-13a. The principle of personal liberty. In matters of conduct over which Christians differ, 2-6, the principle of personal liberty is to operate, 3-13a. This prohibits our despising or judging a weaker brother, because God has received him as a believer, 3, and because there are allowable conscientious differences, 5-6.
14:13b-23. The principle of our neighbor's welfare and God's glory.
15:1-3. Plea to observe these principles. The strong believer ought to put up with the failings of the weaker brother, sacrificing personal pleasure, 1b.

15:4-13. Christian service and God's worldwide glory
4-7. The hope of God's worldwide glory. Human relationships of God's redeemed people are to glorify the Father, 5-7, promoting His praise and honor.
8-13. The world is the ultimate outreach of the gospel. God's goal has always been that the nations of the earth should glorify Him in worldwide adoration.

Quotations from the Old Testament

Paul quotes extensively from the OT to support his argument in Romans. Like several of the NT writers, he draws his quotations from the LXX (Greek Septuagint) rather than the Hebrew text of the OT that serves as the basis of our English translations. Furthermore, the NT writers, under the inspiration of the Holy Spirit, did not feel compelled to always quote the text verbatim, often choosing rather to paraphrase and comment on the text as necessary for their own context.

15:14-16:27. Christian service and Christian fellowship
15:14-33. Paul greets the saints in Rome. Paul expresses his longing to visit the church in Rome, 22-29, and the circumstances delaying his visit. He asks for prayer support, 30-32, ending with a blessing of peace, 33.
Ch. 16. Closing greetings and warnings. He mentions many saints by name—trophies of the gospel of God, 1-16. It is noteworthy that at least nine women are included among those who had done much for him in the service of the Lord.

1 Corinthians
Worldly vs. spiritual Christian living

Outline

1-3	The unity of the church vs. divisions
4-11	The order of the church vs. disorders
12-16	The gifts and doctrines of the church vs. their abuse

Date and purpose. This letter was written from Ephesus, probably in A.D. 55. It was penned to instruct recent converts from the paganism, with its vice and sin, so notably practiced at Corinth. As a center of commerce and wealth, as well as covetousness and unbridled lust, Corinth, with its worldly wisdom, offered a challenge to Christianity. If a church could be planted here where East and West met on the crossroads of the Graeco-Roman world, its influence could be expected to be far-reaching.

The site of the Tribune, Corinth, where Paul was brought before the Pro-Consul Julius Gallio.

1 Corinthians

1. Christ the basis of unity

1-9. The preeminence of Christ. The spotlight is focused on Christ in these opening verses. The believer's position in Christ is the basis of Paul's appeal to correct the faulty practices of the Corinthians.

10-17. The presence of factions. The faults and abuses in the Corinthian church were due to Christians behaving as unregenerate people, as carnal believers instead of spiritual. This resulted in disunity.

18-31. The corrective of the cross. Only the cross can save us from human philosophies and bring us to the true wisdom of God. Faith in the message of the cross releases both the wisdom and the power of God that humanity might not boast before God, 26-29.

2. The Holy Spirit the agent of unity

1-13. The Spirit reveals true wisdom. Apart from the teaching ministry of the Spirit true wisdom is unknown and unknowable, 11-13.

14-16. The unregenerate are totally ignorant of true wisdom. The person "without the Spirit" does not receive true wisdom, because it is mere folly to him.

3:1-8a. The spiritual Christian

1-3a. The spiritual vs. the worldly. The worldly believer is a "mere infant in Christ," 1, but the spiritual Christian is mature, 3.

3b-8a. The results of worldliness. Jealousy, bickering, and divisive cliques were formed.

3:8b-23. The judgment of the believer's works

8b-9. Christian service to be judged. This judgment, which concerns deeds only, not salvation, will determine the believer's reward, 8b.

10-15. The believer's judgment for service. Two kinds of service exist. One is like gold, silver, and precious stones, built by the spiritual believer, 12; the other is like wood, hay, and stubble, built by the worldly believer.

16-23. Solemn warning to worldly believers. The body of *every* believer is a sacred temple in which the Holy Spirit dwells. Sins of the body and of the mind are warned against.

4. The church and its leaders

1-8. The sin of judging God's servants. The church's leaders are to be highly esteemed as ministers of Christ and stewards of the truth revealed by God, 1.

9-21. The holy dedication of the apostles. Apostolic sacrifice and suffering are used to shame the carnal self-secure critics in the Corinthian church, 9-13.

5. The problem of the immoral believer

1-5. Carnality blinds to the presence of gross immorality. In a case of vile incest the incestuous brother was to be abandoned to Satan so that he might be disciplined as a believer possessing eternal life, 5.

6-13. The principle of the yeast of sin. Sin

condoned or unjudged spreads like yeast in a batch of dough. It must, therefore, be purged out, 7.

6:1-8. The disorder of legal suits
1-8. Christian suing Christian. Christian going to law against fellow Christian in pagan courts before pagan judges, 1, is a violation of Christian truth.

6:9-20. The snare of fornication
9-20. The Christian tempted to fornication. Fornication is a sin against the sanctity of the believer's body, 18. The believer's body is "a temple" ("a dwelling place of God"), specifically the most holy place where the Shekinah glory was manifested in the tabernacle or temple, 19.

7:1-24. Regulations of Christian marriage
1-9. The purpose of Christian marriage. Celibacy is best for some, 7-8, but marriage is God-ordained and designed to meet physical and psychological needs as constituted by the Creator, 7, 9.

10-24. Regulations governing Christian marriage. Marriage of believers is for life, 10-11. The general principle is that insofar as possible every effort is to be made to maintain the status quo at the time of becoming a believer, 12-24. Applied to the marriage union, it means the saved partner is to do everything possible to maintain the union and win the unsaved partner to the Lord.

7:25-40. Marriage vs. the unmarried state
25-31. The general principle. The general rule is that the unmarried are well-off as they are, particularly at times when believers are subject to economic and social stress, 25-26.

32-40. Contrast between the married and unmarried state. The unmarried believer of either sex is more at liberty to please the Lord, 32-34, and to serve Him without distraction, 35.

8. Christian liberty
1-13. The law of love the solution, and the law of knowledge inadequate. To most believers, the knowledge of the nothingness of an idol was such an obvious fact of revelation that they were not offended by eating meat first dedicated to a heathen deity, as was often the case in a pagan city like Corinth. Some weaker believers did not have this conviction and were offended, 7. Love must be superior to knowledge if a weaker brother is not to be offended, 8-13.

9. The church and its workers
1-15. Church leaders are to be honored and supported. God-ordained church leaders should not only be honored as such, but financially supported as well, 7-18. As illustrations the apostle uses the cases of the soldier, the vine grower, the shepherd, 7, and the law of Moses, 8-9 (cf. Deut. 25:4).

16-27. True church leaders are to be rewarded. They are under a divine commission and constraint, 16; and if they serve willingly, they will be rewarded in this life, 18, and in the life to come, 19-27.

10:1-15. The church's heritage
1-5. OT typology and its lessons. The Egyptian redemption, the wilderness wandering,

Cenchreae, harbor for ancient Corinth.

symbolizing the death of Christ and the fellowship of the body of Christ, 16, portrays our oneness as believers in union with Christ, 17.

23-33. The law of love and Christian liberty. The believer is not under a legalistic principle, but the law of unselfish love, 23-24.

11:1-16. The church and its women

1-10. The headship of man. In urging the headship of man, 3, Paul presents the woman's headdress as a symbol of her subordination to the man, as the man in turn is subordinated to Christ, 4-6.

11-16. Order under grace. "In the Lord," man and woman are one, and mutually dependent, 11-12.

11:17-34. Disorders at the Lord's Supper rebuked

17-22. The disorder exposed.

23-34. The disorder corrected.
Self-examination is necessary, 28, to avoid condemnation and consequent chastening, entailing weakness, sickness, and even death, 30.

12:1-11. The believer and the sign gifts

1-3. The Giver of the gifts. Those who had been controlled by demon spirits must now be taught the work of the Holy Spirit, called also the Spirit of God.

4-11. The list of the gifts. There are numerous and various gifts, but only one and the same Spirit who gives the gifts and operates them through *each* believer, 4. The Spirit gives the gifts to people for service. Christ gives the gifted people to the church. God the Father controls the numerous and various workings of these

and entry into the land were types or shadows of spiritual truths applicable to NT saints, 6, 11. The "fathers" prefigure NT saints, and the bread they ate and the water they drank in the desert point to Christ, 3-4.

6-15. The warning. Despite God's grace, Israel fell into idolatry, 5, 7, 8; tempted the Lord, 9; and murmured, 10. Many were destroyed, 9-10. Paul warns against proud self-sufficiency, 12, and encourages his readers to trust God and flee from idolatry, 13-14.

10:16-33. The Lord's Supper

16-22. Fellowship at the Lord's Table requires separation. The communion,

gifts, 6. Although under the sovereign control of the Spirit, 11, these are mainly the *sign* or *miraculous* gifts with which the early church was endowed before the full NT revelation was given to guide believers.

12:12-31. The church and the sign gifts

12-27. The church as the body of Christ. The unity of the body is illustrated as a human body, 12a. There is one church, one body; many members, many functions, but all a vital part of the one body.

28-31. The church and the sign gifts. The apostle now relates the church, the body, the aggregate of individual believers, to these gifts. Everyone does not have the same gift, 29-30, nor is expected to have.

13. The church and the permanent gifts

1-8a. Love must control the exercise of all spiritual gifts. This is true of the sign gifts as well as the non-sign or permanent gifts of the church. The "most excellent way," 12:31, is the "love" way, which the worldly, emotional Corinthians had completely missed in their childish desire for the showy gifts to be used for selfish ends.

8b-13. Permanence of love. Love is contrasted with the gifts that would be superseded, 8. They would cease because a time of complete or perfect knowledge and prophecy would come, 9, an event many have linked with the completion of the NT Scriptures.

14. Abuse of the sign gifts

1-11. The superiority of prophecy over tongues. "Keep on pursuing love," 1, and "eagerly desire spiritual gifts"—particularly prophecy, i.e., inspired verbal utterances of truth not yet written down. This is superior to speaking in tongues because it is more comprehensible to man.

12-40. Correction of the abuse of tongues. The believer should desire the superior edifying gifts, and was to pray for the gift of interpretation if he had the gift of tongues. The church was to use tongues only with great restraint, 19, and in any case, only if an interpreter was present, 27-28. The main purpose of the gift, 21-22, as a sign to unbelieving Jews was to be held in mind.

15. The doctrine of resurrection

15:1-19. The importance of Christ's resurrection

1-11. The fact and import of Christ's resurrection. The doctrine of the resurrection of the body was specially denied by the pagan intellectualism of Corinth. By contrast Paul presents Christ's resurrection as central in the gospel of salvation.

12-19. Christ's resurrection the basis of ours. Paul argues for the importance of the doctrine by looking at the alternatives.

15:20-23. Christ's resurrection and ours

20. Christ's resurrection a guarantee of ours. "Firstfruits," 20. On the Feast of Firstfruits (Lev. 23:10-14), the first sheaf of ripened grain was presented to the Lord as a pledge of the ingathering of the whole harvest.

21-23. Christ's resurrection the divine remedy for the Fall. All "in Adam," 22, i.e., all members of the human race, die (physically). All

The Tomb of the Herods, Jerusalem.

"in Christ," 22, *all* redeemed humanity, will enjoy victorious resurrection.

15:24-28. Resurrection and the final consummation
24-26. The final abrogation of death. The destruction of death is the last result of Christ's victory over death in His own resurrection.
27-28. The eternal state. This will entail paradise regained (Rev. 22) as it was lost in Gen. 1-3.

15:29-34. Christ's resurrection and new incentives
29. The incentive to be baptized for the dead. If Christ's resurrection is not a fact, and ours consequently not a living hope, 12-19, then what is the purpose of Christian baptism? If we will die and stay dead, we might as well already be dead; thus, baptism would be a farce.
30-34. The incentive to live dangerously. If Christianity is resurrectionless, why risk one's life, as the apostle did, in fighting against violent

beastlike opposition such as that at Ephesus, 32 (cf. Act 19:23-41)?

15:35-58. Resurrection and conquest over death
35-49. The character of the resurrection body. Three illustrations from nature are used to demonstrate the reasonableness of the new resurrection body: plants, 37-38; flesh, 39; and heavenly bodies, 40-41.
50-58. The change that produces the resurrection body. The need for change is indicated by the creation of our bodies for the natural realm and their fallen corrupt nature, 50. All believers will be changed, 51, and the change will take place in a split second, at the "last trumpet" (cf. 1 Thess. 4:13-18).

16:1-4. The doctrine of stewardship
Periodic, personal, proportionate giving is not to be mere legalistic tithing, but rather a giving on the basis of love for the Savior.

16:5-24. The illustration of brotherly service
5-14. Brotherly concern. This is illustrated by three contemplated visits: Paul's own visit, 5-9; that of Timothy, 10-11; and that of Apollos, 12.
15-24. Service and final salutation, a beautiful illustration of brotherly service.

2 Corinthians
The glory of the Christian ministry

Outline

1:1-2:13   Introductory, personal testimony
2:14-7:16   The glory of the Christian ministry
8:1-9:15   The glory of the ministry of giving
10:1-13:14 The glory of the Christian ministry defended

Author and genuineness. The intimate details of Paul's life and ministry contained in this letter are beyond the reach of a forger. Links with 1 Corinthians, Galatians, Romans, and Acts abound in the biographical touches. The letter was probably written shortly after 1 Corinthians, in A.D. 56, from Macedonia (cf. 2:13; 7:5-7; 8:1; 9:2-4).

Character of the letter. It is the most personal and the least doctrinal of all the Pauline letters, except for Philemon. It lays bare the life and ministry of the great apostle.

Contents. Attacked by critics, Paul presents a grand defense of his life and ministry in ch. 1-7. Chapters 8 and 9 concern the collection for the impoverished believers in Jerusalem, with instructions in proper giving. Chapters 10-13 further defend Paul's apostleship and authority against false legalistic teachers.

The Romans carry in triumph the booty from the Temple in Jerusalem, Titus' Arch, Rome.

2 Corinthians

aromatic herbs strewn along the way.

15-17. The Christian's powerful influence.
Every true minister of Christ is a censer of sweet incense wafting Christ's fragrance abroad upon a corrupt and ill-smelling world.

1:1-11. Divine comfort and its purpose

1-7. God's comfort abounding in times of trouble. The purpose of God's comfort (Greek *paraklesis,* "a calling alongside") is that after we have been comforted we may go to the side of a needy one and minister the divine consolation we have received.

8-11. Thanksgiving for recent deliverance.
Paul's harrowing experience at Ephesus
(cf. Acts 19:23-20:1) is an example of the tribulation through which God's servant passed.

1:12-2:13. Testimony of sincerity

1:12-24. Paul's reason for joy. The sealing of the Spirit, 22, is the guarantee of the believer's security (Eph. 1:13; 4:30); the Holy Spirit is the "seal." A seal signifies ownership (Jer. 32:11-12), security (Est. 8:8), and a completed transaction (Jer. 32:9-10).

2:1-13. Paul's desire to visit them in joy. To avoid a sad visit, 1-2, he corrected their faults in this letter, 3-13.

2:14-17. The glory of the ministry —its triumph

14. The Christian's march of triumph. The illustration is that of a triumphal march through the city of Rome to honor a Roman conqueror. Perfume of incense ascended from the numerous censers borne by captives and from

3:1-6a. The glory of the ministry —its accreditation

1-3. Paul's ministry is not accredited by self-commendation, but by his witness and work.
Paul's Corinthian converts were his credentials, 2, as well as Christ's credentials, 3.
4-6a. It is accredited by God. Paul's qualification was divine. His ministry was attested by Christ, 4.

3:6b-11. The glory of the ministry —its message and grace

6b-11. Its message was spiritual and life-giving. As the gospel of grace is energized by the Holy Spirit, it is contrasted with the law of Moses, a code written on stone.

3:12-18. The glory of the ministry —its transforming power

12-17. It is to exercise great boldness, illumination, and freedom. The glory of the Christian ministry produces such hope that it is to be proclaimed plainly without fear, 12. In place of the regulation of the outer law, the believer finds the dynamic of inner law, 17, "the law of the Spirit of life" (Rom. 8:2).
18. It is to enjoy wonderful transformation.

4:1-7. The glory of the ministry —its sincerity

1-2. It renounces all sin and sham. Such a ministry is grounded in a personal experience of

God's mercy in Christ.

3-7. It advertises Jesus Christ. Satan, the god of this present age, has blinded the minds of unbelievers to the light of the gospel. It is, therefore, essential that if this blindness is to be penetrated, Christ, not we ourselves, must be proclaimed.

4:8-18. The glory of the ministry —its sufferings

8-11. It suffers but benefits spiritually. Believers experience suffering and death so that Christ's life may be revealed and seen in them.

12-18. It has an inner secret of spiritual stature. The secret comprehends self-crucifixion, faith, hope, self-forgetfulness, spiritual strength, proper perspective, and a wise goal.

5:1-13. The glory of the ministry —its fearlessness in the face of death

1-8. Its conviction of the resurrection of the body. The Christian has the strong assurance, 1, 6, of a future life. His redeemed body is called an "earthly tent." Death is the taking down of the tent, 1. The resurrection body is not built by human hands. Immortal, it is described as "an eternal house in heaven," 1.

9-13. Results of the conviction of bodily resurrection. It makes us reckon on the fact that all believers must face a judgment of their life and works since they have been saved. Reward or loss of reward will be the issue, 10.

5:14-21. The glory of the ministry —its motives and dignity

14-17. Its glorious motive. This is "love," both Christ's love for us and our love for Christ. This

mighty dynamic impels us and is the constant drive of Christ's true minister. Being in Christ involves a new creation with a *completely* new order, 17.

18-21. Its wonderful dignity. To be an ambassador, 20-21, means to represent one's country (heaven) and government (the Lord) with prestige, wisdom, maturity, and dignity.

6:1-10. The glory of the ministry —its character

1-3. It is to be blameless, because the ministry is peculiarly liable to criticism and blame from sinful people, as well as from worldly believers, 3. Stumbling blocks are easily erected by wrong conduct.

4-10. It is to be approved. The apostle names nine testings of a minister in which he is to honor God, 4-5, nine ways by which Christ's minister is to be characterized, 6-7, and nine paradoxes, 8-10, which occur in the life of the true minister.

6:11-7:1. The glory of the ministry —its purity

6:11-13. Purity is the basis of affection among believers. To achieve Christian unity and to love one another, God's people must be separate from that which contaminates.

6:14-7:1. A plea for purity. The unequal yoke is anything that unites a believer with an unbeliever in a common purpose, 14 (cf. Deut. 7:2-3; 22:10).

7:2-16. The glory of the ministry —its reflection in Paul's life

2-11. Paul's loving concern for the Corinthian believers. He urges them to open their hearts toward him, 2, protesting his interest in their

The Temple of Apollo, Corinth.

welfare, 3-7.

12-16. He desires them to be assured of his love. Their welcome of Titus assured the apostle that his confidence in them was not misplaced, 13-16.

8:1-15. Example and exhortation in giving

1-8. Christian giving and the example of the Macedonian Christians. Paul uses the example of the generous Macedonian churches in demonstrating the grace of giving, 1.

9-15. Christian giving and the example of Christ. The apostle sets out the grace of giving, i.e., a disposition wrought in the heart by the Holy Spirit, 9; the example of Christ in giving, 9b; pledging in giving, 10-11; willingness in giving, 12; and equality in giving, 13-15.

8:16-9:5. Instruction in wise handling of funds

8:16-24. The Lord's money is to be handled in a manner above reproach.

9:1-5. The Corinthians are urged to meet their share. Paul tactfully commends them, 1-2,

yet sends delegates to them to make sure they will be ready, 3-4, with their gift in hand, 5.

9:6-15. Principles of spiritual giving

6. The principle of harvest. A bountiful sowing will mean a bountiful reaping.

7. The principle of free-will donation. Joyful, spontaneous gratitude to God for what He has done for us in Christ alone can make a "cheerful" (hilarious) giver.

8-15. The principles of grace and thanksgiving. Spiritual giving taps God's boundless resources. God gives to us that we may give to others. Thanksgiving ultimately goes back to God's supreme gift of salvation through Christ, 15, the ground of all spiritual grace.

10. The glory of the ministry defended —commended by the Lord

1-6. The minister commended by his attitude. He is to be characterized by "the meekness and gentleness of Christ," 1, yet by godly boldness, 1-2, and a disciplined prayer life, 3-4, that is highly effective in spiritual results, 5.

7-11. The minister commended by his authority. The authority is not idly presumptuous or dependent upon outward appearance, 7-10, but is from the Lord and genuinely real, 11.

12-18. The minister commended by the Lord. Self-commendation as well as comparison with others is unwise and not to be engaged in, 12.

11:1-15. The glory of the ministry defended by sincerity attested in service

1-6. The sincere motives of service. Paul was sincere in his jealous love for the spiritual welfare of the Corinthians, and it was his desire that they might be chaste and pure in Christ, 2.

7-11. The rewards of sincere service. Sincere service abases self and serves unselfishly, 7-9.

12-15. The counterfeits of sincere service. Paul states that insincere ministers are "deceitful" workmen, 13, under Satan's delusive power, 14.

11:16-33. The glory of the ministry defended by sincerity attested by suffering

16-23a. Paul answers his critics. The apostle resorts to a legitimate type of ridicule and satire to answer his critics forcefully and to prove to them his utter sincerity.

23b-33. Paul cites his sufferings to prove his sincerity.

12:1-10. The glory of the ministry defended by experience of God's dealing

1-6. The experience of God's glory. Paul uses his sublime experience of God's revealed glory to him, 1, to defend his ministry against false workers.

7-10. The experience of God's testing. Paul's "thorn" (Greek *skolops,* "anything pointed," like a stake or a sharp thorn) was a real pain or experience of suffering with a definite purpose to keep him humble, 7.

12:11-21. The glory of the ministry defended by experience of effective service

11-12. Ministry for Christ is to be effective for Christ. Paul authenticated his apostleship by the genuine works of a true apostle, including miracles and the sign gifts, 12 (cf. 1 Cor. 12:8-11).

13-19. Effective service excels in helping others. It acts in sincerity before God in Christ for the edifying of God's people, 17-19.

20-21. Effective service warns against sin.

13:1-10. The glory of the ministry defended—commended by honesty

1-6. Honesty to correct faults. There is such a thing as believers *failing* the test in the race before them, 5-6 (1 Cor. 9:27), facing loss of reward or possible physical death (1 Cor. 3:14-15; 5:5; 1 John 5:16).

7-10 Honesty to demand honesty. He was honest himself and demanded honesty in those to whom he ministered, 7.

13:11-14. Benediction and farewell

Galatians
Maintaining our freedom in Christ

Outline

1:1-2:14	Personal—Gospel revelation
2:15-4:31	Doctrinal—Justification
5:1-6:18	Practical—Sanctification

Occasion. The letter was necessitated by serious defection among Paul's converts in the Roman province of Galatia made on his three missionary journeys (Acts 13:4-14:28; 16:6; 18:23). The apostle is called on to defend the gospel of free grace that he had proclaimed to the Gentiles (Acts 14:27). Judaistic teachers had come in to adulterate Paul's gospel with a mixture of human works and some form of legalism.

The purpose. Paul is forced to defend his apostleship as genuine, the gospel he preached as divinely authoritative, and the doctrine of justification alone, apart from deeds or law-keeping, as valid.

Contrasts in Galatians

Chapters 1-2 Personal

Lost in Adam	**Saved in Christ**
All die physically in Adam	**All live spiritually in Christ**
Another (false) gospel	**The genuine gospel**
Human reasoning	**God's revelation**

Chapters 3-4 Doctrinal

Law	**Grace**
Deeds	**Faith**
The curse of death	**The blessing of life**
Condemnation by deeds	**Justification by faith**
Servants in slavery (defeat)	**Sons in freedom (victory)**
The old covenant	**The new covenant**
(symbolized by Hagar)	**(symbolized by Sarah)**

Chapters 5-6 Practical

Living in the flesh	**Walking in the Spirit**
Deeds of the flesh	**Fruit of the Spirit**
Falling from grace	**Standing firm in grace**
World or self the object of glorying	**The cross the sole object of glorying**

Galatians

1:1-9. Greeting and theme
1-5. The greeting. Paul stresses the divine origin of his apostleship, 1-2, because his enemies in Galatia attacked both him and the gospel he preached

6-9. The gospel—true and false. Here for all time Paul finalizes and fixes the true gospel of redeeming grace from any admixture of legalism or human deeds, 8-9.

1:10-2:14. Paul's true gospel —a divine revelation
1:10-24. Proved by Paul's early experiences and ministry. Paul declares that he had once been a strong supporter of Judaism, which his legalistic foes were trying to mix with the gospel of grace, 13-14, but he had left it for something better.

2:1-14. Proved by Paul's later experiences and ministry. Nothing was added to the divine revelation of Paul's gospel of grace by subsequent contacts with the apostles, 1-6.

2:15-21. Justification and the Jewish law
15-18. Jews (not just Gentiles) must be justified by faith. Paul here proves to the Galatians that whatever false claims were made by the legalistic perverters, he and Peter were in complete concord doctrinally.

19-21. Justification by faith cuts us off from legalism. In a fallen sinner, God's imputed righteousness can come only by Christ's death. Otherwise His death was useless, 21.

3:1-5. Justification and the Holy Spirit
1-3. The gift of the Spirit is by faith. The Galatians in lapsing from grace into legalism were senseless and deluded, especially since Christ's all-sufficient death had been so distinctly expounded before them, 1.

4-5. Christian living is by faith. They began the Christian life in faith, relying on the Spirit. Were they to be made mature in it by the flesh, 3?

3:6-9. Justification and the Abrahamic covenant
6-9. The Abrahamic covenant is the basis of faith. Abraham believed God, 6, and so was justified, as are all those who like him believe God, 7.

3:10-18. Justification and blessing
10-13. Redemption from the curse. The law was intended to demonstrate mankind's helpless sinfulness, 12, that they may be saved by Christ, 13. The curse of the law fell on our Lord, 13. By His death on the tree (the cross) the Sinless One became the Sin Bearer, the Sin Offering (1 Peter 2:24).

14-18. Reception of the blessing. The blessing of justification includes: the blessing given to Abraham, 14-16; the promise through faith, 14; and the covenanted blessing of an inheritance, 17-18. The covenant blessing is wholly by faith. Salvation is by faith *plus nothing*.

The Roman aqueduct, Pisidian Antioch.

3:19-29. Justification and the purpose of the law

19a. The question. If justification is by faith plus nothing, 14-18, and not at all by deeds of the law, what then is the purpose of the law?
19b-29. The answer. It was "added" (i.e., put or placed by the side of grace), "because of transgressions" (i.e., for the divine purpose that it might clearly reveal sin as transgression or personal guilt (Rom. 5:13). It was added to show that all, both Jew and Gentile, are chained to sin, 23. It was introductory to the present age of spiritual adulthood, 25-29.

4:1-7. Justification and sonship

1-3. Sons under faith vs. servants under the law. The apostle illustrates the difference between the Mosaic (legal) age and the gospel (grace) age with the figure of a child heir in a family.
4-7. Sonship by redemption from the law. Christ's incarnation was "when the time had fully come," i.e., when the law had fully discharged its task as a pedagogue to bring us to Christ, 4.

4:8-18. Justification and freedom

8-14. Losing our liberty in Christ. Being set free from bondage to the enslaving deities of paganism, by a knowledge of the one true God revealed in Christ, were the Galatians to be again victimized by a religion of *doing something* to gain favor with God, 9?
15-18. Losing the blessing of freedom. The legalists made a show of affection; however, not for the good purpose of liberating but for enslaving. Indeed, they were determined to shut out their victims from the liberating truth of the grace of Christ that their dupes might show them obedient affection, 17.

4:19-31. The new covenant vs. the old

19-26. The illustrating allegory. The allegory, 22-27, is directed as an illustration to confused but justified *believers,* 19-21, who were attempting to mix two mutually exclusive systems, law and grace.
27-31. The meaning of the allegory. The believer loosed from the law is free in Christ under grace.

5:1-9. The peril of falling from grace

1-3. Falling from grace. Having proved the truth that the believer is not under law but under grace, the apostle warns of the peril of being entangled once more or held in "the yoke of slavery."
4-9. The sad results of falling from grace. It meant losing the race, 7, disobeying the truth, 7, and listening to false teachers rather than the Spirit, 8.

5:10-15. The call to freedom under grace

10-13a. The call. The apostle expresses assurance that the Galatians will heed his warning and the false teachers will be dealt with as they should, 10-12.

13b-15. The warning against license. Freedom in Christ is not to be used as an opportunity for indulging the sinful nature or as a cloak for sin, but for love shown in service, 13.

5:16-18. Sanctification and the Holy Spirit

16a. The human condition. "Live by the Spirit." The imperative (command) is in the present tense and involves a *continuous* reliance on the Spirit, i.e., faith in the Spirit's operation. Sanctification is thus by faith, not by works; by the Spirit of God, not by morality or self-effort.

16b-18. The divine undertaking. When we believe, God undertakes. It is God, not we ourselves, who does the sanctifying work. The unceasing struggle between the old nature and the new, 17, and the futile self-effort of the flesh versus the effective inworking of the Spirit, demonstrates that those who are "led by the Spirit" alone have complete victory, 18.

5:19-26. Acts of the sinful nature vs. fruit of the Spirit

19-21. The acts of the sinful nature listed. These are the outcome of unbelief—failing to walk by means of the Spirit, which involves faith. The old nature in believers is just as vile as the old nature in the unregenerate.

22-26. The fruit of the Spirit specified. "Fruit" is in contrast to "acts." One is by faith, the other by human effort; one by the Spirit, the other by the flesh. One is holy, the other is polluted. One springs out of the renewed nature, the other is produced by the old nature.

6:1-18. Sanctification in action

1-6. Dealing with fellow Christians. The burdened fellow believer, 2-5, is to be helped, 2, in all humility, 3, and faithfulness, 4, realizing everyone has a burden to bear, 5. "The law of Christ," 2, is the law of love for one's neighbor (Luke 6:27-38).

7-9. Sowing to the Spirit. The new life in Christ is presented under the figure of farming.

10-13. Manifesting spirituality. Spirituality is shown by doing good to all, particularly to fellow believers, 10, and by exemplifying a spirit of sacrificial love, 11-13.

14-18. The basis of true spirituality. This is the cross, 14 (cf. 1 Cor. 1:18), because it separates the world from the believer by his death-to-sin position in Christ, and the believer from the world, 14-15, i.e., the satanic world system.

Ephesians
Blessed in the heavenly realm in Christ

Outline

1-3	Our position in Christ (What we are before God)
1:1-23	The believer as God's child
2:1-18	The believer as a member of Christ's body
2:19-3:21	The believer as God's building
4-6	Our practice of Christ (How we are to act before people)
4:1-6:9	A worthy walk

Date and author. This magnificent letter was evidently addressed to the church in Ephesus (cf. Acts 19), but intended also as a circular letter to neighboring churches. Paul had spent three years in Ephesus. He wrote this letter, the first of his so-called prison letters, about A.D. 61 or 62 from prison in Rome.

Significant words in Ephesians. In occurs about 90 times, stressing the believer's union with Christ in death, resurrection, ascension, and present position. **Body** is a metaphor describing our union with Christ. **Live** refers to our behavior within the body of Christ, how we act in union with Him, the Head.

The Graeco-Roman amphitheater at ancient Ephesus, where Paul was taken during the silversmiths' riot.

Ephesians

Divine election

This is the sovereign act of God in grace by which from eternity certain ones are chosen from the human race for Himself (John 15:19; Eph. 1:4). Election applies only to God's people, not to the lost. People are not elected to perdition.

Foreordination

Foreordination is that exercise of the divine will by which what has been determined by God from eternity is brought to pass by Him in time.

Foreordination and free will

Foreordination concerns only God's people. So far as the human race is concerned everyone may accept Christ as Savior and is invited to do so. The basis for this invitation is the work of the incarnate Son, which made the human race savable. Free will concerns people outside Christ. Once they accept the gospel and are "in Christ" their viewpoint changes, as God from His side shows them why believers are accepted.

1:1-6. Chosen in Christ by the Father
1-6. Blessed, chosen, and adopted in Christ by the Father. After the greeting, 1-2, the apostle presents God the Father's role in our salvation, 3-6.

1:7-12. Redeemed by the Son
7. Purchased by Christ's blood. "Redemption" is deliverance by means of a price paid, in this case Christ's blood (Lev. 17:11; Matt. 20:28).
8-10. Enlightened by His grace. His redemption bought us out of the ignorance of the slave-to-sin category into the intimacy of a relationship as a son (John 15:15).
11-12. Given an inheritance in His purpose. The purpose is that we "might be for the praise of his glory," 12. He will be glorified in us, as well as we in Him.

1:13-14. Sealed by the Spirit
13a. The Spirit energizes faith to salvation. The Holy Spirit *applies* our salvation in persuading us to appropriate it (cf. John 16:13-15).
13b-14. The Spirit seals the believer. The Spirit Himself indwelling the believer is the seal.

1:15-23. Prayer for realization of the believer's position in Christ
15-16. The apostle's prayer interest.

17-23. The apostle's prayer. He asks for *knowledge* on the part of God's people concerning their position and possessions in Christ, and for *power* of that position to be shown in their lives by faith, 19-23.

2:1-7. The believer as a member of Christ's body
The results of the work of grace relate to the past, present, and future, 5-7. In the past, we *were* raised from the dead with Christ, 5-6a. In the present, we *are now* seated in the heavenly realms in union with Christ, 6b. In the future,

Reconstructed remains of the Temple of Hadrian, Ephesus.

God *will* display to the universe the unfathomable wealth of His kindness to us through Christ, 7.

2:8-10. The way of salvation in the body

8-9. Saved by grace. The emphasis is on the divine method of salvation, "by grace"; on its free, undeserved character, "the gift of God"; and on its God-glorifying purpose, "so that no one can boast."

10. Saved to serve. Saved apart from deeds, but for good deeds.

2:11-18. The body made one by Christ's blood

11-12. What we were in ourselves. We were "Gentiles by birth," 11a, outside the spiritual privileges of the Jews, 11b, and without Christ, without hope, without God, 12.

13-18. What we are in Christ. We are now united to Christ; brought near to Him; fully accepted by God; a new community of His people, "one new man"; Jew and Gentile together having access to God by one Spirit, 18.

2:19-22. The believer as God's building

Believers are part of a single "building." This involves the Triune God. It is God the Father's "household" into which the believer is born, 19. The holy "temple" into which the believer is corporately built is the Lord's the Son's, 21. The dwelling that He has chosen to indwell is the Spirit's, 22.

3:1-12. The formation of the building revealed

1-6. The mystery and its meaning. The revelation of its meaning was divinely made known to Paul, who expounded the mystery of the church in his letters.

7-12. The mystery and Paul's ministry. The mystery involves the unfathomable riches of Christ, 8, including His person, His work, His intercession, His coming again, His eternal kingdom, and His inheritance in us.

3:13-21. Prayer for knowledge and power

13-19. The petition. The prayer is addressed to the Father, 14-15, seeking the threefold fullness of the Triune God, 16-19.

20-21. The benediction.

4:1-6. A life worthy of Christ

1-3. The life described. The virtues of humility, gentleness, patience, and forbearing love, 2, are basic in maintaining the practical unity of the body of Christ.

4-6. The basis of the worthy life. Scriptural ecumenicity is described in the seven "ones" in these verses.

4:7-16. The ministry and a worthy life

7-11. Christ's gifts for a worthy life. *The* gift par excellence, 7, is the Spirit (Luke 24:49), but other gifts that make possible a worthy life are also included, notably gifted people, 11.

12-16. Purpose of the gifts. They are to prepare God's people for the work of ministering on the Lord's behalf and building up the body of Christ, 12.

4:17-29. The new self and a worthy life

17-22. The old self put off. The "old self," 22, is the unregenerate person ruled by his corrupt, fallen nature (Rom. 6:6). Its characteristics are described in verses 17-22.

23-29. The new self put on. The "new self," 24, is the regenerate person with a new nature in whom Christ is formed (Col. 1:27). Its characteristics are described in verses 23-29.

4:30-32. The Holy Spirit and worthy life

30. The Holy Spirit is grieved by an unholy life. Our safety and security are not to be abused by license.

31-32. The Holy Spirit effects a holy life. He enables us to put away sin and to show Christian characteristics.

5:1-17. Imitators of God and a holy life

1-7. Imitating God as children of love. Since "God is love" (1 John 4:8), family likeness requires that we imitate our Father in worthy behavior as "children of love," 1-2.

8-17. Imitating God as children of light. Since "God is light" (1 John 1:5), family resemblance necessitates that we imitate our Father in a worthy life as "children of light," 8 (cf. 1 Thess. 5:5).

5:18-20. The filling of the Spirit and a worthy life

18. The true elixir of life and the false.

19-20. The results of being Spirit-filled. This involves a life overflowing with joyful song and praise to the Lord (cf. Phil. 4:6).

A soldier's armor depicted in relief, Ephesus.

5:21-33. Husbands, wives and a worthy life

21. The general principle. We are to submit to one another "out of reverence for Christ."

22-24. The duty of wives. The illustration used is the relation between Christ and the church. The dominating note is love—a loving subjection, not a mechanical "obey," a word reserved for children, 6:1, and servants, 6:5.

25-33. The duty of husbands. They are to love their wives, 25, as Christ loved the church and died to sanctify and glorify it, 25-27. The union of Christian husband and wife is to be permanent, intimate, and indissoluble, 31.

6:1-4. Children, parents and a worthy life

1-3. The injunction to children. Children are to obey parents, the only qualification being "in the Lord."

4. The injunction to fathers. They are not to provoke children with unreasonable demands, but to discipline and instruct them in the Lord's Word.

6:5-9. Servants, masters and a worthy life

5-8. Servants are to obey. Servants are to obey their masters, living for Christ in the social status in which they were saved, 5a.

9. Masters and employers. They are to act in the light of Christ's mastery over their lives, bearing in mind there is no respect of earthly positions with Him (cf. Acts 10:34).

6:10-20. Spiritual conflict and a worthy life

10-12. The warrior's resources. When Christians put on their spiritual armor, the Holy Spirit empowers them to resist Satan's attack.

13-20. The warrior's use of his resources. The believer's resources are described under the figure of a Roman soldier's equipment in full battle dress. His secret of victory in spiritual battle is reckoning by faith on those resources which are actually his in Christ, the Victor (Col. 1:13; 2:15). "Put on the full armor" emphasizes the responsibility of so reckoning, 13.

6:21-24. Personal note; closing greeting

Philippians
The joy of knowing Christ

Outline

1 The joy of Christ our life
2 The joy of Christ our example
3 The joy of Christ our goal
4 The joy of Christ our sufficiency

Author and theme. This letter was written while Paul was a prisoner in Rome, perhaps A.D. 62. Its theme is the adequacy of Christ for all the experiences of life—privation, persecution, hardship, and suffering, as well as prosperity and popularity.

Historical background. The account of the Philippian mission (Acts 16:6-40) shows the church there was founded under divine leading (Acts 16:6-7), as a result of a directing vision (Acts 16:8-11), and born in a prison (Acts 16:25-34). A note of triumphant joy in Christ permeates, joy being mentioned 18 times in the letter, despite the apostle's severe testings in the interim (cf. 2 Cor. 11:23-33).

The Agora (market) of Roman Philippi, with the walls of an early Christian basilica beyond.

Philippians

1:1-11. Paul the pastor's joy in Christ

1-2. His pastoral greeting. Paul addresses the local church in Philippi, Macedonia (cf. Acts 16:6-40), which was organized with "overseers" (bishops) and "deacons" (cf. Acts 6:1-7).

3-11. His pastoral joy. Paul's remembrance and prayer ministry for the Philippians were characterized by joy, 3-4.

1:12-30. Paul the prisoner's joy in Christ

12-20. His confident joy in tribulations. He is assured his suffering will result in promoting the gospel, 12, even in the emperor's court itself (cf. 4:22).

21-30. The secret of Paul's confident joy is his Christ-centered life. In the light of his own conflicts, the apostle tells the Philippians to endure suffering joyfully, 27-30.

2:1-11. Exhortation to unity and humility

1-4. The exhortation. The basis for the exhortation is the Philippian believer's position in Christ, 1.

5-11. The example of Christ. His self-humbling, 5-8, led to His exaltation by the Father, 9-11. This great "kenotic" or self-emptying passage is the basis for the apostle's exhortation, 5.

2:12-16. Working out salvation

12-13. The exhortation. Working *out* salvation is vastly different from working *for* salvation. Working out salvation in daily experience is on the basis of obedience to God's Word, 12a, and by "fear and trembling," 12b.

14-16. The result. This will be blamelessness of life, and a character in keeping with the position of God's children, 15.

2:17-30. Paul's example of humble service

17-18. The joy of such service. To realize fully such joy, the apostle is willing to be poured out as a drink offering sacrificially in service, 17.

19-30. The service exemplified. In Timothy, 19-23, in himself, 24, and in Epaphroditus, 25-30, joyful self-humbling service is seen.

3:1-6. Christ the true goal vs. false goals

1. The true goal in life presented. All real rejoicing concentrates in Christ and in what He has done, 1a (cf. 1 Thess. 5:16).

2-6. False goals warned against. The term "mutilators of the flesh," 2, involves a play on the word "circumcision." Paul uses *katatome* ("a cutting up" or "mutilation") instead of *peritome* ("a cutting around" or "circumcision") in order to emphasize the error of the Judaizers who required circumcision of the Gentile believers.

3:7-9. Christ the one goal in life

7-8. Counting all lost. Paul counts all the gains in the old unregenerate life as pure liability, as rubbish (Greek "excrement"), 8b, "for the sake of Christ," 7.

8b-9. Reckoning the gain. "Found in him," 9, is

the position of perfect acceptance in the righteousness of God gained by faith.

3:10-14. Concentration of spiritual purpose

10-11. The apostle's object is Christ. The "resurrection from the dead," 11, refers to the resurrection of believers when separation from sin will be final and conformity to Christ complete.

12-14. Paul presses on to what lies ahead. Paul aimed to possess such intimate knowledge of his Lord, and his position in Him, that the day of judgment would be one of approval and victory instead of shame and defeat.

3:15-19. Another appeal for unity

15-16. The appeal. Those who are "mature" (*teleioi*), i.e., grown-up both doctrinally and experientially, are to have the attitudes that Paul has just expressed in his testimony concerning his own struggle of faith, 15.

17-19. The example. The apostle offers his own way of life as an example, 17a. Those who do not walk in grace are "enemies of the cross of Christ," 18.

3:20-21. Christ the believer's expectation

20a. Our heavenly citizenship.

20b-21. The privileges of our citizenship. When He comes again our Savior will complete our salvation in its future sense of glorification, 21. The resurrection body will be deathless, disease-free, sinless, indestructible, and designed for heaven.

4:1-5. Standing fast in Christ's sufficiency

1. The reason for the injunction. Keep on standing firm because we are a heavenly people enjoying a sure salvation.

2-5. The result of the injunction. Their constant perseverance will heal personal rifts and cause them to "agree with each other in the Lord," 2. It will produce a spirit of helpfulness among believers.

4:6-9. The secret of God's peace

6-7. The prescription for receiving God's peace. A twofold direction: don't worry about anything, and pray about everything in a spirit of gratitude, 6.

8-9. The prescription for maintaining God's peace. (1) Guard our mental life. Meditate on the things that are true, noble, right, pure, lovely, and admirable, 8. (2) Practice the things that were taught by the apostles.

4:10-23. Paul's testimony of God's peace

10-14. His contentment in the Lord. He stressed the fact that he had learned to be satisfied in whatever state he found himself while serving the Lord, 11-12.

15-23. His gratitude for benefit received. He commended the early generosity of the Philippian church, 15-17, and was grateful for their recent gift via Epaphroditus, 18.

Colossians
The supreme glory of Christ's person

Outline

1:1-14	Paul's interest in the Colossians
1:15-29	The glory of Christ's person and work
2:1-23	Christ the answer to doctrinal errors
3:1-4:18	Union with Christ the basis of Christian living

Date and author. One of the Roman prison letters written by the apostle Paul, 1:1, probably in A.D. 61 or 62.

Purpose and theme. The apostle knew about two serious doctrinal errors that threatened the church at Colosse. One was a form of ascetic legalism (2:14-17), and the other was a type of unsound mysticism (2:18-23). So this letter exalts Christ's person and work and the believer's union with Him to combat these errors.

The site of ancient Colosse is marked by the mound in the middle distance in this photograph.

Colossians

1:1-8. The apostolic greeting

1-3. Paul's pastoral solicitude. Paul associates Timothy with himself, 1, in this introductory greeting to the believers at Colosse, a small town in Asia Minor.

4-8. Reasons for Paul's interest. He had a personal connection with them through Epaphras, 7, who had made known their "love in the Spirit," 8.

1:9-14. The apostolic prayer

9-11. The petitions made. Paul's prayer for the Colossians was continuous, 9 (cf. 3).

12-14. The name in which the petition is made. The prayer is directed to God the Father, who has qualified us to share in the inheritance of the saints, 12.

1:15-17. Christ's deity and creatorship

15a. Christ's deity. He is the image (*eikon*), the exact likeness or representation, of the invisible God. In Christ preincarnate and then incarnate, God became visible to mankind (John 1:1, 14, 18).

15b-17. Christ's creatorship. As Creator, Christ is prior to all creation. He is the goal of creation, 16c. All creation centers in Him, and He is the Sustainer of creation.

1:18-19. Christ's headship over the church

18a. He is Head of the church. The church is *His body,* of which Christ is the Head.

18b-19. He is the beginning of the new creation. Through His redemptive work the new creation is brought into being, by virtue of which He is its Head. He was God become human, to create a new people through redemption.

1:20-23. Christ's work of reconciliation

20-21. The meaning of reconciliation. Christ made peace between God and mankind by His "blood, shed on the cross." The sinner is reconciled (thoroughly changed) by divine power from a state of hostility and aversion toward God to loving trust (cf. Rom. 5:10).

22-23. The purpose of reconciliation is to present the believer holy, faultless, and beyond reproof before God, 22 (cf. Eph. 5:27).

1:24-29. Christ's glory proclaimed in Paul's ministry

24-25a. By Paul's sufferings. The apostle rejoices in these sufferings, which are for God's people, 24a.

25b-29. By his fulfilling the word of God. The complete preaching of the Word of God, 25b, involves the revelation and exposition of the "mystery," 26. The epitome of this mystery, or divine truth now revealed, is "Christ in you," which is the truth that the crucified, resurrected, and ascended Christ dwells in the believer, 27b.

2:1-7. Christ the answer to doctrinal error

1-2. The conflict with error. This involves

A Roman slave badge.

intense conflict (Greek *agonia,* "agony"), 1a,
because of demonic opposition directed against
God's truth (cf. 1 Tim. 4:1-5; 1 John 4:1-4).
2c-7. The answer to error. God incarnate, in
whom are "hidden *all* the treasures of wisdom
and knowledge," 3, is the answer to all error,
including any persuasive speech that removes
Christ from the center of spiritual thought and
activity, 4.

2:8-13. The peril of false philosophy
8. The warning. "Philosophy," literally "love of
knowledge," is here any system of religious
thought that does not make the person and work
of Christ central.
9-13. The remedy. The remedy to false religion
centers in Christ and involves adherence to the
truth of His full deity in humanity, 9; recognition
of the believer's complete spiritual life in union
with Him, 10a; and recognition of Christ's

authority as Head of the body, the church, as
well as all earthly rule and authority.

2:14-17. The peril of legalism
**14-15. Legal observances were done away in
Christ.** Christ erased the legal ordinances that
condemned us, nailing, as it were, the certificate
of debt that was against us as sinners to the
cross (cf. Eph. 2:15-16). In Him we have full
emancipation.
16-17. The conclusion. Therefore, no believer
is to pass judgment on another believer in
matters of food or observance of a festal day,
monthly new moon, or sabbath, 16
(cf. Rom. 14:3).

2:18-19. The peril of false mysticism
18. The form of the error. This pseudo-
mysticism took the form of Gnosticism, a
spurious knowledge (Greek *gnosis*) which
inculcated a false humility and a worship or
veneration of angels, 18a.
19. The reason for the error. This false
mysticism came about through losing contact
with the supreme headship of Christ, 19a.

2:20-23. The peril of asceticism
**20a. The believer's emancipation from
legalistic ordinances.** The medium of
emancipation is death. This is the *position* the
believer enjoys in Christ (Rom. 6:3-4). This
position is to be reckoned and converted into the
experience of deliverance from legalistic "dos"
and "don'ts," which the apostle calls "the basic
principles of this world."
20b-23. Result of this emancipation. If freed,
why then "still belong," i.e. allow laws to be
imposed on oneself or permit oneself to be

bound by ordinances, 20b? On the contrary, separate completely from such regulations as "Do not handle! Do not taste! Do not touch!" 21.

3:1-4. Union with Christ and a holy life
1. Basis of a holy life. The basis is the fact of union with Christ in resurrection, 1a, and in His present heavenly position, 1b.
2. Exhortations to a holy life.
3-4. Reasons for these exhortations. A holy life is possible now if we know and act on our position in Christ. It is assured in the future by our glorification.

3:5-7. Pronouncing death on a sinful life
5a. Death sentence declared.
5b-7. Results of failure to pronounce the death sentence. The members of the redeemed body will fall into the sins enumerated in 5b.

3:8-17. Putting on the new self
8-9. Putting off the old. The "old self," 9, is the unregenerate person with his human nature (Rom. 6:6; Eph. 4:22).
10-17. Putting on the new. The new self is put on as a fresh clean garment, with a new divine nature, 10b, and a new unity transcending race and social position, 11.

3:18-4:6 A heavenly walk and domestic relationships
3:18-21. Wives, husbands, children. No Christian wife is to give blind submission to an unsaved husband if such obedience violates her conscience before God. The supreme duty of a husband is to love his wife, 19 (Eph. 5:25), and

Christianity and slavery

Although Paul never condones slavery, arguing to the contrary in Galatians 3:28 that the slave and the free man are one in Christ, he does recognize it as part of the law of the land and an inherent part of Roman culture. As a result, he offers instructions to both slaves and slave owners concerning their behavior under Christ. This should not be interpreted, however, as an acceptance of the practice (cf. Philemon and Onesimus).

everything else will follow in due order.
3:22-4:1. Servants, masters. Slaves are to act under a Christian spirit of service, obedience, faithfulness, and sincerity, 3:22-25. Masters are to act in the light of the example set by their supreme Master in heaven, 4:1.
4:2-6. General principles.

4:7-18. A holy life and Christian fellowship
7-15. The commendation of fellow workers.
16-18. Instructions and greeting. Directions are given about the public reading of this letter to the Colossians at Laodicea, a nearby town.

1 Thessalonians

Picture of an exemplary church

Outline

1	An exemplary church
2	A model minister
3	A holy life
4-5	The coming of Christ and the Day of the Lord

Writer and date. This letter is likely to be the earliest of Paul's letters, written c. A.D. 52.

Purpose of the letter. It was written to encourage a young church in the basic truths of the gospel and to instruct it about the Second Coming of the Lord.

The harbor at Thessaloniki, ancient Thessalonica, capital of the Roman province of Macedonia.

1 Thessalonians

1:1-4. An elect church

1-3. A model assembly. Thessalonica was a very important city on the Thermaic Gulf, southwest of Philippi. The apostle, however, takes pride in the Christians there rather than in the great city.

4. An elect assembly. Election is both individual and corporate. The latter is in view here.

1:5-8. A missionary church

5. Objects of effective evangelism. The gospel that Paul preached came "with power," "with the Holy Spirit," and "with deep conviction," 5a.

6-8. Subjects of effective missionary work. After their conversion they became a Christian example to the believers in Macedonia and Achaia (Greece), 7, and their missionary zeal spread the gospel to the regions beyond, 8.

1:9-10. A serving and waiting church

They served "the living and true God" in contrast to the false, dead idols.

2:1-4. Model ministerial conduct under persecution

1-2. Boldness engendered by suffering. The suffering that Paul endured at Philippi (Acts 16:12-40) had emboldened Paul to declare the gospel with great confidence.

3-4. Faithfulness called forth by

responsibility. Paul viewed the gospel as a sacred trust and its heralds solemnly entrusted with it as something exceedingly valuable and easily despoiled, 4.

2:5-8. Unselfish ministry in love

5-7. The proof of selfless love. Negatively, Paul and his co-laborers never employed flattery, 5. Positively, they were gentle, i.e., mild or kind as a nursing mother who nourishes her own little children and hence showers real love on them, 7.

8. The expression of selfless love. Silas and Timothy, 1:1, with Paul were "delighted" (heartily willing) to communicate not only the gospel but their very own lives.

2:9-20. Devoted ministry for others

9-12. Devoted ministry described. It is marked by sacrifice, labor, and self-denial for others' good and the success of gospel witness, 9.

13-20. Results of a devoted ministry indicated. They became followers (imitators) of the churches of God in Judea, which likewise suffered persecution from apostate Jews, whose unbelief and sins are mentioned, 14-16 (cf. Acts 7:52; 17:5, 13; 18:12).

3:1-8. Standing fast in the Lord

1-5. The apostle's concern. When Paul had arrived in Athens (cf. Acts 17:15; 18:5), he so desired the Thessalonians' spiritual welfare that he preferred to remain alone, 1, in order that Timothy might be sent to look after their spiritual interests, 2.

6-8. The apostle's reward. His godly concern for them was rewarded when Timothy "brought good news" of their faith and love.

3:9-13. Apostolic prayer for holiness
9-10. The question. How can God be thanked
enough for all the joy the Thessalonians have
given Paul by their spiritual perseverance, 9?
11-13. The petition. He prays that God might
direct or clear the way for them, 11; that the
Lord might make them "overflow" in love, 12; to
the end that God might establish their hearts
blameless in holiness.

4:1-12. Divine call to holiness
1-3. The authority behind the call. The
authority behind the call is God. The person
who rejects this call rejects God, 8.
4-8. The call itself. We are called to a life
pleasing to God.
4:9-12. The elements of a holy life. The basic
element is love, "brotherly love," 9. Other
elements enjoined are quietness, industry,
responsibility, and honesty, 11-12.

4:13-18. The believer's hope
13-15. The blessed hope. Hope is faith-
produced confidence and expectation of the
future. The great obstacle to hope for the
unbeliever is death. This obstacle is removed in
Christ.
16-18. The Lord's coming. The answer to the
Christian's hope is the return of the resurrected,
ascended Christ to raise the bodies of those
who died in the Lord and to glorify the living
saints.

5:1-11. The Day of the Lord
1-3. The Day of the Lord—what it is. The
"Day of the Lord," 2, concerns the restoration of

Part of the Arch of Galerius, Thessalonica.

the kingdom of Israel (Acts 1:6-7; 3:19-21) and
the earth judgments that take place prior to the
setting up of that kingdom
(cf. Isa. 2:6-22; Jer. 30:5-9).
4-11. The Day of the Lord and the believer.
God's wrath will not fall on those in Christ, 10,
because they will be glorified and removed

View from the ancient walls of Thessalonica.

(4:13-17) before these end-time manifestations of God's wrath (Rev. 3:10).

5:12-15. Exhortations toward mutual harmony

12-13. Showing honor to those in places of responsibility in the Lord. Paul gives four reasons that believers are to regard these brethren with favor and respect.

13b-15. General admonitions for harmony. The basic principle of living in peace is to rule all relationships, 13b. Believers are to admonish or warn the idle, that is, those who neglect duties, 14. The word "idle" is used of soldiers who desert their ranks.

5:16-22. Various exhortations

Rejoice, pray, and be thankful, 16-18. Thankfulness is God's will for His people, 18. Do not quench the Spirit, 19, by disobeying God.

Four further admonitions follow, 20-22.

5:23-24. Sanctification for the whole person

To be set apart for God is the idea of the Greek adjective *hagios* ("holy"), which in its verbal form means sanctify or make holy. This work of sanctification is the work of "God himself." It is not a human accomplishment, 23. The Christian may be certain of complete sanctification since it is effected by God, 24.

5:25-28. Closing charge

25-26. Request for prayer. The Lord's servants need the constant prayer of God's people.
27-28. Charge concerning reading.

2 Thessalonians
Comfort in persecution

Outline

1   The coming of the Lord and comfort in present persecution
2   The coming of the Lord and the Day of the Lord
3   The coming of the Lord and practical Christian living

Writer and occasion. Paul was the writer (1:1). The occasion was a misunderstanding among the Thessalonians about the coming of Christ for His own (1 Thess. 4:13-17) and the Day of the Lord (1 Thess. 5:1-10). Because these believers were being persecuted severely, they erroneously concluded that the Day of the Lord had arrived (2:2). Paul writes to correct this misconception.

Paul wrote to the Thessalonian church from Rome.

2 Thessalonians

1:1-4. The church commended

1-2. Greeting. 3-4. The commendation. Paul was bound to express thanks to God for the Thessalonians because their faith was growing and their love abounding toward one another, 3.

1:5-10. The church comforted

5-6. The reason for their sufferings. It was really for the kingdom of God that they suffered, 5c (1 Thess. 2:14; Heb. 10:32-33).

7-10. The basis of comfort. The second coming of Christ in glory, 7-8, will witness the vengeance of God on those who do not know Him and have not obeyed the gospel of salvation by believing, 8.

1:11-12. Intercession for the church

The purpose of Paul's prayer was that the Lord might be magnified in the Thessalonians and they in the Lord, according to the grace given them.

2:1-5. The church and the Day of the Lord

1-2. A misunderstanding exposed. The Thessalonians thought their sufferings (1:5-12) meant that the Day of the Lord had arrived, 2, that the end-time period of worldwide judgment (Rev. 6-19) had dawned, making way for the setting up of Christ's kingdom

(Rev. 19:16-20:10).

3-5. The error refuted. *Before* the Day of the Lord bursts on a Christ-rejecting world, there must *first* come the apostasy or falling away. This is not simply the departure from the faith often characterizing the church age, but wholesale rebellion and thoroughgoing lapse into error and demonism. The man of lawlessness, 3, will arrogate to himself divine honors and deceive end-time Jewry regathered to Israel, 4.

Graeco-Roman statue of a slave from Corinth.

2:6-9. The church and the man of sin
6-7. The role of the Holy Spirit. The One who holds back the full development and manifestation of the demonic forces of evil in this era (cf. 8-10) is the Holy Spirit.

8-9. The church and the man of lawlessness. "The lawless one," 8, sums up the full development of last-day miracle-working demonism (Rev. 9:1-21; 12:7-17; 16:13-16). He will be destroyed by Christ's coming in glory, and Satan will be bound in the abyss (Rev. 20:1-3).

2:10-12. The church and rejecters of the truth.
Demonic deception will burst forth with irresistible power. The rejecters of the truth are doomed because they did not love and accept the truth when it was available, 10. God sends them a "powerful delusion" to believe "the lie," i.e., the supreme deception of accepting the Antichrist, 11 (John 5:43; Rev. 13:8).

2:13-17. The Thessalonians
13-14. The Thessalonians were a cause for thanks because they were God's beloved and elect (see notes on "Divine election" and "Foreordination" in Eph. 1).

15-17. The Thessalonians were objects of exhortation and prayer. The exhortation is to steadfastness and faithfulness to the teachings or traditions taught them, 15. The prayer is for comfort and grounding "in every good deed" (practice) "and word" (doctrine).

3:1-5. Apostolic request for prayer
1-2. The request. Paul asks that the Word of God may run without obstruction and that he might be rescued from "wicked and evil" men.

3-5. The basis for the request. The Lord's faithfulness and Paul's confidence in the Thessalonians constituted the ground for the apostle's prayer, 3-4.

3:6-15. Instruction concerning disciplinary separation
6. The general principle of separation.

7-9. The apostolic example. Paul toiled with his own hands as a tentmaker, that he might not be a burden or expense on any of those to whom he ministered, 8.

10-11. The disorder specified. Among the Thessalonian believers were people who did not work and people who were "busybodies," 11. Paul says no work—no food, 10. He puns on the word "work," 11—not just workers (*ergazomenoi*) but workers-around (*periergazamoi*), i.e., intensive workers in the wrong way or "busybodies."

12-15. The cure indicated. They were to "earn the bread they eat," and not mix with the disorderly in order to shame them, warning them as brothers.

3:16-18. Concluding blessing.
"The Lord of peace" was to grant them peace by His personal presence, 16.

1 Timothy
Directions for church order

Outline

1 The discipline of sound doctrine
2 The discipline of prayer and public worship
3 The discipline of church government
4-6 The discipline of the local pastor

The writer and the theme. Paul is the writer (1:1). The general thought of 1 Timothy is on church order, soundness of faith, and ecclesiastical discipline (ch. 1-3). It was inevitable that instruction to local pastors should be given after churches were founded (ch. 4-6).

The Fountain of Trajan, Ephesus. Timothy was pastor of the church in Ephesus.

1 Timothy

1:1-7. The pastor and sound doctrine

1-4. The pastor and unsound teachers. Paul greets Timothy as a pastor and as "my true son in the faith," 1-2. In such a capacity he urges the younger man to assume responsibility against unsound teachers, 3-4.

5-7. The pastor and legalists. Those who have missed the mark through legalism have turned aside to "meaningless talk"—discussion of meaningless words, 6.

1:8-11. The law and the gospel of Christ

8-10. The purpose of the law. In no sense is the law to be used for the righteous (justified) person, either to justify him or to sanctify him. It is intended to reveal to the sinner his sin and its penalty apart from Christ, 9-10.

11. The purpose of the gospel. It heralds God's love for sinners by providing for their salvation.

1:12-17. The gospel of Christ and the sinner

12-15. Salvation and commission of Paul the sinner. The apostle's ministry of salvation was the result of God's saving grace, 12, manifested toward a great sinner, a blasphemer, a persecutor of God's people, and "a violent man," 13 (Acts 8:3; 1 Cor. 15:9).

16-17. Paul's salvation an example for all believing sinners. The apostle was to be a pattern of God's gracious patience and love toward sinners in Christ, 16.

1:18-20. The charge to Timothy the pastor

18-19a. The charge was that Timothy might wage a successful spiritual battle, 18.

19b-20. The warning. By teaching error, Hymenaeus and Alexander (2 Tim. 2:17-18) had destroyed the faith of some.

2:1-8. The church and public prayer

1-2a. The general injunction.

2b-8. Reasons for prayer. (1) That Christians may lead a tranquil and quiet life in godliness and dignity, 2b, in accord with God's will, 3. (2) Because God's desire is salvation in which prayer has an important place, 4. (3) Because the incarnation and work of Christ gave new power and outreach in prayer, 5-6.

2:9-15. The order of women in Christian society

9-10. A Christian woman's demeanor and dress. Without, there is to be befitting dress; within, proper adornment of heart shown by modesty and a serious attitude toward her place in Christian society.

11-15. A Christian woman's reaction to men. A Christian woman is to be characterized by a spirit of teachableness, 11. Paul himself did not permit women to teach men or usurp authority over them, in the sense of acting in independent power or domineering over them, 12. Her great honor is in producing and training godly offspring, 15.

3:1-7. The qualifications of overseers
1. The honor of the office.

2-7. The qualifications of the office. The ideal overseer must possess the fifteen qualities listed in these verses, ranging from being a gifted teacher, 2, to being gentle and not having a love of money, 3.

3:8-13. The qualifications of deacons
8-12. Their qualifications. The deacons were charged with the financial and temporal administrations of the local church, as the overseers were charged with the more directly spiritual aspects. The deacons' qualifications, 8-10, 12, are largely the same as the overseers' qualifications.

13. Their reward. Those who discharge the office well acquire for themselves an "excellent standing," literally a step, or stair, in the sense of dignity of rank.

3:14-16. The church and revealed truth
14-15. The church and its relation to revealed truth. "The church of the living God," 15 (the body of Christ), is the pillar or column in the sense of the support holding up the roof of truth. It is also the "foundation" of truth in that the Holy Spirit teaches the revealed truth of God.

16. The gist of revealed truth. This verse refers to the basic body of divine revelation made known in Scripture and may well have constituted an early Christian hymn. It centers in Christ: His incarnation, His resurrection, His post-resurrection appearance, His church and body, and His ascension.

4:1-6. The pastor and doctrinal error
1-2. Demonism the source of doctrinal error. The well-instructed pastor must know the real origin of false teaching to deal with it adequately. Therefore the Holy Spirit speaks plainly on this point. He declares that error is instigated *not* primarily by the false teacher but by the evil spirits or demons energizing the false teacher.

3-6. An illustration. The apostle selects a current error, a kind of legalistic asceticism, to illustrate the fact that false doctrine is demon-originated. It forbids marriage and the eating of certain foods, which the apostle shows were created by God to be received with thanksgiving and prayer, 3-5.

4:7-16. The pastor and self-discipline
7-11. Self-discipline in public ministry. This involves faithfully teaching the truth, refusing "godless myths," and exercising toward a goal of godliness rather than toward mere physical conditioning, the benefits of which are temporary, 8.

12-16. Self-discipline in public and private ministry. Timothy, the young man, is to give no occasion for anyone to look down on his youth. He is rather to be an example or model to God's people, 12.

5:1-16. The care of widows
1-2. Conduct toward various Christians. These include elders, young men, older women, and younger women.

3-16. Treatment of Christian widows. Widows who are really destitute are to be honored and provided for, 3. Those who have children or other relatives ought to be supported by them, 4.

5:17-22. Concerning elders

17-20. Honor due them. Teaching elders (pastors) are to be considered worthy of "double honor"—honor of position and honor of financial support, 17-18.

21-22. Timothy's responsibility. Timothy is solemnly warned against partiality in dealing with God's people, 21 (cf. James 2:1-12).

5:23-25. Paul's personal advice to Timothy

23. Regarding Timothy's health. Paul suggests that Timothy use a little wine for its medicinal value.

24-25. Regarding the question of people's sins and good deeds. Some people's sins are so evident that they precede the sinner to judgment, but in the case of others, their sins catch up with them and appear as a sequel to their evildoing, 24. Good works, and deeds of love, likewise, are sometimes obvious, and sometimes hidden, but are not hidden from God.

6:1-5. Directions for servants and masters

1-2. The general directive. Paul applies the Christian ethic to the prevailing situation.
3-5. Denunciation of false teachers.

6:6-10. Warning directed to the rich

6-8. The blessing of godly contentment. Gain is not godliness, 5, but godliness with contentedness is *great gain* (emphatic), 6. Contentment is satisfaction with one's lot in the will of God (Heb. 13:5).

9-10. The curse of ungodly wealth. The curse is not in wealth itself, but in the wrong attitude toward it.

6:11-16. Warning directed to godly people

11-12. Their ambition. Godly people run away from the snares of worldly wealth and diligently pursue Christian virtue, 11.

13-16. The apostle's charge. Paul tells them to keep this commandment, 14, concerning worldly wealth (6-13) without stain or cause for rebuke until Christ appears.

6:17-19. Instructions for wealthy believers

17-18. The charge. They are told not to be conceited or to fix their hope on material wealth.
19. The purpose. The goal in view is future reward for faithfulness and the present enjoyment of the spiritual life.

6:20-21. Appeal to Timothy

The young pastor was entrusted with a life and ministry that he was commanded to watch over jealously. He was to avoid empty discussions and to give himself wholly to proclaiming God's revealed truth, 20.

2 Timothy
A good soldier of Jesus Christ

Outline

1. Apostasy and pastoral faithfulness
2. Apostasy and spiritual conflict
3. Apostasy and the Word of God
4. Apostasy and a faithful Lord

The writer. Second Timothy was written, as was 1 Timothy, by Paul the apostle to his "dear son" Timothy (1:1-2).

The purpose. The letter was written to outline the course of a true servant of Jesus Christ in a time of doctrinal decline. The churches of Asia (1:15) had defected from the gospel of grace that the apostle had proclaimed, and they had lapsed into legalism. Paul encourages Timothy to use the divine resources available to the faithful pastor in such a time of apostasy.

Archaeologists excavate part of the ancient Forum, Rome.

2 Timothy

had been divinely appointed as a herald and an instructor of the gospel.

1:1-5. The integrity of a faithful pastor
1-4. Paul's love and prayers for Timothy. In his greeting, 1-2, Paul calls Timothy his "dear son," showing his deep affection for this true child in the faith.
5. Paul's confidence in Timothy. Paul was sure that the same genuine faith that resided in Timothy's mother and grandmother was present in Timothy also.

1:6-8. The afflictions of a faithful pastor
6-7. Afflictions demand a spirit of courage. Timothy's God-given endowment, bestowed on him through the laying on of the apostle's hands at his ordination as a pastor, was not a spirit (attitude) of fear, but of power (the dynamic interior working of an omnipotent God), love, and self-discipline, 7.
8. Afflictions are part of faithful gospel testimony. Timothy was to expect afflictions and not try to avoid them by being ashamed "to testify about our Lord."

1:9-11. The appointment of a faithful pastor
9-10. The gospel described. The good news is divine, sanctifying, gracious, purposeful, preplanned, and revealed.
11. The appointment illustrated. Paul himself

1:12-14. The holy confidence of a faithful pastor
12. The testimony of assurance. Assurance is the believer's conviction that he possesses salvation, which will be safely guarded.
13-14. The results of assurance. One sound in faith is able (1) to enjoin soundness of doctrine on others, 13a; (2) to put sound doctrine into practice, 13b; (3) to guard or keep his ministry for Christ intact, 14a. This is accomplished by means of the Holy Spirit, not self-effort, 14b.

1:15-18. The trials and joys of a faithful pastor
15. The trials. Apostasy had already set in, and two of the deserters are mentioned.
16-18. The joys. The household of Onesiphorus is mentioned. Onesiphorus had refreshed the apostle by not being ashamed of Paul's imprisonment in Rome.

2:1-3. The message of grace and spiritual warfare
1-2. Strength is required to proclaim the gospel of grace. "*You* (emphatic) then, my son, be strong [or strengthen yourself] in the grace that is in Christ Jesus," because the Asian churches had defected from it, 1.
3. Preaching grace arouses conflict. Paul told Timothy to suffer opposition along with him, as a good soldier of Christ Jesus.

2:4-7. Separation and success in God's work
4. The necessity of separation. In the conflict

that the message of grace arouses, there must be disentanglement from worldly pleasures and pursuits on the part of the Christian soldier, for his single aim is to please his Lord.

5-7. The necessity of obedience and effort. Reward for achievement in the Christian race demands (1) separation from sin, (2) discipline and obedience to God's Word, and (3) labor and effort.

2:8-10. Suffering and soul-winning

8-9a. The cause for the suffering. The gospel of grace led Paul to suffer hardship, including imprisonment.

9b-10. The results of the suffering. Paul was in chains, but the Word of God was not, 8b.

2:11-14. Union with Christ and coming glory

11. The believer's position of union. This is a trustworthy statement, a reliable fact, that the believer has been placed by the Holy Spirit into a *position* of union and identification with Christ in death, burial, and resurrection (Rom. 6:3-4; 1 Cor. 12:13; Col. 2:8-10).

12a. The believer's experience of union.
12b-14. The problem of the believer's unfaithfulness. If we continue to be unfaithful, so that our experience is inconsistent with our position, yet "He will remain faithful, for he cannot disown himself," 13. He cannot go back on His word, His promise of our safety and security in Christ (John 10:28-29).

2:15-19. Bible study and godly living

15-18. A discerning use of Scripture—the antidote to error. Setting forth divine revelation without distortion, perversion, or contradiction is possible only as God's workman diligently labors to discern the various subjects in Scripture and to make application accordingly.

19. Bible study—the key to godly living. This divine foundation has a twin seal (mark or token) guaranteeing it: (1) the Lord knows His own, and (2) the Lord's own are to abstain from wickedness.

2:20-23. Separation and spiritual usefulness

20-21. The principle illustrated. The illustration is that of a large household with many utensils, some valuable, others less so.

22-23. The principle enunciated. "Flee the evil desires of youth," but pursue Christian virtues practiced by those "who call on the Lord."

2:24-26. Spiritual victory

24-25a. The servant of Jesus Christ. He must be gentle, gifted and trained to teach, enduring, and patient under evils and injuries.

25b-26. The servant's conquests over Satan. The servant's personal victory, 24-25a, has a twofold strategy: (1) that the Lord might grant his opponents repentance; (2) that they might recover their senses.

3:1-5. The apostasy

1. The time of the apostasy. The time described as "the last days" often refers in Scripture to the messianic period. NT writers viewed Christians as living in the last days, which were to be days of departure from the truth.

2-5a. The nature of the apostates. The difficult times, 1, are made so by the character of the people involved. Nineteen characteristics of

Facsimile of an ancient scroll, such as Paul would have used to write his letters.

these people are listed in these verses.

5b. The attitude toward apostates. Rigid separation is commanded.

3:6-9. Results of apostasy

6-7. Immorality and false intellectualism.
Apostates gravitate into immorality (2 Peter 2:10-14; Jude 4, 8, 10). Here they are represented as entering homes and seducing weak, silly women. Moreover, they are ever learning but are never able to come to any accurate or real knowledge of the truth.

8-9. Opposition to the truth. Not only are apostates unable to arrive at the precise knowledge of the truth, they stoutly "oppose" or

stand against the truth, as Jannes and Jambres did (cf. Ex. 7:11-12).

3:10-13. Persecution and apostasy

10-11. Apostasy leads to persecution.
Persecutions and troubles befell Paul at Antioch in Pisidia, 11 (Acts 13:45-50), Iconium (Acts 14:5-6), and Lystra (Acts 14:19).

12-13. Godliness and persecution. All those who determine to live in a godly way will suffer persecution.

3:14-17. Scripture and apostasy

14-15. The role of Scripture in Timothy's life.
16-17. The inspiration and use of Scripture.

The Odeon, Ephesus.

This declares: (1) The full inspiration of the entire OT and by implication all canonical Scripture. (2) All Scripture is a product of God—God-breathed. (3) As God-breathed it is inerrant and fully authoritative. (4) The whole of Scripture is useful.

4:1-4. The preached word and apostasy

1-2. The solemn charge. So pivotal is the matter of heralding the Scripture, 2, that the apostle stresses the accounting that Christ's ministers will render as to how they have handled the Word of God.

3-4. The reason for the charge. The Word of God alone is the antidote against apostasy.

4:5-8. The reward of the faithful preacher

5. Advice for a faithful preacher. Serve God in full measure, completely discharging your service through maximum effectiveness.

6-7. Testimony of a faithful preacher. Paul states that he is "now ready to be offered" (KJV),

i.e., to pour out his life as a libation or drink offering, having spent it in sacrifice to make known the gospel (cf. Phil. 2:17).

8. The reward of the faithful preacher. The "crown" is the victor's crown, the garland of wild olive or pine given to the winner of the Greek games.

4:9-15. Personal warnings of a faithful preacher

9-13. Advice concerning fellow workers. Paul requests Mark to be brought, 11. The request for Mark is particularly significant since Paul had earlier refused to take him on the second missionary journey because of his unreliability (cf. Acts 15:37-39). Apparently Mark had matured and Paul had forgiven.

14-15. Warnings concerning evil workers.

4:16-18. Testimony of the Lord's faithfulness

Human unfaithfulness, seen at Paul's first defense before Caesar, when all had abandoned Paul, 16, is contrasted with God's faithfulness, 17-18, when the Lord stood with Paul and strengthened him.

4:19-22. Greetings and closing salutation

Titus
The order of God's house

Outline

1 Scriptural church organization
2 Pastoral ministry toward various groups
3 Pastoral ministry and general teaching

Writer and theme. The author is Paul (1:1). Titus had been left on the island of Crete to organize the churches there (1:5). The letter therefore has much in common with 1 Timothy, but with greater emphasis on church organization and administration.

Fair Havens, Crete. Titus had been left on the island of Crete to organize the churches there.

Titus

so that they are silenced, as they corrupt or overturn whole families, teaching "things they ought not to teach" for vile or dishonorable financial gain, 11.

13b-16. The remedy. A severe reprimand is called for, 13b-14. Then a positive note is sounded: Inculcate purity.

1:1-4. Greeting to Titus

1-3. Paul's ministry defined. The apostle defines his offices as being those of God's bondservant and Christ's apostle, 1.

4. Paul's greeting to Titus.

1:5-9. Qualifications of elders and bishops

5. Titus's task outlined. Paul left Titus in Crete to organize the assemblies there according to divine order and appoint church officers (elders and bishops). These officers are called bishops (*episcopoi,* "overseers") and deacons (*diakonoi,* "servers") in 1 Timothy 3:1-13. Bishops and elders (*presbuteroi*) are terms apparently used to designate the same office of one who both preached and taught, in addition to being an administrator. Deacons were concerned with finances and benevolences (Acts 6:1-7).

6-9. Qualification of elders. An "overseer," literally "God's steward," is one who holds a commission from God to serve in the gospel, a trustee of spiritual truth, 7.

1:10-16. Warning against false teachers

10-13a. The legalists especially cited. The churches in Crete were in danger from "the circumcision group," 10, i.e., Jewish legalists. Paul says that they must be curbed or muzzled

2:1-4a. The aged adorning the gospel

1-2. Elderly men. The general responsibility of a true pastor is to teach what is right for sound doctrine, 1.

3-4a. Elderly women. Older women are to be reverent in their behavior and teachers of what is good to the young.

2:4b-6. The young adorning the gospel

Young women, 4-5, and young men, 6, are both told to be "self-controlled."

2:7-8. Titus, the pastor, adorning the gospel

7-8a. The pastoral example. Titus was to be an example for the young men, 6, to imitate (1 Cor. 11:1). "In everything" he was to be a model of good works, 7; displaying the quality of not being corrupted or vitiated by error in doctrine.

8b. The purpose of the pastoral example. Titus was to be so exemplary that the opponent would be put to shame.

2:9-10. Servants adorning the gospel

9-10a. Their conduct enjoined. Servants were to be voluntarily submissive to their own masters, pleasing them in everything without being impudent or insubordinate, 9.

The New Testament World

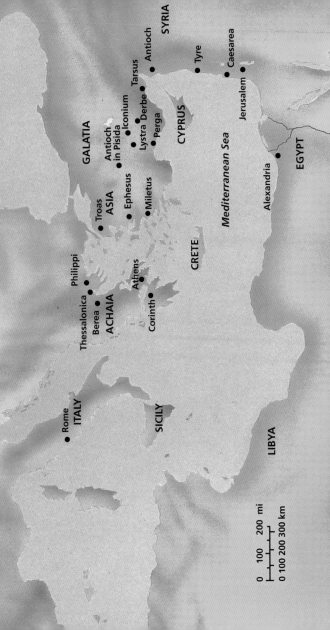

Part of the theater at Laodicea (see opposite).

10b. The purpose stated. "That in every way they [bondslaves] will make the teaching about God our Savior attractive." How significant it is that common slaves should be selected for this high purpose of adorning the gospel.

2:11-15. The gospel and adorned living
11-14. The basis of adorned living. "The grace of God," 11—the unmerited divine favor and mercy bestowed on helplessly lost sinners who trust in Christ's vicarious atonement (Rom. 3:24)—constitutes the foundation of godly conduct.
15. The injunction to enforce these truths.

3:1-7. Adorning the gospel before the world
1-2. The nature of exemplary behavior. Believers are (1) to be subject to established government, (2) to speak evil of no one, and (3) to be "peaceable."
3-7. The reason for exemplary behavior. The gospel of grace is to be adorned before the world because we ourselves (emphatic) were once in the same unsaved state, 3. Thus we are to be examples of God's grace, especially as we realize that our present condition is entirely due to the grace of God, 4-7.

3:8-11. Adorning the gospel with good works
8. The continual affirmation of profitable things. Good deeds are to follow personal faith.
9-11. The avoidance of unprofitable things. Legalistic snares such as "foolish controversies," with which Judaism was honeycombed, and "genealogies," to which the Jews attached great importance, are to be shunned because they have no value.

A heretic, one who creates factions and fosters divisions as a result of false doctrine, is to be shunned after he fails to respond to two warnings, 10 (cf. Matt. 18:17).

3:12-15. Closing greetings
12-13. Instructions concerning fellow workers.
14-15. Instructions concerning Christian industry. One is saved without works but "to do good works" (Eph. 2:10).

Philemon
Christian fellowship in action

Outline

1-7	Paul's greeting and commendation of Philemon
8-21	Paul's intercession for Onesimus
22-25	Concluding word and greeting

Writer and date. The apostle Paul is the author of this personal letter, 1, probably written in A.D. 61 or 62.

Theme. Philemon was a Christian of Colosse, a small city in Asia Minor southeast of Laodicea and south of Hierapolis. His slave, Onesimus, had apparently robbed him and consequently fled to Rome. There Onesimus came into contact with Paul and was saved. The apostle sent him back to his master with this priceless letter preserved for us.

Philemon was from Colosse, a small city in Asia Minor, south of Hierapolis, pictured here.

Philemon

because of the deep affection Paul had for him, but he gives him back to his master, 13. It is a powerful plea for Philemon to forgive his runaway slave.

14-16. Not as a servant but as a brother
14. Paul's courteous tact. Paul's aim was to motivate the best in a person.
15-16. Paul's skillful analysis. Maybe Onesimus was separated from Philemon for a while that his master might have his complete loyalty and permanent service, 15.

1-3. Paul's greeting to Philemon
1-2. The greeting. Mentioned is the church that met in Philemon's house, 2. The homes of believers were the customary places of all the early assemblies.
3. The benediction is characteristic of the Pauline letters.

17-19. Reckon to my account
17. Welcome him as me. Paul gives a further appeal.
18-19. Put any demerit to my account. Paul will pay any debt owing, 19a; but he tactfully suggests that Philemon owes himself to him for the benefit not only of returning a runaway slave, but even more, now a brother in the Lord.

4-7. Paul's commendation of Philemon
4-5. Philemon's love and faith. Paul commends Philemon for his love and faith directed toward the Lord and toward all believers.
6-7. Paul's prayer for Philemon. The apostle prays that the "sharing" of Philemon's faith may be "active" in the sense of being efficiently adapted to work toward others in blessing (cf. James 2:14, 17).

20-21. Paul's confidence in Philemon
Paul had confidence that Philemon would do even more than has been suggested to him.

22-25. A request and closing greetings
The imprisoned apostle asks Philemon to find him lodging, for he, in faith, looks forward to release.

8-13. Paul's plea for Onesimus
8-10. The plea. Although by virtue of his apostolic authority, Paul was free to "order" Philemon concerning the proper action to take with regard to Onesimus, 8, yet out of Christian love he rather pleads with him, as the aged friend and the "prisoner of Christ Jesus."
11-13. Paul's defense of Onesimus. Paul would have desired to keep Onesimus because of his usefulness in assisting him, and also

Hebrews
Christ superior to all

Authorship and date. This great letter is anonymous. It was written before the destruction of Jerusalem and the temple by the Romans in A.D. 70 (cf. 10:11).

Theme. Hebrews meets a pivotal need in showing the relationship of Christianity to Judaism, a burning issue in the Christian church since the apostolic period.

Outline

1:1-2:18 Superiority of the Son to the prophets and angels

3:1-4:16 Superiority of the Son to Moses and Joshua

5:1-8:5 Superiority of Christ's priesthood

8:6-10:39 Superiority of the new covenant to the old covenant

11:1-13:25 Superiority of faith

Orthodox Jews pray at the Western Wall, Jerusalem.

Hebrews

imperceptibly "drift away" from these truths in the strong currents of legalistic ritualism.

2-4. The reason for warning. If judgment fell on those who broke the law given through the mediation of angels, how much more serious will be the state of the one who rejects the word of God's Son!

1:1-3. The Son superior to the prophets

1. The ministry of the prophets. The word through the OT prophets came in many ways and in various modes (dreams, visions, audible voices, theophanies, angels, men, etc.).

2-3. The superior ministry of the Son. The Son's ministry is superior to that of the OT prophets because of His glorious person and His creative and redemptive work. That superiority is seen in the following declarations: Christ's eternal deity, 2a; God's full and final revelation, 2a; the Son's eternal heirship, 2b; Christ's creatorship, 2c; His full divine glory, 3a. The Son is the incarnation of God Himself, 3b, 3c; the sustainer of the universe, 3c; and a finished redemption, 3e.

1:4-14. The Son superior to the angels in His person and work

4-9. Superior in His person. He is *uncreated* Deity; the angels are mere creatures, though lofty celestial spirits. "All God's angels," 6, are commanded to "worship him."

10-14. Superior in His work. Christ is superior to angels in His work as *Creator*, 10-12, and *Redeemer*, 13-14.

2:1-4. Warning against drifting

1. The warning. The danger was that they might

2:5-9. The Son superior to the angels in His authority

5. The Son's kingdom authority. "The world to come" refers to the inhabited earth in the coming age, when Christ the Son returns to rule in His glorified humanity.

6-9. The basis of the Son's authority. This quotation from Psalm 8:4-6, referring to the original estate of the first Adam (man), is applied to Christ, the "second man" (1 Cor. 15:47). Adam, mankind's representative, forfeited his dominion over the earth through sin, but the last Adam (Christ, the perfect man) regained it by virtue of His humiliation and death for everyone.

2:10-13. The Son superior to the angels in His perfect humanity

10. Bringing sons to glory. It was God the Father's purpose "in bringing many sons to glory," i.e., consummating their salvation in resurrection and glorification, to make complete the work of the Pioneer (Leader) of their salvation through suffering.

11-13. Union of the Redeemer and the redeemed. As sons of glory, 10, they are destined for glorification even as Christ their Pioneer is already glorified.

The reference to Psalm 22:22 in verse 12 prophetically sets forth the eternal priestly work of Christ in which He continually reveals God's name to us and sings the praises of God among us His "brothers" (cf. John 20:19).

2:14-18. The Son superior to the angels in His conquest of sin and death

14-16. The purpose of the incarnation. This purpose is threefold: (1) that the Incarnate One might render completely powerless the devil's power over death; (2) that such might be accomplished through the death of the Incarnate One, 14; (3) that those who were in bondage to the fear of death might be delivered, 15.

17-18. The purpose of His priesthood. Christ

must, in order to be a qualified high priest on behalf of humanity before God, "be made like his brothers," whom He was bringing to glory.

3:1-6. The Son superior to Moses

1. Holy brothers. The readers, addressed here for the first time as "holy brothers, who share in the heavenly calling," were no longer simply Jews with an earthly inheritance but members of the body of Christ.

1b-2. Consider the Son. The exhortation here is to contemplate our faithful High Priest so as to fully understand Him as the delegated One sent by the Father.

3-6. The Son contrasted with Moses. Christ built the house while Moses only served in it, 3-5a. Moses was faithful as a servant, Christ was faithful as Son.

3:7-19. Warning against departing from the living God

7-10. The sin of heart-hardening. The danger is that of becoming stubbornly insensitive and rebellious against God, 8a. Such sin leads to error, wandering, and ignorance of God's ways, 10.

11. The penalty—forfeiture of God's rest. God's "rest" is the quiet inner assurance and triumphant sense of peace He gives those who trust Him.

12-15. The deceitfulness of sin. So treacherous is sin in making the heart insensitive to God and His Word that constant exhorting is necessary while opportunity remains, 13.

16-19. The tragedy of unbelief. The Israelites "rebelled," 16, and angered God, 17. Their bodies fell in the desert. They forfeited God's rest, 18, because of their unbelief, 19.

The Jewish-Christian letters

Hebrews, James, 1 Peter, 2 Peter, Jude. These inspired letters are addressed principally to Jewish believers. In the case of Hebrews the purpose is to set forth the finality of Christ's salvation and warn against the peril of Jewish believers going back to the superseded ritualism of Judaism. James instructs them in the practical virtues familiar to OT saints. First Peter is also addressed to Jewish Christians of the dispersion (1:1-2). Second Peter and Jude are more general, like the catholic (universal) letters of 1, 2, and 3 John.

These Jewish-Christian letters deal with the inculcation of the practical expression of salvation in consistent living grounded in the basic doctrines of biblical Christianity.

4:1-8. The Son superior to Joshua in the rest He gives

1-3b. The gospel, the source of rest. A believer should "be careful" (have godly concern) lest he die in unbelief in the "wilderness" like Israel, and never enter Canaan, the place of rest (cf. Num. 14). Faith in the gospel is the key to this rest, 3a (Ps. 95:11).

3c-8. God's creation is rest as a type. On the seventh day of creation God rested and was refreshed (Ex. 31:17; cf. Gen. 1:31-2:3). This serves as a type of the rest that believers may enter spiritually now, in the middle of persecution, as they rely on the finished work of Christ.

4:9-13. The Son superior to Joshua in the redemption He provides

9-10. Redemptive rest is available for God's people. The rest of redemption reposes wholly in the work of the cross, and ceases from all self-effort, human merit, or legalistic claim as a means either to salvation or sanctification, 10 (cf. Eph. 2:8-10).

11-13. The rest to be diligently realized. The instrument God uses to bring people into the rest of faith is the living and dynamic Word of God, 12-13. It strips away all pretense and sham, revealing us as we truly are, 13.

4:14-5:10. Christ's priesthood superior to Aaron's

4:14-16. Our great high priest. Christ, our "great high priest," is great because of His finished work of redemption, attested by His having "passed through the heavens" (ASV), 14.

Christ is also great because He is Jesus, the Son of God, qualified to represent humanity before the throne of God the Father. Further, Christ is great because He transforms God's throne of holy judgment against sinners to a throne of grace for believers, His blood being sprinkled on it.

5:1-4. Qualifications of Aaronic priests. Six qualifications for Israel's high priest are listed in these verses.

5:5-10. Superiority of Christ's qualifications. Six reasons are given that show that Christ was fully qualified to be a high priest. As a result of these perfect qualifications, He became the source of eternal salvation, not a mere covering for sin (as did the Aaronic high priest's sacrifice).

5:11-14. Appeal to maturity

11-13. Characteristics of the immature. Many of the Hebrew believers were still untaught at a time when they should have been qualified to be teachers of deeper truths. As babes, they could receive only milk, or elementary truths, and were unqualified because of a lack of knowledge of the truth of the Word, 12b-13.

14. Contrast of the mature. Those who are mature have an adult diet, able to take the solid nourishment of the Word as applied to life and doctrine.

6:1-3. Pressing on to full growth

1a. Exhortation to spiritual progress. "Leaving," in this passage, means advancement—to advance beyond the elementary truths concerning Christ towards full growth.

1b-2. Danger of spiritual retrenchment. The peril endangering maturity is that of re-laying the foundation instead of proceeding to build the superstructure on it. Six basic truths constituting

Hebrews reminds us of the wilderness journeyings.

Him an impostor and subjecting Him to great indignity and public shame, because it slighted both His person and His work.

7-8. The result of the sin—divine rejection. The result is rejection or disqualification (1 Cor. 9:27) for a prize, with the believer's work being burned, as wood, hay, or stubble, at the judgment seat of Christ (1 Cor. 3:13-15).

6:9-12. The contrast of maturity in Christ

9-10. The better things of salvation. Not only the writer but God Himself would not forget the many acts of kindness that the Hebrew Christians had shown toward their Christian brethren, even in times of persecution.

11-12. The author's desire. It was the writer's longing that their good start (9-10) might continue toward full maturity, 11.

6:13-20. Encouragement to maturity in Christ

13-18a. God's faithfulness to Abraham. This patriarch is introduced here to serve as an example of perseverance in waiting for the promise of God. Abraham persevered because God guaranteed by His own name the covenant He made with Abraham, 13. The divine oath, 14, involved a Hebraism, "I will surely bless [superabundantly bless] you and give you many descendants [superabundantly multiply]." Given to encourage Abraham in patience, it accomplished its purpose, 15, that is, he received the full guarantee of its complete fulfillment.

18b-20. God's faithfulness in Christ. Christ, who is the fulfillment of the Abrahamic covenant, is our assurance, the object of our hope, 18b.

the foundation, while absolutely necessary but not ends in themselves, are listed in these verses.

3. The dynamic of spiritual progress. God can only allow such blessing as believers trust Him in faith and allow Him to work in them (Phil. 3:14).

6:4-8. The sin of lapsing back into Judaism

4-5. The subjects—Hebrew believers. These verses show that the people under discussion were believers.

6. The nature of the sin—defection from the all-sufficient nature of Christ's death. Evidently the Christians in view were those who fell back on Judaistic ritual and sacrifices to atone for their sins. This was tantamount to crucifying the Son of God again, considering

This hope we continually have as an "anchor," 19 (emphatic), for the soul that keeps us from drifting.

7:1-3. Melchizedek, the type of Christ as king-priest

1-3a. The identity of Melchizedek (Cf. Gen. 14:17-24). This man was "king of Salem," an ancient name for Jerusalem. But more important, he was "priest of God Most High" (*El Elyon*, "creator [or "possessor"] of heaven and earth," Gen. 14:18-19, 22), 1a. His superiority to Abraham is revealed in his blessing, 1b, and in his receiving tithes from Abraham, 2a.

3b. Melchizedek, a type of Christ. Melchizedek was made like, or made to resemble, Christ in description and typical significance. The focus is thus placed on Christ's royal authority and His unending priesthood.

7:4-22. The superiority of Melchizedek's priesthood to Aaron's

4-7, 9-10. Aaron paid tithes to Melchizedek. Melchizedek's priesthood was greater than Aaron's because the Aaronic priests (who received the tithes of the people) as descendants of Abraham offered tithes through Abraham to Melchizedek, the greater.

8. Aaron's priesthood was temporary, Melchizedek's permanent.

11-14. The Aaronic priesthood was limited. The Levitical priesthood lacked "perfection," 11, in the sense of completeness of operation and effect. It could neither remove sin, nor grant righteousness or favor with God, 11a. This lack of perfection is recognized: (1) in the need that existed for "another priest," 11b; (2) in the

necessity of a change in the law with which the Aaronic priesthood was inseparably bound, 12; and (3) in the need for a change in the exclusive regulations of the law that limited the priesthood to the tribe of Levi, and thereby excluded Christ on the human plane from serving, since He was from the tribe of Judah, 13-14a.

15-22. The Melchizedek priesthood is final. Six reasons are given in these verses why Christ's priesthood, after the order of Melchizedek, is final and complete.

7:23-28. The superior efficacy and perpetuity of Christ's priesthood

23-24. Its perpetuity. Christ's one permanent priesthood was not to be superseded because He continues forever, 24.

25-28. Its superior efficacy. The efficacy of Christ's priesthood is superior, first, because of its complete ability to save, 25b; second, because its Priest is perfectly suited to our need, 26; third, because the sacrifice of this priesthood is final, 27; and fourth, because it is sealed by divine oath, 28.

8:1-5. Christ, high priest in the heavenly sanctuary

1-2. The reality of His ministry. The main "point," 1, in what has been said is that Christ "sat down at the right hand of the throne of the Majesty in heaven," 1, completely superseding the Levitical priesthood, 1. The early tabernacle was a mere foreshadow of the heavenly, being pitched not by man but by the Lord, 2.

3-5. The typical foreshadowing of His ministry. "Every high priest . . . appointed to offer both gifts and sacrifices" was a type of "this one," who must also have something to offer, 3,

The Jewish high priest in his distinctive costume.

viz., He offered Himself once for all as a completed, final sacrifice to remove sin.

8:6-13. The satisfactory nature of the new covenant

6-9. The limitations of the old covenant. The "old covenant" refers to the legal or Mosaic covenant. It was enacted on promises inferior to those on which the new covenant was established, 6. The old covenant also lacked finality, 7, and efficacy, 8-9. It provided no power to the sinner to keep its conditions.

10-13. The satisfactory nature of the new covenant. In contrast to the old, the new covenant is gracious and unconditional, 10a; spiritually efficacious, 10b-11; resulting in spiritual regeneration, 10b, and universal knowledge of the Lord, 11. It is faultless and final, 12, based as it is on the complete redemption of Christ, settling forever Israel's sin question and superseding the old covenant, 13.

9:1-10. The typical nature of the old covenant

1-5. The ordinances of the sanctuary under the old covenant. The ministry of the priests under the Mosaic covenant is described in relation to the pieces of furniture in the tabernacle. The outer room (the Holy Place) is described in 2, the inner room (the Most Holy Place) in 3-5.

6-10. The sacrifices of the old covenant. The daily repeated activities relating to the sacrifice and worship, which were performed by the priests in the Holy Place, 6, and the sacrifices of the Day of Atonement, which were offered by the high priest once a year in the Most Holy Place, 7, showed that the way of access to God for every believer was not yet open, 8.

9:11-14. Reality under the new covenant

11-12. The essence of the reality. Christ's appearance as High Priest fulfilled the types of both the Melchizedek and the Aaronic priesthoods in bringing "the good things that are already here," 11a. He fulfilled the type of the high priest's entering the holiest once a year (Lev. 16) by having entered "once for all by his own blood" into the real holy place in the tabernacle in heaven, 12.

13-14. The meaning of the reality. If the sprinkling of ceremonially defiled people with animal blood and the ashes of a red heifer (Num. 19:16-18) could purify outwardly to any degree, to how much greater degree will the blood of Christ effect inward cleansing and obtain an eternally complete salvation, 14?

9:15-22. The new covenant sealed by Christ's blood

15-17. Christ's death a necessity. Without Christ's death there could have been no "will" or covenant, 16, nor could He have become the Mediator, acting between a holy God and guilty sinners to the end that they might be reconciled, 15a.

18-22. The necessity of Christ's death foreshadowed by the law. The first or legal covenant was inaugurated by blood, 18, beginning only when Moses had sprinkled with blood both the book of the law and the people, 19. The tabernacle and all the vessels of worship were similarly blood-sprinkled, 21 (Ex. 29:12, 36), thus typically showing the necessity of Christ's death.

9:23-24. The better sanctuary of the new covenant

Our Lord, as both Priest and Sacrifice, has entered into "heaven itself," to present Himself in the immediate presence of God on our behalf, 24, thus securing eternal redemption.

9:25-10:4. The better sacrifice of the new covenant

9:25-28. Christ's sacrifice is final. This finality is indicated by Christ's complete and unrepeatable offer of Himself in contrast to the high priest who entered the Most Holy Place every year "with blood" that was not his own, 25.

The sacrifice of Christ is final because: (1) it involved the blood of His own glorious person, 26, satisfying all the claims of an infinitely holy God against sinners; (2) it perfectly meets the needs of the sinner, 27; (3) it perfectly meets the needs of the believer, 28a.

10:1-4. Levitical sacrifices imperfect and repeatable. These typical sacrifices never cleansed away sin in the worshipers, 2. On the contrary, they only brought a fresh remembrance of sins to be atoned for, 3, because of the utter inability of animal blood to remove sin and guilt, 4.

10:5-10. The new covenant based on Christ's perfect sacrifice

5-7. Christ's perfect sacrifice foretold. Verse 7 predictively sums up our Lord's redemption work: God the Son entering the world to become incarnate, "I have come" (cf. Luke 1:35), and His utter obedience to the Father's will, even to death, "to do your will, O God" (cf. Luke 22:42; Phil. 2:8).

8-10. Christ's perfect sacrifice annuls the old order. The Father's dissatisfaction with the Levitical ritual, 8, is contrasted with His will for the Son, 9.

10:11-14. The new covenant is superior because of Christ's present position

11. The inferior position and ministry of the Levitical priests. The repeated offering of the same sacrifices could never "take away" sins.

12-14. The superior position and work of Christ. The completeness of His work was signified by His having "sat down," thus assuming an exalted position of authority and priestly service "at the right hand of God," 12.

10:15-18. The new covenant is superior because of the finality of Christ's sacrifice

15-17. The witness of the Spirit. Christ in His sacrificial atoning death accomplished remission of sins and transformation of life for all who place their faith in Him, 16-17. It was to this that the Spirit gave witness.

18. A summary statement. Where sins are completely forgiven a need no longer exists for further "offering for sin."

10:19-25. Appeal to a life of faith

19-22. The basis for the appeal. The Hebrew believers are encouraged to enter God's presence with confidence because the blood of Christ has made such access possible, 19; because Jesus has inaugurated a new way "through the curtain" into the immediate presence of God, 20; and because we have a High Priest in the real sanctuary in heaven, 21.

23-25. The further appeal. The writer urges: (1) steadfastness in the hope Christ has given us, 23, (2) consideration for one another, 24, and (3) constancy in public worship, 25.

10:26-31. Warning against lapse into Judaism

26-29. The problem of presumptuous sinning. This sin, which faced the Hebrew believers to whom the letter is addressed, consisted of a deliberate course of action

---

The covenants of Scripture

Covenant and significance

Eternal covenant Heb. 13:20

Abrahamic covenant Gen. 12:1-3

The covenant of promise. In Abraham (through Christ) all the families of the earth were to be blessed (John 8:56-58; Gal. 3:16).

Mosaic covenant Ex. 20:1-31:18

The legal covenant, given solely to Israel. It consisted of the commandments (Ex. 20:1-26); the judgments (social) —(Ex. 21:1; 24:11); and the ordinances (religious)—(Ex. 24:12-31:18); also called the law. It was a conditional covenant of works.

Davidic covenant 2 Sam. 7:4-17; 1 Chron. 17:4-15

New covenant Jer. 31:31-33; Matt. 26:28; Mark 14:24; Luke 22:20; Heb. 8:8-12 The covenant of unconditional blessing based on the finished redemption of Christ. It secures blessing for the church, flowing from the Abrahamic covenant (Gal. 3:13-20), and secures all covenant blessings to converted Israel.

against the full knowledge they had received of the truth, 26a. They are accused of trampling under foot the Son of God, rejecting as common and unholy the covenant blood of Christ by which they were consecrated, and insulting the Holy Spirit who imparts the gracious blessing of God.

30-31. The punishment. This punishment refers to "his people," and may be executed by present disciplinary action or at the future judgment seat of Christ (cf. 1 Cor. 3:11-17).

10:32-39. A call to patient faith
32-34. The call to remember their early faith. The vacillating Hebrew believers are called on to remember the days past, in which, after they had been spiritually enlightened concerning Christ's eternal redemption, they demonstrated their faith by enduring a "great contest in the face of suffering," 32.

35-39. The call to continue in patient faith. Their present need is perseverance (*hupomone*, that quality of remaining under trial and difficulty with persevering endurance), so that they may receive the promised reward, 36-37.

11:1-3. The superiority of persevering faith
1. The definition of persevering faith. Such faith is (1) the assurance of things hoped for—hope being faith in action with regard to the future reality of present promises, and (2) a settled conviction of things not yet actual but certain to become so.

2-3. The accomplishments of persevering faith. Faith enables people to receive divine approval, 2, and to understand spiritual truth, 3.

11:4-40. Faith that envisioned the promise—Christ
Abel and Enoch
4. Abel's sacrifice of faith. Cain's offering was a presentation of his own works and secured no acceptance with God. In contrast, Abel's sacrifice secured God's declaration that he was righteous, testifying for all time that salvation is by faith in the atoning death of an acceptable substitute (John 1:29).

5-6. Enoch's walk of faith. Enoch's life was an illustration of the truth that the way of faith is the only way of pleasing and approaching God, 6.

Noah
7. Noah's action of faith. Noah built the ark because of his faith in God's predictive word concerning events of which there was as yet no visible sign.

Abraham and Sarah
8-10. Abraham's obedience of faith. In leaving his home in Ur, and later Haran (Gen. 11:31-12:4), for Canaan, Abraham displayed an obedient faith that was unwavering in that the land he set out for was still not promised to him, and when it was, the Canaanites still possessed it.

11-12. Sarah's strength by faith. By faith Sarah received physical strength to conceive Isaac, the child of promise in the line of Christ, even when she was long past the age of childbearing, because she considered God, who had given her the promise, faithful and trustworthy in keeping His word, 11.

The reality and hope of faith
13-15. Its reality. The genuineness of the faith of OT saints is shown by their death, their

Hebrews recounts again the story of Moses' flight of faith from Egypt.

unwavering trust, their pilgrim walk, and their words and actions.

16. Its hope. The genuine faith of the OT saints expressed itself in their hope for a better country (heaven).

Abraham and Isaac
17-19. Abraham's severely tested faith was triumphant. The supreme test of Abraham's faith was his presenting of Isaac as a sacrificial offering. Abraham conquered the fear of death, as he "reasoned that God could raise the dead."

Isaac, Jacob, and Joseph
20-21. Isaac and Jacob's blessing of faith. Isaac by faith, when blessing Jacob and Esau, assigned things still in the future as if they were present (Gen. 27:27-29, 39-40).

22. Joseph's instructions of faith. Joseph believed God would keep His word in bringing about the Exodus and Israel's restoration to Canaan (Gen. 15:13-21), and ultimately would resurrect his physical body for the heavenly Canaan.

Moses in Egypt
23. His parents' act of faith.
24-26. Moses' choice of faith. Moses preferred to endure ill treatment with God's people rather than enjoy the passing pleasures of a sinful life, 25.

Moses leaving Egypt
27. Moses' flight of faith. Moses fled without fear of Pharaoh, enduring because he saw "him who is invisible."

28-29. Moses' Passover of faith. Simple faith prompted Moses to institute the Passover and the sprinkling of the blood on the doorposts, so that the destroyer of the firstborn might not touch the Israelites (Ex. 12:21-30).

Joshua and Rahab
30. Joshua's march of faith. Faith, not the marching or the trumpet blaring, released the power of God to level the walls (Josh. 6:12-21).
31. Rahab's hospitality of faith. She received the Israelite spies into her home and thus exhibited personal faith in her confession (Josh. 2:9-11).

From Gideon to Samuel and the prophets
32-37. Their exploits and suffering. Six heroes of faith appear in verse 32, and their exploits (and other people's) are detailed in verses 33-34, and their sufferings in 35-37.
38. Their evaluation. The world was not worthy of them.
39-40. The faith of Old Testament saints and ours. OT saints gained approval as a result of their faith. They will "be made perfect," 40, along with NT saints, when Christ returns.

12:1-4. The race and goal of faith
1. The race of faith. The figure of an amphitheater filled with OT saints (11:4-38) witnessing NT believers run the race of faith constitutes an incentive for Christians as they run.
2-4. The goal of faith. The goal is "Jesus," the all-sufficient Savior; therefore sight is to be fixed on Him throughout the race.

12:5-11. Chastening as an incentive to faith
5-9. The discipline of faith. Divine discipline is an encouragement to press on toward the goal because it is a token of the Lord's love for His own, 5-6.
10-11. The results of disciplined faith. The first result is our permanent eternal good, and the second result is sharing God's holiness, 10.

12:12-17. A warning from Esau
12-14. The exhortation. The call is to pursue peace in the sense of constantly and diligently following it, 14, so as to live harmoniously with everybody. Urged also is the diligent pursuit of holiness.
15-17. The warning. Verse 15 is a warning against defaulting from the grace of God, resulting in a bitter spirit that poisons many in the Christian community.

12:18-24. The result of faith that has obtained the promise
18-21. It delivers from a law of terror. God's presence, under the law, brought fear and trembling, even to Moses, 21.
22-24. It brings the blessings and relationships of grace. Grace, under the new covenant, brings Hebrew believers to Mount Zion, the city of the living God, the "heavenly Jerusalem," in contrast with the earthly Jerusalem and the fearful Mount Sinai, 22.

12:25-29. Warning against refusing to heed God's voice
25-27. The danger of sin. If the Israelites who refused to listen and obey Moses' warning on earth suffered God's judgment, how much

The Dome of the Rock is probably built over the site of the Jerusalem Temple.

greater peril do those face who refuse to heed the voice of God's own Son from heaven, 25?
28-29. The preventive against sin. Realizing that they are heirs of the unshakable kingdom, believers are to show their gratitude.

13:1-6. The expression of faith in daily living
1-4. In social relationships. Love for the brethren is to be a normal course of action, 1. The marriage bond, and the sexual life within that bond, are to be held in high honor, 4.
5-6. In financial matters. Freedom from the love of money and contentment with present possessions are to characterize believers.

13:7-9. Faith's expression in a stable testimony
7-8. The example. Both the spiritual leaders who had spoken the Word of God to these Hebrew believers and the Lord Jesus Himself constitute examples of stability.
9. The exhortation. "Do not be carried away by all kinds of strange teachings" is an obvious reference to the legalistic teachings that had been added to Judaism. Legalism was barren of spiritual reality; grace is full of it. Feeding on grace will lead to stability of life and testimony.

13:10-14. Faith expressed in separation from Judaism
10-12. The basis of separation. The life of faith was no longer related to the practices of Judaism.
13-14. The exhortation to separation. Separation would require pilgrim faith, fixing their hope not on the temporal but on the eternal, "the city that is to come," 14.

13:15-17. Faith expressed in spiritual worship and obedience
15-17. Sacrificial worship. This includes the sacrifice of praise, 15, and the sacrifices of substance and of good works, 16, sharing oneself with others in need, and obedience, 17.

13:18-25. Concluding benediction
18-19. Personal request. The writer requests specific prayer from his readers, particularly for honorable conduct and for restoration to their company.
20-21. Benediction. This prayer contains essential elements for the spiritual well-being of the Hebrew believers to whom he has been writing.
22-25. Closing greeting.

James
The necessity of a living faith

Outline

1   Living faith tested by trial
2   Living faith proved by deeds
3-4   Living faith evidenced by conduct
5   Living faith exercised by persecution

The author. There is strong evidence for the traditional view that James, the half brother of our Lord (Mark 6:3), was the author of this letter.

The character of the letter. There is no more Jewish book in the NT. The letter could be described as an interpretation of the OT law and the Sermon on the Mount in the light of the gospel of Christ.

The church order and discipline it displays are very simple. The leaders are called "teachers" and "elders," with no mention of "bishops" or "deacons." Believers still met in the synagogue, with little organization since various members set themselves up as teachers.

The traditional setting of the Serrmon on the Mount, on the shores of the Sea of Galilee.

James

1:1-4. The purpose of trials
1. The author. James, the brother of our Lord, humbly styles himself simply "a servant (*doulos*, "slave") of God and of the Lord Jesus Christ."

2-4. His message. James's chief ministry was to comfort Jews who had turned to Christ. They were targets of intense persecution from their unbelieving countrymen. James urges them to "consider it *pure* joy" (emphatic), 2, the occasion of becoming involved for Christ's sake in various temptations.

1:5-12. Wisdom for trials
5-8. The need and supply of wisdom for trials. In no sphere is wisdom so essential and folly so disastrous as in the matter of life's reverses. If anyone is deficient in this God-given faculty let him ask for it from God, and ask without doubting, 5-6.

9-12. The rewards of exercising wisdom in trials. Wisdom enables the brother of "humble circumstances" to rejoice in his exalted position in Christ, 9. Wisdom enables the rich brother to rejoice in his lowliness apart from his salvation, 10-11. Wisdom also reveals the blessedness of the believer who endures testing, 12.

1:13-18. God and trials
13-15. God tempts no one to sin. Wisdom shows us that solicitation to evil is not from God as the initiating agent, 13. The cause of sin is in ourselves, 14, and the progress of sin is inexorable, 15.

16-18. God is good to people. God's goodness is shown by His gifts, 17. So far from bringing temptation and sin into our lives, He is the Bestower of every benefit we enjoy.

1:19-25. God's Word and trials
19-21. God's goodness and the believer's responsibility. The injunctions of these verses are: (1) be quick to listen, (2) be slow to talk, (3) be slow to get angry, (4) get rid of everything vile, and (5) receive the Word of God.

22-25. God's Word and the believer's obedience. So important is God's Word in living and facing trials that we must "do what it says," 22, rather than be mere hearers who know the Word only theoretically and are deluded into thinking that hearing is enough.

1:26-27. False and true religion.
To be genuine, outward religious observance must be accompanied by inner godliness. Inner godliness is revealed in curbing the tongue, in compassionate love, and in separation from sin.

2:1-9. Dead faith manifested in partiality
1-5. How the sin nullifies genuine faith. Partiality is the sin of displaying undue respect or disrespect for certain people. It nullifies genuine

faith by violating equality within the Christian brotherhood and by detracting from God's glory revealed in Christ.

6-7. Why the sin is serious. Partiality dishonors the poor, 6, and honors the rich, who so frequently are oppressive and godless, 7.

8-9. Partiality breaks the royal law. This is the law of love, "royal" or "kingly" because it is the monarch of all laws, the quintessence of the Ten Commandments. The sin of partiality infringes on this royal law, "love your neighbor as [you love] yourself" (Lev. 19:18).

2:10-13. Dead faith results in judgment
10-11. The reason for judgment. The law is like a chain. The chain is broken when one link of the chain is broken, 11. Unless people have saving faith in Christ, they stand condemned by the law, 12.

12-13. The reason for mercy. Because God has shown mercy on sinners, they are to be merciful in their dealings with others, 13.

2:14-20. Dead faith is useless
14-16. The principle stated and illustrated. The uselessness of dead faith is illustrated by the case of a fellow believer who is destitute, 15-16.

17-20. The inseparability of faith and works. To offer God a faith separated from works is little better than the faith of demons who believe and shudder, 19.

2:21-26. Living faith proves a person righteous
21-24. The case of Abraham. James asserts that Abraham was justified by works when he offered up Isaac, 21 (Gen. 22:9-12). James here is not contradicting Paul, Romans 4:2-4. (1) James uses the term "justified" in the sense of actually demonstrated *before people*; Paul uses the term in the sense of being judicially declared righteous *before God*. (2) James is correcting an abused truth; Paul sets forth the truth itself.

25-26. The case of Rahab. Her saving faith was seen when she hid the spies, sent them back another way, and hung out the red cord (Josh. 2:1-21; Heb. 11:31).

3:1-5. Living faith and the influence of the tongue
1-2. Our weighty responsibility for what we say. The tongue has great influence for good or bad. For this reason James warns against haste in becoming a teacher, 1.

3-5. The power of the tongue illustrated. Three analogies are used to show the great effect produced by a relatively insignificant cause: the horse's bit, 3, the ship's rudder, 4, and the spark of igniting fire, 5.

3:6-12. Living faith and the treachery of the tongue
6-8. Its unruly nature. Not only is the tongue powerful; it is treacherous. Its treachery is shown by its distinctive character as a fire, its defiling character, its corrupting quality, and its evil source.

9-12. Its unpredictable inconsistencies.

James shows how inconsistent the tongue is by two illustrations from nature and so demonstrates that the tongue is guilty of what is absolutely contrary to nature, 12.

3:13-18. Living faith and wisdom

13-16. Earthly wisdom. Every believer must choose which wisdom will guide his life, earthly, 14-16, or heavenly, 17-18. Earthly wisdom cannot produce a truly wise teacher, endued with discreet knowledge, who demonstrates by good behavior his works with genuine humility, 13. It produces jealousy and ambition.

17-18. Heavenly wisdom. True or heavenly wisdom, which has righteousness as its fruit, sows in peace because possessors of this wisdom are those who make peace, 18.

4:1-5. Living faith and worldliness

1-4. The manifestations of worldliness. This sin, rooted in unbelief, is seen by: (1) tensions generated by "desires that battle" inside a person, 1, (2) dissatisfaction, 2, (3) prayerlessness, 2, (4) prayer with the wrong motive, 3, (5) spiritual adultery, 4, and (6) hostility against God, 4.

5. The cure for worldliness. This is submission to the Holy Spirit who lives in the redeemed body of every believer (1 Cor. 6:19), allowing Him to control the whole life.

4:6-10. Living faith and humility

6. The source of humility. God is the source of this grace.

7-10. The way to humility is to submit to God, resist the devil, draw near to God, separate from evil, repent in abject contrition, and humble yourself.

4:11-12. Living faith and evil speaking

11a. The injunction is to stop speaking loosely against fellow believers in a spirit of criticism.

11b-12. The reason for the injunction. Such evil speaking is sinful because it not only is against Christian brothers, 11a, but against the law.

4:13-17. Living faith and secularism

13. The spirit of secularism. Supreme and well-nigh exclusive attention to the affairs of this life with little or no thought of God stems from a lack of living faith.

14-17. The folly of secularism. Secularism is a violation of the meaning of life, which is to serve God, not self, 14.

5:1-6. Living faith exercised by persecution

1-3. Oppressors' doom predicted. These oppressive rich people represent the unsaved, who will face judgment in the last days.

4-6. Oppressors' crimes exposed. Their oppression of the godly poor has reached the ears of "the Lord Almighty," 4.

5:7-11. Living faith exercised by patience under persecution

7-9. Ground for patience. Note the double, and therefore emphatic, exhortation: "Be patient . . . be patient," 7-8. James refers to the coming of the Lord as

Elijah prayed effectively, with God's glory in mind.

5:13-18. Living faith exercised in prayer

13. Exhortation to the suffering. Affliction of any sort is to lead the suffering saint to prayer.

14-15. Instructions to the physically ill. The sick believer was to call the *elders* of the assembly, never one elder. The use of oil for anointing the sick was a general Jewish practice, and one that the Lord's disciples adopted (Mark 6:13). However, the emphasis is on "the prayer offered in faith." Such a prayer is divinely given and operates when it is God's will to heal.

16. Exhortation to persevering prayer. Power in prayer is evidently conditioned on one's being in fellowship with both the Lord and fellow believers.

17-18. The example. Elijah prayed "earnestly" ("prayed with prayer," a Hebraism for "prayed intensely," cf. 1 Kings 17:1); he prayed effectively, with God's glory in mind.

5:19-20. Living faith exercised by a diligent witness

The blessing of reclaiming a brother who errs in being led astray from the truth of the gospel and its precepts is set out.

being "near," the Greek expressing present time and a settled state, so that the event is always imminent, 8, with the Judge (the returning Christ) "standing at the door," 9 (cf. Matt. 24:33).

10-11. Encouraging examples of patience. The case of Job is the classic illustration of God's purpose in the trials of His people and steadfast endurance, 11.

5:12. Living faith exercised by avoiding oath-making

12a. The warning. Swearing or cursing shows impatience and pride, which are foreign to the meek endurance just commanded.

12b. The reason for the warning.

1 Peter
Living in the light of future glory

Outline

1:1-25	Present suffering and future inheritance
2:1-4:6	The Christian's suffering in view of Christ's passion
4:7-5:14	The Christian's suffering in view of Christ's coming

Authorship. That the letter was written by the apostle Peter is indicated by the intimate acquaintance the author shows with the life of Christ and His teachings (cf. 5:5 with John 13:3-5; 5:2 with John 21:15-17).

Theme. The letter is predominantly addressed to Jewish believers. The subject of the letter is "suffering," with seven different words used for it in the one letter. Hope in the middle of suffering is engendered by the prospect of a future inheritance (1:4-5) and the coming of the Chief Shepherd (5:4). Suffering is purposeful (1:6-7; 2:19-20; 3:14; 4:14). It is to be expected (4:12), not to be dreaded (3:14); it is to be borne patiently (2:23; 3:9) and rejoiced in (4:13). The sufferings of Christ are featured (1:11; 2:21; 5:1) as the believer's example (2:21; 4:12). Suffering is often in God's will (4:19).

The harbor, Antalya. Peter's letter was addressed to believers in Asia Minor.

1 Peter

1:1-5. Encouraged for suffering

1-4. A basis for courage. The strangers of the dispersion were believing Jews scattered throughout Roman provinces in Asia Minor. Their spiritual wealth provided a basis for courage in the middle of severe persecution from fellow Jews. It included their election, 2; their sanctification by the Holy Spirit, 2; their new birth, 3; and their future glorification and inheritance, 3-4.

5. Present status of the sufferers. They were "shielded by God's power" as though garrisoned with a military contingent, and so kept secure.

1:6-9. Tested for suffering

6. The proper attitude toward suffering. Suffering should be endured with joy and seen as transient.

7-9. The purpose of suffering. God's aim in suffering is that the believer's faith may be proved genuine and that it may result in "praise, glory and honor" to Christ.

1:10-12. Salvation and suffering

10-11. The search of the prophets. The OT prophets were intrigued by the plan of salvation that was hinted at in their utterances about God's grace, 10. This grace was to be displayed in the vicarious sufferings of the Messiah-King, 11.

12. The benefactors of the prophetic message. This message was intended for a future age (ours).

1:13-21. Holy living and suffering

13-17. The exhortation to holy living. This so great salvation demands a once-for-all attitude of separation from sin.

18-21. The reason for holy living. The apostle reminds his readers of the greatness of our great redemption, which is the essential basis for a holy life.

1:22-25. Regeneration and behavior

22. The responsibility of regeneration. The new birth is to be seen in a transformation of character. Their love is to be "from the heart," a genuine and permanent attitude.

23-25. The means of regeneration. Being "born again," 23, rests on the authority and testimony of God's Word.

2:1-3. The believer's growth and suffering

This involves, negatively, a distinct separation from evil, 1; and, positively, an intense appetite for the Word of God, 2.

2:4-10. Spiritual identity, an encouragement in suffering

4-8. Identity with Christ. Peter's Jewish readers may be ostracized by the world and by unbelieving Jews, but they are gloriously identified with their Lord and His church in a personal and intimate way. The figure of a building is used to describe this relationship.

9-10. Identity with God's own. Identification with Christ also brings one into living relationship with the whole company of believers, who are described as "a chosen people," "a royal priesthood," "a holy nation," and "a people belonging to God."

2:11-20. The believer's pilgrimage and suffering

11a. The pilgrimage described.

11b-18. Pilgrim conduct enjoined. Pilgrims must lead good "lives among the pagans," so that the unsaved might glorify God by the good works of His own in the "day he visits us," the day of Christ's coming in judgment, 12.

19-20. Pilgrim conduct and suffering. Pilgrims will often be called on to endure pain as a result of suffering unjustly, 19.

2:21-25. The believer's suffering and Christ's example

21a. The believer's call to suffering.

21b-25. The example of Christ's suffering. Christ left us an example for imitation, a pattern for guidance, desiring His redeemed ones to "follow [closely] in his steps," 21b.

3:1-7. God's pattern for wives and husbands

1-6. Pattern for wives. Following OT examples, particularly Sarah (Gen. 18:12), wives are to be women of faith, inner adornment, submission, obedience, and courage, 5-6.

7. Pattern for husbands. The husbands are to live with their wives with the understanding of what marriage means.

3:8-12. The believer's suffering and harmonious living

8-11. Requirements for harmonious living.

Believers must be likeminded in the faith, sympathetic toward one another, humble in spirit, not vengeful toward others.

12. Reason for harmonious living. They are the objects of the gracious care of the Lord (cf. Ps. 34:15-16).

3:13-17. Maintaining a good conscience under suffering

13-15. The way to a good conscience. Keeping a good conscience entails facing persecution fearlessly, 14, reverencing Christ as Lord; and maintaining a proper witness before people, 15.

16-17. The result of a good conscience. A good conscience puts persecutors to shame, 16.

3:18-22. Christ's example of triumph and encouragement

18. Christ's triumph over suffering. Christ's example argues for patience under suffering because He Himself chose not to be exempt from suffering.

19-20. Christ's encouragement in suffering. These Jewish believers were engulfed in the pagan world. Peter encouraged them by a reference to Christ's ministry to the antediluvian generation through Noah.

21-22. Christ's triumph in providing salvation. Christ's sufferings resulted in our salvation. This makes our suffering not only bearable but glorious. The outward figure of this salvation is water baptism. The ark on the flood water is the type; our salvation in Christ (the true Ark) the antitype.

4:1-6. Suffering and Christ's example for victorious living

1-2. The basis for victorious living. Believers are to arm themselves, as soldiers putting on armor, "with the same attitude" (and purpose) Christ had—purposing to suffer rather than to sin, 1.

3-6. The case against sinful living. Six sins are cataloged, 3, characteristic of the unregenerate. Believers, because of their changed lives, bring condemnation to the ungodly, resulting in Christians being maligned for their purity of life, 4.

4:7-11. Judgment and service in the middle of suffering

7. Living in the light of coming judgment.
8-11. Serving in the spirit of love. Foremost is the injunction to "love each other deeply, because love covers over a multitude of sins," 8. Lack of love broadcasts and uncovers these sins to the detriment of God's work. Peter is speaking merely of a loving spirit of forgiveness versus an unloving spirit of criticism, not of the expiation of sins. Peter also enjoins the practice of ungrudging hospitality, 9, and the use of one's spiritual gifts for the welfare of one another, 10.

4:12-19. The Lord's return and trials
12-14. The source of courage for trials.
Trials are to be expected, not viewed as unusual in the believer's life, and are allowed in order to test the genuineness of their faith.

15-19. Courage for trials and Christian duty.
Suffering is to be welcomed when it is "according to God's will," and the sufferers are to commit their souls to a faithful Creator, who made them and can certainly take care of them in suffering, bringing them through it to His glory, 19.

5:1-5. The Lord's return and daily duty
1-4. Duty of elders. The elders are exhorted to oversee "God's flock" (the body of believers) voluntarily, not under compulsion, and eagerly without being motivated by personal gain, 1-2.
5. Duty of the young.

5:6-11. The Lord's return and Christian maturity
6-9. Developing maturity. This involves a spirit of continued submission to God, 6-7, and an attitude of continued resistance to Satan, 8-9.
10-11. Enjoying maturity. Believers are to perpetually recognize God's glory and dominion, 11.

5:12-14. Concluding greeting
12. Personal testimony. Peter wrote with ringing authority because he himself was a brilliant trophy of God's grace.
13-14. Final greetings. "Babylon" probably refers to the church of Jewish converts at Babylon on the Euphrates.

2 Peter

Growing in grace

Outline

1 Secret to Christian growth
2 Antidote to error
3 Key to certainty of the future

Occasion and date. Second Peter was evidently penned to the same people as 1 Peter, namely Jewish Christians. It was apparently written after 1 Peter and before Jude, as the doctrinal defection it describes is not as fully developed as in Jude. The date is probably A.D. 66 or 67.

The Colosseum, Rome. Tradition has it that Peter was executed in this city.

2 Peter

1:1-4. The basis of Christian growth
1-2. The common faith of believers. The apostle addresses those who have received "a faith as precious as ours," that is, a faith equally precious to all believers.

3-4. The spiritual endowment of believers. Facilitating Christian growth, this endowment consists of "his divine power" (the dynamic of the Holy Spirit), "knowledge of him," 3, His Word, a new nature, 4, ability and means to live in a holy manner, 4b.

1:5-9. The way to Christian growth
5-7. Employment of one's spiritual endowment. Because of the spiritual endowment God has committed to us, 3-4, let us "make every effort" to cooperate with Him. Love fittingly completes the choir of graces as in Colossians 3:14, and encompasses them all, being the badge of spiritual adulthood (cf. 1 Cor. 13).

8-9. The resultant manifestation of spiritual maturity. This adulthood will reveal itself in fruitfulness, 8, and will shield the believer from spiritual shortsightedness.

1:10-15. The consummation of Christian growth
10. Assuring our calling and election. Although their election is certain, from the divine point of view, believers are to employ their spiritual resources, 5-7, in manifesting maturity, 8-9, in order to make their calling and election certain to men.

11-15. Entering the eternal kingdom. The entrance spoken of here is the entrance into the eternal kingdom of our Lord and Savior Jesus Christ at the resurrection of the body and its consequent glorification (Phil. 3:20-21; 1 Thess. 4:13-17; 1 John 3:1-3).

1:16-21. Christian growth and biblical authority
16-18. The authority of apostolic testimony. Peter himself points believers to the real authority of the Word of God, declaring that the inspired testimony for the apostles rules out deception, 16. On the mount of transfiguration Peter was an eyewitness of Christ's "majesty."

19-21. The authority of the written Word. The Scriptures are of divine origin, for they are divinely inspired, 20-21.

2:1-3a. False teachers—their rise
1. Their activity. They stealthily introduce destructive heresies.

2-3a. Their influence. The influence of these prophets is shown by their popularity: "many" people follow them.

2:3b-9. False teachers—their doom
3b. Their certain judgment declared.

4-8. Their certain ruin illustrated. The first illustration is of fallen angels, 4; the second example is that of the ancient world, 5; the third illustration is that of Sodom and Gomorrah, 6-8.

9. The divine principle enunciated.

The traditional site of Peter's betrayal, Jerusalem.

2:10-16. False teachers
—their presumption and greed
10-12. Their sin of presumption specified.
These ungodly teachers are given particularly to
sensuality and lawlessness, both seemingly
stemming from the more basic sin of
presumption, 10c-12.
12b-13a. The punishment of their sin. They
will "perish," the Greek word expressing
"corruption" and "destruction."
13b-14. Their moral dishonesty. The false
teachers' love of luxurious pleasure leads to
lives addicted to revelry.
15-16. Their mercenary character illustrated.

2:17-18. False teachers
—their empty intellectualism
17. They are devoid of God's Spirit. Several
metaphors show this emptiness.

18. They are snared by empty intellectualism.
These teachers of error employ arrogant
language with a view to deceive.

2:19-22. False teachers
—their bondage to sin
19-20a. Their empty promise of freedom.
They are common slaves (*douloi*) of moral
depravity, and thus helpless to free others.
Having rejected the truth of the gospel, they
have spurned the only source of liberty. The
liberty they offer is spurious.
20b-22. The plight of their victims. As
enlightened but unsaved moralists, the followers
of these false teachers at least avoid the more
obvious sins, but by rejecting the light of Christ
they are exposed to greater darkness and
deeper sins (Phil. 3:18-19).

3:1-7. Last-day scoffers
and the Second Coming
1-3. The warning concerning scoffers. Peter's
specific purpose in writing was to alert them to
the peril of last-day scoffers, scorners, and
mockers who laugh at or make jest of anything
(Jude 18).
4-7. The nature of their scoffing. These
mockers will scorn the truth of the Second
Coming, 4. The restoration of the earth, the
Noahic flood, 6, and the coming earth-renovating
catastrophe by fire, 7, exhibit the truthfulness of
God's Word versus the scoffer's claim, 4.

3:8-10. God's patience
and the Day of the Lord
8-9. God's time schedule. The apostle
proceeds to answer the scoffers, pointing out
that our limited time concepts are not the context

Peter was present at the Transfiguration, which probably took place on Mount Hermon.

in which God operates to bring His purposes to pass.

10. The certainty of the Day of the Lord. Peter gives a new revelation concerning the Day of the Lord as it relates to the cataclysm of fire.

3:11-13. Present conduct and the eternal state

11-12a. The impetus to holy living. The coming judgments of the Day of the Lord furnish ample reasons for godly living.

12b-13. The glorious expectation. This anticipated event is promised by God's own Word, 13a, is expected by faith, 13b, and entails a sin-cleansed universe, 13c.

3:14-18. The believer's hope and growth in grace

14-17. The incentive to growth. The realization of this hope (of new heavens and a new earth in which righteousness dwells) is a further stimulus for a holy life, 14.

18. The plea for growth. Believers are urged to keep on growing in grace—God's method not only of saving people, but of maturing them.

1 John
Fellowship
of father and children

Outline

1-3   Family fellowship and the Father
4-5   Family fellowship and the world

God. Both also have the same simple, direct Hebrew style.

Author. The writer was the apostle John, also the author of the fourth gospel. This fact is demonstrated by the similar vocabulary in both the gospel and the letter. They contain such expressions as *light, new commandment, works of the devil, take away sins, eternal life, love, abide, Paraclete, Savior of the world, born of*

Occasion and date. The letter was written about A.D. 85-90, apparently from Ephesus, where Irenaeus says John lived during the latter part of his life, and where he seems to have overseen surrounding churches (cf. Rev. 2-3).

St John's Tomb, St John's Church, Ephesus.

1 John

1:1-4. The basis of fellowship
1-2. The incarnation and eternal life. The apostle presents his authority as an eyewitness to the central fact of the gospel. "The Word of life," 1, is a reference to Christ as the One who came to bring eternal life to sinners dead in sin (John 3:16).

3-4. The incarnation and fellowship. The aim of John in writing was that his Christian readers might have fellowship (*koinonia*, fellowship in common participation of an experience) with him in sharing communion with God, 3.

1:5-10. The conditions of fellowship
5-8. Walking in the light. Requirements for walking in fellowship are having a right concept of God, 5; living a life separated from sin, 6; claiming the cleansing power of Christ's sacrifice, 7; and recognizing the presence of the old nature, 8.

9-10. Confessing our sins. Confession of our sins to God brings forgiveness and cleansing. Such involves our frankly admitting and openly avowing our known sins, 10.

2:1-2. The advocacy of Christ and fellowship
1. Fellowship maintained Godward by Christ's advocacy. The remedy for sin when a believer does sin is based on the work of a continually present advocate who is none other than Jesus Christ the righteous. An advocate is one who is summoned alongside to serve as a helper.

2. The efficacy of Christ's advocacy. Christ Himself is the all-sufficient Advocate because *He Himself* (Greek intensive) is the personal "atoning sacrifice."

2:3-6. Obedience and fellowship
3-5. Assurance of being in fellowship. Knowledge of Christ is inseparably linked to obeying Him and loving Him, 5b-6.

6. The duty of the believer claiming to be in fellowship. Christians are bound to imitate Christ in His walk if they claim to "live in Him."

2:7-11. Brotherly love and fellowship
7-8. Love, the expression of fellowship. The command was "new" in that it had a fresh dynamic, because it was realized in Christ and is realized in the believer when he walks as Christ walked, 8. Jesus also called it "new" and gave it a new motive, "as I have loved you" (John 13:34-35).

9-11. Hatred, the denial of fellowship. Hatred not only kills fellowship but breeds spiritual ignorance and blindness, 11.

2:12-14. Spiritual maturity and fellowship
12. The Father's family. John describes his readers as "dear children" (*teknia*, "born-again ones").

13-14. Fellowship and Christian growth. Those who develop spiritually and enjoy the full privilege of fellowship are described in these verses, from the most mature to the babies.

2:15-17. The peril of worldliness and fellowship

15a. The peril warned against. This warning is couched in a twofold command: (1) "Do not love the world," the world system under which Satan has organized fallen mankind on his God-opposing principles, (2) "or anything in the world," such as its pleasure.

15b-17. The reason for the warning. (1) Love for the world excludes love for God, 15b-16. (2) The world is impermanent, 17a. The doer of God's will is destined for permanence, 17b.

2:18-23. Loyalty to the faith and fellowship

18-21. Doctrinal defection, the foe of fellowship. The entire present age may be characterized as "the last hour" with an acceleration of defection as the Second Coming draws nearer. "Antichrist" means one who is opposed to Christ but who deceitfully comes under the guise of Christ, 18. This letter was written because of the existence of the antichrists who stood opposed to the truth and because John's readers knew the truth, 21.

22-23. The essence of doctrinal defection. Writing against the background of the Gnostic heresy, John identifies the defectors as those who deny the deity of Jesus, 22. The Gnostics ("liars") denied that Jesus was the God-man, stating that the Christ-spirit came on Jesus at His baptism and left before His death.

2:24-29. Abiding in Christ and fellowship

24-26. Adherence to the truth. This delivers believers from "those who are trying to lead you astray"—those actively attempting to deceive, 26.

27-29. Reliance on the Holy Spirit. The Holy Spirit is the "anointing," 20, which believers receive at the time of their conversion. He abides in believers, teaching them all things, and guiding them into all truth (John 16:13), 27.

3:1-10. Righteous living and fellowship

1. God's bestowed love, an incentive to a holy life. John states that the Christian's life should be a holy one because of God's past work for us.

2-3. Christ's coming, an incentive to a holy life. God's future work of transforming the believer by glorification at the coming of Christ should also motivate him to a righteous life.

4-5. A holy life, the intent of salvation. Christ appeared as the answer to the sin problem. He, the sinless Savior, is also our example, 5b.

6-10. A holy life and fellowship. The person who is abiding in Christ does not sin habitually (present tense, "does not go on sinning continually"), 6a. Righteous deeds are the fruit of a righteous character and proof of regeneration, 7. Such holiness is the family likeness, 7b.

No member of God's family habitually practices sin because the new nature (God's "seed") abides in him and he cannot sin as a pattern of life, 9.

3:11-18. Brotherly love and fellowship

11-15. The fellowship of love. A constant exhortation of God's Word is "Love one another," 11. The fellowship of God's family is to be permeated by the atmosphere of love.

16-18. The manifestation of love. The supreme manifestation of love was Christ's incarnation and death (Rom. 5:8), which furnishes an example of love in action, 16.

3:19-24. Christian assurance and fellowship

19-21. The nature of assurance. Assurance, or certainty of salvation and acceptance with God, depends on the practice of genuine love, 19.

22-24. The realization of fellowship. Experiential communion with the Father is enjoyed through a dynamic prayer life and constant obedience, 22-23.

4:1-6. Discernment of error and fellowship

1. The presence of error. Error threatens the fellowship of God's own. Teachers who are not from God are false prophets, energized by demon spirits.

2-6. The acid test of error. The essence of this test is the confession of Christ's deity and incarnation, and it is this confession that distinguishes between those energized by the Spirit of God and those false teachers empowered by the spirit of error (Antichrist), 2-3a.

4:7-18. Love and the manifestation of fellowship

7-8. Love, a family characteristic. True love (*agape*) has its source in God and is a characteristic of every one who has been born of God, those who personally know Him, 7. Their behavior is to reveal their character in their loving one another, 7a.

9-10. The supreme manifestation of love. The nature of God's love is seen in His loving us apart from any reciprocal love on our part—it

is impossible for fallen people to love God, 10a.

11-12. The obligation to love. Believers have a moral obligation ("ought") to love one another since God loved us to the extent of giving His only born Son, 11.

13-16. Love and the indwelling presence of God. The Holy Spirit, who indwells every believer, imparts knowledge of God's presence and of our union with Him (cf. John 15:1-10), 13.

17-18. The perfection of love in us. Mature love results in the assurance that we will be unashamed "on the day of judgment," 17, because of our likeness to Christ.

4:19-21. The incentive to love and fellowship

19. The incentive to love. If God's love was so great "first," then it is expected that His children will love as a result.

20-21. The fellowship of love. The circle of fellowship is complete when we show our love for God by loving our brother. This is the express command of God, 21.

5:1-5. Faith and fellowship

1-3. Faith introduces us to fellowship. Faith in Christ, bringing the experience of the new birth, is the basis of fellowship, 1. This is a fellowship of love, 1b-2a, and a fellowship of obedience, 2b-3.

4-5. Faith gives victory. Victorious faith is centered in the person of Christ who conquered the world Himself (John 16:33); therefore we overcome the world through Him.

5:6-12. Testimony and fellowship

6-10. The testimony concerning the Son. The first witness is external and is to Christ's

The Temple of the Emperor Trajan, Pergamum.

righteousness and to His redemption, 6. The second witness is internal and is that of the Holy Spirit, 6b.

11-12. God's testimony believed. The testimony is: "God has given us eternal life, and this life is in his Son," 11.

5:13-15. Prayer and fellowship
13. The importance of assurance. The apostle's purpose in writing to believers was that they might have assurance of eternal life.

14-15. Power in prayer. Assurance of salvation gives believers confidence of access to God's presence, 14a; breadth of petition, 14b; consciousness of God's will, 14c; faith to believe, 14d; confidence we will receive an answer, 15.

5:16-21. Prayer fellowship and the sinning Christian
16-17. Prayer and the problem of serious sin. If a true believer falls into sin, a fellow believer is to pray for him. The "sin that leads to death," 16, is persistent, willful sinning.

18-20. Sin and its remedy. The believer's new birth and new position are a remedy for sin, 19. He is born of God and into His family. In contrast, the world (all unsaved) is in the power of Satan, 19.

21. Concluding charge.

2 John
Living in truth and love

2 John

Writer and destination. Second John is a personal note, sent by the apostle John to "the chosen lady and her children." The identity of this woman (or church?) is not known.

Purpose. John's purpose in penning the letter was to warn this influential and esteemed lady (1-2) against false teachers. She apparently sponsored meetings with visiting preachers in her home (10). The apostle encourages her and warns against unsound doctrine by suggesting she sponsor no one who teaches less than the full deity and humanity of Christ.

St John's tomb, Ephesus.

1-6. Living in truth and love
1-3. The greeting. John professes to love the chosen lady and her children "in the truth," 1. True Christian love rests on "the truth," i.e., the revealed Word of God focused in the person and work of Christ. Such truth is the sure basis of genuine love, both in the present and in the future, 2.
4-6. The exhortation. John urges the practice of Christian love as the natural outcome of the truth.

Refusing the false fellowship of error
7-9. The presence of error indicated. The presence of error calls for self-examination on the part of the believers, lest the false teachers undo in the fellowship what the apostles had accomplished, thus resulting in loss of reward for the Christian, 8.
10-11. Refusal to admit false teachers. Evidently false teachers were being entertained in Christian homes under the cloak of hospitality. The apostle forbids believers to carry on doing this.
12-13. Conclusion.

3 John
Help and hospitality toward itinerant ministers

3 John

Date and place of writing. According to Eusebius, John returned from his exile on Patmos to Ephesus after the death of Domitian (A.D. 96), spending his closing years visiting the Asiatic churches (cf. 2 John 12; 3 John 10, 14), ordaining elders and ministering. Therefore, 2 John and 3 John were written after the book of Revelation, if Eusebius is correct.

Street of the Curetes, Ephesus.

1-8. Gaius's example of living in truth and love
1-4. The apostle's greeting to Gaius. John's greeting to his "dear friend Gaius," 1, includes a prayer for his spiritual and physical well-being, and expresses joy for his life in the truth.
5-8. Gaius's life in the truth. This was demonstrated by his life of good works, hospitality, and love.

9-11. Example of a contrary life
9-10. The example. Diotrephes, in contrast to Gaius and Demetrius, did not walk in love and the truth because he loved "to be first," 9, and was uncharitable and domineering, 10.
11. The warning.

12-14. Demetrius's good example
12. Demetrius's good report. The good testimony to the life of Demetrius (unknown) was universal.
13-14. Closing observations.

Jude
Contending for the faith

Occasion and date. Little is known of the circumstances or date of writing, except that the apostasy it describes is more developed than in 2 Peter, and so appears to be written after A.D. 66 or 67.

The author. The author was evidently the brother of James, who was the bishop of Jerusalem and the writer of the letter of James (James 1:1; cf. Matt. 13:55; Mark 6:3), and the (half) brother of our Lord, 1. At first an unbeliever (John 7:3-5), he became convinced of Jesus' deity (Acts 1:14).

Jude reminded his readers of the fate of the cities of the Plain, Sodom and Gomorrah, by the Dead Sea.

Jude

1-4. Contending for the faith

1-2. Greeting. Jude addresses believers in general, citing their election, their preservation, and their status as "loved by God the Father."

3-4. The occasion of the letter. The author's original purpose was to write a doctrinal letter, 3a, "about the salvation we share." False teachers threatened the teaching of this general truth involving Christ's person and finished work. Jude, therefore, switched to an exhortation to militantly defend the faith, 3b.

5-7. Historical warnings of God's judgment

5. The Israelites in the wilderness. Jude's readers knew all these facts, so he only had to remind them of these things.

6. The fallen angels. Evidently, the sin of these specially designated angels was that they "did not keep their positions of authority," their own initial distinctive order as purely spirit beings (cf. Gen. 6:1-6).

7. The sinners of Sodom and Gomorrah. Their judgment served as an example to warn others of the judicial punishment of eternal fire.

8-16. False teachers

8. Their presumption indicated. The sin of the false teachers is revealed in their sexual immorality, their insubordination, and their slander.

9-10. Their presumption illustrated. These men "speak abusively against" anything they do not understand, showing no reverence for any authority.

11. Reasons for their woe. These teachers of error are self-willed religious naturalists, gone "the way of Cain" (Gen. 4:3-8). Cain was a type of the religious natural man who rejects God's plan of redemption and molds his own religion of human merit to suit himself.

12-13. Their spiritual sterility. Their spiritual emptiness is seen in their peril, their barrenness, 12, and their shame and deception, 13.

14-15. Their judgment predicted. Jude declares that Enoch prophesied about these false teachers in dim antiquity.

16. Their character reviewed.

17-25. Exhortations and closing blessing

17-23. Exhortations to God's own. The children of God are to remember the apostolic prophetic warnings, 17-18. Seven more exhortations follow in verses 19-23.

24-25. Closing benediction. Praise is ascribed to God for His ability to keep us from stumbling into sin and to present us in a glorified state in His glorious presence.

Revelation
Christ's unveiling and kingdom

The title. This great prophetic unfolding is called "the Revelation [Greek *Apocalypse*] of Jesus Christ." It is *His* revelation given to Him by the Father to be made known to His servants, 1:1.

Background and date. Evidence, both internal and external, places the book toward the end of Emperor Domitian's reign (A.D. 81-96). It was Domitian who had the apostle banished to the rocky island of Patmos in the Aegean Sea (1:9).

Nature of the book. Revelation is the central terminal where all the great trunk lines of the prophetic Word converge, and is thus the consummation of all revealed truth. It was meant to be understood for the following reasons: (1) it is revelation, "a making known" or "unveiling." (2) It promises blessing to those who hear and keep its words of prophecy (1:3). (3) The book is not sealed (1:3b; 22:10). (4) A simple key is furnished to understand the book (1:19). (5) The apocalyptic symbols, which are the vehicles of its interpretation, are found explained elsewhere in Scripture.

Methods of interpretation
The spiritualizing method. This interpretation takes a mystical or allegorical approach to most of the book. It sees the book dealing primarily with the general struggle between the church and evil throughout the entire age, thereby giving encouragement to tested saints. It practically ignores the book's claims to be prophetic.

The praeterist method. This interpretive school holds that the book has already been practically fulfilled.

The continuous-historical method. Those who hold to this method maintain that Revelation covers the entire span of church history from John's time to the end of the world. However, this view fails to correlate the book with Bible prophecy as a whole and leaves the details of Revelation without adequate explanation.

Outline

1	The Patmos vision (*what you have seen*, 1:19a)
2-3	Letters to the seven churches (*what is now*, 1:19b)
4-22	Climactic events of history (*what will take place later*, 1:19c)
4-5	The divine throne in heaven
6-18	The Great Tribulation on earth
6:1-8:1	Seal judgments
8:2-11:19	Trumpet judgments
12-13	Seven personages
14	Preview of the end of the Great Tribulation
15-16	Bowl judgments
17-18	Judgment of Babylon
19	The Second Coming and Armageddon
20-22	The Millennium, the last judgment, the eternal state

Great prophetic themes consummated here

The Lord Jesus Christ, the central subject of all Scripture Gen. 3:15; Rev. 1:1
The church Matt. 16:18; Rev. 2-3
The resurrection and glorification of the saints Rev. 20:4-6
The Great Tribulation Deut. 4:29-30; Jer. 30:5-7; Rev. 4-19
Satan and the world system Isa. 14:12-14; Ezek. 28:11-18; Rev. 12:3-17; 20:1-3, 10

The judgment of the nations Joel 3:1-10; Matt. 25:31-46; Rev. 16:13-16
The Antichrist Ezek. 28:1-10; 2 Thess. 2:7-10; Rev. 13:1-10; 19:20
The times of the Gentiles Dan. 2:37-44; Luke 21:24; Rev. 6:1-19:16
Paradise lost Gen. 3
Paradise regained Rev. 21-22
The judgment of the wicked Ps. 9:17; Rev. 20:11-15
The eternal state with the new heaven and earth Isa. 65:17; 66:22; Rev. 21-22

The futurist method of interpretation. This school uses the key of 1:19 as a guide in placing most of the book (ch. 4-22) still in the future, grounding interpretation in OT prophecies. NT prophecies that refer to Christ's return are correlated with the events recorded in Revelation.

Monastery of St John, Patmos.

Revelation

1:1-3. Introduction

1-2. The nature of the book. It is *the*
Revelation, the great unveiling of the future. It
deals with things that "must" come to pass
"soon" and so are of vital import to God's people
now. It is an unveiling from Christ, given through
an angel to John in signs or symbols.

3. The purpose of the book. Its purpose is to
bless those who read it, especially those
undergoing persecution.

1:4-8. Greeting from the author

4a. The author and recipients of the book.
John the apostle is evidently the human author.
The recipients are seven representative
churches in western Asia Minor. These are
representative of conditions in the universal
church in every locality during the entire church
age.

4b-8. Benediction from the Triune God.
"Grace and peace" are the two great
possessions of the church in Christ. They come
from God the Father, 4b, God the Spirit, 4c, and
God the Son, 5-8. Jesus, the center of the book,
is described in full detail: His obedient earthly
life, 5a; His glorious resurrection, 5b; His future
title and kingdom glory, 5c; His redemptive work
and accomplishment, 5d, 6a; His worthiness of
all praise, 6b; His Second Coming, 7; and His
personal testimony, 8.

Part 1. The things seen
—The Patmos vision, 1:9-20

1:9-20. The circumstances and the vision

9-11. The circumstances.

12-16. The vision itself. Christ, the glorified
One, appears intimately associated with His
church on earth, 13. He is in the middle of the
church, denoted by the seven lampstands or
lightholders, Christ Himself being the Light (John
8:12). He appears as "son of man," here
primarily as Judge, evaluating the service of His
church on earth.

17-18. John's response to the vision.
Prostrated at the sight of the glorified Son of
Man, John is given assurance by the resurrected
Christ.

19. The key to all the visions of the book. This
verse, indispensable to the correct interpretation
of Revelation, suggests a threefold division of
the book: (1) "what you have seen," i.e., the
vision of the Son of Man as Judge (1:10-20);
(2) "what is now," i.e., the seven churches,
representative of the church during the entire
church age (ch. 2-3); (3) "what will take place
later," i.e., after the church period ends
(ch. 4-22).

20. The meaning of the first vision. The
"seven stars" are messengers, and the "seven
lampstands" are the churches.

Part 2. The things which are
—The church age, Ch. 2-3

2:1-7. Ephesus—the loveless church

1-3. Greeting and commendation. The letter is
addressed to the "angel" of the church at

Ephesus. The church is commended for its good works, patient endurance, and intolerance of evil, 2-3.

4-5. Complaint and warning. The Ephesian church's sin was departure from its initial heartfelt affection for the Lord.

6-7. Praise and promise. The church is commended for detesting "the practices of the Nicolaitans," a symbolic name apparently of a party attempting to introduce a false freedom into the church.

2:8-11. Smyrna
—the persecuted church

8-9. The persecution. The Jews of the "synagogue of Satan," 9, were Jews nationally but not spiritually. They bitterly opposed Christianity, so that in rejecting the truth their synagogue became that of Satan.

10-11. The encouragement. Four encouraging reasons are given why they should not fear these things that they were about to experience.

The seven sevens of the Apocalypse

1. The seven churches
2:1-3:22
2. The seven seals
6:1-8:1
3. The seven trumpets
8:2-11:19
4. The seven personages
12:1-13:18
The woman, 12:1-2
The dragon, 12:3-4
The Man Child, 12:5
The archangel Michael, 12:7
The remnant, 12:17
The beast out of the sea, 13:1-8
The beast out of the earth, 13:11-18
5. The seven bowls
15:1-16:21

6. The seven dooms
17:1-20:15
Ecclesiastical Babylon, 17:1-18
Political Babylon, 18:1-24
Antichrist and the false prophet, 19:20
Antichristian nations, 19:21
Gog and Magog, 20:8-9
Satan, 20:10
The wicked dead, 20:11-15
7. The seven new things
21:1-22:21
New heavens, 21:1
New earth, 21:1
New city, 21:9-23
New nations, 21:24-27
New river, 22:1
New tree, 22:2
New throne, 22:3-5

2:12-17. Pergamum
—the worldly church

12-13. Where Satan's throne was. As a center of pagan religion, including Caesar worship, it was called "where Satan has his throne."

14-15. The teaching of Balaam, and the teaching of the Nicolaitans.

16-17. Warning and promise. The warning is to repent, 16, and the promise concerns Christ as "the hidden manna," 17, His glorified humanity preserved in the heavenly tabernacle until manifested at His second coming.

2:18-29. Thyatira
—the paganized church

18-23. Commendation and complaint. Christ, depicted as Judge, 18, charges the church with tolerating the false prophetess Jezebel, 20, even though it was a church full of good works, 19.

24-29. Promise to the overcomer. "Satan's so-called deep secrets," 24, is an arresting reference to demonism and false teaching. Overcomers will participate in Christ's messianic rule, 27.

3:1-6. Sardis—the lifeless church

1-3. Dead orthodoxy. This church had a "reputation" for spiritual life, but "the seven stars" (the messengers of the seven churches) judged it spiritually dead, 1.

4-6. Blotting names out of the book of life. This symbolism refers to the ancient practice of a city enrolling its citizens with the names of the dead erased. So, by analogy, those who have a "name" (as belonging to the visible church) but are "dead" (unregenerate) are "erased" from God's roll of heavenly citizens.

3:7-13. Philadelphia
—the missionary city

7-9. An open door of witness. This letter, together with the one addressed to the church at Smyrna, contains no word of rebuke. The Philadelphian church's vigorous missionary activity won many Jews of the city.

10-13. Kept from the hour of testing. The promise, 10b, seems to indicate that the church, of which the Philadelphian church was representative, will be glorified and taken to heaven before the Great Tribulation begins, 10.

3:14-22. Laodicea
—the lukewarm church

14-19. Insufferable lukewarmness. Christ calls this church's lukewarm profession nauseating, 15-16, and utterly deceptive of its true spiritual condition, 17. He advises the church "to buy from me gold refined in the fire," 18, the real wealth of a divine-human Savior cleansing the heart, and to buy the "white clothes" of a truly regenerated and sanctified life and the eye salve of faith granting true spiritual insight and knowledge.

20-22. Christ shut out. Christ, who had been ousted, appears on the outside knocking on the doors of individual hearts, waiting for them to receive Him, 20.

Part 3. The things which shall be hereafter, Ch. 4-22

4-5. The divine throne in heaven

Chapters 4 and 5 introduce the source of the visions and judgments that are to follow. The setting is in heaven and the chief person is Christ.

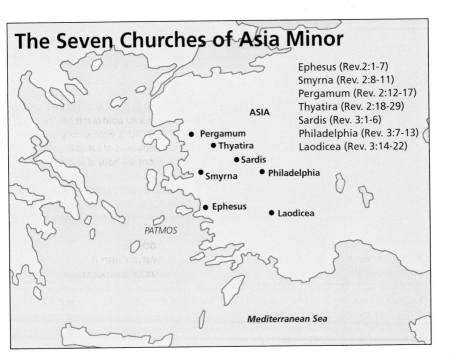

The Seven Churches of Asia Minor

Ephesus (Rev.2:1-7)
Smyrna (Rev. 2:8-11)
Pergamum (Rev. 2:12-17)
Thyatira (Rev. 2:18-29)
Sardis (Rev. 3:1-6)
Philadelphia (Rev. 3:7-13)
Laodicea (Rev. 3:14-22)

ASIA

● Pergamum
● Thyatira
● Sardis
● Smyrna   ● Philadelphia
● Ephesus   ● Laodicea

PATMOS

Mediterranean Sea

4:1-5. The throne introduced

1. The heavenly door. The scene is changed from earth to heaven.

2-5. The heavenly throne. Christ now occupies the throne of God the Father, 2, until His second coming. God's glory is symbolized in terms of precious gems, 3. The rainbow is a token of God's mercy based on the accepted sacrifice of His Son, as the Noahic rainbow was the sign of a covenant based on the sacrifice offered by Noah that looked forward to Christ.

4:4, 10-11. The twenty-four elders

These "elders" evidently represent redeemed OT and NT saints, for the term is never applied to angels. The crowns the elders wear are victors' crowns, 4. Their being "dressed in white," 4, displays them as a redeemed royal priesthood (1 Peter 2:9), engaged in priestly services (Rev. 5:8).

The term "elder" is commonly employed in Scripture of the representative head of a nation, tribe, city, or family. The number 24 represents the OT saints under the 12 tribes of Israel and the NT saints by the 12 apostles of the Lamb (cf. the 12 foundation stones of the 12 apostles of the Lamb and the 12 gates of the 12 tribes of Israel, Rev. 21:10-14).

4:6-11. The four living creatures

6-8. Their identity. They are a special order of created beings associated with the throne of

God, apparently combining characteristics both of the cherubim, concerned with the public governmental glory of God (Gen. 3:24; Ex. 25:17-20; Ezek. 10:1-22), and the seraphim, concerned with the holiness of God (Isa. 6:1-7).

8-11. Their worship. They adore the Lord God Almighty, 8-9, and are joined in worship by the 24 elders, 10-11.

5:1-4. The seven-sealed book

1. What the book is. The seven-sealed book is the title deed to the forfeited inheritance of the earth lost by Adam when he fell. "Sealed with seven seals" symbolizes the completeness of the sealing till one legally qualified to open the tightly closed legal document should appear.

2-4. Who is worthy to open it? "No one" was able to open it: not angelic beings or any of Adam's descendants.

5:5-10. The one worthy to open the book

5-6. The Lion of the tribe of Judah. He alone is worthy because (1) He is the "Lion of the tribe of Judah" (the royal tribe), a second advent title of the Messiah as "King of kings" (19:16; Gen. 49:8-10), who in majestic might would secure the blessing of Israel and the whole earth and in His lionlike character crush His foes. (2) He is the root of David. (3) As the God-man He has triumphed, 5. (4) He is the Lamb slain, 6.

7-10. His sublime action. It was the case of a kinsman (the God-man) being able to do what no one else could do (3-4; cf. Lev. 25:23-24).

5:11-14. Universal worship of the Lamb

11-12. Worship of the heavenly beings. This great scene depicting the kingdom rights and glories of Christ (ch. 4-5), evokes the praise of myriads of angels, the living creatures, and redeemed humanity in heaven, 11.

13-14. Participation of all creation.

6:1-8:5. The seven-sealed book opened

6:1-17. Seals one to six

1-4. Seals one and two. The opening of the seals precipitates the Day of the Lord and the period of tribulation on the earth to dispossess Satan and wicked people. The rider on the white horse, 2, is the Antichrist who imitates Christ (19:11). The rider on the red horse, 3-4, symbolizes war and carnage.

5-8. Seals three and four. The rider on the black horse symbolizes famine, and the rider on the pale horse represents pestilence and is called "Death," 7-8.

9-11. Seal five. The souls under the altar are the martyrs. "The word of God" is that for which they suffered death, and their "blood" cries for vengeance, 10.

12-17. Seal six. This seal apparently symbolizes governmental anarchy under the figures of earthquake, darkening of sun and moon, and falling stars.

(Ch. 7. First parenthesis)

7:1-8. The sealing of Israelites

1-3. A remnant of Israel preserved. The preservation is symbolized by a "seal." It is a public preservation, for "the servants of our God" are to be sealed on their foreheads, 3, involving no secret discipleship.

4-8. The number of sealed Israelites specified. These are the earthly Israelites living in the time of "Jacob's trouble" (Jer. 30:5-7). Dan and Ephraim are omitted, probably because of their complicity in idolatry (Deut. 29:18-21; 1 Kings 12:25-30).

7:9-17. The salvation of Gentiles

9-14. Elect Gentiles preserved. This company of saved people is an elect body of Gentiles, like the elect body of Jews, 1-8, which will be preserved through the end-time Tribulation, 14, to enter the kingdom.

15-17. Their kingdom bliss assured. The sufferings of their tribulation experiences will be past, 16, and Christ the kingdom Shepherd (Ezek. 34:23) will provide for them, 17.

8:1-5. Seal seven

1. Seal seven opened. This concludes the complete opening of the seven-sealed book (5:1) so that its full contents (the trumpets and bowls) might be released on the earth and its wicked inhabitants.

2-5. The prayer of the saints answered by earth judgments on the wicked.

8:6-11:18. The seven trumpets blown

8:6-13. Trumpets one to four

7. Trumpet one. The first six trumpets introduce more severe judgments. Trumpet one is blown resulting in hail and fire mixed with blood, which affects vegetation and suggests severe drought.

8-13. Trumpets two to four. Trumpet two results in judgment on the sea, 8-9; trumpet three affects the fresh water supply, 10-11; and trumpet four affects the heavens themselves, 12-13.

9:1-12. The fifth trumpet—the first woe

1. The abyss opened. John sees "a star that had fallen from the sky to the earth." This "star" is the angel custodian of the pit of the Abyss, the prison house of the demons (Luke 8:30-31). He is an angel *fallen* from heaven, not a fallen angel.

2-12. The loosing of myriads of demons. The symbolism, 2-11, describes the invisible spirit world in terms visible and comprehensible to men and women. The name of the king of the demons is *Abaddon*, meaning "destruction," 11, or in Greek *Apollyon*, meaning "destroyer" (cf. 2 Thess. 2:7-12).

9:13-21. The sixth trumpet —the second woe

13-19. Gathered armies loosed. From the altar of intercession, the golden altar of incense, God answers the prayers of His suffering and martyred saints. Toward the altar their prayers ascend (8:3). From it the answer goes out, 13, specifically from the "four [expressing universality] horns" (denoting power and efficacy of the saints' prayers and the answer).

20-21. The purpose of the woe. The divine design is twofold, punishment and reformation.

(10:1-11:13. Second parenthesis)

10:1-7.The angel and the little scroll

1-6. The identity of the mighty angel. This angel is an actual angel who symbolizes Christ (cf. 5:2; 8:3). His stupendous act of setting his feet on land and sea shows Christ's right to claim the earth as His own, 2 (Ps. 95:5; Eph. 1:13-14).

7. The mystery of God fulfilled. "The mystery

of God" is the theme of the "little scroll," and concerns Christ as incarnate Redeemer of the earth. This truth is the grand theme of the rest of Revelation where "the mystery of God" (a previously hidden truth, now fully revealed) is "accomplished," i.e., completed.

10:8-11. John and the little scroll

As a result of eating the little scroll (book) John must prophesy again, as he had done in the previous section, "about many peoples."

11:1-2. The end of the times of the Gentiles

1-2a. Restoration of temple worship. This point marks the Lord's dealing again with Israel and its worship in a restored temple in "the holy city," Jerusalem (cf. 2 Thess. 2:3-4).
2b. End of the times of the Gentiles. This period, which began with Judah's captivity under Nebuchadnezzar, will not end until the Second Coming (Dan. 2:34-35, 44; Rev. 19:11, 21).

11:3-13. The two witnesses

3-7. Their identity. These witnesses are evidently two members of the latter-day remnant.
8-13. Their destiny. Their corpses are dishonored in Jerusalem, 8, but God resurrects, 11, and translates the two witnesses in "*the* cloud" (Greek), 12, i.e., the Shekinah glory (cf. Ezek. 10:19; Matt. 17:5).

11:14-19. The seventh trumpet —the third woe

14-18. Anticipation of Christ's worldwide kingdom. Verses 15-19 give a panorama of the rest of the book, future events being seen as already present. They envision the establishment of Christ's worldwide reign, 15-17.
19. God's temple in heaven opened. "The ark of his covenant," seen within the temple, speaks of God's faithfulness to His covenants and promises to Israel (Rom. 9:4-5).

12-13. Seven personages performing during the last days of the Tribulation

12:1-2. Person one—the woman, Israel

1. The woman. The characters who will be on the stage during the final days before Christ's return are introduced. The great "wondrous sign" is the "woman," 1. She evidently symbolizes Israel, for she is dressed in regal and governmental splendor, the twelve stars illustrating her twelve tribes, as Joseph's dream shows (Gen. 37:9).
2. The woman's pregnancy. This travail refers to Israel's agony during the Great Tribulation, as the context clearly illustrates.

12:3-4. Person two—the dragon, Satan

3. Dragon in prophetic view. The dragon is identified as "that ancient serpent, called the devil or Satan" in verse 9. He is "an enormous red dragon," which symbolizes him as the proud, cruel energizer of the "beast." Red portrays his murderous character.
4. The dragon in historical perspective. This includes a panoramic sketch of his original fall.

12:5-6. Person three —the male child, Christ

5. The male child. Four things are declared: His birth, His destiny, His ascension, and His position on God's throne.

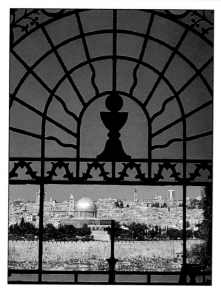

Jerusalem from the Mount of Olives.

12:13-16. Satan persecutes the woman

13-14. Reason for Satan's persecution. Knowing that his defeat has been occasioned by the exaltation of the Man Child, Christ, the dragon vents his fury on the sun-clothed woman (Israel) who gave the Man Child birth, 13.

15-16. Israel's preservation. Verse 16 points to friendly nations, that, having heeded the preaching of the gospel of the kingdom, protect these persecuted Jews.

12:17. Person five —the Israelite remnant

17. The godly remnant. Satan now turns against the godly remnant of Jews still in the land.

13:1-10. Person six —the beast out of the sea

1-5. The beast—the Roman prince. This last great ruler of Gentile world power arises out of an unsettled political condition ("the sea," Isa. 57:20), 1a. He heads a confederated ten-kingdom empire covering the sphere of the ancient Roman Empire, Daniel's fourth beast (Dan. 7:24-28). The beast is worshiped together with the dragon who energizes him, 4.

6-10. The beast's wicked career. He is permitted unrestrained power over all earth dwellers except over the elect, 8-10.

13:11-18. Person seven—the beast out of the earth, the false prophet

This third member of the unholy trinity arises out of the earth, 11a. He is the first beast's (Antichrist's) prophet, 11b, though disguised as a lamb.

6. The woman's flight. Verse 6 describes Israel's flight into the wilderness, to be sustained for three and a half years during Satan's terrible persecution.

12:7-12 Person four —Michael, the archangel

7-9 Michael. Michael is the special protector of Daniel's people the Jews, 7a (Dan. 12:1; cf. Dan. 10:13-21).

10-12. Rejoicing over Satan's expulsion. This joyous shout is a prelude to the establishment of Christ's kingdom, 10a, which begins with Christ's return.

14. Foreview of the end of the Tribulation

14:1-5.The Lamb and the 144,000
1-3. Identity of the 144,000. They are evidently the living Jewish remnant spared from death and moral contamination during the Great Tribulation. They are identical to the Israelites of 7:1-8. They belong to the Lamb and have His mark on their foreheads, 1c. Having gone through great tribulation, their song of God's grace is a "new song," a song of redemption at the cost of the Lamb's blood, 3 (cf. Rom. 3:24).
4-5. Their character and destiny. Their practical godliness is shown in their separation from wickedness, 4a, their obedience, 4b, and their truthfulness, 5.

14:6-8. The fall of Babylon foreseen
6-7. Proclamation of the everlasting gospel. This gospel proclaims mercy in the middle of judgment.
8. Fall of Babylon anticipated. Babylon is a symbol of the satanic world system, the center of all that is false and evil.

14:9-13. The punishment of the wicked
9-11. Worshipers of the beast and their fate. The doom of these rebels is announced by an angel with a "loud voice" so that all may hear and be without excuse, 9. Unutterable anguish is symbolized by the "burning sulfur," 10.
12-13. The bliss of the martyrs. The blessedness of those who die rather than worship the beast is indicated, 13.

14:14-20. Preview of Armageddon
14-16. The harvest. This is heaven's view of the climax of God's judgment. The figure of the harvest portrays judgment that separates the righteous from the wicked. The judge sits on "a white cloud," white signifying the purity and absolute righteousness of the judgment to take place, the cloud indicating the divine presence (10:1; Ezek. 10:4; Matt. 17:5; 24:30).
17-20. The vintage. This is God's wrath poured out on sinners. The terrifying carnage of Armageddon is symbolized by the picture of blood flowing as high as a horse's bridle for "1,600 stadia" (about 200 miles), 20.

15-16. The seven bowls

15:1-8. Preparation for the final plagues
1. The sign of the seven angels. This symbol is called "great and marvelous" because these angels have the seven last plagues and in them God's fury is completed.
2-4. The victorious martyrs. The song of Moses (concerning redemption out of the Red Sea, Ex. 15) combines with the song of the Lamb (redemption from sin and exaltation of the Lamb of God).
5-8. Ministers of God's wrath. The four living creatures (see notes on 4:6-11), as executors of the judicial government of God, perform accordingly, 7.

16:1-12. Bowls one to six
1-3. Bowls one and two. The bowl judgments are the consummation of the wrath of God poured out on mankind's wickedness and are characterized by severity, finality, and brevity.

The first bowl, 2, is poured out on the earth-organized government under the leadership of the beast. The second bowl, 3, is poured out on the sea, which becomes blood and is symbolic of the complete moral and spiritual death of godless society.

4-9. Bowls three and four. Fresh waters become blood in the pouring out of the third bowl, 4. God's absolute authority over creation is exhibited in the fourth bowl, 8.

10-12. Bowls five and six. The fifth bowl causes darkness to fall over the empire of the beast, 10. Morally, politically, and spiritually his kingdom is plunged into solitary darkness. The sixth bowl, 12, causes the drying up of the Euphrates River, 1,780 miles in length, western Asia's longest river. This symbolizes the removal of every barrier for the advance of "the kings from the East" to Armageddon.

(16:13-16. Third parenthesis)

16:13-16.The three frogs
13-14, 16. Satanic trinity and Armageddon. "Frogs" symbolize the demons who will be the spiritual dynamic behind Armageddon (cf. 1 Kings 22:20-28). The dragon (Satan), the beast (the Antichrist), and the false prophet symbolize the satanic trinity of evil, the source of the "spirits of demons," 14, i.e., demon spirits. **15. Warning to the remnants** to stay awake and alert.

16:17-21. The seventh bowl
17-18. The consummation of judicial wrath. The seventh angel pours out his bowl "into the air," the realm of Satan (Eph. 2:2). This judicial action, symbolized by voices, thunders, and

lightnings, precedes the great earthquake, 18. **19-21. The results of God's wrath.** "Babylon the Great," the counterfeit political and religious center of ch. 17 and 18, experiences God's full wrath, 19.

17-18. Judgment of Babylon

17:1-6.The vision of the prostitute, ecclesiastical Babylon
1-5. The prostitute and her identity. The prostitute represents ecclesiastical Babylon (personified religious revolt against God) in its final form, ripened for judgment. She is guilty of prostituting truth and purity, 2. She is spiritually destitute, 3. The "desert" symbolizes the place of drought, where those who are thirsty can never be satisfied, 5.

6. The woman and her crimes. Her most horrible sin is her murder of the true saints of God. Both OT "saints" and NT martyrs of Jesus suffered under this prostitute.

17:7-18. The prostitute and her doom
7-14. The instrument of her doom. The *revived* Roman Empire with its end-time emperor (the beast) appears as the agent of the prostitute's destruction (16-18). It will be the time of great deception, 8-9.

The type of government of the revived Roman Empire is indicated, 10. The seven heads are not only seven hills (on which Rome is built and the harlot sits, 9), but they are also seven kings, 10. These "seven kings" evidently refer to seven distinct forms of government that characterized the empire (32 B.C.-.A.D. 476). Five have fallen, "one is," 10, the imperial form of John's day. "The other," the seventh, has yet to come, and when it comes it must remain only "a little while" (its full power is only three and a half years, 13:5).

15-18. The account of her doom. The prostitute finds that the beast turns against her at the end to utterly destroy her, 16.

18:1-24. Judgment of commercial Babylon

1-8. Her destruction announced. A great angel announces her utter ruin, 1. She is "fallen, fallen" (completely fallen) because of her corrupting sin of commercialism, 2-3.

9-19. Her destruction is lamented by those who grow wealthy on her traffic, 9-11.

20-24. Her destruction is effected. The boulder thrown into the sea symbolizes Babylon's utter destruction, 21-23, for she is guilty of the blood of God's people, 24.

19. The Return of Christ

19:1-5. Rejoicing at Babylon's fall

1-4. Heaven rejoices. Wicked earth dwellers lament (18:9-19) but heaven rejoices (18:20-19:6) over Babylon's fall.

5. The voice from the throne speaks. This symbolizes God Himself speaking from the center and source of His government.

19:6-10. The marriage of the Lamb

6-8. The wedding. The bride, spoken of as wife to be, represents the NT church (Eph. 5:32). The figure of "wife" symbolizes the glorified church joined to Christ her Head in royal administration and dignity in the kingdom.

9-10. The guests. The bliss of the invited guests is stressed in 9b. It is called a "wedding supper,"

9b, as it is a blessed reward for God's own in contrast to the supper of judgment (19:17).

19:11-16. Christ's second coming

11-14. The conqueror and His victorious army. Christ's coming is described in a symbolic vision. The vision is the departure of Christ from heaven with His saints and angels to claim His kingship over the earth. He exercises omniscient judgment, 12a, symbolized by "His eyes are like blazing fire," and He has absolute authority, 12b, shown by His many crowns (diadems). He comes on a white horse, 11, in victorious conquest. His redeemed share His triumph, and are also seen coming on white horses, 14.

15-16. The conqueror and His conquest. He conquers supernaturally, 15a. The "sharp sword" is the omnipotent, irresistible Word of God that spoke the universe into being and that slays His enemies. He comes with absolute royal sovereignty, 16. Universal dominion is His. His name, denoting His full kingship and lordship over all the earth and people, is His right as Creator and Redeemer. The descriptive title "King *par excellence* and Lord *par excellence*" ("King of Kings and Lord of Lords") is on His "robe" and on His "thigh," where one would expect His sword, showing that He conquers by His word and not by a literal sword.

19:17-21. Armageddon

17-18. The great supper of God. This great supper symbolizes the destruction of Christ's enemies on earth.

19-21. The total destruction of Christ's foes. The beast and the false prophet are both cast alive into Gehenna (eternal hell).

Babylon

The Babylon of ch. 18 is the satanic world system in its godless commercial and economic aspects. This system honeycombs all phases of the life of unregenerate mankind organized as a system under Satan. The satanic world system of Babylon is mentioned in more than 30 NT passages. Satan is directing its head (John 12:31; 14:30; 1 John 5:19). The system is pronounced by God as wholly evil (Gal. 1:4; James 4:4; 2 Peter 2:20). It is shown to be limited and temporary (1 John 4:4), as Revelation 17-18 proves. It is doomed to destruction at Christ's second coming (1 John 2:17; Rev. 17-18; 19:11-16; 20:1-3).

20. The Millennium and final judgment

20:1-3. Satan bound
1. The vision of the angel. The angel represents the agent of God's authority over the underworld. The "key" and the "chain" portray in figurative language the divine authority itself.
2-3. The binding of Satan. This is signified by the angel's laying hold of the dragon in the sense of subduing and vanquishing him. The duration of Satan's binding is the length of the Millennium. This binding is necessary because the kingdom has for its object the restoration of the divine authority over the earth (Acts 15:14-17), against which Satan is the chief opponent.

20:4-6. The saints reign
Those involved in "the first resurrection," 5, find that "the second death," Gehenna (the lake of fire), has no power over them, 6b. They will be king-priests of God associated with Christ the King-Priest and will reign during the thousand-year Kingdom Age, 6c.

20:7-10. Satan loosed
7-9. Satan's last rebellion. After His thousand-year imprisonment, Satan is liberated from the abyss to test people's loyalty to God. He successfully deceives "the nations." The result of Satan's revolt will be the complete supernatural destruction of the rebels, 9.
10. Satan's final doom. Satan is now consigned to "the lake of burning sulfur," which speaks of inexpressible conscious torment (14:10; Isa. 30:33).

20:11-15. The final judgment
11. The throne and the judge. This scene of judgment closes the Millennium and marks the beginning of eternity. The judgment concerns the wicked dead.
12-15. The dead and their judgment. Each sinner is face to face with God alone, 12. The Book of Life is opened, containing the name of not one unsaved person, demonstrating that this is purely the sinner's judgment, 15.

21:1-22:5 The City of God and the eternal state

21:1-8. The eternal state
1-7. Eternity and the righteous. Eternity is characterized by a new heaven and a new earth, 1. The new Jerusalem, 2, represents the glorified church (3:12) after the millennial reign. All traces of sin are removed, 4. The authentication of this grand finale of divine redemption is by God Himself, 5.
8. Eternity and the unrighteous.

21:9-10. The vision of the city introduced

9. The angelic invitation. The angel invites John to view the Lamb's wife, the bride.

10. The view of the great city. This city supersedes the historical Jerusalem, which passed away with the first earth, 1, and becomes part of the new earth, 2.

21:11-21. A description of the city

11-14. Her identity. The city is the magnificent symbol of the eternal abode and destiny of the redeemed of all ages. Both Israel and the church appear prominently in the city, 12, 14.

15-17. Her size. The dazzling city's measurements reveal a solid cube of golden construction 1,500 miles broad, wide, and high.

18-21. Her splendor. The glorious destiny of the redeemed is symbolized by the city's adornment with every divine beauty, her wall being of jasper, and the city itself of pure gold, both crystal-clear, 18.

21:22-22:5. Life within the city

22. Her temple. No visible temple will adorn the city of God, for God the Almighty and Christ the Lamb dwell there.

23-24. Her light. God will illuminate the city.

24b-26. Her gates and her honor. Nations will bring their glory to the city, which has open gates, as all her enemies are defeated.

27. Her citizens. Nothing unclean will live there, only the redeemed.

22:1-5. Paradise restored. The complete removal of the curse brings even more than paradise ever enjoyed before the Fall. The environment will be perfect. Fullness of life ("river of the water of life") flows from the source of eternal life, God the Father through the Son (the Lamb), 1.

22:6-21 Closing testimonies

22:6-11. The testimony of the angel and of Christ

6. The angel authenticates the prophecy. The truth of these great predictions is attested and the OT foundation and NT fulfillment are declared.

7. Christ Himself announces that He will come soon.

8-11. The angel pronounces the book unsealed. The reason for not sealing this prophecy is that "the time is near," 10.

22:12-21. The concluding testimony of Christ

12-15. His coming and rewards. Christ announces again the certainty and nearness of His coming. He declares the rewards He will give for works, 12b.

16-19. His person and relationships to mankind. He who has sent His angel to give "this testimony" (the whole content of the book) to the churches, 16a, describes Himself in His relation to Israel, 16b; in His relation to the church, 16c; and in His relation to every soul that thirsts, 17.

20a. Christ declares that He is coming soon.

20b. The church replies to her Lord. John, representing the church, as well as his own keen desire, cries, "Amen. Come, Lord Jesus."

21. The closing blessing.